**HISTORICAL DICTIONARIES OF RELIGIONS,
PHILOSOPHIES, AND MOVEMENTS
Edited by Jon Woronoff**

HISTORICAL DICTIONARY
OF
TERRORISM

by
Sean Anderson
and
Stephen Sloan

*Historical Dictionaries of Religions,
Philosophies, and Movements, No. 4*

The Scarecrow Press, Inc.
Metuchen, N.J., & London
1995

British Library Cataloguing-in-Publication data available

Library of Congress Cataloging-in-Publication Data

Anderson, Sean, 1952–
    Historical dictionary of terrorism / by Sean Anderson and Stephen
Sloan.
        p.   cm. — (Historical dictionaries of religions, philosophies,
and movements ; no. 4)
    Includes bibliographical references.
    ISBN 0-8108-2914-2 (alk. paper)
    1. Terrorism—History—Dictionaries.   2. Terrorists—History—
Dictionaries.   I. Sloan, Stephen,   II. Title.   III. Series.
HV6431.A537   1995
909—dc20   94-17408

TABLE OF CONTENTS

This book is dedicated by Sean to his parents,
Nora Helen and Simon Kendall Anderson,
and by Steve to
Robin and Arnold Kanarek,
Michael and Ruth Sloan,
and Scott and Virginia Sloan.

ACKNOWLEDGMENTS

The authors wish to thank those who have made this work possible in so many ways. First and foremost we wish to thank Lisa Evans who undertook much of the initial planning, painstaking background research, writing and revision necessary to produce the initial draft and who undertook these tasks conscientiously and attentively. We also wish to thank Karl G. Blanke, Ambassador Edwin G. Corr, Arthur Dolsen, Justin K. Elledge, Erich Frankland, Alan C. Frantz, Maria Refugio Pearson, Alvin F. Sherman, Jr., and Eric Y. Shibuya, who each put their expertise and documentary materials at our disposal.

Sean K. Anderson wishes also to thank his parents, Nora Helen and Simon Kendall Anderson, for their unwavering moral and material support, and also to thank Tim Conway, Steve Dile, Mike Hawley, Oystein Mageroy, Mike Means, Mike Moorman, and David Nehrenz for their faithful encouragement and spiritual support.

EDITOR'S FOREWORD

Terrorism has constantly dogged this supposedly modern and enlightened age. It has merely adopted new shapes and forms in keeping with the times. It has also gone high-tech, like everything else. But, as we all know, terrorism has been around for centuries, indeed, millennia. And, as this book convincingly shows, it will remain with us in the future even if, with the end of the Cold War, it again mutates. So it is essential to get a better grasp of what the phenomenon consists of, by whom it is practiced . . . and against whom.

That is not an easy task, not when terrorism is so widespread and diversified. Nor is it even simple to explain just which acts or groups are terrorist. Still, this latest volume certainly makes the situation much clearer by tracing an amazing number of acts and groups in literally hundreds of informative entries. It further inserts terrorism in its historical context through a detailed chronology. Of no less significance is an introduction that helps us understand the whys and wherefores. For all these reasons as well as its comprehensive and well-structured bibliography, this volume is bound to become a standard reference work.

This *Historical Dictionary of Terrorism* was written by Sean Kendall Anderson and Stephen Sloan, each of whom specializes in different aspects of a worldwide phenomenon. Dr. Sloan had his first encounter in Indonesia in 1965–1966. During his stay, an abortive coup d'état killed more than 100,000 people and was examined in his first book, *A Study in Political Violence: The Indonesian Experience*. While teaching political science at the University of Oklahoma, a post he has held since 1966, Dr. Sloan pioneered simulations of terrorist incidents and formulated counter-terrorist doctrine. He worked for the private and public sectors and wrote *Simulating Terrorism* and coauthored *Responding to the Terrorist Threat: Security and Crisis Management.* "Andy" Anderson has focused on the Middle East since returning from a stint as chief editor of the International Department of the Pars News Agency in Tehran in the early 1980s. He has lectured and written on Iran and Islamic fundamentalism. They have both thoroughly researched manifestations in North America, Latin America, Africa, Asia, and Europe for this volume.

Jon Woronoff
Series Editor

LIST OF ABBREVIATIONS

Note: All abbreviations used in this dictionary are included in this list, including abbreviations of names of organizations and agencies that are not terrorist groups.

AAA   *Alianza Apostólica Anti-Communista,* Anti-Communist Apostolic Alliance [Spanish group]

AAA   Argentine Anti-Communist Alliance

AD   *Action Directe,* Direct Action

ADC   Arab-American Anti-Discrimination Committee

ADL   Anti-Defamation League of B'nai B'rith

AISSF   All-India Sikh Students' Federation

ALA   Armenian Liberation Army

ALF   Animal Liberation Front

ALF   Arab Liberation Front (group within PLO)

AN   *Avanguardia Nazionale,* National Vanguard

ANAPO   National Popular Alliance

ANC   African National Congress

ANO   Abu Nidal Organization

ANS   *Aktiongemeinschaft Nationaler Sozialisten,* Action-Front of National Socialists

APRA   American Popular Revolutionary Alliance

ARA   Armenian Revolutionary Army

ARDE   *Alianza Revolucionaria Democrática,* Nicaraguan Democratic Alliance

ARENA   *Alianza Republicana Nacional,* Republican National Alliance

ARM   Animal Rights Militia

ASALA   Armenian Secret Army for the Liberation of Armenia

ASALA-M   ASALA-Militant, extremist wing of ASALA

ASALA-RM   ASALA-Revolutionary Movement, moderate wing of ASALA

AVC   Alfaro Vive Carajo Organization

AYM   Aryan Youth Movement, youth wing of WAR

BKA   German Federal Office of Criminal Investigations

BLA   Black Liberation Army

BR   *Brigate Rosse,* Red Brigades

BSO   Black September Organization

CALN   Armed Commandos for National Liberation

CCC   Communist Combatant Cells

CERF   *Frente Clara Elizabeth Ramírez,* Clara Elizabeth Ramirez Front

CIA   Central Intelligence Agency

CNPZ   Nestor Paz Zamora Commando

CON   *Coordinatora Opositora Nicaragüense,* Nicaraguan Opposition Coordinator

C-PDL   Christian-Patriots Defense League

CPP-ML   Communist Party of the Philippines, Marxist-Leninist

CSA   The Covenant, the Sword, and the Arm of the Lord

DFLP   Democratic Front for the Liberation of Palestine (group within PLO)

DGSE   General Directorate for State Security of the Interior Ministry (Nicaragua)

DRFLA   Democratic Revolutionary Front for the Liberation of Arabistan

EGP   *Ejército Guerrillero de los Pobres,* Guerrilla Army of the Poor

ELA   *Epanastatikos Laikos Agonas,* Revolutionary Popular Struggle

ELN   *Ejército de Liberación Nacional,* National Liberation Army, name of a Colombian and a Bolivian group

EOKA   *Ethniki Organosis Kyprion Agoniston,* National Organization of Cypriot Fighters

EOKA-B   *Ethniki Organosis Kyprion Agoniston-Beta,* National Organization of Cypriot Fighters-B

EPL   *Ejército Popular de Liberación,* Popular Liberation Army

ERCA   *Ejército Rojo Catalán de Liberación,* Red Army for the Liberation of Catalonia

ERP   *Ejército Revolucionario de Pueblo,* People's Revolutionary Army (member of FMLN; also name of Argentine group)

ESA   *Ejército Secreto Anticommunista,* Anti-Communist Secret Army

ETA   *Euzkadi Ta Askatasuna,* Basque Fatherland and Liberty

ETA-M   *Euzkadi Ta Askatasuna-Militar,* Basque Fatherland and Liberty-Militant branch

ETA-PM   *Euzkadi Ta Askatasuna-Politico-Militar,* Basque Fatherland and Liberty-moderate branch

FAL   *Fuerzas Armadas de Liberación,* Armed Forces of Liberation (member of FMLN)

FALN   *Fuerzas Armadas de Liberación Nacional,* Armed Forces of National Liberation

FANE   *Fédération d'Action Nationale Européene,* Federation for National European Action

FAR   *Fuerzas Armadas Rebeldes,* Rebel Armed Forces (Guatemala)

FAR   *Fuerzas Armadas Revolucionarias,* Revolutionary Armed Forces (Argentina)

FARC   *Fuerzas Armadas Revolucionarias de Colombia,* Revolutionary Armed Forces of Colombia

FARL   *Factions Armées Révolutionnaires Libanaises,* Lebanese Armed Revolutionary Faction

FARN   *Fuerzas Armadas de la Resistencia Nacional,* Armed Forces of National Resistance (member of FMLN)

FARN   *Fuerzas Armadas Revolucionarias Nicaragüenses,* Revolutionary Armed Forces (contra group)

FBI   Federal Bureau of Investigation

FDN   *Fuerza Democrática Nicaragüense,* Nicaraguan Democratic Force

FDR   Democratic Revolutionary Front (political front of FMLN)

FLN   *Front de Libération National,* National Liberation Front of Algeria

FLNC   *Frente de Liberación Nacional Cubana,* Cuban National Liberation Front

FLNKS   *Front de Libération Nationale Kanake Socialiste,* Kanak Socialist National Liberation Front

FLQ — *Front de Libération du Québec,* Quebec Liberation Front

FMLN — Farabundo Martí Liberation Front, or, Farabundo Martí National Liberation Front

FNE — *Faisceaux Nationalistes Européens,* European Nationalist Fascists

FNLC — *Front de la Libération Nationale de la Corse,* National Front for the Liberation of Corsica

FP-25 — *Forças Populares do 25 Abril,* Popular Forces of 25 April

FPL — *Fuerzas Populares de Liberación,* People's Liberation Forces (member of FMLN)

FPM — *Frente Patriótico Morazaniste,* Morazanist Patriotic Front

FRANCIA — *Front d'Action Nouvelle Contre l'Indépendence et l'Autonomie,* New Action Front Against Independence and Autonomy

FRC — Fatah Revolutionary Council (Abu Nidal organization)

FRELIMO — Mozambican Liberation Front

FRPL — Lautaro Rebel Forces, also known as Lautaro Youth Movement

FRP-LZ — *Fuerzas Revolucionarios Populares Lorenzo Zelaya,* Lorenzo Zelaya Popular Revolutionary Forces

FSLN   *Frente Sandinista de Liberación Nacional,* Sandinista National Liberation Front

FULK   *Front Uni de Libération Kanak,* Kanak United Liberation Front

GAL   *Grupos Antiterroristas de Liberación,* Anti-Terrorist Liberation Groups

GBR   *Grupo Bandera Roja,* Red Flag Group

GRAPO   *Grupo de Resistencia Antifascista, Primero de Octubre,* October First Antifascist Resistance Group

GSG-9   *Grenzschutzgruppe 9,* Border Protection Group No. 9, West German anti-terrorist unit of Border Patrol

IDF   Israeli Defense Forces

IE   Invisible Empire (Ku Klux Klan group)

IFLB   Islamic Front for the Liberation of Bahrain

ILO   Islamic Liberation Organization

IMRO   Inner Macedonian Revolutionary Organization

INLA   Irish National Liberation Army

IRA   Irish Republican Army

IRGC   Islamic Revolutionary Guards Corps, *Sipah-i Pasdaran-i Inqilab-i Islami*

JCAG   Justice Commandos of the Armenian Genocide

JDL   Jewish Defense League

JRA   Japanese Red Army

KDP   Kurdistan Democratic Party

KISAN   *Kus Indian Sut Asla Nicaragua Ra,* United Indigenous Peoples of Eastern Nicaragua

KKK   Ku Klux Klan

KKKK   Knights of the Ku Klux Klan (major Klan group)

LEHI   *Lohame Herut Israel,* Fighters for the Freedom of Israel

LTTE   Liberation Tigers of Tamil Eelam

M-19   *Movimiento 19 de Abril,* April 19th Movement

MAPU/L   United Popular Action Movement—Lautaro, also known as Lautaro Youth Movement

MAS   *Muerte a Secuestradores,* ''Death to Kidnappers'' Colombian drug smugglers' antileftist death squad

May 1   Revolutionary Organization of May 1

May 15   Arab Organization of May 15

M19CO   May 19th Communist Organization, also called May 19th Communist Coalition

MILPAS   *Milicias Populares Anti-Somocistas,* Popular Anti-Somocista Militia, later known as, *Milicias*

Populares Anti-Sandinistas, Popular Anti-Sandinista Militia

MIR   *Movimiento Izquiereda Revolucionario,* Revolutionary Movement of the Left

MIR   Mujahideen of the Islamic Revolution

MJL   Lautaro Youth Movement

MK   *Umkhonto we Sizwe,* "Spear of the Nation," military wing of African National Congress

MLAPU   Marxist-Leninist Armed Propaganda Unit

MLB   Movement for the Liberation of Bahrain

MLF   Moro Liberation Front, or, Moro National Liberation Front

MLN   *Movimiento de Liberación Nacional,* also known as the Tupamaros

MNR   Mozambique National Resistance, until 1982 the name of the current RENAMO

MPL   Cinchoneros Popular Liberation Movement

MRPF   *Frente Patriótico Manuel Rodríguez,* Manuel Rodriguez Patriotic Front

MRTA   *Movimiento Revolucionario Tupac Amaru,* Tupac Amaru Revolutionary Movement

NAFF   New Afrikan Freedom Fighters

NAP   National Action Party

NAR	*Nuclei Armati Rivoluzionari,* Armed Revolutionary Nucleus
NDM	Nicaraguan Democratic Movement
NORAID	Irish Northern Aid Committee
November 17	*Epanastatiki Organosi 17 Noemvri,* Revolutionary Organization of 17 November
NPA	New People's Army
NSF	National Salvation Front
NSLF	National Socialist Liberation Front
NSWPP	National Socialist White People's Party
NWLF	New World Liberation Front
OAAS	Organization for the Armed Arab Struggle
OAS	*Organisation de l'Armée Secrète,* Secret Army Organization
OIRA	Official Irish Republican Army
ORDEN	*Organización Democrática Nacional,* National Democratic Organization
ORPA	*Organización Revolucionaria del Pueblo en Armas,* Revolutionary Organization of the People in Arms
OVPR	Organization of Volunteers for the Puerto Rican Revolution

PALIKA	*Parti de Libération Kanak,* Kanak Liberation Party
PCES	Communist Party of El Salvador
PFLA	Popular Front for the Liberation of Arabistan
PFLP	Popular Front for the Liberation of Palestine (group within PLO)
PFLP-GC	PFLP-General Command
PFLP-SC	PFLP-Special Command
PFLP-SOG	PFLP-Special Operations Group
PIR-1	People's Information Relay No. 1
PIRA	Provisional Irish Republican Army
PKK	*Partiya Karkaran Kurdistan,* Kurdistan Workers' Party
PL	*Prima Linea,* Front Line group
PLA	Palestine Liberation Army
PLF	Palestine Liberation Front (group within PLO)
PLO	Palestine Liberation Organization
PNC	Palestine National Council
PNV	Basque Nationalist Party
PPC	Communist Party of Colombia
PPM	Patriotic People's Movement

PRTC   *Partido Revolucionario de los Trabajadores Centroamericanos,* Revolutionary Party of Central American Workers (member of FMLN)

PSF   Popular Struggle Front (group within PLO)

RAF   *Rote Armee Fraktion,* Red Army Faction

RATF   Revolutionary Armed Task Force

RENAMO   *Resistência Nacional Moçambicana,* Mozambique National Resistance

RFF   *Frente Ricardo Franco,* Ricardo Franco Front

RGR   Red Guerrilla Resistance

RUC   Royal Ulster Constabulary

RZ   *Revolutionäre Zellen,* Revolutionary Cells

SAIRI   Supreme Assembly for the Islamic Revolution in Iraq

SAS   Special Air Service, elite British antiterrorist and special operations units

SASOL   South African Coal, Gas and Oil Conversion

SDS   Students for a Democratic Society

SGPC   Shiromani Gurdwara Parbandhak Committee

SIM   ''Imperialist State of Multinationals,'' [Red Brigade idiom for modern Italian state]

SL	*Sendero Luminoso,* Shining Path, Peruvian Maoist group
SLA	Symbionese Liberation Army
SPLA	Sudanese People's Liberation Army
SSNP	Syrian Social Nationalist Party
TL	*Terra Lliure,* Free Land, Catalonian separatist group
TPLA	Turkish People's Liberation Army
TPLF	Turkish People's Liberation Front
TULF	Tamil United Liberation Front
UDA	Ulster Defense Association
UFF	Ulster Freedom Fighters
UFF	United Freedom Front
UGB	*Unión de Guerreros Blancos,* or, *Unión Guerrera Blanca,* White Warriors' Union
UKA	United Klans of America
UNL	*al Qiyada al Wataniyya al Muwahhada,* Unified National Leadership
UNO	*Unidad Nicaragüense Opositora,* Unified Nicaraguan Opposition
UP	Patriotic Union (FARC front)

URNG   Guatemalan National Revolutionary Union

USIS   United States Information Service (overseas offices of United States Information Agency of U.S. Department of State)

UVF   Ulster Volunteer Force

WAR   White Aryan Resistance

WPA   White Patriot Army

YAMATA   *Yapti Tasba Masraka Aslika Takanda,* Miskito Indian acronym for ''United Nations of Yapti Tasba [Sacred Motherland]''

ZOG   ''Zionist Occupation Government'' [Neo-Nazi idiom for United States government]

CHRONOLOGY OF INCIDENTS, HISTORY OF IDEAS, AND PERSONALITIES PERTAINING TO TERRORISM

A.D. 66 to 70 — Jewish nationalist Zealot (*Sicarii*) movement creates mass insurrection in Roman province of Judea, leading to Roman destruction of Jerusalem and Second Temple and mass suicide of Zealots besieged at Masada fortress.

A.D. 1090 to 1256 — The Ismaili Fedayeen cult of "assassins" conducts a terror campaign against the religious and political establishment of the Abbaside Islamic empire until the cult is exterminated by the Mongol invaders.

May 1793 to July 1794 — French revolutionary Committee of Public Safety undertakes purge of real and suspected enemies of the revolution, leading to 300,000 arbitrary arrests and 17,000 executions. This "Great Terror" lasts until Robespierre, its original instigator, is executed himself.

24 December 1865 — Ku Klux Klan founded in Pulaski, Tennessee, by Confederate Civil War veterans.

1869 — *Catechism of the Revolutionist* written by Sergey Nechayev provides an idealized model of the political terrorist that inspires later terrorist theoreticians and practitioners.

January 1878 to March 1881	Narodnaya Volya (People's Will) Russian terrorists conduct bombing campaign against Tsarist government, culminating in assassination of Tsar Alexander II on sixth attempt.
September 1901 to March 1902	An American, Ellen M. Stone, is kidnapped by the Inner Macedonian Revolutionary Organization and held for ransom of $66,000. After the U.S. government refused to pay this ransom, Stone's sponsoring organization raised and paid the required sum.
28 June 1914	Austrian Archduke Francis Ferdinand is assassinated by Serbian terrorists in Sarajevo, Bosnia-Herzegovina. Event sets World War I in motion.
21–23 February 1931	First recorded hijacking of an airplane: Rebel soldiers in Peru force two American pilots to fly them about and to drop propaganda leaflets over Lima.
9–10 November 1938	German Nazis undertake *Kristallnacht* terror against German Jews, smashing shop windows of Jewish-owned businesses and burning synagogues. Marks beginning of genocidal policy against Jews as part of Nazi state terror lasting until collapse of Third Reich in May 1945.
16 January 1939 to 22 February 1940	Irish Republican Army carries out first major bombing campaign within England proper with over 50 bombings of public places within a 13-month period.
6 November 1944	Jewish terror group Lehi assassinates Lord Moyne, the British minister for Middle Eastern affairs, in Cairo.

11 March 1946   The Fidaiyan-i Islam, an Iranian Islamic fundamentalist terror group, initiates 10-year-long assassination campaign against Westernized Iranian intellectuals and political leaders by murdering Ahmad Kasravi, prominent anti-Shiite secularist intellectual and historian.

22 July 1946   Jewish terror group Irgun bombs British administrative headquarters located in King David Hotel, Jerusalem, killing 91 people.

30 January 1948   Mohandas K. Gandhi is assassinated by Hindu extremist.

9 April 1948   Jewish terror groups Irgun and Lehi massacre Arab villagers of Deir Yassin located on Jerusalem-Tel Aviv road. News of massacre creates panic among other Palestinians, who flee former mandatory Palestine at onset of first Arab-Israeli war.

1 November 1950   Puerto Rican nationalists plotting to assassinate U.S. President Truman exchange gunfire with security guards at Blair House, Washington, D.C.

September 1952   Mau Mau insurgency erupts in Kenya, lasting until October 1956.

1 March 1954   Four Puerto Rican nationalists open fire on House of Representatives from visitors' gallery, wounding five representatives. All four captured by security guards.

20 August 1955   Algerian National Liberation Front terrorists undertake wholesale slaughter of 37 European

men, women, and children in Philippeville massacre.

20 March 1960   South African police massacre 69 black civil rights demonstrators in Sharpeville incident, which moves African National Congress to abandon its policy of nonviolence.

10 October 1967   Ernesto Che Guevara, guerrilla leader and author of *The Guerrilla War,* is captured and executed by U.S.-trained Bolivian anti-insurgency forces.

22 July 1968   Popular Front for the Liberation of Palestine begins hijacking campaign against El Al airliners with hijacking of El Al flight from Rome to Tel Aviv, diverting it to Algeria.

28 August 1968   Guatemalan Rebel Armed Forces gunmen assassinate U.S. Ambassador John Gordon Mein in Guatemala City, the first assassination of a U.S. ambassador in the line of duty.

4 November 1969   Carlos Marighella, terrorist and author of *Minimanual of the Urban Guerrilla,* written in June 1969, is killed in gunfight with Brazilian police in São Paulo.

12 December 1969   The Avanguardia Nazionale, an Italian neo-Fascist group, bombs Agricultural Bank of Milan, killing 16 and wounding 90 others.

31 July 1970   Uruguayan Tupamaros kidnap and murder Daniel A. Mitrione, U.S. AID public safety adviser.

6–9 September 1970	PFLP terrorists hijack five commercial airliners to Dawson's Field, outside Amman, Jordan, and hold 400 hostages. Three-week crisis provokes Jordanian government to expel Palestinian guerrilla groups in an armed confrontation, an event recalled by Palestinians as ''Black September.''
5 October 1970	Quebec Liberation Front (FLQ) terrorists kidnap James Cross, British trade commissioner to Quebec.
10 October 1970	FLQ members kidnap and murder Pierre LaPorte, Quebec Minister of Labor. Canadian government invokes War Powers Act, suspending civil liberties, in order to crack down on FLQ.
1 March 1971	U.S. Senate Office Building is bombed by Weather Underground.
28 November 1971	Jordanian Prime Minister Wasfi al Tall is assassinated by Black September assassins while in Cairo.
30 January 1972	British troops fire on Catholic civil rights demonstrators in Londonderry, Northern Ireland, killing 13. Incident, known as ''Bloody Sunday,'' marks renewal of IRA and sectarian violence in Northern Ireland.
30 May 1972	Three Japanese Red Army members, acting on behalf of PFLP, open fire on travelers at Israel's Lod Airport, killing 25 and wounding 76.

21 July 1972	Provisional Irish Republican Army (PIRA) conducts over 20 bombings in Belfast, killing 11 and wounding over 100, on ''Bloody Friday.''
5–6 September 1972	Eight Black September terrorists seize Israeli team at Munich summer Olympics after killing two team members. Eventually all hostages are murdered and all but three terrorists killed when Bavarian police open fire on terrorists moving the hostages.
1 March 1973	Eight Black September members seize Saudi Arabian embassy in Khartoum, Sudan, and murder U.S. Ambassador, his chargé d'affaires, and a Belgian diplomat.
29 March 1973	Irish navy seizes cargo ship *Claudia* filled with Libyan-supplied arms and explosives being smuggled to Northern Ireland by 4 PIRA members.
28 September 1973	Two Saiqa terrorists seize five Jewish hostages on ''Chopin Express'' train used to transport Soviet Jews emigrating to Israel from Austria, forcing Austria to close transit facilities for émigré Jews.
20 December 1973	Basque Fatherland and Liberty members assassinate Spanish Prime Minister Luís Carrero Blanco by exploding mined road as his automobile passes over charges.
31 December 1973	Venezuelan terrorist ''Carlos'' attempted assassination of Teddy Zeiff, Jewish owner of British Marks and Spencer department store chain, but failed when his gun jammed.

5 February 1974   Symbionese Liberation Army abducts Patricia Hearst.

11 April 1974   PFLP terrorists attack Israeli town, Qiryat Shemona, killing 18 and wounding 16.

13 April 1974   New People's Army murders three U.S. Navy personnel outside Subic Bay Naval Base in Philippines.

15 May 1974   Democratic Front for the Liberation of Palestine gunmen seize school together with over 100 students and teachers as hostages in Israeli town of Maalot. Gunmen kill 27 students as Israeli troops try to storm building.

17 May 1974   Core group of Symbionese Liberation Army is killed in shoot-out with Los Angeles police.

19 August 1974   Cypriot right-wing nationalist EOKA-Beta gunmen stage riot at U.S. Embassy in Nicosia and murder U.S. Ambassador Rodger P. Davies in revenge for perceptions of U.S. support for Turkey.

13 September 1974   Three Japanese Red Army members seize French Embassy in The Hague in order to free comrade from prison. All four allowed to leave for Syria.

6 October 1974   Puerto Rican nationalist group FALN initiates mainland U.S. bombing campaign striking five New York City banks.

9 November 1974   Red Army Faction (Baader-Meinhof Gang) murders head of West German Supreme Court, Günter von Drenkmann, at his Bonn home.

21 November 1974	PIRA bombs two Birmingham pubs, killing 21 and wounding close to 200 others.
24 January 1975	FALN bombs Fraunces Tavern in Wall Street district during lunch hour, killing 4 and wounding another 60.
29 January 1975	Weather Underground bombs U.S. State Department main office in Washington, D.C., causing extensive damages.
27 February 1975	June Second anarchistic leftists kidnap West German Christian Democrat leader, Peter Lorenz, who is released in exchange for five Red Army Faction prisoners.
4 August 1975	Ten Japanese Red Army gunmen seize the U.S. Consulate in Kuala Lumpur with 52 hostages, who are released in exchange for freedom of seven imprisoned JRA members in Japan.
21–23 December 1975	Venezuelan terrorist "Carlos," leading 5 terrorists, captures 11 oil ministers meeting at the OPEC Secretariat in Vienna, along with several other hostages, who are released in exchange for an as yet undisclosed ransom.
23 December 1975	November 17 leftists murder Athens CIA station chief Richard Welch.
27 June to 1 July 1976	Hijacking of Air France flight 139 from Tel Aviv to Paris to Entebbe, Uganda, by PFLP and Red Army Faction members with the support of Ugandan president Idi Amin. Israeli rescue operation was carried off with great success, although four hostages lost their lives

as did the Israeli commander of the rescue mission.

10 September 1976	Six Croatian nationalists hijack a TWA 727 New York-to-Chicago flight, ultimately to Paris. The hijackers demand publication of a manifesto for the release of the passengers.

21 September 1976   Former Foreign Minister Orlando Letelier of Allende government of Chile is assassinated by agents of Chilean secret police in Washington, D.C.

9 March 1977   Washington, D.C. Islamic Center and B'nai B'rith headquarters, together with 134 hostages, is seized by Muslim sectarians motivated by intrasectarian grievances. Hostage-takers surrender after two days.

23 May 1977   South Moluccan terrorists seize passenger train near Assen, the Netherlands, and a primary school in a coordinated action. As situation with hostages on train deteriorated markedly Dutch Marines stormed both the train and the school, killing all six terrorists on the train but capturing all four alive at school.

5 September 1977   Red Army Faction kidnaps West German businessman Hanns-Martin Schleyer, holding him hostage against release of Andreas Baader, Ulrike Meinhof, and nine other gang members. On 18 October 1977 Schleyer is murdered.

13–18 October 1977   PFLP members hijack Lufthansa plane to Mogadishu, Somalia, demanding release of Red Army Faction (RAF) members from West German jails. After pilot is murdered, West

German antiterrorist commandos storm plane on October 17, killing three of four terrorists and freeing hostages. On learning of the hijackers' failure the RAF prisoners in Germany commit suicide and RAF kidnappers murder Hanns-Martin Schleyer in reprisal.

16 March 1978   Italian Red Brigades kidnap former Italian Premier Aldo Moro for release of imprisoned comrades. Moro was murdered and his body found on 9 May 1978.

27 August 1979   PIRA bombs yacht of Earl Louis Mountbatten, killing him and two others and wounding four.

4 November 1979   Iranian university students storm U.S. Embassy in Tehran, with apparent blessing of Ayatollah Khomeini. They hold 53 American hostages for 444 days, resulting in severance of diplomatic relations between Iran and the United States but also ascendance of Islamic fundamentalists within Iran's revolutionary regime.

20 November 1979   On first day of the year 1,400 of Hegira (Islamic) era, Sunnite Muslim fundamentalists seize Masjid al Haram, Islam's holiest shrine, in Mecca, which is regained by Saudi Arabian national guards only after fierce fighting and bloodshed. Rumors of alleged U.S. involvement in the desecration of the shrine lead to riots in Pakistan in which U.S. Embassy is burned and an Embassy guard killed.

24 March 1980   Archbishop of El Salvador and critic of Salvador government, Oscar Romero y Galdames, is

assassinated while saying Mass, presumably by a right-wing death squad.

22 July 1980

David Bellfield, an American follower of the Ayatollah Khomeini, murders Ali Akbar Tabatabai, an Iranian anti-Khomeini activist, at the latter's home in a suburb of Washington, D.C.

4 December 1980

Four American church workers found murdered outside San Salvador, believed to be victims of right-wing death squads. Incident creates backlash against Salvadoran regime among U.S. public.

13 May 1981

Turkish gunman wounds Pope John Paul II in assassination attempt in St. Peter's Square. Evidence emerges of Bulgarian secret police and possible Soviet involvement in plot.

6 October 1981

Anwar Sadat assassinated by Islamic fundamentalists during review of parade commemorating October 1973 War.

17 December 1981

NATO Southern Europe Ground commander, U.S. Army General James Lee Dozier, is kidnapped by Red Brigades but is released 42 days later by Italian counterterrorist commandos.

2 February 1982

President Hafiz al-Asad orders destruction of Syrian city of Hama after its occupation by Muslim Brotherhood forces seeking to topple Syrian regime. Estimates of total deaths in this city of 180,000 ranged from 10,000 to 25,000 killed.

3 June 1982   Abu Nidal's followers wound Israeli ambassador to Britain in assassination attempt. Israel invades Lebanon in reprisal, ultimately besieging Beirut and forcing Palestine Liberation Organization to remove its troops and offices from Lebanon.

20 July 1982   PIRA bombs Royal Household Cavalry regiment in Hyde Park and also Royal Green Jacket military band at Regent's Park.

16 September 1982   Lebanese Phalangist troops begin two-day massacre of Palestinian refugees at Sabra and Shatila camps in revenge for assassination of Lebanese President and Phalangist leader Bashir Gemayel two days earlier in bombing by member of pro-Palestinian Syrian Social Nationalist Party.

18 April 1983   U.S. Embassy is partially destroyed by Islamic Jihad suicide truck bomber, killing 49 people and forcing removal of U.S. Embassy from West Beirut.

23 October 1983   U.S. Marines temporary barracks at Beirut Airport is destroyed by Islamic Jihad suicide truck bomber, killing 241 U.S. Marines. Islamic Jihad conducted similar operation the same day against the French military headquarters, killing 56 soldiers.

6 November 1983   U.S. Senate cloakroom is bombed by Armed Resistance Unit leftist group in protest against U.S. invasion of Grenada.

12 December 1983   Suicide truck bombers of al Dawa, a pro-Iranian Islamic fundamentalist group, at-

tack U.S. and French embassies in Kuwait City.

16 March 1984   Beirut CIA station chief, William Buckley, kidnapped by Islamic Jihad as part of its hostage-taking campaign against westerners in Lebanon. Buckley was later murdered, possibly in late 1985, and his remains returned only by December 1991.

17 April 1984   Libyan diplomats open fire from Libyan Embassy on anti-Qaddafi protestors in St. James Square, killing British policewoman. Diplomats were subsequently besieged and expelled from Britain while diplomatic relations between Libya and Britain were severed.

5–6 June 1984   Indian Army storms the Golden Temple, the Sikhs' holiest shrine, to end terrorist agitation directed by Sikh leaders from within sanctuary. Hundreds are killed and relations between Sikhs and Indian government reach new low.

18 June 1984   Neo-Nazi group, the Order, murders Alan Berg, a controversial Denver radio talk-show host, at his home.

12 October 1984   PIRA bombs Brighton hotel hosting meeting of top members of British Conservative government.

31 October 1984   Indian Prime Minister Indira Gandhi assassinated by two Sikh bodyguards, apparently in reprisal for her orders for June 5 attack on Golden Temple.

14 June 1985   TWA flight 847 hijacked to Beirut by Hezbollah terrorists. Hijackers murder U.S. Navy diver, Robert Dean Stethem. Last 39 of original 145 hostages were released by June 30.

23 June 1985   Air India flight 182 is destroyed off western coast of Ireland. Evidence suggests it was bombed, possibly by Sikh terrorists, as Dashmesh Regiment, a shadowy Sikh group, claimed credit for bombing this flight.

1 October 1985   Israeli jets strafe and bomb PLO headquarters outside Tunis in retaliation for murder by al Fatah operative of three Israeli tourists in Larnaca, Cyprus, on 25 September.

7 October 1985   *Achille Lauro* cruise ship hijacked by Palestine Liberation Front terrorists, who murder elderly Jewish American hostage, Leon Klinghoffer.

27 December 1985   Abu Nidal gunmen open fire at Rome and Vienna airports in coordinated attacks, killing 18 holiday travelers.

5 April 1986   Bombing of West Berlin discotheque, killing 3 and wounding 200 others, leads United States to bomb Libya, the suspected sponsor of the bombing, on April 15.

6 September 1986   Abu Nidal gunmen attack Istanbul synagogue, killing 21 worshippers before killing themselves.

20 January 1987   Islamic Jihad kidnaps hostage negotiator Terry Waite after media speculation links him to Iran-Contra affair.

9 December 1987	Palestinian protest over Israeli motorist's accident killing Palestinian pedestrians in Gaza Strip erupts into rioting, marking beginning of intifada uprising.
5 April 1988	Iranian-sponsored terrorists seeking release of comrades from Kuwaiti jails hijack Kuwait Airways flight 422, killing two hostages and holding rest of crew and passengers captive two weeks before abandoning airplane in Algeria.
14 April 1988	Naples USO club is car bombed, killing five people. Japanese Red Army operatives acting on behalf of Libya carried out operation to mark second anniversary of U.S. raid on Libya.
15 November 1988	Palestine National Council, legislative organ of PLO, declared independent Palestinian state to exist in West Bank and Gaza Strip and accepts, in principle, Israel's right to exist within pre-1967 borders contingent on Israeli recognition of Palestinian state.
21 December 1988	Pan Am flight 103 is destroyed over Scotland by radio bomb, killing all 259 persons aboard as well as 11 villagers of Lockerbie struck by falling debris. Suspicion has focused on the Ahmad Jibril's PFLP-General Command, a renegade PLO faction as well as on Iran and Libya as possible state sponsors.
14 February 1989	Ayatollah Khomeini issues *takfir* against British author Salman Rushdie, for the writing of *Satanic Verses,* a book regarded by many Muslims as a thinly veiled attack on the char-

acter of the Prophet Muhammad. The verdict of *takfir* anathematizes Rushdie as an apostate and enemy of Islam and authorizes any true believer to kill him on sight.

31 July 1989 | U.S. Marine Lt. Colonel William R. Higgins, kidnapped on 17 February 1988 by Hezbollah elements while serving in Lebanon as truce observer, murdered by captors in reprisal for Israeli capture of Hezbollah leader Sheikh Abdulkarim Ubaid on previous day.

16 November 1989 | Salvadoran soldiers murder six Jesuit priests and two maids at the José Simeón Canas University of Central America. For the first time in Salvadoran judicial history the officers involved in this death squad killing are eventually convicted for their participation.

25 February 1990 | Violeta Chamorro defeats Daniel Ortega in Nicaraguan presidential elections, so ending formal Sandinista domination of Nicaragua. U.S.-supported contras begin demobilization while formal Nicaraguan state support for leftist insurgency in El Salvador also is ended.

30 May 1990 | Israeli forces thwart sea-borne attack on Tel Aviv beaches by members of Palestine Liberation Front. PLO refusal to condemn attack leads U.S. government to discontinue talks with PLO representatives.

14 August 1990 | Sendero Luminoso terrorists attempt car bombing of Presidential Palace in Lima, Peru, but fail to kill or wound newly elected President Fujimori.

12 October 1990	Speaker of the Egyptian National Assembly is murdered in an assault on his motorcade, possibly by pro-Iraqi agents in retaliation for Egypt's support of Operation Desert Storm.
7 February 1991	PIRA launches mortar attack on British Prime Minister's residence while Prime Minister John Major and members of his cabinet were in session there. This attack resulted in no deaths or injuries.
21 May 1991	Former Indian Prime Minister Rajiv Gandhi assassinated by Liberation Tiger of Tamil Eelam suicide bomber in southern India.
6 August 1991	Shapur Bakhtiyar, last prime minister of pre-revolutionary Iranian monarchy, is assassinated by Iranian agents in Paris.
11 August to 4 December 1991	All remaining six U.S. hostages held by Islamic Jihad, and several other Western hostages, including Terry Waite, are released before end of year. Remains of William Buckley and Colonel William R. Higgins also released and returned to United States.
17 March 1992	Islamic Jihad claims credit for car bombing of Israeli embassy in Buenos Aires, killing 20 and wounding over 200, in reprisal for Israeli killing of Hezbollah leader in air raids on Hezbollah bases.
29 June 1992	Armed Islamic Movement, believed to be the armed wing of the Islamic Salvation Front, assassinates Algerian President Muhammad Boudiaf.

16 July 1992   Sendero Luminoso begins offensive to topple Peruvian government with two massive car bomb attacks, killing 18 and wounding over 140 others in Lima.

13 September 1992   Abimael Guzman, leader of Sendero Luminoso, is captured by Peruvian security forces along with top lieutenants during a strategy session held in Lima, Peru.

26 February 1993   World Trade Center building in New York City car bombed by followers of Shaykh Umar Abdul Rahman, the exiled leader of the Egyptian fundamentalist *Jamaa al Islami* group. Four suspects were found guilty by a Federal jury on 4 March 1994 while another two suspects remained at large.

13 September 1993   Israeli-Palestinian peace agreement signed in Washington, D.C., by Israeli Prime Minister, Yitzhak Rabin, and Palestine Liberation Organization Chairman, Yasir Arafat. Those opposed to the accord, including Palestinians affiliated with HAMAS group or with dissident PLO factions, as well as Israeli settlers and ultra-nationalists, seek to scuttle peace settlements through terrorist attacks in following months.

2 December 1993   Pablo Escobar, fugitive head of Medellín cocaine cartel responsible for narco-terrorist bombing and kidnapping campaign against Colombian police and government officials, is shot to death by security forces in Medellín.

25 February 1994   Dr. Baruch Goldstein, a militant follower of Rabbi Meir Kahane, opened fire on Palestinian

Muslims praying at the Tomb of the Patriarchs in Hebron, killing at least 29 and wounding an estimated 150. Event triggers anti-Israeli rioting in occupied territories and leads to temporary hiatus in Israeli-Palestinian negotiations on autonomy.

15 August 1994   French Interior Ministry announces arrest of ''Carlos'' in the Sudan by French counterintelligence agents.

INTRODUCTION

THE SUBJECTIVITY OF TERRORISM

The study of terrorism has been burdened by a continuing and often acrimonious debate over the definition and consequent nature and scope of terrorism. The overused platitude "one man's terrorist is another man's freedom fighter" aptly illustrates how subjectivity has obscured the identification of terrorism without which there can be no systematic study of this matter. This subjectivity stems from several related factors. At the outset, the very mention of "terrorism" evokes a fearful image of slaughter, an image that has been perpetuated and magnified through the mass media. The vision of unarmed civilians taken hostage, being wounded or murdered has seared the consciousness of a global audience. Terrorists themselves have skillfully exploited that image to force their message on a mass audience with the stereotypical picture of an armed and hooded perpetrator pointing an AK-47 or M-16 at helpless victims. This frightening imagery of terrorism in turn has often provoked an emotional response equally in the lay observer, the scholar, or the policymaker who cannot ignore their gut reactions to the threats and acts of bloodshed. All too understandably such indignation and condemnation act as impediments to a detached assessment of the causes, dynamics, and outcomes of terrorism. Blanket condemnation of terrorists as crazed killers may act as a catharsis, but it does not provide any foundation for understanding the phenomenon.

This moralistic blanket condemnation of terrorism makes it

difficult to arrive at any dispassionate objectivity in understanding terrorism, and even the attempt to study terrorism without immediate condemnation of it may be viewed as tacit acceptance of what is judged to be pernicious and reprehensible. The disturbing questions of morality are carried over into the equally heated debate over the nature of terrorism in which competing interpretations of what terrorism really is also complicate the debate on terrorism.

ELEMENTS OF TERRORISM

Many view terrorism as, first and foremost, criminal acts that cannot be justified. Terrorist acts are accordingly viewed as assaults upon the civil order that should not be dignified by being regarded as instruments for pursuing some higher cause. Viewed in this manner, terrorism is nothing more than a form of criminal violence.

Another approach recognizes that even while terrorism may consist of criminal actions, they are nonetheless actions meant to achieve certain goals. However brutal or reprehensible terrorism may be it cannot simply be dismissed as mindless violence. Accordingly terrorism can be defined as:

> a purposeful human activity directed toward the creation of a general climate of fear designed to influence in ways desired by the protagonists, other human beings, and through them some course of events.[1]

This attempt to define terrorism as purposeful action may provide, in turn, the basis for an objective analysis, for it offers a functional means for understanding the major common elements of terrorism irrespective of the differing goals of various perpetrators.

---

[1]H.H.A. Cooper. *Evaluating the Terrorist Threat: Principles and Applied Risk Assessment.* Clandestine Tactics and Technology Series, Gaithersburg, Maryland: International Association of Police Chiefs, 1974, p. 4.

The first common element of terrorism is the use, or threat, of violence. The mere threat of violence alone is not enough, however. Ultimately there must be the use of violence, or else the threat, however ominous, will lose its credibility. There may be some disagreement on whether such violence must be physical. Do different forms of mental cruelty, for example, constitute a form of terrorism? Even while there is no consensus on the answer to this question, a second common element of terrorism helps to clarify the problem, for the use of terrorism, irrespective of its goal, involves "violent . . . behavior . . . designed to generate fear in the community [or individual]."[2]

The intent to generate fear is the second common element that distinguishes terrorist violence from other forms of violence. One authority aptly notes that terrorism ultimately is "a form of psychological operations."[3] This psychological component of seeking to create fear as a primary goal, whether in an individual, a community, a state or a corporation, is essential to the concept of terrorism.

Another common element of terrorism as purposeful action is that the terrorist act is a form of communication meant to send a message of fear and intimidation not just to the immediate victim but also to a broader audience. As an often-quoted definition notes:

> Terrorism is the threat of violence and the use of fear to coerce, persuade, and gain public attention.[4]

Terrorism, then, is a form of "armed propaganda," a potent way not only to communicate but also to send a message in an age dominated by the mass media.

---

[2]Thomas B. Thorton. "Terror as a Weapon of Political Agitation," in *Internal War,* Harry Eckstein, ed., New York: Free Press, 1964, pp. 71–91.
[3]Michael T. McEwen. "Psychological Weapons Against Terrorism: The Unused Weapon," *Military Review,* 66, 1 (January 1986), p. 62.
[4]National Advisory Committee on Criminal Justice Standards and Goals. *Report of the Task Force on Disorders and Terrorism.* Washington, D.C.: U.S. Government Printing Office, 1976, p. 3.

TYPES OF TERRORISM: THE PRIMACY OF POLITICS

While in practice it is not always clear whether a given terrorist act is the work of "crusaders, criminals, or crazies,"[5] since even criminals will try to disguise or justify their acts on a political basis, there is basic agreement that terrorism is a form of political violence and action. There is, however, a reluctance to append the word "political" to a terrorist act since it is feared that doing so will transform the criminal into a political actor and so confer some degree of legitimacy upon the act. Nevertheless the political content of terrorism has largely been accepted in the scholarly literature. While there are many definitions of political terrorism, Grant Wardlaw's pioneering effort tightly defines its major characteristics:

> Political terrorism is the use, or threat of use, of violence by an individual or a group, whether acting for or in opposition to established authority, when such action is designed to create extreme anxiety and/or fear-inducing effects in a target group larger than the immediate victims with the purpose of coercing that group into acceding to the political demands of the perpetrators.[6]

Starting from this base point scholars have sought to establish typologies to identify different types of terrorism as a foundation for comparative analysis. One of the most useful is the dichotomy developed by T. P. Thorton, who differentiates between "enforcement terrorism" and "agitational terror." The former is also called "terror from above," which is used by governments and authorities to maintain their control and to suppress threats to their own power. The latter is used by those who wish to replace, transform, or destroy the existing order.[7] This basic typology is exceedingly useful for it recognizes that terror is not an instrument

---

[5]Taken from the title of Frederick J. Hacker's *Crusaders, Criminals or Crazies: Terror and Terrorism in our Time.* New York: Bantam, 1978.
[6]Grant Wardlaw. *Political Terrorism: Theory, Tactics, and Counter-Measures.* Cambridge: Cambridge University Press, 1982, p. 16.
[7]Thorton in Eckstein, ed. p. 72.

used just by those supporting the status quo, a liberal view often used to justify violence against the state, nor is it an instrument used only to attack the civil order, a conservative view often used to condemn terrorism and to justify harsh countermeasures.

There are more elaborate typologies such as the well-known classification system by Richard Schultz, who identifies three general categories: (1) "Revolutionary Terrorism . . . the threat and/or development of extranormal forms of political violence, in varying degrees, with the object of successfully effecting a complete revolutionary change (i.e., a change of fundamental political-social processes) within the political system. Such means may be employed by revolutionary elements indigenous to a particular political system or by similar groups acting outside the geographic boundaries of the system." (2) "Sub-Revolutionary Terrorism . . . the threat and/or employment of extranormal forms of political violence, in varying degrees, with the objective of effecting various changes in the particular political system . . . The goal is to bring about certain changes in the body politic, not to abolish it in favor of a complete system change. Perhaps the broadest of the three categories, groups included here span the political spectrum from left to right . . . Such means are employed primarily by groups or movements indigenous to the particular political system, though similar elements beyond the system's geographic boundaries may also rely on such means." (3) "Establishment Terrorism . . . the threat and/or employment of extranormal forms of political violence in varying degrees, by an established political system, against both external and internal opposition. Specifically such means may be employed by an established political system against other nation-states and groups external to the particular political system, as well as internally to repress various forms of domestic opposition/unrest and/or to move the populace to comply with programs/goals of the state."[8]

---

[8]Richard Schultz. "Conceptualizing Political Terrorism: A Typology," in *International Terrorism: Current Research and Directions,* Alan D. Buckley and Daniel D. Olson, eds. Wayne, New Jersey: Avery Publishing Group, Inc., 1980, pp. 9–15.

Schultz's definitions, however, may be culturally bound. How one determines what constitutes "extranormal forms of political violence" may depend largely on what is "normal" for the particular culture and political tradition in which the violence takes place. What is regarded as "extranormal political violence" in the Netherlands may be viewed as normal, indeed as routine, political violence in Lebanon.

The other unexamined assumption within this typology lays in the distinction between "revolutionary" and "subrevolutionary" political violence, which appears to reflect a tendency largely unquestioned in contemporary Western political thought to link the idea of revolution connotatively with that of political development or progress, and specifically with leftist or socialistic political movements, while regarding rightist or fascist political movements as atavisms, which cannot be classified as truly "revolutionary."

In fact, right-wing authoritarian states and left-wing totalitarian states resemble each other structurally far more closely than does either type resemble Western liberal democracy while they and their state functionaries, or else state-sponsored agents and proxies, also behave very similarly. The implied claim that true revolutionary movements achieve systematic transformation while subrevolutionary ones do not actually begs the question whether the supposedly "true" revolutionary movements ever do live up to their aspirations of holistic change and transformation. Historically it seems more evident that on seizing power the new revolutionary order usually incorporates large structural elements of the systems it replaces. Thus the Bolshevik revolutionaries replaced the Tsarist Okhrana with their own Cheka that eventually became the Soviet Union's KGB, so perpetuating in a more efficient form an instrument of statist absolutism. Moreover even "subrevolutionary" nationalistic or secessionist political movements often claim to seek the same types of social and economic transformations sought by avowedly socialist and internationalist movements. Despite these reservations Schultz's typologies, and others like it, have provided a valuable comparative framework in which to analyze terrorism in its many forms.

THE IMPACT OF TECHNOLOGY ON CHANGING TYPES OF TERRORISM

While the common elements described above provide lines of continuity running through terrorism's long and complex history, nonetheless a strong case can be made that technological innovation has created a new form of terrorism:

> Non-Territorial Terrorism—a form of terror that is not confined to a clearly delineated geographical area.[9]

That is, as a result of a joint revolution in the 1960s with the large-scale introduction of jet aircraft into international travel and the proliferation of television, terrorists could literally strike at global targets of opportunity in a matter of hours and force their message upon a mass audience undreamed of by their most dedicated and skillful predecessors. Moreover, their objective might not be the seizure of territorial power but rather regional or even global destabilization. Faced with this challenge authorities were forced to recognize that traditional means of prevention and control of terrorism appropriate within a specifically identifiable strife zone would not be effective against those who might be many thousands of miles away from their intended target. In reality nonterritorial terrorists had at their disposal, and used, an intercontinental delivery missile rivaling the missiles of mass destruction that, fortunately, were never employed in any general war. This was something new and invidious under the sun.

THE HISTORICAL DIMENSIONS

Despite these innovations and the emphasis on contemporary terrorism as being, as one authority deemed it, ''A New Mode of

---

[9]Stephen Sloan. *The Anatomy of Non-Territorial Terrorism: An Analytical Essay.* Clandestine Tactics and Technology Series, Gaithersburg, Maryland: The International Association of Chiefs of Police, 1978, p. 3.

Conflict,"[10] terrorism actually comes from a very ancient tradition. As one author notes,

> We tend to think of political terrorism as a modern development . . . But the terrorizing of humans by fellow humans on political or political-ethnic grounds goes much further back, in many forms. As a missionary in Burundi sadly said about the massacre of 10,000 Hutu tribesmen by the ruling Tutsi in 1972 . . . "This has been going on for centuries and will happen again."[11]

The same could be said for the tragic ethnic violence in the former republics of Yugoslavia and the disintegrated Soviet Union, the relentless attacks against the Kurds and any other number of primordial conflicts in both industrialized and agrarian societies.

In the long history of terrorism the names of certain groups surface repeatedly; they share the tendency to use violence to promote and exercise their religious beliefs. The Zealots were religious nationalists in first-century Judea who revolted against the Roman occupation. Hidden in crowds they would stab secular officials, priests, and soldiers with their daggers (sicarii) and then escape by merging back into the crowds. Their actions created an environment of fear where no one was to be trusted and everyone was feared. The Zealots pioneered the techniques of pure terror that would be used by future generations of true believers.

The word "assassin" came from another religious-political group. In the eleventh and twelfth centuries Ismaili Shiite activists in southwest Asia organized corps of assassins, known as the Fedayeen, literally the "self-sacrificers." These assassins were willing to undertake attacks against Sunnite rulers in spite of the certainty of their own death or capture, as they were assured of their place in Heaven if they fell as martyrs fighting in the path of

---

[10]Brian Jenkins. *International Terrorism: A New Mode of Conflict.* Los Angeles: Crescent Publications, 1974.

[11]Albert Parry. *Terrorism: From Robespierre to Arafat.* New York: The Vanguard Press, 1976, p. xi.

God. To counter the awe and respect these bold attacks created among the common people, apologists of the Abbaside dynasty targeted by the Ismailis gave out that the attackers were really "Hashshishin," those acting under the influence of hashish. This official disinformation became the source of the word "assassin." The car and truck bombers of the 1980s who blew up the U.S. Embassy in West Beirut, and later bombed the U.S. Marine barracks and French military headquarters there all within one year, reproduced in a modern setting the same tactics used by the earlier Ismaili Fedayeen.

Other English words have come from the ancient lexicon of terrorism. The term "thug" was taken from the name of a secret sect in India that also employed terrorism as part of its ritual worship of Kali, the Hindu goddess of destruction.

The genesis of modern terrorism took place during the French Revolution and the reaction that followed it. Under Citizen Robespierre and his Committee of Public Safety, the "Great Terror" was directed against the real and imagined enemies of the revolution. In excess of 17,000 people were victims of this first exercise of mass state terrorism. It is sad to note how this figure pales into insignificance when compared with the statistics of the mass terrorism of modern totalitarian states, which have refined with murderous efficiency the ability to engage in genocide, whether in the gas chambers of the Third Reich or the killing fields of Kampuchea.

The resort to terrorism as an instrument of revolutionary transformation was more fully developed in Imperial Russia. In the *Catechism of the Revolutionist,* written in 1869, Sergey Nechayev provided an idealized guide that would be employed by later generations as the model of a terrorist dedicated to his or her cause to the death. As he noted in this *Catechism:*

> The revolutionary is a doomed man. He has no interests of his own, no affairs, no attachments, no belongings, not even a name. Everything in him is absorbed by a single thought, a single passion—the revolution . . . . The revolutionary enters into the world of the state, of class, of so-called culture, and lives in it only

because he has faith in its speedy and total destruction. He is not a revolutionary if he feels pity for anything in this world. If he is able to, he must face the annihilation of a situation—everything and everyone must be equally odious to him. All the worse for him if he has family and loved ones in this world; he is no revolutionary if he can stay his hand.[12]

The antecedents of modern terrorist tactics were also developed during this period. The Narodnaya Volya (People's Will) organization employed dynamite in its assassination campaigns against the officials of the Tsarist regime.

The use of terrorism as a weapon of propaganda and communication was further developed during this period by the followers of anarchism. The leading advocate of anarchism, Mikhail Bakunin, recognized that violence sent a potent message to both allies and enemies. This message, through the medium of violence called "propaganda by the deed," is still practiced today before the lens of the video camera.

The impact of technology on communications and control of information heightened the capacity of those who utilized terrorism as a form of propaganda not only to convey a message but, more ominously, to exert social and political control over subject populations that went far beyond the capability of the most repressive dictators of the past. The penetration and consequent control of all levels of political, social, and economic life by a repressive regime led to the development of the modern totalitarian state. The reign of terror pioneered by the French revolution was expanded with murderous efficiency by Stalin through the massive purges and show trials of the 1920s and 1930s and reached its zenith in the genocide attempted under the Third Reich with its concentration camps and crematoria. The murderous combination of technology and attendant organizational capabilities led to the maturation of "terrorism from above." Modern

---

[12]Reprinted from M. Confino, *Daughter of a Revolution.* London: Alcove Press, 1974 in Walter Laqueur, ed. *The Terrorist Reader: An Historical Anthology.* New York: New American Library, 1978, pp. 68–70.

state terrorism, which is aptly defined in what follows, had come of age:

> . . . state terrorism can be seen as a method of rule whereby some groups of people are victimized with great brutality, and more or less arbitrarily by the state, or state-supported actors, so that others who have reason to identify with those murdered, will despair, obey, or comply. Its main instruments are summary arrest and incarceration without trial, torture, political murder, disappearances, and concentration camps.[13]

CONTEMPORARY TERRORISM

In the 1960s, "terror from below" continued as a new generation of revolutionaries attempted to overthrow what they regarded as repressive regimes. In Latin America the use of terror as part of insurgent movements was accelerated by the Cuban revolution and the attempt to export it to Central and South America. Ernesto Che Guevara perhaps best embodied the mystique that surrounded the new revolutionaries. Guevara emphasized the need to employ terror tactics in an essentially rural guerrilla war. He emphasized the importance of the *foco*—a small clandestine group of rebels who could ignite the fires of revolution. Guevara, however, overlooked the importance of slowly developing a foundation of support among the indigenous peasantry. His failure to rally the peasants led to his capture and death in Bolivia. In spite of Guevara's failure, his mystique would influence other real and self-styled revolutionary terrorists.

In contrast to Guevara's rural-based approach, Carlos Marighella emphasized the importance of employing terrorism in the cities as a means of dramatizing the rebels' cause and provoking the government to overreact. In turn this overreaction was supposed to antagonize the general population, either neutralizing

---

[13]P. Timothy Busnell, Vladimir Shlapentokh, Christopher K. Vanderpool, and Jeyaratnam, eds., *State Terror: The Case of Violent Internal Repression.* Boulder, Colorado: Westview Press, 1991, p. 31.

their support for the established order or else prompting them to join the revolutionary cause. Marighella's *Minimanual of the Urban Guerrilla*[14] provided a tactical guide instructing future urban terrorists on how to finance their operations through bank robberies among other things. In the United States the Symbionese Liberation Army would follow Marighella's approach, even using the kidnapped Patty Hearst in their short-lived and violent history. During this period groups such as the Red Army Faction in Germany (better known to the public then as the Baader-Meinhof Gang), the Red Brigades in Italy, and the Weather Underground in the United States in reality revived and renewed the anarchistic tradition even though they conceived of themselves as bona fide internationalist socialist revolutionaries.

During the late 1960s the scope and impact of terrorism was greatly expanded, as was earlier noted, as a result of the large-scale global introduction of jet aircraft. The Popular Front for the Liberation of Palestine (PFLP) engaged in a number of highly dramatic operations in the period from 1968–1970 that would be copied by numerous terrorist groups in the following decades.

With the seizure of 53 American hostages at the U.S. Embassy in Tehran in November 1979, another chapter in modern terrorism was opened:

> . . . the behavior of Iran, Libya, and other countries points to the development of rogue, or outlaw states, who no longer use terror [solely] as an instrument of maintaining internal control, but rather as a technique in a new diplomatic method—'armed diplomacy'— as a means of carrying out foreign policy.[15]

In the 1980s states increasingly supported various terrorist groups in pursuit of their foreign policy objectives. "State-sponsored terrorism" by the Soviet Union, the United States, Iran,

---

[14]See, "Appendix: Minimanual of the Urban Guerrilla," in Robert Moss, *Urban Guerrilla Warfare*. London: International Institute for Strategic Studies, 1971.

[15]Stephen Sloan, "International Terrorism, Conceptual Problems and Implications," *Journal of Thought: An Interdisciplinary Quarterly,* 17, 2 (Summer 1982), p. 23.

Iraq, Syria, North Korea, and other governments enabled terrorists to have levels of financial, logistical, and tactical support unavailable to them in the past. The linkages between various terrorist groups and their state sponsors were hotly debated, particularly by the United States, which sought to verify the degree of Moscow's involvement with terrorists during the waning days of the Cold War. Such diverse groups as the West German Baader-Meinhof Gang, the Provisional Irish Republican Army (PIRA), and the Popular Front for the Liberation of Palestine (PFLP) received funding from their respective state sponsors.[16] State sponsorship, particularly in the Middle East, continues to enhance the capability of various terrorist groups to pursue their objectives.

FUTURE TRENDS

In trying to forecast future trends in terrorism one must be cautious to avoid inferring too much on the basis of limited information. New groups may rapidly emerge, whether pursuing new issues or perpetuating old animosities. Moreover old-line groups may be subject to fragmentation, generational disputes, and decline in the face of effective counterterrorism strategies. Keeping these caveats in view, a broad assessment of future trends follows. This assessment essentially covers two areas of change: (1) Geographically specific changes, that is, where is a group located and what are its goals and objectives, and (2) functionally specific changes, that is, how does a geographically specific terrorist group change its strategy based on technological innovations.

On the broadest geographical level, the fall of the Berlin Wall and the disintegration of the Soviet Union has unleashed, and will continue to unleash, forces of nationalism that had been repressed or long hidden under communist rule. These nationalisms, based on primordial loyalties fueled by ethnicity, language, and race,

---

[16]Claire Sterling. *The Terror Network: The Secret War of International Terrorism.* New York: Holt, Rinehart and Winston, Reader's Digest Press, 1981.

have already led to violence within the borders of the former Soviet Union that has spilled over into the Yugoslavian civil war. One can anticipate that terrorism "from above" and "from below" will not only intensify as groups assert their independence and as the states they threaten respond with repression in an attempt to survive, but that such terrorism will spill over into surrounding states fueled by émigré or exile groups who are seeking a territorial base from which to assert their own claims to a separate identity.

This assertion of ethnicity in the form of political terrorism may be in part a reaction by various ethnic groups against what they perceive to be the growing domination of an assimilating, cosmopolitan consumer mass culture as well as against the penetration of their societies by multinational corporations. With the envisioned integration of the European Community, one might hope that the erasure of traditional borders would lessen ethnic hostilities, but it is quite plausible that the romanticizing of its own idealized past by each of the various subnational groups could lead equally to a reaction against the present including the resort to terrorism.

Such a reaction against perceived domination by the technologically modern societies is already taking place in a most potent form. The rise of Islamic fundamentalism, not only in Southwest Asia but also within Africa and within the former borders of the Soviet Union, is likely to increase under a call for the reaffirmation of the Muslims' traditional values and unique cultural identity. Supported by Iran, a new generation of Muslim fundamentalist terrorist groups may follow in the tradition of Hezbollah and Islamic Jihad to strike at targets of opportunity, not only in the Middle East, but also in the "Great Satan"—the United States, and its European allies.

The resort to "agitational terror" will most likely continue throughout the Third World as a wide variety of groups react to the growing disparity between the "have" and "have-not" nations. In addition, the industrialized states of the West will not be immune from their own enduring and growing underclasses.

Finally one can anticipate that issue-oriented terrorist groups will continue to exist and grow. One can anticipate, for example, that extremists within the ecological movement may employ terrorism as a means of reacting against what they view to be the pernicious impact of modern technology.

Functionally, modern terrorism is entering a very dangerous period. The disintegration of the Soviet Union has led to the end of the nuclear "balance of terror" between Washington and Moscow. As a result, many states wishing to become regional powers will seek to use the threats of chemical, biological, and nuclear weapons to assert their hegemony over particular geographic areas. An even more alarming possibility is that such states may provide the technology of mass destruction to terrorist groups under their sponsorship. Even without such sponsorship terrorist groups may still be able to acquire such weapons, especially portable nuclear weapons and chemical weapons, as they pursue their own goals.

The changing landscape of terrorism will probably include additional dangerous innovations. Armed with high-technology weapons various terrorist groups may engage in highly profitable criminal activities that now threaten states, much as the narco-terrorists threaten Latin American governments, but on a regional or global scale. The impact of technological innovation may ultimately lead to a more insidious development likely to be exploited by the practitioners of "regime" and "enforcement" terrorism. Armed with the technological capabilities not only to kill or physically maim large numbers of people but also with the capacity to invade the privacy and security of the individual, a new generation of mercenaries may offer their services to the highest bidders, whether these be corporations or governments. State-organized terrorism in particular,

> . . . will continue to decide the fate of mass populations. It will probably become more invidious and more intrusive. The firing squad and torture chamber will continue but one must be particularly concerned that the information revolution (in the form of computer technology) does not provide authoritarian regimes with the capability of not only effectively controlling subject people, but

also effectively placing a human face on their activities by no longer having to rely on brute force.[17]

In the next generation the physical brutality of terrorism will unfortunately not only be ''enhanced'' by the proliferation of modern weapons of mass destruction, but also by the capabilities of both states and nonstates to breach the already fragile security zone of the individual who may be targeted by new techniques of ''unarmed propaganda'' as opposed to the old ''armed propaganda.''

THE CLASSIFICATION SYSTEM EMPLOYED IN THE DICTIONARY

Because of the great diversity of terrorist groups presented in the following pages a classification system has been provided to enable the reader not only to identify the unique features of each group but also to have the means to acquire a comparative perspective on terrorism. As is true of all classification systems this one is arbitrary and a given group may fit into more than one category. Nevertheless this classification scheme meets the requirement that it be sufficiently broad in scope to discern patterns that may be obscured by the outward diversity that characterizes the landscape of terrorism.

A thorough encyclopedia of terrorism will need to identify and describe other terrorist phenomena besides the various terrorist groups, such as the principal doctrines motivating such groups, biographic sketches of important theorists, tacticians and operators, and chronologies of events associated with particular groups or movements. Properly conceived, a regular scheme of description and comparative analysis should not preclude some discussion of the distinctive political beliefs, unique organizational features, motivations, and tactics of a group.

---

[17]Stephen Sloan, ''Technology and Terrorism: Privatizing Public Violence,'' *IEEE Technology and Technology Magazine,* 100, 2 (Summer 1991), p. 14.

The scheme for classifying terrorist groups presented here is derived, in part, from Richard Schultz's proposed typology of terrorism.[18] Each entry on a given group addresses two essential questions: First, "Who are they?," that is, what sort of *group* or *actor* is behind the given terrorist action(s)? Second, "What do they want?," that is, what are the *long-range political goals* that the group is seeking? Together these two characteristics define the overall type of each group. Once one grasps the overall type of group one may proceed to note the peculiarities of doctrine, strategy, tactics, targets, group origins, and history and leadership that distinguishes each group within a single type from others belonging to that same basic group type.

TYPES OF TERRORIST GROUPS

Following both Paul Wilkinson[19] and Richard Schultz[20] this classification recognizes three main types of terrorist actors:

I. *State Actors:* Governments and their agencies can use terrorism against their own people to preserve their rule. Sovereign states can also use terrorism to topple other governments or else to force them to change their politics.

Examples would include the Tonton Macoutes of the former "Papa Doc" Duvalier regime in Haiti used to terrorize political opponents of the regime. In Nicaragua under Sandinista rule the *turbas divinas* ("divine mobs") and Iran's *hezbollahi* street mobs are also examples of state-directed and controlled terror groups.

II. *Revolutionary Actors* use terrorism to overthrow a regime, or to force a regime to change fundamentally how it conducts its public business, or else to establish a new state within the territory

---

[18]Schultz, Richard. 1980. "Conceptualizing Political Terrorism: A Typology," in Alan D. Buckley and Daniel D. Olsen ed. *International Terrorism: Current Research and Future Directions.* (Wayne, New Jersey: Avery Publishing Group, 1980), pp. 9–14.

[19]Wilkinson, Paul. 1974. *Political Terrorism.* (London: Macmillan, 1974).

[20]Richard Schultz., pp. 1–11.

of an existing state. Although nationalist insurgents seeking to secede from an existing nation-state appear to pursue a more modest goal than those who seek an overall sociopolitical transformation within that nation-state, both nationalist secessionists and self-styled revolutionaries are seeking fundamental changes in the status quo, which is basically the essence of revolution. Radical socialism and radical nationalism may not resemble each other in substance but if the goal that each strives to achieve is so radically different from the existing state that realizing it requires the end of the current state then each would be equally revolutionary.

An example of this can be found in the relationship of the two groups, Dev Sol (the Revolutionary Left) and the Armenian Secret Army for the Liberation of Armenia (ASALA) with respect to the existing Turkish Republic. The former would overthrow its current regime to establish a Marxist-Leninist state within the existing Turkish borders. The latter would establish a new Armenian state within the eastern one-third of the modern Turkish state's territory. Both are counted as ''revolutionary'' groups since each seeks an absolute transformation of the existing status quo in Turkey, one redefining the social and economic system within Turkey and the other redefining the scope of Turkish jurisdiction and sovereignty over territory and nationalities.

III. *Entrepreneurial Actors* are those transnational terrorist groups that have achieved a degree of group identity, making them autonomous from any given nation-state. While Wilkinson and Schultz count ethnic nationalist terror groups as representing forms of ''Sub-Revolutionary Terrorism'' under the classification system used in this text they would be considered examples of revolutionary groups rather than entrepreneurial groups. In effect, entrepreneurial groups either hire themselves out for service to various regimes on a contract basis or else pursue an agenda of limited goals distinct from any nationalistic or revolutionist program. As the Abu Nidal Organization and Ahmad Jibril's Popular Front for the Liberation of Palestine-General Command have separated themselves from the mainstream Palestinian nationalist movement, they have transformed themselves into self-sustaining criminal organizations that sell their terrorist skills to various Arab and non-Arab regimes. Criminal organizations may also maintain their own in-house terrorist capacity as has been the case with the Colombian drug syndicates' proprietary death squads known as "the Extraditables" and MAS (Muerte a Secuestradores, "Death to Kidnappers"). Less insidious examples of entrepreneurial groups include ecological activists and animal-rights activists who pursue a terrorist version of single-interest politics cutting across several national jurisdictions. One of the most prominent examples of such a group that has embarked on a terrorist campaign is the Animal Liberation Front, which has carried out sabotage of private and public research facilities and harassment of animal researchers in the United States, Canada, and Great Britain.

The category of entrepreneurial groups often contains groups that at an earlier stage in their history would have been more readily classified as revolutionary organizations. This can be explained often by such groups' failure to achieve their original revolutionary goals coupled with their members' inability to separate themselves from the cohesive identity of the group, for which they have often sacrificed the prime years of their lives and which has absorbed so much of their energies and devotion. Such members also often have no alternative skills with which to pursue a nonterrorist livelihood and so the group continues to exist by selling its services to various buyers. Examples would include, again, the Abu Nidal group as well as the Mujahideen-i Khalq-i Iran ("People's Strugglers of Iran"), a revolutionary group that has turned entrepreneurial due to the destruction of its membership base in Iran by the current Iranian regime and the group's need to attach itself to Iraqi sponsorship in order to continue its activities from outside Iran's borders.

Identification of Goals: There are three main types of goals, namely, I. regime maintenance, II. regime change, and, III. seeking limited advantage(s).

As an example of the first, state actors use repression as a means of ensuring regime survival. Likewise revolutionary actors seek to change a political status quo. Entrepreneurial groups specialize in coercive types of terror that may be aimed only at gaining marginal, or relative, political or economic goals, e.g., hostage-taking in order to exact the profits of extortion.

The generation of a typology from these two sets of characteristics is illustrated in Figure 1 below along with specific examples of each:

		TYPES OF OBJECTIVES		
		REPRESSIVE	REVOLUTIONARY	LIMITED
T Y P E O F A C T O R	STATE	Tonton Macoutes	Islamic Revolutionary Guards Corps	Wrath of God
	REVOLUTIONARY	Force 17	Sendero Luminoso	Black September
	ENTREPRENEURIAL	The Extraditables	PFLP-General Command	Animal Rights Groups

Figure 1. Typology for Classification of Groups and Group Activities and Functions. Examples of each are given for each typological combination.

The types found in the upper left to lower right diagonal in Figure 1 represent the most natural congruence of actor types with goal types. State actors have a primary interest in self-maintenance. The Tonton Macoutes of Haiti are a state-sponsored repressive group. Revolutionary groups generally pursue a revolutionary agenda while entrepreneurial groups will be primarily motivated by goals other than maintaining or overthrowing state systems. The main characteristics of actor types and of types of goals are summarized on the following page.

Although this congruence of actor types and goals seems intuitive, it does not tell the entire story. In fact, each basic type can use terrorism in each of the three ways described earlier. While the main upper-left to lower-right diagonal contains the most favored position for each of the actor types, the off-diagonal

SUMMARY OF TYPOLOGICAL CLASSIFICATION SCHEME:

I.   Type of Actor

   STATE

   -   acting against their own people to preserve their regime, sometimes called state repression, regime terrorism, or "state terror"

   -   acting against other states to topple their governments, known also as state sponsorship of terrorism

   -   acting against other states to force political changes, that is, changes in the policies of targeted governments, also called state sponsorship of terrorism

   REVOLUTIONARY

   -   acting to overthrow a regime to establish a new regime

   -   acting to create a new state out of the territory of an existing state, e.g., nationalist insurgents

   -   acting to create a fundamental change in the nation-state system, e.g. pan-nationalist or anarchistic movements

   ENTREPRENEURIAL

   -   acting autonomously from any _existing_ nation-state but also from any _aspirant_ would-be nation-state

   -   operating transnationally, may hire themselves out to states or other groups

   -   engaging in criminal actions but usually as a means to other political ends, e.g., bank robberies and kidnapping for ransom in order to finance operations or else to drive out some foreign presence

2.   Goals of Actors:

   -   Regime Maintenance

   -   Regime Change

   -   Limited Advantage
       (sub-systematic changes)

positions are roles that such groups can occupy as situations require. Thus, although al Fatah is primarily a revolutionary group seeking the establishment of a Palestinian state, it also has a "regime maintaining" goal of keeping other Palestinians in line and punishing dissidents. Therefore it created Force 17 as its own version of a security police and intelligence force within the Palestinian community. Following the expulsion of the PLO from Jordan, al Fatah also sought the limited goal of punishing Jordanian government and military authorities. To that limited end Fatah created the Black September Organization, which very quickly expanded its list of targets to include Israel and the Western nations.

The example of the "Extraditables," an extension of the Medellín drug cartel, which is essentially a criminal entrepreneurial group, shows how even entrepreneurial groups can act as protectors of a status quo or as a revolutionary group. In this case the status quo would have been the cartel's domination over much of the economic life of Colombia and over the rural communities producing the coca crop. It has also behaved in a revolutionary manner in seeking to destabilize the Colombian government through wholesale terrorism against not only the Colombian government but even against terrorist guerrilla groups that have interfered in the drug cartel's operations and profits.

State actors also can seek to produce revolutions in other nations or else use terror to achieve limited goals. Iran has sought to export its Islamic revolution to neighboring Muslim states and the very same Islamic Revolutionary Guards Corps that acts as an organ of state repression within Iran has set up training camps in Lebanon's Bekaa valley to train Hezbollah guerrillas and terrorists bent on establishing an Islamic state in Lebanon and on destroying the State of Israel. Israel meanwhile developed its own corps of quiet killers, known as the "Wrath of God," who engage in the limited pursuit of tracking down and killing Palestinians, or others, considered to be responsible for terrorist actions against Israel, such as the Black September operatives who planned and executed the Munich Olympics massacre, or else considered to be public enemies of Israel, such as Khalil al Wazir. In fact, it is this wide range of possible motives enjoyed by each of the actor types that makes state sponsorship of terrorism at all possible.

Of course, classification schemes do not accommodate all cases perfectly. There are at least two types of terrorist groups that are anomalies, namely what this dictionary describes as "anarchistic leftists" and state co-opting groups.

Augustus Norton and others have used "anarchist" or "anarchistic" as an additional classification. One can argue that anarchists, too, should fall under the heading of "Revolutionary" since they also seek a revolutionary transformation of the nation-state system to a nonstate system, which also entails the overall transformation of existing regimes. While few groups today openly identify themselves as being "anarchists," there is a type of revolutionary group that espouses tentatively revolutionary socialist goals while behaving for all practical purposes as if its goals were anarchistic. During the student radicalism of the late 1960s a number of similar student groups emerged in Europe, North America, and Japan that spoke the language of the New Left but ultimately appeared to pursue terrorist violence as an end in itself rather than as a strategy to achieve revolution. In spite of their self-identification with a world socialist revolution, they amounted to little more than practicing anarchists, or perhaps even nihilists, insofar as they limited their purposes to destroying the existing capitalist states rather than building the foundations of some successor socialist state. While this type of group does form a subspecies of the revolutionary terrorist groups it is sufficiently different from other revolutionary groups to deserve its own distinctive label of "anarchistic leftist terrorists."

The other anomalous group type are those nonstate groups that are so powerful relative to a weak, or weakened, state that they are able to penetrate the apparatus of state power and to usurp government power for their own ends. Examples of this can be found in the penetration of the Salvadoran transitional government's military and security forces in the early 1980s by privately run "death squads," or EOKA-Beta's penetration of the Cypriot national guard and judiciary prior to the coup d'état against Archbishop Makarios in 1974.

Although these cases seem anomalous, the ''anarchistic leftists'' are simply a variation of the revolutionary actor while the state co-opters are entrepreneurial or revolutionary actors that exploit opportunities to usurp control over a weakened state for achieving limited ends. Having established a classification scheme broad enough to encompass even these subspecies, the reader can proceed to study who and what the various terrorist groups are and what it is each is seeking.

To provide further qualitative and quantitative information regarding the various groups that will better facilitate comparison between groups the authors have provided brief tallies of the numbers of various actions attributed to each group. These tallies are also analyzed as percentages of the total numbers of actions attributed to each group. The figures used have been based largely on the statistical database appended to Edward F. Mickolus's three major chronologies spanning the period from 1968 to 1987.

Note on transliterations of Arabic and Persian words and names: The authors have not adopted a single, consistent phonetic transliteration of the various names or words cited in this *Dictionary* that were originally written in the Arabic script. Having already familiarized most readers with inexact transliterations of certain Arabic or Persian words, popular literature and journalistic usages have completely outpaced the efforts of linguistic purists to devise a consistent, univerally-observed scheme of transliteration for such words. For instance, most readers are already more acquainted with Koran than with the more precise Quran, or with Hezbollah rather than Hizballah. Therefore, to make this reference volume relatively more accessible to a wider readership, those current and more common spellings have been kept in preference to more unfamiliar alternative spellings. Other Arabic or Persian names have been phonetically transliterated whenever a popular usage was not already current.

THE DICTIONARY

- A -

ABDUL RAHMAN, SHEIKH UMAR. (b. 1938) Islamic fundamentalist cleric and leader of *Jamaa al Islami* fundamentalist
group in Egypt. Abdul Rahman was along with the Munazzamat al Jihad (q.v.) defendants accused of assassinating
President Anwar Sadat in 1981. Abdul Rahman, who is
blind, was considered an accessory due to his issuing the
Islamic judicial decree to the assassins that authorized the
killing of Sadat but was acquitted. After his release, Abdul
Rahman led a puritanical Islamic fundamentalist movement
which aims to topple the Mubarak regime in order to create
an Islamic state. The *Jamaa al Islami* has tried to accomplish
this in part by attacks upon non-Muslim tourists in Egypt,
particularly those visiting the archaeological remnants of
pre-Islamic Egypt.

    Although banned from entering the United States as a
person known to be associated with terrorist groups and
activities, Abdul Rahman nonetheless obtained a tourist visa
in the Sudan and came to New Jersey where he became the
prayer leader of a small mosque in Jersey City. Following the
World Trade Center bombing (q.v.) he was implicated in that
conspiracy as well as in a broader conspiracy to bomb other
public places in New York, including the Holland and
Lincoln tunnels and the United Nations building. He was
also implicated in a plot to murder U.S. Senator Alfonse
d'Amato (R., N.Y.) and U.N. Secretary General Boutros-
Ghali. In June 1993, Abdul Rahman and seven others were
arrested in connection with this plot.

Abdul Rahman was also the spiritual mentor of El Sayyid A. Nosair who assassinated JDL founder Rabbi Meir Kahane on 5 November 1990. See Munazzamat al Jihad, Takfir, and the World Trade Center Bombing.

ABU NIDAL. (b. 1935) Sabri Khalil al Banna was born in Jaffa, Palestine, but fled with his family to Beirut in 1948. He joined Al Fatah (q.v.) after the 1967 Arab-Israeli war, adopting the nom de guerre Abu Nidal, meaning "father of the struggle." He became a high-ranking member of the Palestine Liberation Organization, being put in charge of its diplomatic mission in the Sudan in 1970 and afterward being appointed chief PLO representative in Iraq. After the October 1973 war he grew disillusioned with the direction of the PLO under Yasir Arafat's leadership and founded his own rival group, the Fatah Revolutionary Council (q.v.) in 1974.

Abu Nidal reputedly has tried to assassinate Arafat on a number of occasions and therefore is under a death sentence by the PLO. In addition to the Fatah Revolutionary Council, Abu Nidal has founded and directs other groups such as Black June (q.v.), the Revolutionary Organization of Socialist Muslims, and the Arab Revolutionary Brigades, which may be either separate groups or merely different names for the same group. As the organizational relationship of these groups to one another is unclear, analysts tend to speak of an "Abu Nidal Organization" rather than the Fatah Revolutionary Council or its satellite groups.

Abu Nidal has enjoyed the state sponsorship of Iraq from 1974 to 1983, Syria from 1983 to 1987, and Libya since 1987. The notoriety of his terrorist actions has moved each of his sponsors to distance themselves from him. Although the Iraqi government, with which Abu Nidal had the longest-standing relationship, ordered his organization to leave Iraq in 1983 during the 1990–1991 Persian Gulf crisis and Operation Desert Storm, Abu Nidal's organization is believed to have carried out assassinations on behalf of Iraq against Arab officials critical of Saddam Hussein, in particular, the Speaker of the Egyptian National Assembly, killed on 12 October 1990, and also PLO official Salah Khalaf, killed on 14 January 1991. Currently Abu Nidal is headquartered in Libya.

ABU NIDAL ORGANIZATION. Name by which Western intelligence and law-enforcement agencies refer to the umbrella organization comprising the Fatah Revolutionary Council and other Palestinian terrorist groups all headed by Sabri Khalil al Banna (aka, Abu Nidal). See Fatah Revolutionary Council

ACTION-FRONT OF NATIONAL SOCIALISTS. The *Aktiongemeinschaft Nationaler Sozialisten* (ANS) was a German neo-Nazi offshoot of the defunct right-wing National Democratic Party. This group has engaged in paramilitary training and terrorist activities to overthrow the Federal Republic of Germany and restore a right-wing authoritarian nationalist regime. The ANS was formed in 1977 by former West German Army lieutenant Michael Kühnen, who led the group in violent attacks against foreign immigrants, Jews, and leftists. Apart from conducting this violence and vandalism, the approximately 270 ANS members were heavily involved in paramilitary training, stealing military arms, and committing robberies.

ANS leader Michael Kühnen was first arrested in late 1977 for painting swastikas on shop windows in Hamburg. In 1978 an antipolice riot in Schleswig-Holstein broke out when German police tried to prevent about 120 ANS members from dedicating a plaque honoring Adolf Hitler. Michael Kühnen and 19 other ANS members were arrested then and later released. Four other ANS members were arrested in August 1978 for plotting to bomb the Kiel office of the Communist Federation party.

Kühnen was sentenced to four years in jail for incitement to racism and glorification of violence. In 1980 his followers in Hamburg ''tried'' an ANS member whom they suspected of being an informant and a homosexual, who was accordingly murdered on 28 May 1981. During Kühnen's imprisonment his lieutenant, Christian Worch, led the ANS until he, too, was arrested on bombing charges in March 1980. Kühnen was released from jail in 1982 on condition that he not employ, train or shelter neo-Nazis. Defying the terms of his probation he reconstituted the ANS group under the new name "Action-Front of National Socialists/National Activists" until it was also banned in 1983.

Although Kühnen died in mid-1991, he left behind a network of similar neo-Nazi groups which relied on cellular structures to elude penetration and suppression by German authorities. Kühnen reputedly also masterminded the strategy of building up support for the neo-Nazi movement in Germany by exploiting widespread anti-foreigner resentment against guest workers and immigrants fleeing Eastern European countries in the post-Communist era.

AFRICAN NATIONAL CONGRESS. The ANC, founded in 1912, is the oldest and largest black nationalist political party in South Africa and has been the leading group there in the struggle against apartheid. From 1912 to 1961 the ANC was a purely political movement but, following the 20 March 1960 massacre of some 69 demonstrators by South African police in Sharpeville, it was banned by the South African government. The political apparatus of the ANC went into exile while Nelson Mandela (b. 1918) and other ANC leaders remaining in South Africa created the armed wing of the ANC, *Umkhonto we Sizwe*, to carry out limited violence against the South African regime to gain redress of grievances.

As Umkhonto we Sizwe has used indiscriminate bombings of civilian areas and has targeted white farmers as well as South African military and security forces to attain its political agenda, it can be properly classified as a terrorist group. Accordingly, the U.S. Department of Defense 1990 publication *Profiles of Terrorist Groups* listed the African

National Congress among the terrorist groups operating in Africa. Other observers and institutions, viewing the ANC in the context of South African apartheid and state repression of its black and colored citizens, argue that the African National Congress should be considered a legitimate political group and are therefore reluctant to classify it as a terrorist group. Accordingly the U.S. Department of State Office for the Coordinator for Counterterrorism does not include the ANC among its listing of the major terrorist groups.

It should be noted that the legitimacy of the ends sought by the African National Congress and the heinous nature of the apartheid it fights are matters logically distinct from the questions of the legitimacy of the tactics elected by the ANC to achieve its ends and to fight apartheid. The African National Congress, like the Sinn Fein of Ireland, can be regarded as a primarily political entity, while its armed wing, like the Irish Republican Army, may be studied as a military phenomenon and assessed accordingly. Therefore the terrorist actions attributed to the ANC are analyzed under the heading given for the armed wing of the ANC. See Umkhonto we Sizwe.

AIR INDIA BOMBING. On 23 June 1985 Air India flight 182, a Boeing 747 carrying 307 passengers and 22 crew members, en route from Montreal to New Delhi disintegrated at 30,000 feet and 180 miles off the west coast of Ireland. All aboard perished, most of them naturalized Canadian citizens of Indian origin. The same day luggage from an Air India flight originating in Vancouver, British Columbia, exploded at Tokyo's Narita Airport, killing two Japanese baggage handlers. While forensic evidence from the fragments of flight 182 have not conclusively proven that the airplane was bombed, most experts familiar with these incidents concluded that flight 182 contained a radio bomb similar to the one reconstructed from remains of the bomb that exploded at Narita airport.

The Royal Canadian Mounted Police learned that two

Sikhs had checked in bags at Vancouver to be transferred to flight 182 in Montreal but neither of them later joined that flight. Credit for bombing the Air India flight was claimed in the name of the Dashmesh Regiment (q.v.) but also by the Kashmir Liberation Army. Canadian Sikhs have angrily denied that Sikhs had any role in the incident.

ALFARO VIVE CARAJO ORGANIZATION. The Alfaro Vive Carajo ("Alfaro Lives, Damn It!") Organization is a non-state, Ecuadoran revolutionary group that seeks to overthrow "oligarchic and imperialist" institutions and to force the withdrawal of foreign interests from Ecuador. AVC has received material aid from the M-19 (q.v.) group in Colombia and possibly from Nicaragua, Cuba, and Libya.

While founded in the late 1970s this group surfaced in August 1983 with the theft of the swords of the early twentieth-century Ecuadoran revolutionary and national hero, Eloy Alfaro. In May 1984 the group bombed the U.S. Embassy compound in Quito. In October 1984 it then séized the Costa Rican Embassy to protest the extradition of AVC leader Rosa Cardenas. On 16 October 1985 it seized the Mexican Embassy, telexing messages to other Latin American countries condemning the severing of diplomatic relations between Ecuador and Nicaragua and denouncing U.S. support for the contras. In May 1986 it kidnapped a Constitutional Court member, who was later freed after a negotiated surrender. In April 1987 it bombed a police station in Quito.

At its height AVC had 200 to 300 members and financed itself primarily by bank robberies. AVC exploited its activities as means to gain publicity for its cause, once even seizing a radio station in February 1986 to broadcast a propaganda tape celebrating its third anniversary. Due to deaths and arrests of its leaders in 1986–1987 the organization lost its strength and has shown little activity since then.

ALIANZA APOSTOLICA ANTI-COMMUNISTA (AAA). The "Anti-Communist Apostolic Alliance" was a formerly

Spanish state-sponsored guerrilla group with the limited aims of suppressing leftism and separatism. AAA conducted attacks on Basque separatists of the Basque Fatherland and Liberty (q.v.) group within the Basque regions of Spain and France and bombed both the Catalan Center in Madrid and the Catalonian paper *El Papus* in Barcelona in 1977. In January 1977 two AAA gunmen killed four prominent leftist lawyers in Madrid. The arrest of these gunmen led to more convictions of other AAA activists. The activities of this group ceased in the early 1980s.

AMAL. Amal (Arabic: "Hope," also the acronym of Afwaj al Muqawama al Lubnaniya, "Lebanese Resistance Detachments") is a political and paramilitary organization representing the Shia of Lebanon. Although a nonstate actor, Amal has a political infrastructure and has gained territorial control over large areas of West Beirut and southern Lebanon during the Lebanese civil war. After the 1978–1979 revolution in Iran, Amal enjoyed some support from the Iranian revolutionary government. After 1982, however, Iran began to form the rival Hezbollah militia (q.v.) under its sponsorship and Amal turned to Syrian sponsorship instead.

Since Amal seeks to change the terms of power in Lebanon in favor of the Shia by setting aside the 1946 "national covenant" between Lebanon's Christians and Sunnite Muslims it may be considered a revolutionary actor. Yet it has neither sought to exclude other confessional groups from participation in Lebanese politics nor has it sought to create a full-scale Islamic state in Lebanon after the Iranian model. For these very reasons more militant Amal members deserted Amal for the splinter group Islamic Amal (q.v.). Most of these defectors were absorbed later into Hezbollah, a Shiite militia created under Iranian sponsorship that seeks to establish an exclusively Islamic state in Lebanon.

While Amal is indigenous to Lebanon it was founded by an Iranian clergyman, Musa Sadr, who arrived in Lebanon in

1957 and established the "Movement of the Deprived" in 1974 to help the Lebanese Shia gain political power. With the outbreak of civil war in 1975 Musa Sadr authorized the creation of a military branch, which properly was the organization called "Amal." The Israeli invasion of southern Lebanon in 1978 and continual Palestinian-Israeli clashes in the largely Shii south of Lebanon increased the Shia's acceptance of Amal as representing and protecting their community. The subsequent victory of an Islamic revolution in Shii Iran also bolstered the confidence of Lebanon's Shia and their support for Amal.

Amal's relationship with Iran's revolutionary government was initially friendly but deteriorated rapidly. With the disappearance of Imam Musa Sadr during a visit to Libya in August 1978, Amal's leadership had passed into the hands of more secular nationalistic Shii politicians who had less sympathy for the ideal of creating a theocratic Islamic state in Lebanon. Also due to the enmity that had grown between the Lebanese Shia and Palestinian guerrillas operating in the south of Lebanon, Amal, in effect, welcomed the 1982 Israeli invasion in the naive hope that Israeli forces would shortly leave and return the south of Lebanon to Shii control. Iran's diplomatic overtures to Libya also antagonized Amal members who believed that the Libyan leader Muammar Qaddafi was responsible for Imam Musa Sadr's disappearance. The falling out between the Iranian government and Amal as well as the defection from Amal of more militant fundamentalists led Iran to sponsor the creation of the Hezbollah militia, which absorbed much of the strength of Amal's following.

Amal's notoriety as a terrorist group stems largely from a mistaken association between it and the rival Hezbollah, which carried out a highly visible campaign of vehicle bombings, assassinations and hostage takings against U.S. and other Western targets in Lebanon. By late 1988 Amal had carried out 18 notable terrorist actions affecting non-Lebanese nationals, including a major bombing, a hijacking, and six kidnappings. From the founding of Hezbollah in

1982 until late 1988, that group, acting sometimes under its nom de guerre "Islamic Jihad," had carried out 137 note-worthy terrorist acts, including 38 bombings, 26 kidnap-pings, 4 hijackings, 7 assassinations, and 6 rocket attacks. Amal's role in assuming custody of the hostages taken in the hijacking of TWA flight 847 in 1985 likewise was secondary to that of Hezbollah in planning and carrying out the original hijacking. Following the TWA 874 incident, open warfare erupted between Hezbollah and Amal. Amal has since then accepted Syria as its main foreign sponsor in place of Iran and has acted more like one Lebanese communal militia among many than as a Pan-Islamic revolutionary vanguard.

AMAL. The Islamic Action [= Amal] Organization is one of a number of Shiite Muslim fundamentalist groups within Iraq seeking to overthrow the Bathist government in that country. Despite the similarity between the transliteration of its Arabic name and that of the Amal (q.v.) group in Lebanon these are different organizations having no direct ties with one another. The Amal group was independent of the al Dawa (q.v.) group in Iraq, which is the largest of the Shiite Muslim fundamentalist groups in Iraq. Both organizations have become affiliated with the umbrella group known as the Supreme Assembly for the Islamic Revolution of Iraq, created in 1982 and headquartered in Tehran, Iran.

ANANDA MARG. The Indian Hindu group, Ananda Marg ("Path of Eternal Bliss") is a nonstate mystical and religious sect devoted to the worship of Kali, the Hindu goddess of destruction. Followers of this sect undertook terrorist activities in the period 1975–1978 for the limited purpose of freeing their founder, Prabhat Ranjan Sarkar, who had been imprisoned in India for murder. This sect comprises a large number of American, Australian, and European followers both in their home countries as well as in India. These non-Indian followers had engaged in attacks on Indian diplomatic targets abroad, giving an international terrorist

character to what otherwise might have been dismissed as a
rather minor sectarian, domestic Indian phenomenon.

Within India on 2 January 1975 Ananda Margists killed
Narayan Mishra, India's Minister of Railways, in a bombing,
killing 2 and wounding 25 others. In March 1975 they
attempted to kill the Chief Justice of India in a grenade
attack. On 4 July 1975 the group was banned under the
Indian government's declared state of emergency. Although
the ban was lifted in 1977, the group carried out a series of
bombings against Indian government targets in Australia. On
15 September 1977, an Australian Ananda Margist stabbed
the Indian military attaché in Melbourne, and on 19 October
1977 another stabbing attempt was made in Melbourne
against an Air India official. In February 1978 they bombed
a conference of the Asian and Pacific Commonwealth heads
of government being held at the Sydney Hilton Hotel killing
two people. American members of the sect were involved in
an assault against an Indian Embassy official in the Philippines on 25 March 1978 and were implicated, along with two
Australians, in a plot to bomb the Indian Embassy in
Thailand on 21 April 1978.

Since 1978 the group, numbering around 1,000 members,
has largely ceased terrorist activities and operates openly in
India, principally in the West Bengal region.

ANARCHISTIC LEFTIST TERRORISM. During the late 1960s
the antiwar protest movement among university students in
Europe, Japan, and the United States gave rise to several
terrorist groups that defy ready identification as revolutionary or entrepreneurial terrorist groups. The Red Army Faction (q.v.) in West Germany, Direct Action (q.v.) group in
France, the Red Brigades (q.v.) and Prima Linea (q.v.) in
Italy, the Communist Combatant Cells (q.v.) in Belgium, the
Weather Underground (q.v.) in the United States, and the
Japanese Red Army (q.v.) all rationalized their terrorism in
revolutionary leftist terms but ultimately appeared to pursue
terrorist violence as an end in itself rather than as a strategy to

achieve revolution. These groups could be considered "leftist" only insofar as they despised capitalism, believed in the superiority of a socialist state, and often spoke in Marxist jargon. For the most part they consisted of alienated middle-class youth who subsisted on their support groups or from the proceeds of robberies and kidnappings. They were also anarchistic insofar as they limited their purposes to destroying the existing capitalist states rather than building the foundations of some successor socialist state.

Many of these groups envisioned themselves as vanguard groups in a world revolutionary movement and sought contacts and working relations with such groups as the Popular Front for the Liberation of Palestine, which often provided them with training and experience. The Red Army Faction eventually became co-opted by the East German communist regime while the Japanese Red Army has similarly become dependent on the Libyan and Syrian regimes. These groups were characterized by a certain heady romanticism and utopianism that drew forth the scorn of more orthodox Marxist thinkers and activists who generally criticized such groups as seeking to substitute the volunteerism of vanguard groups for patient construction of class-based revolutionary consciousness. Although the writings of Herbert Marcuse were much admired by such anarchistic leftists, he himself derided their movement as the "pubertarian struggle."

Because most of the members of these groups reject their family origins or ethnic and religious backgrounds, they are isolated from a community support system that ensures steady recruitment of younger members into their ranks and therefore the survival of these groups is somewhat doubtful. In part for the same reason ethnic and sectarian-based terrorist groups and movements have supplanted anarchistic leftist terrorist groups as the main source of antistate and international terrorist violence in the 1990s.

ANGRY BRIGADE. The "Angry Brigade" was a nonstate British group of ultraleftist university students who adopted more antiauthoritarian, anarchistic ideas in the wake of the 1968 student uprising in France. Their goal of revolutionary anarchism was sought through a series of bank robberies and some 27 bombings in the period from 1968–1971, including two bomb attacks on the home of Robert Carr, British Secretary of State for Employment. Apparently the group intended these bombings as acts of armed propaganda but sought to avoid causing human casualties. The arrest of the so-called Stoke Newington Eight in August 1971 effectively smashed the core of the group and ended its activities.

ANIMAL LIBERATION FRONT. The Animal Liberation Front (ALF) is a nonstate group with the limited aim of protecting ''animal rights,'' specifically by stopping the use of animals as foodstuffs or experimental subjects and also by freeing captive animals. ALF emerged as one of the more radical animal rights groups when founded in 1978 by Ronnie Lee in England. Its membership now includes several thousand in both Britain and the United States.

On 17 November 1984, ALF announced that it had contaminated Mars candy bars manufactured in Southampton, England, with rat poison to protest the manufacturer's use of monkeys in tooth decay research. Around 3,000 tons of candy bars were recalled and destroyed, equivalent to a loss of sales of 15 million pounds sterling. ALF was believed to be responsible for the arson of a livestock disease laboratory under construction at the University of California at Davis that caused $3.5 million in damages. On 3 April 1989, ALF freed 1,200 experimental rabbits, frogs, and mice from a University of Arizona research lab and then torched the lab as well as the University administration building. On 6 July 1990, British police defused a bomb ALF had planted in London's Regent Park.

In the United States since June 1991 ALF has targeted facilities supporting mink fur production beginning with the arson of a mink feed storage barn at Oregon State University. In this campaign ALF has destroyed the equivalent of 130 years of data on mink fur production. In February 1992 ALF torched a Michigan State University researcher's office, destroying 10 years of toxicology research data even though the experiments had used animal semen samples rather than direct testing upon live animals.

Other animal rights activists, such as People for the Ethical Treatment of Animals and the University Students Against Vivisection, have criticized ALF's activities for drawing the animal rights movement into disrepute.

ANIMAL RIGHTS MILITIA. The Animal Rights Militia is a more radical British splinter group of the Animal Liberation Front (q.v.). While having the same limited aims as its parent group of stopping the use of animals in foodstuffs and experimental research, ARM has resorted to more violent tactics of direct attacks upon researchers rather than limiting itself to vandalism of research facilities or economic sabotage. In January 1986 ARM planted bombs under two cars and at two homes of four different victims, all involved either in the commercial breeding of animals or in research involving animal subjects. Although ARM gave prior warnings about its bombs, none of which exploded, the British government regarded this group as a grave public menace at that time.

ANTI-COMMUNIST SECRET ARMY. The *Ejército Secreto Anticommunista* (ESA) was a state-sponsored, repressive organization aimed at silencing leftist dissent and activism in Guatemala that operated largely as a death squad (q.v.). ESA emerged in 1977 during a period when the leftist guerrilla movement was reconsolidating its forces. ESA involved members of the Guatemalan security forces who participated in assaulting and killing students at San Carlos University. ESA published death lists of leftist intellectuals and labor leaders and forced many left-wing politicians to flee Guatemala. ESA is thought to have been responsible for the bombing of the Soviet Tass News Agency office in Guatemala City in 1988.

ANTI-IMPERIALIST INTERNATIONAL BRIGADE. The Anti-Imperialist International Brigade is a nonstate, revolutionary leftist group that is a front for the Japanese Red Army. (See Japanese Red Army)

ANTI-TERRORIST LIBERATION GROUPS. The *Grupos Antiterroristas de Liberación* (GAL) was a Spanish government-sponsored group that acted largely as an anti-Basque death squad, killing Basque Fatherland and Liberty (ETA, q.v.) members and other prominent Basques whether within Spain or France. Spanish police comprised much of the membership of this group, who in turn recruited, financed, and directly aided hit men to assassinate as many as 30 Basques in France during the period from 1983–1987.

In November 1984 GAL killed a popular Basque leader, Santiago Brouad, and in September 1985 killed four Basques in France. GAL members were well-equipped killers who were provided with surprisingly good intelligence about the whereabouts of ETA members. Within France alone GAL killed over 20 ETA members and suspected sympathizers during the 1980s. In 1991 two GAL members were tried and convicted for attempted murder.

ARAB LIBERATION FRONT. The Arab Liberation Front is an Iraqi-sponsored Palestinian militia group numbering about 500 militants. While this group's purported goal is to establish an independent Palestinian state, the Iraqi government created it in 1969 mainly to extend Iraqi influence within the Palestinian movement and within Lebanon. This has brought the group into conflict with other groups in Lebanon enjoying Syrian state sponsorship, such as Amal (q.v.). Apart from its role in Lebanon, the Front has conducted some armed raids into Israeli territory. This group helped form part of the Rejection Front in 1974 opposed to the peace overtures of PLO Chairman Yasir Arafat and is led by Abdul Rahim Ahmad, one of Arafat's critics.

ARAFAT, YASIR. (b. 1929) Given name, Abdul-Rahman Abdul-Rauf Arafat al Qudwa al Hussayni, nom de guerre, Abu Ammar, Yasir Arafat has been the head of the al Fatah (q.v.) group since the early 1960s and is concurrently chairman of the Palestine Liberation Organization (q.v.) since February 1969. Arafat was born in Jerusalem into a Palestinian family related to the Grand Mufti of Jerusalem who played a key role in organizing and leading Palestinians against the Israelis during the first Arab-Israeli war. Arafat studied engineering at Cairo University in the 1940s and 1950s, where he met other Palestinians such as Khalil al Wazir and Salah Khalaf, who become cofounders with Arafat of al Fatah in 1957, originally a secret group that surfaced in 1959.

Following the defeat of the Arab states in the 1967 war, al Fatah undertook guerrilla warfare with Israel, and its popularity, together with that of Arafat, grew among the Palestinians, allowing Arafat and other guerrilla leaders to take over control of the PLO in 1969.

Arafat has survived a number of challenges to his preeminence in the leadership of the PLO. In 1974 leftist and pro-Syrian groups, which coexisted with Fatah within the framework of the PLO, formed a "Rejection Front" (q.v.) in protest to Arafat's willingness after the October 1973 War (known also in the West as the Yom Kippur War and among the Arabs as the Ramadhan War) to adopt diplomatic initiatives on behalf of the Palestinians rather than relying on armed struggle alone. Although Fatah was responsible for the terrorist actions committed by the Black September (q.v.) group, in 1974 Arafat committed Fatah to abstaining from terrorist actions outside of the borders of former mandatory Palestine, a declaratory policy not always observed in practice as shown by the activities of the Fatah-controlled Hawari (q.v.) group and Force 17 (q.v.) group. In 1982 the Israeli army forced the PLO and Arafat out of Lebanon although both returned in 1983. In 1983 Syria instigated a revolt against Arafat among extremists within the PLO including some members of Fatah, and he was again forced to flee from Lebanon when his new base in Tripoli was besieged by PLO mutineers.

Arafat used the opportunity afforded by the intifada to shift the attention of PLO leaders and subgroups from their intramural quarreling to adopting a common strategy. The nineteenth Palestine National Council held in Algiers in November 1988 vindicated Arafat's approach with its implicit endorsement of the right of Israel to exist alongside a Palestinian state in the West Bank and the Gaza Strip and by its adopting a resolution renouncing the use of terrorism outside the borders of former mandatory Palestine. While Arafat explicitly denounced the use of terrorism, he regarded subsequent armed struggle within Israel and the occupied territories as a form of insurgency rather than terrorism. With his signing of the 13 September 1993 peace accord with Israel on behalf of the PLO, Arafat has renounced such further insurgent or terrorist activity within Israel proper or the occupied territories. [See al Fatah, Force 17, Hawari Group, and Palestine Liberation Organization]

ARENA. The *Alianza Republicana Nacional*, the "Republican National Alliance," is a Salvadoran right-wing political party that has sponsored, or directly engaged in, repressive violence against Salvadoran leftists. On 28 March 1982 ARENA won a plurality of the seats in the Constituent Assembly elections, and its leader, Roberto D'Aubuisson (d. 1992), was elected president of that body. Due to ARENA's substantial role both in shaping the Salvadoran polity and later in winning the Salvadoran presidency, it cannot be accurately described as being either a nonstate actor or a state-sponsored actor but rather as a state-co-opting one. (See State Co-Optation.)

With the intensification of leftist guerrilla attacks in the early 1980s, right-wing death squad (q.v.) activity soared. In 1982 Roberto D'Aubuisson led a coalition of Salvadoran businessmen and rightist politicians in forming the ARENA party on whose ticket D'Aubuisson made an unsuccessful bid for the presidency in 1984. Many ARENA members, including D'Aubuisson, appear to have been directly involved in death squad activity both before and after ARENA was formed. ARENA itself was believed to have been behind the assassinations of political rivals both in the centrist Christian Democrat party and the leftist Democratic Revolutionary Front.

On 19 March 1989, ARENA candidate Alfredo Cristiani won the Salvadoran presidential election, which was preceded by an intensification of death squad activity, rising from an average of 21 deaths per month in 1987 to 30 deaths per month in the first three months of 1988. The rate then fell to 16 deaths per month following Cristiani's election. Since then, during the early 1990s ARENA has largely desisted from terrorist activities, having achieved most of its political aims.

ARGENTINE ANTI-COMMUNIST ALLIANCE. The Argentine AAA consisted of policemen and security forces who began in 1973 to take the law into their own hands in intimidating and killing leftist politicians, journalists, and intellectuals. The AAA may be considered a nonstate death squad (q.v.) precursor to the state-sanctioned death squad terror from 1976 to 1983 known as the "dirty war" (q.v.). The AAA would publish notices signed "AAA" listing targeted persons who were warned to leave the country. Victims included not only Argentine Communists and left-wing Perónistas but also persons of moderate political opinions whose statements or actions incurred the ire of AAA members. While AAA activity may have originated spontaneously among disgruntled policemen, by 1976 the military dictatorship that came to power took over death squad activity in a much more conscious and brutal manner.

ARMED FORCES OF NATIONAL LIBERATION. The *Fuerzas Armadas de Liberación Nacional* (FALN) is the name of two unrelated groups:

1. Puerto Rican FALN: This group seeks Puerto Rican independence through terrorist attacks in Puerto Rico and the United States. The group was formed from the merger of the remnants of the Armed Commandos of National Liberation (CALN, q.v.) and the Armed Independence Revolutionary Movement in 1974.

The group's first operation was to bomb five banks in New York City on 26 October 1974. FALN has concentrated largely on bombing symbolic targets such as banks, corporation headquarters, government offices, and military installations, thus usually avoiding harm to life and limb. On 25 January 1975, however, FALN bombed the Fraunces Tavern, a site close to Wall Street. The site apparently was chosen for its symbolic value because George Washington bade farewell to his troops there at the conclusion of the War of Independence. Since the bomb exploded at the height of the lunch hour 4 diners were killed and 63 others injured the first time an FALN bombing had caused fatalities. Afterwards FALN expanded its targets to include department stores and hotels, striking the Chicago area as well as New York and Puerto Rico. Despite a hiatus caused by the arrest of several members in April 1980, FALN continued its bombing campaign until 1983. With the capture of FALN bombing expert William Morales in June 1983 the bombing campaign on the mainland U.S., totaling around 160 bombings, came to a virtual halt. The arrest of several FALN and Macheteros (q.v.) leaders in Puerto Rico on 30 August 1985 appears to have set the group back; it has remained relatively inactive since then.

FALN differs from other Puerto Rican groups insofar as it appears to include in among its roughly 50 members a large number of Puerto Ricans born and raised in the United States. This may explain why it was the only active Puerto Rican separatist group that regularly carried out terrorist acts on the U.S. mainland. FALN also has the distinction of being one of the few terrorist groups that has ever threatened to use nuclear terrorism. In a communiqué published on 21 March

1980, FALN hinted that it would not hesitate to sabotage nuclear reactors. Such sabotage has never occurred, but FALN and other groups have attacked several non-nuclear energy-related facilities in Puerto Rico, such as power pylons, substations, and even an oil refinery.

2. Venezuelan FALN: Younger members of the Venezuelan Communist Party, more attracted to the Cuban model of revolution, joined forces with the Venezuelan Revolutionary Movement of the Left (MIR), a left-wing faction of the ruling Democratic Action party, to form this Marxist guerrilla group active in the 1960s and 1970s. With Cuban backing FALN managed to carry out an urban terrorist campaign and also engaged in sabotage of foreign businesses and oil production facilities. FALN used kidnapping and hijacking as means to embarrass the Venezuelan government and to create publicity, at one point kidnapping the U.S. Army attaché, Colonel James Chenault, on 27 November 1963, and releasing him after the government freed several imprisoned leftists.

In 1969 after Cuba abandoned support for leftist guerrillas in Venezuela, MIR abandoned FALN to return to legality. FALN became inactive and its leader, Douglas Bravo (b. 1933), eventually accepted a presidential pardon in 1979.

ARMED PROPAGANDA. Armed propaganda, or "propaganda by the deed," refers to the use of violent force not so much to achieve a tactical objective through the direct physical effects of the action, but rather to focus attention on the symbolic, political importance of the action or else to draw attention to the executing group's demands. In its earliest activities the Basque Fatherland and Liberty (q.v.) group tended to bomb or vandalize Spanish Civil War memorials, actions of armed propaganda that had little effect on Spanish domination in the Basque provinces but ones that strongly signaled a Basque rejection of Spanish hegemony.

While campaigns of armed propaganda can be directed toward symbolic, nonliving targets, they can also be more lethal. The Kurdish Workers' Party (PKK, q.v.) used to occupy villages in southeastern Turkey, murder scores of Turkish civilian men, women and children, and then leave before the Turkish army could arrive on the scene. While the murder of those civilians could hardly serve any military purpose, such events would serve to portray the Turkish army as ineffective in protecting Turkish nationals, who would then be terrorized into leaving those regions claimed by the PKK terrorists as Kurdish lands. Similarly the seizure of the U.S. Embassy in Tehran can be considered an act of armed propaganda meant to demonstrate the powerlessness of the United States to intervene in Iranian affairs.

Armed propaganda is by no means solely a tactic of nonstate terrorist groups. Brilliantly executed counterinsurgency actions or police raids on terrorist hideouts, orchestrated with favorable mass media coverage, could also be undertaken to produce a psychological impact on insurgent or terrorist groups far out of proportion to the physical effects of the act itself. An action such as the FBI's capture of the Lebanese hijacker Fawaz Younis on the high seas is meant not only to bring one suspected terrorist to trial, but also to serve notice to other would-be hijackers that a similar fate could await them, and so to deter them from future hijackings.

ARMED RESISTANCE UNIT. Pseudonym for the Revolutionary Armed Task Force (q.v.).

ARMED REVOLUTIONARY NUCLEUS. The *Nuclei Armati Rivoluzionari* (NAR) is an Italian right-wing terrorist group seeking to overthrow the current constitutional democracy in Italy to replace it with a Fascist-style authoritarian regime. This group appeared in December 1977 when it bombed the Rome offices of the Christian Democratic and Communist parties. In June 1980 NAR assassinated Roman judge Mario Amato, who had been instrumental in uncovering and convicting rightist groups violating Italy's ban on neo-Fascist groups, in particular NAR. In the period from 1977–1981 the group perpetrated at least 25 terrorist acts, and Italian police have implicated it in the 2 August 1980 bombing of the Bologna train station. On 2 May 1985 some 53 members of NAR were sentenced to prison for their role in the terror campaign of 1977–1981.

ARMENIAN LIBERATION ARMY. ALA was a nonstate Armenian guerrilla group with the revolutionary goal of restoring formerly Armenian portions of eastern Turkey to Armenian sovereignty. While this group bombed Turkish targets in Western Europe in the 1970s it has since sunk into obscurity.

ARMENIAN SECRET ARMY FOR THE LIBERATION OF ARMENIA. ASALA is a formerly Soviet-sponsored, revolutionary organization with the triple aims of regaining portions of eastern Turkey claimed as parts of historic Armenia, avenging the Armenians killed by the Ottoman forces during World War I, and forcing the Turkish government to acknowledge responsibility for the events of 1915. ASALA is a Marxist-Leninist organization that has also declared its opposition to "imperialism," that is, only the imperialism allegedly committed by western countries. ASALA never similarly criticized the Soviet Union for imperialism and always maintained that Soviet Armenia was already liberated. It is suspected that the Soviet Union sponsored ASALA as a means of pressuring Turkey to play a less accommodating role within NATO. ASALA also has received aid from radical Palestinian groups with which it has collaborated within Lebanon. Interestingly ASALA, an anti-American group, has committed few terrorist acts in the United States, one being the bombing of the Swiss Bank Corporation in New York in May 1982, while a plot to bomb an Air Canada cargo building in Los Angeles was foiled in the same month.

ASALA was founded in 1975 and has concentrated on the assassination and terrorization of Turkish diplomats in the name of avenging Armenians killed in the pogroms in eastern Turkey. By 1981 it had engaged in at least 40 attacks in 11 countries. By mid-1982 ASALA had killed 24 Turkish officials and had carried out about 100 bombings, including an attack at Ankara airport in August 1982. It also attacked French targets under the name "the Orly Organization" and Swiss targets under the names "October Movement" and "June 9" in order to punish France and Switzerland for cracking down on ASALA agents traveling under falsified passports. The 15 July 1983 attack on Orly Airport that killed seven persons reportedly caused a split in the organization due to the disaffection of less militant members over the harm to the Armenian cause due to such "blind" acts of terrorism. The dissident group became known as the ASALA-Revolutionary Movement, while the main group became known as ASALA-Militant.

As its headquarters were located in Beirut, ASALA suffered some disruption, having been forced to flee due to the Israeli siege and bombardment of Beirut in the summer of 1982. ASALA bombed the French Embassy in Lebanon in October 1987. It is believed that the leader of ASALA-Militant, Hagop Hagopian, was killed on 28 April 1988 by members of his own group. The head of ASALA-Revolutionary Movement is Monte Melkonian.

The power struggle within, and between, ASALA factions has led to a reduction in its terrorist acts since the mid-1980s, although ASALA members were suspected in playing a role in the September 1986 bombing campaign in Paris aimed at pressuring the French government into releasing three convicted terrorists, one of whom was an ASALA member. In the early 1980s ASALA also began using the front name of the New Armenian Resistance. (See also Justice Commandos of the Armenian Genocide)

ARYAN NATIONS. The Aryan Nations is a nonstate, revolutionary organization dedicated to the creation of an independent, "Whites-only" homeland in the Pacific northwestern states and to the overthrow of the "ZOG," that is, the "Zionist Occupation Government" of the United States. The visible corporate organ of the Aryan Nations is the Church of Jesus Christ Christian headed by Richard Butler, a minister of the Identity Christian movement (q.v.). While Butler's church is headquartered on the Aryan Nations compound outside Hayden Lake, Idaho, in fact the Aryan Nations refers also to Butler's umbrella organization that seeks to unite disparate right-wing groups sharing white-supremacist, anti-Semitic, or populist ideologies, such as the Ku Klux Klan, American Neo-Nazi groups, the Posse Comitatus, and the Covenant, the Sword and the Arm of the Lord. Aryan Nations achieves this coordination through conferences held at its Hayden Lake compound each year since 1979 and through the creation of the Aryan Nations Net, a computer bulletin board system that allows members of like-minded groups to share ideas and plans year-round. The Aryan Nations has an outreach ministry to the Aryan Brotherhood, itself a network of white supremacist prison gangs whose members are recruited into the Aryan Nations upon their release from prison.

While the visible Butler organization itself does not directly participate in executing terrorist actions it has given moral encouragement to such groups as the Posse Comitatus and White Aryan Resistance and has spawned terrorist splinter groups such as The Order (q.v). The Aryan Nations is estimated to have 150 to 500 members in about 18 states. Richard Butler denies that the Aryan Nations has any involvement in terrorism or sedition, but in 1987 two Aryan Nations members were convicted on counterfeiting charges and another convicted for a series of bombings in Idaho in 1986 in connection with a bizarre plot to terrorize anti-Aryan Nations residents into leaving the Coeur d'Alene area. Richard Butler was acquitted in April 1988 by the U.S. District Court in Ft. Smith, Arkansas, of sedition charges arising from the links between the Aryan Nations and the Order, with the latter's involvement in armed robberies and the deprivation of Alan Berg's civil rights. Later on 19 October 1990 three other Aryan Nations members were convicted for conspiracy to bomb a Seattle nightclub patronized by homosexuals. (See also the Covenant, the Sword and the Arm of the Lord; Posse Comitatus; and Ku Klux Klan)

ASSASSINATION. The deliberate murder or killing of political or military figures, or of ordinary civilians, for political ends, assassination is perhaps the oldest and most fundamental of the terrorist tools. The Ismaili Fedayeen (q.v.) attacked high secular and religious authorities using corps of assassins willing to undertake attacks against Sunnite rulers in which the individual assassin was certain to be killed or captured. To counter the awe and respect these bold attacks created among the common people, apologists of the Abbaside dynasty targeted by the Ismailis alleged that the attackers were really "Hashshishin," those acting under the influence of hashish. This term became the source of the word "assassin."

While the term assassination has usually been restricted to the murder of high-ranking or prominent personages, this dictionary considers all instances of deliberate killings of either civilians or official persons, prominent or obscure, as instances of assassination or political murder.

AVANGUARDIA NAZIONALE (AN). The "National Vanguard" is an Italian right-wing terrorist group founded in 1959 by Stephano Delle Chiaie (q.v.). During the 1960s the group collaborated with other right-wing groups throughout Europe in an umbrella organization known as the "Black Orchestra." On 12 December 1969 the group bombed the Banca del Agricultura in Milan, killing 16 people and wounding 90 others, in an attempt to create a backlash against leftists whom they tried to frame as the perpetrators. The AN attempted a coup d'état on 7 December 1970 against the Italian government. AN, along with other smaller right-wing organizations, merged with the Black Order (q.v.) after 1973.

- B -

BAADER-MEINHOF GANG. Journalistic name for the *Rote Armee Fraktion*, or Red Army Faction (q.v.), founded by the German leftists Andreas Baader and Ulrike Meinhof. (See Red Army Faction)

BABBAR KHALSA. Babbar Khalsa is a small Sikh terrorist group originally formed for the limited purpose of avenging the deaths of Sikh fundamentalist followers of Sant Jarnail Bhindranwale who were killed on 13 April 1978 by Nirankari Sikhs when the latter had been attacked by Bhindranwale's followers as "heretics." The moving figure of the group was Bibi Amarjit Kaur, a widow of one of those slain, who became embittered toward Bhindranwale and refused to cooperate with him. The group otherwise embraced the same goals held by Bhindranwale of creating an independent Sikh homeland of Khalistan and assassinating perceived enemies of Khalistan among both Sikhs and non-Sikhs.

The group consisted of only a few scores of youths operating out of the sanctuary of the Golden Temple complex in Amritsar prior to its destruction by the Indian Army in its raid of 5 June 1984. Bibi Amarjit Kaur, along with 400 other Sikh activists, surrendered in the course of the Indian Army attack. Following the death of Bhindranwale in the course of this attack, he achieved the status of a Sikh martyr, and Babbar Khalsa activists maintained that Bibi Amarjit Kaur and Bhindranwale had buried their differences in the face of the Indian Army siege of the Golden Temple. Some Sikh terrorist actions in India, Canada, and Germany have been claimed in the name of Babbar Khalsa, though very little is known of the actual membership of this group.

BANDERA ROJA. The *Bandera Roja*, "Red Flag" group (also referred to by the initials GBR), is a Venezuelan revolutionary group, operating independently of any state sponsor, dedicated to achieving a Marxist-Leninist state in Venezuela through armed struggle. GBR rejects assimilation into peaceful politics and broke with the Venezuelan Revolutionary Movement of the Left (MIR) in 1969 after Cuba abandoned support for leftist guerrillas in Venezuela. The armed wing of GBR is called the Americo Silva Front.

Like many other guerrilla groups in South America formerly sponsored by Cuba and the Soviet Union, GBR has taken to financing its activities through kidnapping for ransom and extorting protection payments from wealthy individuals and firms. In 1972, GBR began a campaign of abducting wealthy businessmen for ransom, kidnapping Caracas industrialist Carlos Domínguez Chávez in a joint operation with MIR activists, and releasing him for $1 million in ransom. After GBR leaders Carlos Betancourt and Gabriel Puerta Aponte were captured in 1973, GBR arranged for both to escape from Caracas's San Carlos Prison in January 1975 along with 21 other guerrillas, by means of a 60-meter tunnel that GBR had dug into the prison, apparently with the cooperation of other leftist guerrillas. In March 1975 GBR renounced all ties to leftist parties working within the constitutional order and published a death list against 20 prominent landowners.

From 1976 to 1977, GBR conducted sporadic attacks on military convoys and temporarily captured small towns. After Betancourt was recaptured in 1977, Bandera Roja activity experienced a hiatus. In December 1981, GBR hijacked three domestic flights, demanding the release of Betancourt and other prisoners; the Venezuelan government rejected those demands, however. In April 1982 Puerta was captured in a firefight in which 25 militants were killed.

Bandera Roja operates mainly in eastern Venezuela and along the Colombian border and has had contact with Colombia's M-19 and ELN (q.v.) groups. Membership in the armed wing is estimated at no more than 50.

BANNA, SABRI KHALIL AL. See Abu Nidal

BASQUE FATHERLAND AND LIBERTY. The *Euzkadi Ta Askatasuna* (ETA), is a nonstate Basque separatist group that has undertaken terrorist operations in order to win independence for *Euzkadi*, the Basque fatherland, consisting of the Spanish provinces of Vizcaya, Alava, Guipuzcoa, Navarra, as well as the French Basque provinces. Due to the general antipathy of France and other European states toward the Franco regime the French government tolerated the presence of ETA terrorists who used France as a base and sanctuary. Since the return of democracy in Spain after Franco's death and the appearance of signs of ETA radicalization of French Basques, France has shed its previous toleration of ETA activities within its territory and undertaken closer cooperation with Spanish authorities to combat Basque terrorism.

The ETA organization has enjoyed moral and material support from the PLO in training camps in Lebanon, South Yemen, and Algeria. The Cuban and Sandinista Nicaraguan governments gave safe haven and training to ETA members. The ETA and Provisional IRA (q.v.) also were reported to cooperate with each other. The Colombian M-19 group, and other Latin American guerrilla groups, have declared their support for ETA while immigrant communities of Basques in Venezuela and elsewhere have also materially contributed to the ETA cause.

The ETA is an offshoot of the Basque Nationalist Party (PNV). In 1957 the youth movement of the PNV met in Paris with the exiled PNV leadership to persuade them to undertake an armed struggle against the Franco regime. Failing in this, many of the PNV youth created ETA on 31 July 1959. Because most of the other non-Basque anti-Franco groups were Marxist many ETA members also adopted a Marxist-Leninist ideology whereas PNV had been, and remains, solidly Catholic and nationalistic. Disagreements over the correct ideological interpretation of the Basque struggle have split ETA into several factions. The two major factions are the ETA-Militar (ETA-M), which advocates unending armed struggle until full independence is won, and ETA-Politico-Militar (ETA-PM), which has laid down arms since formal autonomy was granted to a designated Basque region in January 1980.

ETA activities began in 1961 with the derailment of a train carrying Spanish Civil War veterans en route to a celebration in San Sebastian. During the 1960s ETA concentrated on symbolic targets such as defacing Civil War monuments and symbols of Spanish domination. The murder of a Basque in 1968 by the Spanish Civil Guard led to the first assassination by the ETA of the security chief of Guipuzcoa, which in turn triggered severe regime repression against Basques, which in turn further radicalized many Basques. ETA actions are largely intended as armed propaganda, called *ekintzak*, meant to focus attention on the symbolic, strategic, and political importance of the action. ETA has shown itself to be very selective in choosing targets and means of attacks and also great care in avoiding injury to noncombatants so that over 70 percent of those killed or wounded by ETA have been members of the Spanish security forces or government.

An analysis of 86 major ETA incidents since 1970 reveals that 63 percent involved bombings, including several car bombings; 12 percent involved kidnappings for ransom; 7 percent assassinations; 7 percent armed attacks; and 3 percent sabotage and arson; and the rest involved arms smuggling, bank robberies, and extortions of "revolutionary taxes" from wealthy businesses operating in the Basque country. Generally the ETA has targeted facilities or persons symbolizing Spanish hegemony: army and Civil Guard barracks, government buildings, Spanish military and political figures. Kidnapping for ransom plays a role in financing the ETA, but even then victims are chosen not simply for their potential ransom but usually have been figures of consequence who have spoken out against the ETA. Prior to most bomb attacks ETA has given warnings to allow civilians a chance to remove themselves from the target area. Yet, as France began cooperating with Spain in 1987 in an antiterrorist crackdown aimed at Basque separatists, the ETA began a campaign of terrorization against French targets in

Spain, including tourist transit and hotel facilities, which have victimized increasing numbers of civilians.

From 1961 to 1970 only three deaths resulted from ETA actions. From 1971 to 1975, the year of Franco's death, ETA caused 31 deaths. From 1976 to 1980, when limited Basque autonomy was granted, ETA caused 253 deaths. From 1981 to 1985 the figure dropped to around 190 and from 1986 to 1990 the figure fell to around 159. Each year since 1990 has witnessed in excess of 50 ETA-caused deaths. Most of the 50 victims killed by ETA in 1991 were involved in preparatory projects for the Barcelona Olympics, the fifth centennial celebrations of Columbus's voyage, and the Seville World's Fair, since these events are used by Spanish authorities to stress Spanish social and economic progress since the Franco era. Ironically, as democratization has proceeded in Spain, ETA violence has risen, and as more autonomy has been granted to the Basque region, ETA violence has increased even further, despite the laying down of arms by ETA-PM.

Figures of persons killed by ETA violence vary from source to source depending on whether the actions of certain breakaway groups, such as Iraultza (q.v.), are counted. If only the confirmed actions of ETA are considered from 1968–1990, the total is just over 500 deaths, but if the actions of other Basque terrorist groups are counted, the figure is in excess of 750 deaths.

Some of the more notable ETA actions are mentioned here: The most notorious ETA action was the 20 December 1973 assassination of Spanish Prime Minister Luís Carrero Blanco (b. 1903), whose limousine was blown five stories into the air by the detonation of an explosives-packed 25-foot-long tunnel under the pavement over which the Prime Minister's car would pass on his daily trip to attend Mass. The ETA had spent a year digging and rigging this tunnel. On 28 March 1978, ETA bombed a nuclear power plant under construction near Bilboa, killing two and wounding 14 others. The nuclear plant had been repeatedly attacked by the ETA. On 29 July 1985, ETA-M gunmen shot and killed the Spanish Director of Defense Policy, Rear Admiral Fausto Estigas Estrada (b. 1926). On 21 July 1986, ETA-M fired by remote control several antitank rockets at the Ministry of Defense building, injuring two officers. The booby-trapped launcher exploded when police tried to examine it, wounding another 10 people. On 12 September 1989, ETA-M assassinated public prosecutor Carmen Tagle in Madrid, the first time ETA had struck at the Spanish judiciary. ETA also began making attacks on Spanish targets outside of Spain that year. On 24 October 1989, ETA firebombed the parked car of Spain's ambassador to the Netherlands and bombed two offices of the Spanish Embassy on 26 October. ETA then launched rockets at the Spanish Ambassador's residence in The Hague in the Netherlands on 6 December 1989. ETA continued this trend with over a dozen attacks on Spanish targets in Italy during 1991. On 29 May 1991 ETA-M bombed a Civil Guard barracks, which included family housing units, killing 9, including dependents, and wounding over 50 others.

The ETA members, known as *eterras*, are organized into three to five member cells, known as *comandos*. Most *eterras* are *legales* who may never, or only occasionally, participate in an illegal action. Most live openly but help the *ilegales*, or underground ETA activists, by material aid, communications, information gathering, and the like. The total number of underground activists has been estimated at 200 members, while the total numbers of *legales* is not known. *Comandos* are activated by the ETA directorate, which usually is in France. Few *eterras* therefore will know who is an *eterra* outside of his own *comando*, which helps protect ETA against police penetration should the members of one *comando* be arrested and interrogated. Spanish and French coordinated counterinsurgency measures have not cracked the ETA organization.

BEIRUT AIRPORT BOMBING. On 23 October 1983 a truck bomb driven by a suicide-volunteer demolished the building at Beirut International Airport being used as a temporary barracks, killing 241 U.S. Marines. This bombing was one in a series of anti-Western bombings, including the 18 April 1983 bombing of the U.S. Embassy in West Beirut, the bombing of the French military headquarters in Beirut on the same day as the Beirut Airport bombing, and the 4 November 1983 bombing of the Israeli Defense Forces headquarters in Tyre. All these attacks used suicide drivers, were executed with great precision, and resulted in great damages and loss of life.

According to Lebanese security sources, the truck hit the airport building near a specific pillar where the planners of the bombing had determined that the explosion would do the most structural damage and thus kill the most people. The U.S. Federal Bureau of Investigation estimated that the truck bomb was the equivalent of 12,000 pounds of TNT, making it larger than any conventional bomb used in World War II. The bomb was made of a combination of TNT and hexogen, a highly sensitive and powerful explosive, packed around cylinders of gas to create an air-fuel bomb effect. The sheer cost of this bombing, the quality of intelligence about the U.S. forces needed to execute it, the technical precision needed to build the bomb, and the reluctance of any group to claim immediately their responsibility for this act all pointed to state sponsorship of the bombing. Hezbollah (q.v.), a militia under Iranian state sponsorship, on 16 February 1985 claimed responsibility in the name of Islamic Jihad.

On 4 October 1984, U.S. intelligence agencies identified Hezbollah as the local agent that supplied the suicide driver and Iran as the supplier of the explosives used in the attacks on the Marines and the U.S. Embassy. As early as 6 November 1983, an article in the Israeli daily *Ma'ariv* had identified the Iranian Ambassador to Damascus, Ali Akbar Muhtashami, as having been assigned by the Iranian government to be a liaison with Syrian intelligence in directing terrorist activities through the group that eventually assumed responsibility for the bombing of the U.S. Marines barracks. This article identified Islamic Jihad as being the responsible group headquartered in Baalbak under tutelage of the Islamic Revolutionary Guards Corps (q.v.) of Iran. According to a *Le Monde* report, dated 6–7 November 1983, citing an otherwise unspecified "confidential British document," the principal mastermind of the October 23 operations was one "Abu Muslih," actually Imad Maghniyah, the commander of the 800 or so IRGC troops in Baalbak. This report stated also that Iranian Deputy Foreign Minister Husayn Shaykhulislami, one of the leaders of those students who seized the U.S. Embassy on 4 November 1979, visited Damascus twice secretly, once on April 16, 1983, and again on October 19, 1983, that is, each time a few days ahead of a bombing of a major U.S. target in Lebanon. The Foreign Ministry of Iran and other officials and representatives of the regime have repeatedly denied any knowledge of, or involvement in, these bombings.

The shock of this bombing and the unpreparedness of the Reagan administration or the U.S. public to face the levels of lethal violence that had become commonplace in the Lebanese civil war led to an abrupt withdrawal of U.S. troops from Lebanon.

On 20 July 1987, however, the former commander of the Islamic Revolutionary Guards Corps, Muhsin Rafiqdust, revealed in an interview to the Iranian newspaper *Reselat* that Tehran had supplied the explosives used in the bombings.

BLACK BRIGADES. An obscure Kuwaiti Shiite revolutionary group active in Iraq and Kuwait, possibly a nom de guerre of Dawa al Islami or other groups enjoying Iranian state sponsorship. On 11 July 1985, the group attacked a restaurant in Kuwait, killing a high-ranking Kuwaiti security official. Kuwait was the target of numerous Iranian statesponsored terrorist actions during a period beginning with an assassination attempt against the Emir of Kuwait on 25 May 1985 and ending with the hijacking of a Kuwait Airways Boeing 747 on 5 April 1988. While these actions were partly in retaliation for Kuwait's support of Iraq during the Iran-Iraq war, they were also meant to pressure the Kuwaiti government into releasing those al Dawa terrorists convicted for the attempted truck bombings of the French and U.S. embassies on 12 December 1983.

BLACK JUNE. Black June is a non-PLO Palestinian group founded by Sabri al Banna (Abu Nidal), a onetime Fatah member who later opposed the PLO's increasing reliance on diplomacy rather than armed struggle. Black June is an Iraqi state-sponsored group with the revolutionary aim of destroying Israel and establishing a Palestinian state by force of arms. Secondary objectives include the use of terrorist coercion against the PLO to punish it for retreating from the use of armed struggle as the primary means for the liberation of Palestine. The Iraqi government also uses Black June as a means of maintaining its own influence over the Palestinian movement and within Lebanon. Black June is one of a number of different groups founded by Abu Nidal and numbers about 500 members.

Black June took its name from June 1976 when Phalangist troops with Syrian backing massacred the Palestinian fighters and civilians within the besieged Tal az Zatar refugee camp. Black June tried to kill the Syrian Foreign Minister in 1977 but missed him, killing instead a bystander, the visiting United Arab Emirates's Minister of State for Foreign Affairs. Black June has made numerous attacks on PLO representatives and offices abroad. In the period from 1978–1979 they killed Said Hammami, the PLO representative in London, Ali Yassin, PLO representative to Kuwait, Izzidin Qalaq, PLO representative in Paris, and bombed a PLO office in Istanbul in August 1978, killing four people.

Following a truce with Fatah, Black June turned to attacks on Jewish and Israeli targets. On 3 June 1982, a Black June gunman attacked and wounded Shlomo Argov, Israeli Ambassador to Britain, which occasioned Israel's invasion of Lebanon a few days later. On 9 August 1982, Black June made a grenade attack on a Jewish restaurant in Paris and then opened automatic weapons fire on the restaurant and on a crowd outside a nearby synagogue, killing 6 and wounding

27. On 10 April 1983, Black June again struck at the PLO, killing its delegate Issam Sartawi at a meeting of the Socialist International in Portugal. (See Fatah Revolutionary Council)

BLACK LIBERATION ARMY. One of the two most violent left-wing nonstate, revolutionary groups in the United States during the 1960s, the other being the Weather Underground (q.v.). Born out of the social unrest of the 1960s, the BLA particularly targeted law enforcement officers and was responsible for eight killings in the period from 1971–1973, including two New York City policemen on 27 January 1972. An FBI crackdown led to arrests of leading members of the group after which the group's activities subsided. In the early 1980s, however, remnants of the BLA merged with the Weather Underground to form the Revolutionary Armed Task Force (q.v.), which engaged in a series of bombings against offices of the federal government and multinational corporate firms as well as an attempted robbery of a Brinks armored carrier in October 1981.

BLACK ORDER. The *Ordine Nero* is an Italian nonstate, revolutionary Fascist group that seeks to destroy the democratic government in Italy. The Black Order was the violent successor to the New Order party, which had been suppressed as a proscribed neo-Fascist organization in 1973 and is thought to have ties to the Italian Social Movement, another neo-Fascist group.

Among its terrorist actions, in 1976 the group killed Judge Vittorio Occorsio, who had earlier helped ban the New Order. The group targeted left-wing supporters usually by indiscriminate bombings of public places. On 4 August 1974 the group bombed a train on the Munich-Bologna route, killing 12 people. On 2 August 1980, they bombed the Bologna railway station, killing over 80 and wounding around 200 people. Bologna was targeted apparently because of the domination of the city government by Italian Communists.

At its height, the Black Order numbered around 300

followers. Following the conviction in 1978 of its leader, Pierluigi Concutelli, for the murder of Judge Occorsio the group's prominence in the far right was overtaken by that of the Revolutionary Armed Nuclei (q.v.).

BLACK PANTHERS. Name given to two unrelated groups:
1. The Black Panther Party was a group founded in October 1966 by Huey Newton (b. 1942) and Bobby Seale (b. 1937) and was devoted to promoting a revolutionary black nationalism. While Panthers sought, among other things, amnesty for all black prisoners, comprehensive welfare benefits for black Americans, and exemption from military service for all black Americans, the more problematic aspect of the group was its drift into revolutionary violence. Like many other radical groups born out of the radicalism of the late 1960s, such as the Weathermen (q.v.) and the Red Army Faction (q.v.), the Panthers were revolutionary insofar as they sought to fight what they perceived to be a racist capitalist system but also appeared to be anarchistic insofar as they lacked a clear program for creating an alternative social order.

The appeal for "black power" drew a response from other politically disaffected young black Americans. Among those drawn into the group were Stokeley Carmichael, James Forman, Rap Brown, and Eldridge Cleaver. By 1970 the group had around 2,000 members in some 61 cities in 26 states, mainly outside of the south. Following the 4 April 1968 assassination of Rev. Martin Luther King, Jr., the Panthers advocated arming themselves and conducting military training for its members. Not only were the Panthers viewed by FBI Director J. Edgar Hoover, and other public officials, as being a subversive organization, but many of the Panther leaders also had criminal records and had in some cases jumped bail. This created a situation in which armed conflict between the group and the police was unavoidable. In June 1969, a gunfight erupted between the Sacramento police and the Panthers in which 13 policemen were wounded before the Panthers fled their headquarters. Other similar clashes occurred with police. Eldridge Cleaver (b. 1936), who had jumped bail in November 1968, went to Cuba, then to Algeria, and then to North Korea seeking refuge and support for the Panthers.

By mid-1970 most of the original Panther leadership had either fled the country or gone underground. Rap Brown was arrested in October 1971 on armed robbery charges. Bobby Seale was imprisoned for contempt of court while Huey Newton renounced armed struggle by May 1971. While two hijackings did occur in June and July of 1972 by Panthers and some sympathizers wishing to find asylum abroad, by that time the Black Panther movement had spent itself out. While the militant image of the Panthers inspired fear in the public, in retrospect Panther violence appeared to be more sporadic and reactive than to be tactics serving a comprehensive plan to foment a revolution. Nonetheless the Black Panthers were the predecessors of the Black Liberation Army (q.v.), which in turn, together with remnants of the Weathermen (q.v.), helped form the Revolutionary Armed Task Force (q.v.) that continued a campaign of leftist revolutionary terrorism within the United States until 1986.

2. The "Black Panthers" is also the name given to an obscure group of Palestinian militants in the West Bank who murder Palestinians suspected of collaborating with Israeli authorities. The group appears to be centered in the West Bank town of Jenin and began its activities after the beginning of the intifada uprising.

BLACK SEPTEMBER. The Black September Organization (BSO) was a clandestine group created by al Fatah (q.v.) in December 1971 for the limited purpose of avenging the suppression and expulsion of the PLO from Jordan in the "Black September" of 1970. During that September the PFLP (q.v.) had hijacked several airplanes to Dawson's Field in Jordan and was holding about 400 western hostages there. King Hussein ordered the Jordanian Army to rescue the hostages and, in the course of the fighting that followed, the Palestinians suffered enormous losses and their survivors were expelled to Lebanon. As Fatah held a declaratory policy of not involving itself in the domestic politics of Arab nations, yet nonetheless planned to kill King Hussein and those who shared responsibility in carrying out his orders, it was essential that Fatah be able to maintain a plausible deniability of responsibility for the BSO. In actuality the scope of targets of the BSO grew to include Israeli, U.S., and other Western targets, while their attacks rivaled those of the PFLP in ferocity and media impact. During its period of activity from 1971 to 1974, the BSO was run by Salah Khalaf (aka, Abu Iyad), one of Yasir Arafat's closest deputies.

On 28 November 1971 BSO assassinated Jordanian Prime Minister Wasfi al Tall in Cairo. BSO tried, but failed, several times to assassinate King Hussein. The most notorious BSO action, however, was its attack on the Israeli team at the 1972 Summer Olympics in Munich in which all 11 Israeli hostages and 5 of the 8 terrorists were killed in a shoot-out with West German police. On 29 October 1972, BSO members hijacked a Lufthansa plane and forced West German authorities to release the three surviving BSO gunmen from the Munich attack in exchange for the lives of the Lufthansa hostages. On 16 September 1972, BSO also mailed out 64 letter bombs to Israeli and non-Israeli Jewish targets, most of which were intercepted and deactivated, but some of which succeeded in killing Israeli diplomats, other Jews, and some postal workers. On 1 March 1973 BSO gunmen seized the Saudi Arabian Embassy in Khartoum and murdered U.S. Ambassador Cleo A. Noel, Jr., the U.S. chargé d'affaires and a Belgian chargé d'affaires.

From 1971 to 1974 the BSO carried out at least 34 noteworthy actions, 47 percent (=16) being bombings; 32 percent (=11) being assassinations; 9 percent (=3) being hijackings; another 9 percent (=3) being hostage seizures; and the remaining 3 percent (=1) being a rocket attack upon the U.S. Embassy in Beirut. On 5 September 1973, Italian police foiled a BSO plot to shoot down an El Al airplane with two SAM-7

Strela antiaircraft missiles. Israel, whose citizens and diplomats abroad had become the primary targets of the BSO assassination and letter-bombing campaigns, undertook covert and overt operations to quash BSO. Israeli Wrath of God operatives began killing BSO operatives in Cyprus and Europe while the Israeli Defense Forces launched a raid on Beirut on 10 April 1973 in which they attacked the BSO headquarters, killing 17 terrorists, and destroyed the BSO letter-bomb factory.

In spite of Fatah's desire to conceal its connections with BSO, the arrests of a BSO agent in Jordan and of another in France produced evidence linking the two organizations. Although the BSO was dissolved by Fatah in December 1974 many former BSO operatives then joined either the PFLP or else Abu Nidal's Fatah Revolutionary Council (q.v.). The murder of Israeli diplomat Yosef Alon in December 1975 in Washington, D.C., was once believed to be the work of local proxies acting on behalf of Black September. From 1981 to 1987, about 17 actions were claimed in the name of the Black September Organization, but these were most likely the work of Abu Nidal operatives.

- C -

CALN. The Armed Commandos for National Liberation was a Puerto Rican separatist group formed in 1969. CALN bombed five U.S. businesses in Puerto Rico on 14 November 1970 as well as bombing the San Juan consulate of the Dominican Republic on 23 November 1970. The Puerto Rican police broke up this group, but its members later reorganized themselves and joined with members of another separatist group forming in 1974 the Armed Forces of National Liberation (FALN, q.v.).

CARIBBEAN REVOLUTIONARY ALLIANCE. The Caribbean Revolutionary Alliance is a leftist group seeking Guadeloupe's independence from France. On 13 March 1985, a bomb exploded at a restaurant at Point-à-Pitre owned by a member of France's right-wing National Front, killing 1 person and wounding 11 others.

CARLOS. Carlos "the Jackal," (b. 1950) whose true name was Ilyich Ramírez Sánchez, was a Venezuelan-born terrorist who became briefly notorious in the mid-1970s before sinking into obscurity. Born into a middle-class but Communist family, Sánchez was named in honor of Lenin. Later he went to a Cuban youth camp and ultimately attended Patrice Lumumba University in Moscow from which he was expelled in 1971 for frivolity. Others maintain that he was really recruited as a KGB agent and that the expulsion was faked in order to maintain his cover.

Using the nom de guerre "Carlos," Sánchez went to Paris where he took command of a Popular Front for the Liberation of Palestine cell in the early 1970s. Sánchez is believed to have made an assassination attempt on 31 December 1973 against Marks and Spenser magnate Teddy Zieff, who was wounded but not killed due to a malfunction of the gun. Sánchez was implicated in terrorist bombings of three pro-Israeli newspapers and an attempt to destroy an El Al airliner at Orly airport in 1975. Sánchez is best remembered for his role in the siege of the OPEC Secretariat in Vienna on 21 December 1975 (See OPEC Siege, Vienna) in which he held 11 OPEC oil ministers hostage and collected a massive ransom from the governments of Iran and Saudi Arabia, reportedly over $50 million.

After that episode he dropped out of view. From 1981 onward Carlos entered the service of Syria organizing covert operations against the Iraqi government. After French police arrested two of his agents in February 1982, Carlos threatened the French government with a terror campaign. As this message contained his fingerprints it confirmed that Carlos was still alive six years after the OPEC siege. In 1983 a group calling itself the Organization for the Armed Arab Struggle (q.v.) surfaced under Sánchez's leadership which carried out the threatened terror campaign. In May 1985 the French government released the two agents of Carlos one of whom, Magdalena Kopp, a West German terrorist, later married Carlos. From 1985 on Carlos lived in Damascus with his wife and a daughter, Rosa.

On 15 August 1994 the Interior Ministry announced that French counterintelligence agents had arrested Carlos in the Sudan and was extraditing him to France for trial.

CELLULAR ORGANIZATION. In order to protect themselves from penetration and also to maintain control over members, most terrorist groups opt for a cellular organization. Cells are groups of 3 to 10 members headed by one leader. Rudimentary terrorist organizations, such as the Symbionese Liberation Army, by default have a cellular structure but in the case of larger organizations, such as the Basque Fatherland and Liberty group having hundreds of members, the cellular organization protects the entire organization from penetration. While the ordinary bureaucratic organization is pyramidal, hierarchical, and transparent, the cellular system is better described as a circular, or "solar," system, whose links to other cells or parts of the organization remain hidden.

Within each cell the ordinary members may know one another but have no knowledge of the existence of other cells or of their members and have no link to the rest of the organization except through the cell leader. Cell leaders, in turn, may have no other link to the rest of the organization except through group leaders subordinate to a central operations committee. In the event members of one cell are captured and interrogated they can reveal only what they know of their own cell. Even that knowledge can be limited through the use of false names among the group members while the cell itself may adopt a distinctive name in order to mask its relationship with the parent organization.

The circumstances under which terrorists operate perhaps ensure that only those organizations having cellular structures can continue to survive for long. The Irish Republican Army originally conceived of itself as being a regular army and so produced general orders, official handbooks, rules and records of courts-martial, and the hierarchical command structure of a regular army. The need of clandestinity to protect the organization from penetration by informers or the confessions of captured members forced both the Official and Provisional wings of the Irish Republican Army to adopt cellular structures.

It should be noted that many or even most cells in a terrorist organization may be merely support groups that do not directly execute terrorist activities. Their members may run businesses or operate safe houses that provide support to persons whose identities and about whose activities they may know nothing.

CHRISTIAN IDENTITY. See Identity Christianity

CHRISTIAN-PATRIOTS DEFENSE LEAGUE (C-PDL). The C-PDL is a nonstate group of right-wing survivalists who aim to create a militia and fortified encampments to preserve white, Christian Americans against a coming Communist invasion and racial war. Although the group's aims might appear to be limited by the remoteness of the imagined future holocaust insofar as the group forms part of the network of white supremacist and anti-Semitic groups, such as the Aryan Nations and Ku Klux Klan, it may be assumed to hold the same revolutionary goals of resisting and destroying the United States government, or what such circles refer to as the "Zionist Occupation Government."

Despite the similarity in names, the C-PDL is not directly related to the Identity Christianity preacher Wesley Smith's Christian Defense League. Rather it is the brainchild of current leader John Robert Harrell ("Johnny Bob"), a former mausoleum salesman who devoted himself to the Identity Christian message after experiencing an apocalyptic vision during an illness in 1959. Convinced that a Jewish conspiracy was leading to a Communist invasion of the United States as well as a racial war, Harrell sought to train militia to defend a "Mid-America Survival Zone." He became an associate of

Robert dePugh, founder of the Minutemen, and became a frequent contributor to the Minutemen's tabloid *On Target*.

Harrell gave refuge to a Marine who had gone AWOL after embracing the Identity creed, and in August 1961 Federal agents overran Harrell's fortified Louisville, Illinois, estate where they found four underground two-man bunkers and stockpiles of food and ammunition. Harrell and his followers did not resist arrest, and Harrell was sentenced to four years in prison for harboring a Federal fugitive and on various tax evasion charges. After DePugh was imprisoned in 1968 on a conspiracy conviction, Harrell created four organizations to fill the void left by the defunct Minutemen: The religious organization was the Christian Conservative Church of America, which teaches a synthesis of Christianity, nationalism, anti-Semitism, and anti-Communism. The political branch is the Christian-Patriots Defense League. The military branch is the Citizens Emergency Defense System, a private militia. The fund-raising branch is the Paul Revere Club. One may be a member of the religious branch without having to belong to the other branches, while members of the military and political branches are not required to believe in the group's Identity Christian doctrine so long as they otherwise support its white supremacist and anti-Semitic program.

The C-PDL operates a 220-acre compound beside the Mark Twain National Forest, near Licking, Missouri; a 55-acre paramilitary training facility near Flora, Illinois; and its "Survival Base" near Smithville, West Virginia. The group hosts an annual "Freedom Festival" in Flora in which survivalist and Identity groups conduct weapons workshops and hold Identity doctrine speeches and seminars.

CHUKAKU-HA. The "Central Core" or "Nucleus Faction" is a Japanese revolutionary Marxist group that seeks to overturn Japan's constitutional system and monarchy. Chukaku-Ha is not only the largest faction out of the 23 factions that make up the Japanese New Left movement but also the largest militant domestic opposition group in Japan. The group's ''anti-Imperialist'' position finds practical expression in its protests against the U.S.-Japan Security Treaty while its rejection of the Japanese corporate state is concretely expressed in its frequent attacks on the construction of the New Tokyo International Airport and against the subway and railroad mass-transit systems.

Even though Chukaku-Ha can be considered typically leftist because of its membership in the Japanese New Left and its stated objectives and ideals, this group must also be considered anarchistic insofar as its program seems more intent on destroying the existing Japanese corporate state rather than building an alternative socialist state. Chukaku-Ha is not known to have any foreign state sponsors. Almost all of their activities have taken place within Japan while their base membership of 3,500 members supports the 200 or so full-time activists. Among the full-time activists are members of the Kansai Revolutionary Army, the group's covert active measures group that actually carries out most of the group's terrorism.

The group relies on the use of homemade but sometimes surprisingly sophisticated incendiary bombs, flamethrowers, mortars, and rockets. Most of their targets have been property, whether the headquarters of the Japanese Liberal-Democratic Party, the national railroad system, U.S. Armed Forces facilities, the Imperial Palace grounds, or government offices. Of 41 major incidents from 1984 to 1991, about 46 percent (=19) involved arson using incendiary bombs and devices; 24 percent (=10) involved the use of crude mortars and rocketlike devices; 19 percent (=8) involved assaults and beatings; 5 percent (=2) involved bombings; 2.5 percent (=1) involved sabotage; and another 2.5 percent (=1) involved murder. The group has used mass rallies of its general membership as feints to draw police attention away from actual targets. On one occasion in the frequent clashes at the construction site of Narita airport, throngs of Chukaku-Ha members armed with Molotov cocktails rushed a police barricade and created a small riot. While police concentrated on holding back the demonstrators, the Chukaku-Ha covert operations specialists burglarized the control tower of the airport, entering through underground service corridors, and then smashed much of the computer equipment there.

Some actions included the 19 September 1984 assault on the headquarters of Japan's ruling Liberal Democratic Party. A truck with a flamethrower device was driven into the side of the building and gutted six of its nine floors. Meanwhile the same group exploded a bomb near the Israeli Embassy. On 25 March 1986, they launched three of their homemade rockets at the Imperial Palace and another three at the U.S. Embassy. On 4 May 1986 they launched five rockets at Akasaka palace where the economic summit of the seven major industrialized powers was meeting. The rockets flew 3.5 kilometers and landed within 550 meters of their target. Because of the coincidence of this attack following the U.S. bombing raid on Libya some observers speculated a Libyan connection; Chukaku-Ha had been engaged in a spree of rocket launching that year even before that raid, however. On 23 February 1991, they fired rockets upon U.S. Navy housing outside Yokohama. Most of these rocket attacks have caused little damage and no harm to life or limb due to the missiles' inaccuracy.

CINCHONEROS POPULAR LIBERATION MOVEMENT. The Cinchoneros Popular Liberation Movement (MPL) is a state-sponsored revolutionary group seeking to overthrow the Honduran government and to oppose U.S. interests in the region. Its own ideology represents an eclectic blend of Marxist-Leninist and populist notions. The MPL is the armed wing of the People's Revolutionary Union, a splinter group of the Honduran Communist Party that appeared in 1980. The name "Cinchoneros" is derived from the nickname of Serapio "Cinchonero" Romero, a Honduran peasant leader supposedly executed in the late 1800s.

The group's activities include bombings and hostage taking. While it has largely financed itself through bank robberies and kidnapping for ransom, the MPL is suspected of receiving training, arms, logistical support, and funds from Cuba. Salvadoran Farabundo Martí National Liberation Front (FMLN, q.v.) guerrillas reportedly have trained Cinchonero forces within Honduras and have participated with them in kidnapping operations. The Sandinista government allowed Cinchonero guerrillas safe haven in Nicaraguan territory and had used them as auxiliary forces in fighting the contras.

On 24 March 1980, five Cinchoneros hijacked a Honduran Airlines 737 to Managua, Nicaragua, in order to force the release of 15 Salvadoran leftists imprisoned in Honduras. The hijacked plane was flown to Panama before the captive passengers and crew were finally released. On 17 September 1982, they took 105 hostages at an economic conference at the Chamber of Commerce in San Pedro Sula, killing one guard and wounding two businessmen in the takeover. When their demands for the release of imprisoned comrades were not met, they traded the hostages for safe passage to Cuba. From August 1983 to March 1985, the group bombed U.S., Honduran, and Costa Rican business and airline offices in retaliation for these countries' military cooperation against the Sandinista regime in Nicaragua. On 17 July 1988, the group claimed credit for an attack in San Pedro Sula in which some U.S. servicemen were wounded. On 25 January 1989, the group killed the former head of the Honduran army, General Gustavo Alvarez Martínez.

From late 1984 onward the group appeared to withdraw into a period of reorganization. Little is known about its leadership, while its membership was estimated to consist of, at most, about 200 combatants.

CLARA ELIZABETH RAMÍREZ FRONT (CERF). The *Frente Clara Elizabeth Ramírez* is a splinter group that broke away in 1983 from the Popular Liberation Forces, one of the five major groups united into the Farabundo Martí National Liberation Front (FMLN, q.v.). As such, it has essentially the same revolutionary objectives that the FMLN held at the time the group separated, namely, to overthrow the Salvadoran government and create a revolutionary state in El Salvador after the Nicaraguan model. Due to its defection from the FMLN front, however, it cut itself off from Cuban or Sandinista backing.

CERF is a small (estimated 10 to 20 members), well-trained, urban terrorist group that has succeeded in preventing infiltration by security forces. CERF has concentrated on assassinations and has targeted in particular U.S. military personnel and advisers, as well as Salvadoran military and police officials. Its record is short but rather impressive: On 23 May 1983, CERF shot Lieutenant Commander Albert Schaufelberger (USN), deputy commander of the U.S. military advisory mission in El Salvador. On 17 November 1984, CERF assassinated the security supervisor of the U.S. Embassy, who was a Salvadoran national. On 7 March 1985, CERF shot and killed Lieutenant Colonel Ricardo Cienfuegos, chief Salvadoran military spokesman, at a downtown San Salvadoran health club. On 23 March 1985, they followed up with the assassination of General José Alberto Medrano, founder of ORDEN (q.v.) and patron of extreme right-wing groups and politicians.

On 19 June 1985, the Central American Workers' Revolutionary Party, a member group of the FMLN, publicly machine-gunned off-duty U.S. Marines and other patrons sitting in a sidewalk café in the Zona Rosa district, killing four and wounding nine others. The Salvadoran government responded with intensive counterterrorist operations that, in addition to capturing the responsible culprits, crippled but did not totally destroy the CERF. Since that time, CERF has been struggling to rebuild itself through recruitment efforts among university students.

CNPZ. See Nestor Paz Zamora Commando.

COMMUNIST COMBATANT CELLS. The CCC was a nonstate Belgian leftist group active from 1984 to 1985 that engaged in bombings for the limited purposes of protesting against "the Americanization of Europe," capitalism, and the NATO alliance. The CCC did not enjoy any state sponsorship but briefly formed an alliance with the Red Army Faction (RAF, q.v.) and Action Directe (AD, q.v.) known as the "Anti-Imperialist Armed Front" to coordinate their actions against NATO member governments. Unlike RAF and AD, however, the CCC tended to pick symbolic and strategic targets for bombings and to target property rather than human life, using the terrorist event as "armed propaganda" for publicizing their own specific issues or causes rather than as direct military tactics to achieve revolution. Two fire fighters were killed as an unintended result of a bombing attack in May 1985, while a security guard was wounded by a bombing in November 1985.

CCC activities consisted solely of bombings against international corporate offices, banks, and NATO facilities. Out of 14 major bombings by the CCC, 6 were directed against offices of large U.S. and international firms, such as Litton Data Systems (2 October 1984), Honeywell (8 October 1984), Motorola (21 November 1985), and the Bank of America (4 December 1985); 6 others were directed against NATO facilities, such as bombing several points along a NATO fuel pipeline (11 December 1984), a NATO support facility (15 January 1985), and the NATO Central Europe Operating Agency in Versailles, France, inflicting very minor damage (6 December 1985). The remaining two attacks were against the Belgian Employers Association building (May 1985), in which two fire fighters died, and one of the central offices of the Belgian police.

In late December police arrested Pierre Carette, the founder and leader of the CCC, along with three of his followers. These four were convicted on 14 January 1986 for the attempted murder of the security guard wounded in a series of bank bombings conducted on 5 November 1985. Since then there has been no CCC activity and the organization is presumably dormant or dissolved.

CONTRAS. The "contras," short for "counterrevolutionaries," were the armed groups that began fighting to overthrow the Sandinista (FSLN) regime that seized power in Nicaragua in 1979. Originally they were trained by Argentinean military advisers, enjoyed safe haven in Honduras and Costa Rica, and obtained private financial support from Cuban and Nicaraguan exiles. The Argentineans withdrew their advisers from Honduras in 1981 following the collapse of the military junta after their defeat in the Falklands war. Beginning in October 1982, the contras enjoyed U.S. sponsorship, including CIA advisers, military and humanitarian aid. Due to an ongoing and inconclusive political debate between the Reagan administration and the U.S. Congress, U.S. military aid was cut off in 1984, resumed in 1985, but again cut off after the revelation of the Iran-Contra affair in late 1986.

To fulfill a condition for receiving future U.S. aid, on 12 June 1985 the contras united in an umbrella organization, the Unified Nicaraguan Opposition (UNO), which comprised the following groups:

1. The Nicaraguan Democratic Force (FDN), formed out of the September 15th League, the National Liberation Army, and Nicaraguan Democratic Union, the latter group originally made up of ex-Sandinistas and other opponents of the Somoza regime. This group numbered some 18,000 to 22,000 members and was led by Adolfo Calero, former head of the Nicaraguan Conservative Party. Of the top 56 FDN leaders, about 13 were former National Guardsmen and about 26 were former Sandinistas. These forces were based in Honduras and fought in the north of Nicaragua.

2. The Revolutionary Armed Forces (FARN), numbering 1,000 fighters led by a former Sandinista, Fernando "El Negro" Chamorro, who had fought Somoza since 1960, based in Costa Rica and fighting in the south of Nicaragua.

3. The United Villages of the Nicaraguan Atlantic Coast (KISAN), an alliance of Miskito, Sumo, and Rama Indi-

ans and also English-speaking black Creoles, numbering some 4,000 fighters who fought in the northeastern region of Nicaragua.

4. The Nicaraguan Opposition Coordinator (CON), not an armed group but rather the political front organization of political parties, business organizations, and trade unions in exile.

Another contra group was the Nicaraguan Democratic Alliance (ARDE) numbering 3,000 fighters based in Costa Rica and led by Alfonso Robello Callejas, once a member of the post-Somoza junta, and Edén Pastora Gómez, former leader of the Sandino Revolutionary Front and Sandinista hero. ARDE did not join UNO largely due to the opposition of Edén Pastora to certain of UNO's leaders. Pastora quit the contra struggle in 1986. In May 1987, UNO merged with the Southern Opposition Bloc of Alfredo César to form the *Nicaraguan Resistance*, while KISAN was reorganized as YATAMA separate from the Nicaraguan Resistance command.

Instances of terrorization of the civilian population by the contras and of mistreatment of FSLN prisoners have been documented, in itself hardly surprising given the bitterness that existed between the FSLN and their opponents and given the large proportion of contra fighters who lacked both education and the discipline of previous military training. Public debate over U.S. sponsorship of the contras focused on the questions, 1) were such instances of terrorism part of a deliberate policy to suppress popular support for the FSLN regime rather than random cases?, and if so, 2) did the United States aid, abet, or otherwise encourage such systematic terror? A CIA-sponsored Spanish-language training manual produced for training the contras in techniques of armed propaganda entitled *Psychological Operations in Guerrilla Warfare* has often been cited as evidence of a systematic contra terror campaign inspired by U.S. advisers. This manual was presented by the FSLN in its briefs to the International Court of Justice as evidence of U.S. support of contra terror but key cited passages were ambiguous. Quite apart from any deliberate systematic terrorization by the contras, with or without U.S. sponsorship, the record of the rank and file contras' respect for human rights remained, in the words of a former contra political officer, "depressing and testified to a lack of political discipline." (Pardo-Maurer, 55)

Another more substantial problem connected with the contras were the arrangements made by U.S. National Security Adviser Admiral John Poindexter and his aide Lt. Col. Oliver North, to sell arms to the Iranian government in order both to secure the release of U.S. hostages held in Lebanon and also to generate revenues independent of congressional approval with which to sustain the contras' military needs. Apart from the issue of whether this violated congressional restrictions on funding for the contras, there remained a serious question as to whether the Reagan administration was violating its own executive orders banning arms sales to Iran, having itself earlier certified Iran as a state sponsor of terrorism, and whether the arms-for-hostages aspect of the arrangement violated long-standing U.S. declaratory policy barring the payment of ransom for hostages. The private supply network also had the effect of releasing Calero's FDN, which alone controlled these secret funds prior to the reorganization of UNO, from the necessity of having to reform itself, and its human rights record, to conform to the standards demanded by the U.S. Congress as conditions for its support for the contras.

Before 1982 the FSLN had dismissed the contras as a minor nuisance, but after the contras bombed two bridges spanning the Coco and Negro rivers on the Honduran border on 14 March 1982, the FSLN declared a state of emergency the next day. This state of emergency was not lifted until 16 January 1988. In August 1985 the contras suffered reverses in the battlefields as the FSLN army acquired Soviet Mi-24/5 helicopter gunships as well as Mi-17 troop transports. Within two years, by March 1987, the tide turned when the FSLN army suffered the loss of several Mi-24 helicopters to the contras' U.S.-supplied Red-Eye antiaircraft missiles and failed to seal off the Bocay region in northern Nicaragua against contra infiltration. By October 1987 the contras had severed the Rama road that connects Managua to the Atlantic coast and maintained their offensive for the remainder of the year. Shortly after U.S. aid to the contras lapsed on 29 February 1988, the FSLN army invaded Honduras to capture the contras' headquarters, a move countered by President Reagan's deployment of 3,000 U.S. paratroopers to Honduras on 15 March 1988 and Congress's humanitarian aid package of $17.7 million for the contras on 31 March 1988.

Under the pressure of its Central American neighbors, the Sandinista regime finally agreed to a truce and talks with the contras. While the talks began on 23 March 1988, the FSLN negotiators temporized so that the contras would exhaust their recently received U.S. aid and lose their bargaining position. While this strategy succeeded in diminishing the fighting capability of the contras, political unrest within Nicaragua, and the continuing diplomatic pressure from neighboring Central American states forced the FSLN to agree to democratization. Following the U.S. election of 1988 the contras were supplied with only sufficient nonlethal aid to maintain them pending the results of the elections the FSLN had agreed would be held in Nicaragua in February 1990. Following the Sandinista defeat by the election of Violeta Chamorro as president, the contras began their demobilization, which was completed on 25 June 1990.

COVENANT, THE SWORD, AND THE ARM OF THE LORD (CSA). The CSA was a nonstate religious-revolutionary group that developed out of a fundamentalist Christian commune in the Arkansas Ozarks from 1978 until 1985. The CSA was the military wing of the Church of Zarephath-Horeb, a commune founded and led by a former Disciples of Christ minister, Jim Ellison, who eventually led his following to adopt the teachings of Identity Christianity (q.v.), an amalgam of fundamentalist Christianity with white-supremacist, anti-Semitic and populist ideologies.

Ellison's commune, first organized in the Ozarks outside Elijah, Missouri, from 1970 to 1976, was originally nonpolitical and intended to shelter its members through the tribulations of the apocalyptic end times, which they believed were at hand. In 1976 the commune relocated near Bull Shoals, Arkansas, and in 1978 Ellison, after embracing the Identity Christianity creed, then affiliated his group with the Aryan Nations (q.v.). The commune created its own militia, the "Covenant, the Sword and the Arm of the Lord," set up an automatic-weapons shop, and ran a survivalist-commando training camp used by survivalists and members of groups affiliated with the Aryan Nations. The gun shop supplied the modified MAC-10 machine gun later used by the Order (q.v.) to kill Denver radio talk-show host Alan Berg. The commune also ran a press that marketed Identity Christianity literature.

In August 1983, CSA members firebombed both a Metropolitan Community Church in Springfield, Missouri, and a Jewish Community Center in Bloomington, Indiana. In November 1983, CSA members robbing a Texarkana pawnshop murdered the owner because they assumed him to be Jewish. In June 1984, a CSA member killed a black Arkansas state highway patrolman. Following the FBI crackdown on the Order in December 1984, the FBI captured David Tate, an Order member, en route to the CSA compound. On 23 April 1985, a combined force of FBI commandos, Missouri and Arkansas state police, and national guardsmen stormed the CSA compound. After two days of negotiations, CSA members besieged within the compound surrendered themselves along with the wanted Order members Randall Evans and Thomas Bentley. Jim Ellison was arrested and convicted on racketeering charges and also for conspiracy to manufacture, possess and distribute illegal firearms.

When raided by the FBI Zarephath-Horeb held around 200 men, women, and children. Since 1982 the commune has gone into decline. As the commune proved unable to support itself economically, Ellison had sanctioned car thefts and robberies to make mortgage payments on the commune property. Claiming to obey special divine revelations, Ellison also began to practice polygamy taking followers' wives to be his own. These practices disgusted many members who left Ellison during the last three years of Zarephath-Horeb's existence.

CROATIAN NATIONAL RESISTANCE. The Croatian National Resistance was a nonstate group that sought Croatia's independence from Yugoslavia. Using the name "Croatian Freedom Fighters" this group carried out terrorist actions against Yugoslavian diplomatic and commercial targets abroad. Their most spectacular action was the September 1976 hijacking of a TWA Boeing 727 jet en route from New York to Chicago, which the hijackers diverted to Newfoundland, from there to Iceland, and lastly to Paris. In addition the terrorists had planted a bomb in Grand Central Station whose location they would reveal only after authorities would publish communiqués of the group. After authorities complied and the bomb's location was revealed, one policeman was killed and another injured when they tried to deactivate it.

From 17 March 1980 to 4 July 1982, the group carried out five bombings in the United States. On 17 March 1980, the U.S. office of a Yugoslavian bank was bombed. On 3 June 1980, the home of the acting Yugoslavian ambassador was bombed. A pipe bomb also exploded at the Manhattan New York State Supreme Court on 23 January 1981, for which prior notice was given by the group. On 4 July 1982, a travel agency office was pipe bombed in Astoria, N.Y., while on the same day New York City police defused a bomb set at the Yugoslavian Airlines office. None of these incidents caused any injuries.

CUBAN NATIONAL LIBERATION FRONT. The *Frente de Liberación Nacional Cubana* (FLNC) was a nonstate Cuban émigré group with the revolutionary goal of overthrowing the Castro regime in Cuba. It was one of the five main anti-Castro Cuban exile groups in the United States, the others being Alpha-66, Brigade 2506, the Cuban Nationalist Movement, and Omega-7.

The Cuban National Liberation Front was active mainly in the late 1960s and early 1970s and engaged in assaults and bombings against persons or institutions perceived to be pro-Castro. The group had ceased to function by the 1980s, due to the diminished hopes among the Cuban exile community that Castro's government would ever be overthrown, and Omega-7 (q.v.) remained as the only functioning anti-Castro émigré group.

- D -

DAL KHALSA. The Dal Khalsa is a Sikh political-religious group that seeks the creation of an independent state of Khalistan as a Sikh homeland out of the current Punjab State in India and certain adjacent Punjabi-speaking areas. This group has resorted to terrorism to radicalize Sikh opinion, to gain public attention to its demands, and also to avenge certain alleged wrongs committed against Sikhs or the Sikh religion. Oddly enough this group, which seeks to carve a state of Khalistan out of the Union of India, originally had covert support from the ruling Congress Party. Currently it is believed to have state support from Pakistan even though the irredentist claims for Khalistan would encompass the Punjab districts of Pakistan as well.

In Sikh history the original *Dal Khalsa,* literally "the army of the Pure," was an assemblage of Sikh clans (*misl*) who all submitted to the command of a common leader for accomplishing some limited purpose, originally to battle the Mughals. The modern Dal Khalsa began as the result of an intramural sectarian quarrel among the Sikhs. On 13 April

1978, several Nirankari Sikhs held a religious gathering in the Sikh holy city of Amritsar. A prominent Sikh religious leader, Sant Jarnail Singh Bhindranwale (b. 1947), who anathematized the Nirankari Sikhs as heretics, led a demonstration to break up the Nirankari gathering. Thirteen of Bhindranwale's followers armed with swords were shot dead by the Nirankaris. Bhindranwale turned his attention to taking vengeance on the Nirankaris and on the moderate Sikh and Hindu politicians who protected them. This disaffection led him later to endorse the idea of an independent Khalistan.

In August 1978 several Sikh political youth groups, disaffected with the ineffectiveness of the moderate Akali Dal party in securing Punjabi interests against the central government, formed a group assuming the historically charged name of Dal Khalsa. Their proclaimed goal was to preserve the purity of Sikhism from Nirankari influence, which in practical terms meant opposing those who tolerated the Nirankaris, i.e., the Akali Dal. In the elections to the Shiromani Gurdwara Parbandhak Committee (SGPC), that is, the high Sikh council that oversees management of the Sikh shrines, Bhindranwale backed Dal Khalsa while the Congress party leaders encouraged both Bhindranwale and Dal Khalsa in the hope of weakening the Akali Dal party.

The idea of Khalistan came to the fore later on 16 June 1980, when a National Council of Khalistan announced its formation. On 13 March 1981, the Dal Khalsa endorsed the idea of Khalistan to upstage the more hesitant Akali Dal. That year witnessed a rise in communal tensions between Sikhs and Hindus when the head of the All India Sikh Students' Federation (AISSF), who was closely connected to Bhindranwale, demanded special laws to protect the sanctity of Amritsar. Bhindranwale led a demonstration on 31 May 1981 that clashed with police, leading to several deaths. The subsequent murder on 9 September 1981 of a Hindu publisher, whose paper heaped scorn on the idea of Khalistan and who happened to be an enemy of Bhindranwale, led to the latter's arrest on 20 September 1981 on suspicion of murder.

On 29 September 1981, five Dal Khalsa members hijacked an Indian Airlines Boeing 737, flying from Delhi to Srinagar with 111 passengers and 6 crew, to Lahore, Pakistan, where they released 66 passengers but held the rest pending the release of Bhindranwale and the creation of Khalistan. The hijackers were overcome by Pakistani soldiers on 30 September 1981. Bhindranwale was released from custody on 15 October 1981 but not before many shootings, bombings, and attacks between Hindus and Sikhs in Punjab took place. Bad federal relations between Indira Gandhi's government and the Punjab government added to these sectarian and communal tensions. Due to the role played by Dal Khalsa in instigating anti-Hindu violence in Punjabi cities the organization was banned on 1 May 1982, while the head of AISSF was arrested on 19 July 1982.

Beginning 20 July 1982, Bhindranwale joined other Sikh leaders in the Golden Temple of Amritsar to make a ''peaceful agitation'' to seek redress of Sikh grievances. While Bhindranwale remained within the temple sanctuary outside the effective reach of the law, his followers, presumably with his blessing, began a campaign of terrorism against religiously lax Sikhs, political opponents, and Hindus living in Punjab. Two hijackings were attempted while an assassination attempt was made against the Chief Minister of Punjab. On 25 April 1983, Deputy Chief Inspector of Police, Atvar Singh Atwal, who had visited the Golden Temple purportedly to worship, was shot dead as soon as he left its premises. The Indian government held Bhindranwale and his followers responsible for this and the massive outbreaks of sectarian violence, which Dal Khalsa often instigated. Bhindranwale moved into the innermost sanctum of the Golden Temple, the *Akal Takht,* on 15 December 1983, and on the following day the Indian government issued a warrant for his arrest. On 5 June 1984, the Indian Army began Operation Blue Star in the course of which they overran the Golden Temple complex and destroyed the Akal Takht with tank fire. All told, about

700 troops perished along with 5,000 civilians, among them Bhindranwale.

Following the desecration of the Golden Temple, Sikh extremists began killing not only Indian government officials known to have participated in formulating or executing Operation Blue Star but also moderate Sikhs willing to settle for anything less than an independent Khalistan. On 10 August 1986, Dal Khalsa claimed credit for the assassination of General A. S. Vaidya, who was the Chief of the Indian Army Staff, during Operation Blue Star. In June 1987, Dal Khalsa members killed at least 12 people in two attacks in the village of Udhwuk.

The Dal Khalsa remains under a ban, and its presumed leader, Gurbachan Singh Manochahal, has a reward on his head. The organization is estimated to have ranged between 500 and 1,000 member supporters and has carried out its activities largely within India. The AISSF, with 40,000 members, was banned in March 1984, but the ban was lifted one year later.

DASHMESH REGIMENT. The *Tenth* Regiment is reputed to be a Sikh militant group that aims to establish an independent nation-state of Khalistan as a homeland for the Sikhs in present-day Punjab and adjoining Punjabi-speaking areas. This group has been credited with the assassinations of prominent persons, even other Sikhs, who have criticized the cause of Khalistan. Groups using this and other names have also terrorized Hindus living in, or traveling within, their designated area of Khalistan and have engaged in at least one bombing of a commercial air carrier. The name "Dashmesh" means "tenth," referring to the tenth Guru of the Sikhs, Guru Gobind Singh, who transformed the Sikhs into a warrior society.

Knowledge about the origins, composition, and leadership of the Dashmesh regiment is fragmentary and conjectural. Unlike the Dal Khalsa (q.v.) or the All India Sikh Students'

Federation (AISSF), this group has no history prior to the onset of secessionist troubles in Punjab, and some observers within India have concluded that it is a phantom group, a name being used to hide the culpability of those actually responsible for terrorist actions or to throw outsiders off their scent (*India Today* [New Delhi], 31 August 1984, p. 55).

Supposedly the group was founded in 1984 with the blessing of Sant Jarnail Singh Bhindranwale, a Sikh fundamentalist leader who became closely identified with the Khalistan idea (See Dal Khalsa). As Bhindranwale was also closely associated with the banned Dal Khalsa and All India Sikh Student Federation (AISSF) groups, it is likely that if the Dashmesh Regiment exists, it has drawn its leaders and members from these groups or from the immediate circle of Bhindranwale's followers.

On 28 March 1984, the Regiment claimed credit for the shooting death of Harbans Singh Manchanda, a pro-Congress overseer of the New Delhi Sikh temple. A letter purportedly written by the Dashmesh Regiment addressed to *Indian Express* in April 1984 threatened to assassinate Indira Gandhi. On 14 April 1984, Sikh extremists attempted to burn down at least 34 railroad stations, actions credited to the Regiment. The Regiment also claimed credit for the shooting death of Ramesh Chander on 12 May 1984, editor of the *Hind Samacher* newspaper and son of an enemy of Bhindranwale who had also been assassinated on 9 September 1981.

In the years following the Indian Army's assault on the Golden Temple during June 1984, in which Bhindranwale was killed and the *Akal Takht* (the Golden Temple's holy of holies) destroyed, a number of murders, massacres, and pillagings have been perpetrated both by Sikhs against Hindus and by Hindus against Sikhs. By the Punjab Home Department's estimates, in 1985 there were 61 deaths due to such terrorism; in 1985 there were 520 such deaths; 1987 witnessed 1,199 deaths; and 1988 witnessed 1,964 deaths. The Dashmesh Regiment claimed credit for at least five major incidents following the attack on the Golden Temple, including an assassination attempt on Rajiv Gandhi on 2 October 1986. But the identities of parties responsible for other terrorist actions have been masked by their use of noms de guerre, e.g., on 30 November 1986 Sikh gunmen stopped a bus and shot dead 24 Hindu passengers. This action was repeated on 7 July 1987 with two buses, killing 38 and wounding 32 in one, and killing 4 and wounding 32 in the other bus. Although this action was claimed in the name of the "Khalistan Commando Force" the perpetrators turned out to be AISSF members. Similarly the Regiment may turn out to be in fact an extension of Dal Khalsa, AISSF, or other Sikh groups.

Most of these actions have been confined to India, mainly to the Punjab and nearby Haryana state. The Dashmesh Regiment claimed responsibility for two major terrorist actions outside India, namely the premature explosion of a bomb intended to be loaded onto an Air India Boeing 747 at Tokyo's Narita Airport and the aerial bombing on 23 June 1985 of an Air India Boeing 747 carrying 329 people from Toronto, Canada, to London. (See Air India Bombing.) Wreckage of this plane found off the coast of Ireland indicated it may have been bombed. It should be noted that the Kashmir Liberation Army also claimed credit for these events. In 1985 the FBI foiled a Sikh extremist plot to assassinate Indira Gandhi during her visit to the United States as well as another plot to assassinate the Chief Minister of Haryana State during his visit to New Orleans.

These international terrorist events appear to be anomalies. Although militant Sikh separatists have had ample opportunity to strike at Indian targets outside India, such as diplomatic or government-managed commercial offices abroad, Sikh militants abroad have largely limited themselves to making demonstrations outside Indian embassies and consulates. It appears likely that Sikh militants realize such actions would alienate world opinion from the cause of Khalistan and would compromise the position of the diaspora of Sikh merchant communities living abroad who form a valuable support network.

DAWA, AL. The *Hizb al Dawa al Islamiyya,* or Islamic Call [to faith] Party, is a Shiite Muslim fundamentalist party founded in Iraq by radical junior Shiite clergymen that seeks to overthrow the secular Bathist regime in Iraq in order to create an Iranian-style Islamic Republic. Iraq's population is nearly 60 percent Shiite while the governing Bathist party is predominantly Sunnite. On the other hand, most of the Shiite religious leaders in Iraq come from families that either originated in Iran or else have intermarried with Iranian clerical families, thus undercutting the nationalistic credentials of potential Shiite leaders. While this party is one of the oldest radical Shiite political parties, having been founded in 1968–1969 at the latest, it has had to accept Iranian state sponsorship after having been virtually eradicated within Iraq by severe state repression.

Beginning in 1974 the Iraqi regime responded to Shiite unrest in the shrine cities of Karbala and Najaf by executing five Dawa leaders and eight others in 1977 when riots broke out again. Following the Islamic revolution in Iran in 1979, the Iraqi regime put the pro-Khomeini Ayatollah Muhammad Baqir al Sadr under house arrest in order to deprive Iraqi Shiite fundamentalists the rallying point of a charismatic leader. Shortly after the holding of an Islamic Liberation Movements conference in Tehran in early 1980, an "Islamic Liberation Movement of Iraq" proclaimed its existence in Europe and named the confined Ayatollah Baqir al Sadr as its leader.

Dawa activists joined with other anti-Bathist guerrilla fighters and, with Iranian material and moral support, undertook attacks on police stations and Bathist party offices. On 1 April 1980, Dawa members aided by Iranian revolutionaries attempted to assassinate Tariq Aziz, deputy premier of Iraq and close associate of Saddam Hussein. Reprisals included making Dawa membership a capital offense, the expulsion of over 15,000 Shiites suspected of pro-Dawa sympathies, and the summary execution of Ayatollah Baqir al Sadr and his sister sometime during the week following the assassination attempt. In what amounted to a declaration of war, Ayatollah Khomeini responded to the news of al Sadr's execution by issuing a decree of *takfir* [anathema] on 18 April 1980, against Saddam Hussein and the Bathist regime of Iraq and calling on the Iraqi Armed Forces to overthrow their Bathist rulers. By the end of 1980 over 500 Dawa members were summarily executed in Iraq, although assassinations of government officials and sabotage against the Iraqi military continued even after the outbreak of the Iran-Iraq war in September 1980.

Members of the al Dawa group have joined Hezbollah (q.v.) in Lebanon and formed cells in other Arab lands, particularly Kuwait, where they have received arms and explosives through Iranian diplomatic offices. The spiritual leader of Hezbollah, Sheikh Muhammad Hussein Fadlullah, was a former member of a Lebanese branch of the al Dawa party. At least three of those involved in the 12 December 1983 truck bombing attempts against the U.S. and French embassies in Kuwait were Dawa members who claimed also to be Islamic Jihad (q.v.) members. On 25 May 1985, a Dawa member attempted to assassinate the Emir of Kuwait in a suicidal car bomb attack. The seizing of the U.S. hostages in Lebanon began in earnest after the conviction of the 17 perpetrators of the Kuwait City truck bombing attempts. The hijackers of TWA flight 847 on 14 June 1985 and of Kuwait Airlines flight 422 on 5 April 1988 also included release of the convicted truck bombers among their demands. During the 2 August 1990 Iraqi invasion of Kuwait, prison authorities there released the remaining 15 convicted bombers, 2 having completed their terms earlier. These and other Dawa members participated in the partisan resistance against the Iraqi occupiers of Kuwait. Later Dawa members aided by Iranian Islamic Revolutionary Guards (q.v.) attacked Iraqi troops in Basra during the later stages of the 1991 Persian Gulf war.

In Iran former Dawa party members appeared to form the nucleus of the Supreme Assembly for the Islamic Revolution in Iraq (SAIRI), an umbrella group of Iraqi Shiite dissident groups formed under Iranian auspices in early July 1982 as a government-in-exile of a future Islamic republic in Iraq. SAIRI is headed by Hujjatulislam Baqir al Hakim, son of Muhsin al Hakim, a native Iraqi religious leader claimed by Dawa members as the founder of their party. SAIRI used to form contingents of anti-Saddam Iraqi émigrés to fight alongside Iranian troops in the Iran-Iraq war and also collaborated with antiregime Kurds in the northern war fronts within Iraqi territory.

Although SAIRI attempted to unify the Dawa and other Iraqi Shiite groups under its standard, the main body of the Dawa party remained aloof and maintained its own separate organization.

DEATH SQUADS. Death squads are military, paramilitary, or irregular forces sponsored by a regime or political group to engage in violent repression against a population to prevent it from supporting the opponents of the regime or group. The term ''death squad'' is believed to have originated in Brazil in the 1960s where off-duty policemen formed ''Esquadraos de Morte'' to kill off criminal elements. Later these spontaneously generated vigilantes were co-opted by the Brazilian military regime to kill off dissidents.

The most frequently cited instances of death squads have been those sponsored by right-wing regimes in Central and Latin America to suppress leftists and suspected leftist sympathizers through kidnapping, torture, and murder. Human rights organizations have particularly faulted the Guatemalan security forces for campaigns of state terror in the 1970s and 1980s involving the use of death squads that terrorized not only leftists but also many innocents, particularly Indians in areas of rural insurgency. Among the more notorious of these groups were the White Hand (q.v.) group and the Anti-Communist Secret Army (q.v.). El Salvador had death squad activity during the 1970s involving such groups as the rural militia ORDEN (q.v.), which was declared disbanded in November 1979. In fact, its members appear to have entered newer death squads such as the White Warriors' Union (q.v.) and the Maximiliano Hernández Martínez Anti-Communist Brigade (q.v.). From 1979 until 1982 killings by Salvadoran death squads sometimes exceeded 800 people each month and included among their victims Archbishop Oscar Romero y Galdamez killed on 24 March 1980 and four American church workers on 4 December 1980. This death squad activity created much controversy regarding the Reagan administration's support of the Salvadoran transitional regime against the FMLN leftist insurgency since it was clear that many of the leaders and members of such groups were themselves members of the Salvadoran military and police. By the mid-1980s, however, the murder rate had dropped to less than 100 killings per month and by late 1988 was about 16 killings per month, a figure that may be accounted for by ordinary murders rather than death squad activity.

Examples of death squads can be found outside of Latin America. Many of the Ulster Protestant militias have been accused of acting as anti-Catholic death squads, such as the Red Hand Commandos (q.v.) and the Ulster Volunteer Force (q.v.). South Africa's military Civil Cooperation Bureau was closed on 31 July 1990, following revelations that it had sponsored death squad activities.

While death squads are usually state-sponsored groups in cases where the state is relatively weak a marginally stronger political group or economic elite could sponsor its own death squads without having to rely on the state. Actually such was the situation in El Salvador following November 1979 when a weak transitional government was unable to control its own security personnel involved in death squads being financed and run by Salvadoran oligarchs opposed to agrarian and social reforms. Likewise the Medellín drug cartel formed its own death squad, MAS (q.v.), in order to kill off leftist guerrillas who had been interfering in the smugglers' operations.

Although the term "death squad" has usually been used only to describe right-wing terror groups, there are leftist regimes and groups that have sponsored their own death squads. In El Salvador the Clara Elizabeth Ramírez Front (q.v.) acted as a selective hit squad while the People's Revolutionary Army (See Farabundo Martí Liberation Front) used to kidnap and murder functionaries of the Salvadoran government. In the Philippines the communist New People's Army (q.v.) has been using death squads known as "Sparrow Squads" to murder Philippine government and military authorities as well as U.S. servicemen. The Peruvian Maoist group Sendero Luminoso (q.v.) has also engaged in selective and systematic murder of its opponents. In Turkey, prior to the military coup and crackdown of September 1980, right-wing death squads, such as the Grey Wolves (q.v.), and left-wing death squads, such as Dev Sol (q.v.) and the Turkish People's Liberation Front (q.v.), were operating simultaneously.

Death squads seem to function best as repressive tools when their targets are limited to the leaders of the opposing groups. Once death squad activity becomes random, killing not only opposition followers but also the ordinarily politically uninvolved mass public, then the latter group becomes more politicized and emboldened to resist the sponsors of the death squads.

In conclusion it should be noted that although death squads are usually used to achieve repression of rival political groups once they cease to be sponsored by a state or party, they sometimes revert to becoming free-lance entrepreneurial killers. Such was the case with the members of the disbanded ORDEN group in El Salvador and such is the case with Brazilian policemen today, many of whom have reverted to vigilante actions against petty criminals and homeless street children.

DELLE CHIAIE, STEPHANO. Italian neo-Fascist terrorist and founder of the Avanguardia Nazionale (q.v.). This group carried out a bombing campaign from 1969 to 1973. It merged with the Black Order (q.v.), which in turn produced the Armed Revolutionary Nucleus (q.v.) group responsible for the 2 August 1980 bombing of Bologna's main railroad station. These groups have been affiliated with each other, and with similar right wing extremists outside of Italy, through the ''Black Orchestra,'' originally masterminded by Delle Chiaie.

Delle Chiaie himself had fled to Spain in 1970 following an abortive right-wing coup d'état attempt in Italy in which he participated. In Spain Delle Chiaie became active in state-sponsored death squad activities directed against members of the Basque Fatherland and Liberty (q.v.) group. Following Francisco Franco's death in 1976, Delle Chiaie reportedly moved to Latin America where he collaborated with the former right-wing military regimes in Argentina and Chile in their internal campaigns to suppress domestic leftists and other political opponents. Following his involvement in an abortive coup attempt in Bolivia in 1980 and the fall from power of his right-wing state sponsors in Argentina, Delle Chiaie went into hiding, having been last seen in October 1982.

DEMOCRATIC FRONT FOR THE LIBERATION OF PALESTINE (DFLP). The DFLP is a Palestinian Marxist-Leninist guerrilla organization and PLO member that advocates the creation of an independent Palestinian state on the West Bank and Gaza Strip. It also advocates revolutionary working-class struggle throughout the Arab world as part of an international anti-imperialist and anticapitalist revolution but has limited its own use of armed struggle or terrorism to achieving the independent Palestinian state. Formerly the DFLP enjoyed some support from Libya and South Yemen while its major sponsor was Syria; however, the DFLP lost Syrian support when it refused to join the Syrian-sponsored National Salvation Front in 1987. Since then the DFLP has tried to limit its dependence on any external sponsors. DFLP members have received Soviet training and Cuban aid and are believed to have had contact with the Sandinistas (q.v.).

The DFLP was born out of a division between extreme leftists and Pan-Arabists within George Habash's Popular Front for the Liberation of Palestine (q.v.) (PFLP). This factionalism escalated to armed clashes in Amman, Jordan, during February 1969 until Fatah (q.v.) intervened, recognizing the breakaway leftists as a group separate from the PFLP. Until August 1974 the group was known as the Popular Democratic Front for the Liberation of Palestine. The DFLP consists of Marxist-Leninists who reject the chauvinistic Pan-Arabism of the PFLP in favor of socialist internationalism and who also reject the use of international terrorism. The DFLP believed terrorist or guerrilla actions should be conducted only within Israel and the occupied territories, a position that Fatah adopted five years later in 1974 and that eventually was declared official PLO policy on 15 November 1988 in the nineteenth Palestinian National Council meeting. The DFLP also preceded Fatah in diplomatic initiatives, making contact with Israeli socialist internationalist counterparts such as the Israeli Matzpen group in 1970 but later opposed any negotiations with the former Likud government of Israel. The DFLP also pioneered in 1973 the idea of the establishment of an independent Palestinian state on the West Bank and Gaza Strip that Fatah also later adopted.

During the 1970s the DFLP carried out several attacks within Israel, usually involving hostage takings or bombings. Their most notorious action was the 15 May 1974 assault on the Israeli town of Maalot in which three DFLP terrorists took 90 schoolchildren as hostages to be released in exchange for freeing 23 Arab prisoners as well as Kozo Okamoto, the Japanese Red Army terrorist who had participated in the Lod airport massacre on 30 May 1972. When the negotiations broke down, the Israeli troops stormed the dormitory, but not before the terrorists machine-gunned the children, killing 16 outright and wounding 70 others, 5 of whom later died. Seven other Israelis, two of them Arabs, were also killed and 69 other Israelis were wounded in the course of this action. This massacre prompted Israeli air force retaliatory strikes against Palestinian refugee camps in southern Lebanon believed to have been the bases of the attackers. A similar attack took place in Beit Shean on 19 November 1974 in which all three attackers were killed along with four Israelis. In July 1977 and March 1979, the DFLP carried out several bombings in public markets and buses. In January 1979, a DFLP terrorist team tried to repeat a hostage taking at Maalot but was intercepted by a routine Israeli military patrol. Following 1982, DFLP actions within Israel consisted of grenade and small firebomb attacks throughout Israel, the West Bank, and the Gaza strip, but after 1988 DFLP actions were limited to small border raids.

The importance of the DFLP derives more from its swing votes within the PLO organization than from its declining record of terrorist activities. DFLP support was essential for Fatah to rally the votes needed to have the Palestine National Council (PNC) accept U.N. resolutions 242 and 338, contingent on creation of a Palestinian state in the occupied territories, in the nineteenth PNC meeting held during 12–15 November 1988. The deputy head of the DFLP, Yasir Abdul Rabbo, led the first PLO delegation to meet officially with U.S. diplomats following President Reagan's authorization of direct U.S.-PLO talks on 14 December 1988. In 1991 the DFLP split into two factions with the original leader, Naif Hawatmeh, leading a faction opposed to Arafat and Abdul Rabbo leading the pro-Arafat faction. This split reflected a general dissatisfaction felt within the PLO over the slowness and indirection of efforts on the diplomatic front.

The DFLP had about 1,000 followers in the early 1970s and perhaps as many as 2,000 on the eve of Israel's invasion of Lebanon in the summer of 1982. Currently its two factions together may have about 500 followers.

DEMOCRATIC REVOLUTIONARY FRONT FOR THE LIBERATION OF ARABISTAN. Originally a Marxist-Leninist splinter group of the Popular Front for the Liberation of Ahwaz, both organizations appear to have been Iraqi-sponsored groups ostensibly seeking the independence of the largely Arab-inhabited regions of Khuzistan province in southwestern Iran.

In reaction to a long-standing dispute with Iran over sovereignty of the Shatt-al-Arab estuary, the Iraqi government began in 1960 to support irredentist Arab claims to Iran's Khuzistan Province on the eastern banks of the disputed waterway by supporting the Popular Front for the Liberation of Ahwaz. With the signing of the 1975 Algiers Accord in which Iraq ceded its previous claims to the waterway, Iraqi support of the PFLA insurgency ceased.

The Democratic Revolutionary Front for the Liberation of Arabistan emerged from the remnant of the PFLA, which acquired Iraqi support once again following the Islamic revolution in Iran in 1978–1979 and the outbreak of hostilities between Iraq and Iran in September 1980. The DRFLA emerged into the limelight with its seizure of the Iranian Embassy in London from 30 April 1980 to 5 May 1990 in which 6 terrorists held 26 hostages. Commandos of Britain's 22nd Special Air Service Regiment executed a daytime assault on the Embassy in which five terrorists and two hostages were killed. Within Khuzistan Province, which became a major battleground between Iranian and Iraqi troops, the DRFLA played little effective role in supporting the Iraqi invasion or in harassing Iranian troops.

DEV SOL. The *Devrimci Sol,* or Revolutionary Left, of Turkey is a Marxist-Leninist grouping seeking to unite the Turkish proletariat to carry out a socialist revolution. This group has acted largely as a leftist death squad, attacking Turkish rightists from 1978 to 1983 and striking at retired Turkish security officials as well as U.S. and other nationals of NATO countries from the late 1980s to the present. The group is not known to have had foreign state sponsorship, although it is believed to have had contact with radical

Palestinian groups as well as with Greek leftist terrorists and the Kurdish Workers' Party (q.v.).

Dev Sol emerged in 1978 as a splinter group from Dev Yol (Revolutionary Road), which itself split from the Turkish People's Liberation Army (q.v.) in 1975. Dev Sol engaged in numerous murders of rightist politicians, writers, and students. Following the Turkish military coup and crackdown in September 1980, many members of the group were arrested or killed in clashes with security forces. On 2 October 1980, Dev Sol bombed U.S. Army buildings in Izmir, causing but minor damages. Two days later an unoccupied U.S. Air Force staff sergeant's car was firebombed by Dev Sol. On 24 May 1981, a Turkish Airlines DC-9 with 112 passengers and 7 crew members was hijacked by 4 Dev Sol members from Istanbul to Bulgaria where eventually the terrorists were overpowered by the passengers and captured. On 5 November 1982, the Turkish tourism office in Amsterdam was seized by 10 Dev Sol members who took two hostages for three hours until Dutch police rushed and overpowered the terrorists.

During 1983 to 1989 the group disappeared from view due to the severe repression of leftist terrorists within Turkey in that period. Unlike many other Turkish leftist groups, however, Dev Sol has made a comeback. During 1990–1991 they killed at least 4 active and retired Turkish generals and some 30 police officers. Beginning in 1991, they resumed attacks on Western businessmen and military personnel within Turkey. During 1991, Dev Sol murdered two American contractors and one British businessman in Turkey, attempted to murder one U.S. Air Force officer in his home in Izmir, and conducted over 30 bombings of Western diplomatic, commercial, and cultural targets in Turkey.

Most of Dev Sol's activities have occurred in the environs of Istanbul, Ankara, Izmir, and Adana. The group numbers a few dozen armed militants and several hundred supporters who also maintain a support network among Turkish expatriates in Europe.

DIRECT ACTION. *Action Directe* (AD) was a group of French anarchistic, leftist terrorists active from 1 May 1979 until February 1987. AD, the Red Brigades (q.v.), the Red Army Faction (RAF, q.v.), the Communist Combatant Cells (q.v.), and Prima Linea (q.v.) rationalized their terrorism in revolutionary leftist terms but appeared to pursue terrorist violence as an end in itself rather than as a strategy to achieve revolution. These groups can be considered ''leftist'' insofar as they despised capitalism, believed in the superiority of a socialist state, and often spoke in Marxist jargon. They were also anarchistic insofar as they limited their purposes to destroying the existing capitalist states rather than building the foundations of some successor socialist state. While AD did not appear to have state sponsorship, the group did collaborate with the Red Brigades and the Communist Combatant Cells.

The name of the group derives from a statement made by the group outlining its anarchistic program: ''[We will] wreck society through direct action by destroying its institutions and the men who serve it.'' AD divided itself into two wings, one specializing in international targets, which has deliberately killed and maimed persons connected with West European business or military defense, the other wing striking domestic targets but usually in such a way that human life would not be taken, usually by bombing buildings after closing hours.

An analysis of 35 noteworthy actions committed by AD from 1979 to 1987 shows that 49 percent (=17) of these involved bombings, killing at least 5 and wounding at least 58 others; 23 percent (=8) involved assassination attempts, half of them successful; 14 percent (=5) involved armed attacks with automatic weapons; and the remaining 14 percent (=5) involved theft, threats, and arms smuggling.

Bombing targets have included the European headquarters of the World Bank (4 June 1982); the European Space Agency (2 August 1984); and the officers' club at the Rhein-Main U.S. Air Force Base, which was car bombed,

killing 2 and wounding 19 others (8 August 1985). Successful assassinations included the killing of French General
René Audran (25 January 1985); Georges Besse, chairman of
Renault (17 November 1986); and an American serviceman,
murdered merely to get his car to be used in the Rhein-Main
car-bombing attack.

The Rhein-Main attack is one of the few in which AD
crossed borders to carry out its operations. It was also done in
partnership with the RAF, which may account for its more
calculated brutality. In February 1987, four AD leaders were
arrested outside Orleans for the murder of Georges Besse. In
November 1987 Max Frerot, the AD bombing expert, was
also arrested. The organization appears to have been ended
with these arrests.

DIRTY WAR. Name used to describe the Argentinean military
junta's campaign of state terror to annihilate leftist guerrillas,
politicians, students, unionists, and intellectuals, which lasted
from 24 March 1976 until the fall of the military junta in 1983.
The junta began a massive death squad campaign using both
the military forces and the Argentine Anti-Communist Alliance (q.v.) to arrest tens of thousands of Argentines who were
tortured to death in prisons and their bodies disposed of in river
estuaries, the sea, or unmarked graves.

It is estimated that between 20,000 and 30,000 persons
perished and disappeared in the junta's so-called process of
national reorganization. Although the campaign was originally directed against leftists and enjoyed some support from
middle-class, conservative Argentineans exasperated with
the violence of the Montoneros (q.v.) and similar leftist
terrorists, toward the end of the junta's rule all classes of
Argentinean society had suffered from the death squad
campaign. The dirty war allowed no formal process of
documentation or defense of those considered to be enemies
of the regime and consequently many nonleftists and politically inactive persons also entered the ranks of the "disappeared."

DOUKHOBORS. Also known as the "Sons of Freedom," or "Freedomites," the Doukhobors are members of a Russian Christian sect who emigrated to Canada around the turn of the century. They are a nonstate communal religious group who adhere to a radical ideal of freedom and antiauthoritarianism, rejecting both secular and religious hierarchical authority. A long-standing Doukhobor ritual meant to demonstrate the Doukhobors' radical freedom even from their material possessions has been the periodic communal burning of all their worldly goods. In the course of this ritual, participating Doukhobors would ultimately strip off their garments to burn as well until all participants were naked. Like the Amish, the Doukhobors deny the authority of the government to send their children to public schools but, unlike the pacifistic Amish, the Doukhobors have used arson and bombing of public property as means of protesting and resisting Canadian federal and provincial government intervention in their lives.

There are about 20,000 Doukhobors in Canada, of which some 2,500 are the more radical "Sons of Freedom," located mainly in eastern British Columbia, who have been responsible for most Doukhobor terrorism. Most of these terrorist acts occurred in the period from 1961–1962, although incidents occurred as late as 1972, and consisted of burnings and bombings directed at other Doukhobors, businesses, railroads, power pylons, and government buildings. In the period from 1960–1985 Doukhobor violence accounted for 38.3 percent (=130 events) of all terrorist incidents in Canada and was second only to Québécois separatism (=166 events) as the largest source of political terrorism in Canada. The primary targets in 57 of these 130 attacks were public buildings, transportation, power, or communications facilities. Sixteen attacks were directed at commercial buildings and 17 attacks at community buildings. Although some have described this violence as being religiously motivated, and therefore presumed to be nonpolitical, it is clear that the religious doctrine of independence from all external authority also implies a rather thoroughgoing political anarchism as well as legitimizing instrumental revolutionary violence.

Although Doukhobor terrorism has greatly subsided, its future demise is hardly a foregone conclusion. Those leaders among the Sons of Freedom who were tried and convicted for the terrorism of the period from 1961–1962 are due to be released during the 1990s. Observers who had been predicting the inevitable demise of both Doukhobor religion and violence did so on the assumption that the younger generation of Doukhobors were being inevitably secularized and assimilated into mainstream Canadian society. The resurgence of Jewish, Christian, and Islamic fundamentalist movements in the last quarter of this century belies this assumption of inevitable and irreversible modernization.

- E -

ELA. See Revolutionary Popular Struggle

ELN. See National Liberation Army

ENTEBBE HIJACKING. On 27 June 1976, Air France flight 139 from Tel Aviv to Paris, carrying 245 passengers and 12 crew members, was hijacked out of Athens by seven members of the Popular Front for the Liberation of Palestine (q.v.) to Benghazi, Libya, where the plane was refueled. From there it flew to Entebbe Airport, Uganda, where the hijackers were aided by Ugandan troops in guarding the hostages. The hijackers demanded the release of 53 terrorists held in French, Israeli, Kenyan, Swiss, and West German jails, including Kozo Okamoto, sole surviving terrorist involved in the May 1972 Lod airport attack. Three of the terrorists were non-Arabs believed to be associates of Ilyich Ramírez Sánchez, known as ''Carlos.'' Throughout the hostage seizure the Ugandan dictator, Idi Amin, fully supported the terrorists.

By 1 July 1976, the terrorists had released nearly all non-Jewish and non-Israeli hostages, leaving 103 at Entebbe. On 2 July the Israeli cabinet decided upon Operation Thunderbolt, a plan to send Israeli commandos to Entebbe to rescue the hostages. On 4 July 1976, the Israelis rescued all but four of the hostages, three having been killed by the cross fire at the rescue scene, while another passenger, Dora Bloch, age seventy-five, was absent, having been hospitalized in Kampala. The rescuers killed 7 of the terrorists and about 20 Ugandan soldiers, while the Israeli officer leading the rescue, Jonathan Netanyahu, was the only Israeli soldier killed in the attack. The Israelis destroyed 11 Ugandan air force MIGs to prevent any attempt to interfere with the rescue mission on its return to Israel.

Following the rescue Dora Bloch was reportedly murdered and her body burned, while Idi Amin carried out a widespread purge and executions of Ugandan officials charged with guarding Entebbe airport and the hostages.

ENTREPRENEURIAL TERRORISM. Apart from state terrorism meant to preserve an existing social-political status quo or revolutionary terrorism meant to change that status quo in part or in whole, there are other instances of terrorism and terrorists having much more limited aims that do not fit into the foregoing two categories. The term entrepreneurial terrorism is used to designate this third category since very often the limited end(s) being sought are merely the profits the group can extract from either extortion or from the sale of its terrorist abilities to whatever buyer. Sometimes a revolutionary group that is never able to achieve its original goals will become entrepreneurial, an example being the Inner Macedonian Revolutionary Organization, which began as a nationalist society in 1900 but had degenerated to becoming a criminal for-hire hit squad by World War II. This term, however, is also used in this dictionary to refer to terrorist groups that are essentially single-interest groups. Thus groups like the Animal Liberation Front or the Ananda Marg cult, which each sought only a very limited and specific goal, quite apart from changing or maintaining a social-political status quo, are also considered entrepreneurial insofar as they are absorbed in the marginal gain or loss of their limited ends. Another example concerns hijacking: Hijacking in order to gain passengers as hostages with which to put pressure on a government to comply with political demands could be either a revolutionary or, if the group is a state-sponsored proxy, a state terrorist act. Hijacking a plane merely to fly to a desired country could be considered an entrepreneurial act.

EOKA. The *Ethniki Organosis Kyprion Agoniston* (National Organization of Cypriot Fighters) was a Greek Cypriot revolutionary nationalist group dedicated to winning Cypriot independence from Britain and uniting Cyprus with Greece. This group also had Greek state support from 1971 to 1974. Beginning on 31 March 1955 up to 1958, EOKA conducted anti-British terrorist bombings and shootings throughout Cyprus. In 1958, the British granted Cyprus independence under a constitution that, however, recognized and protected the rights of the island's Turkish minority and allowed the British to maintain control over certain military bases, conditions that blocked the unification with Greece EOKA had sought.

As the original EOKA-Alpha, disbanded in 1960, had failed to achieve reunification, it was reactivated as EOKA-Beta and tried to force the issue of unification during the period from 1971–1974 after the EOKA founder, George Grivas, returned from Greece assured of Greek military support. EOKA-Beta engaged in terrorism against the Turkish Cypriots and played a role in the 15 May 1974 coup d'état overthrowing Cypriot President Archbishop Makarios. This prompted Turkey to invade Cyprus and to impose a de facto partition of the island into Turkish and Greek zones.

Frustrated over a perceived U.S. tilt toward Turkey in these hostilities, EOKA-Beta instigated an anti-U.S. riot on

19 August 1974 at the U.S. Embassy compound in Nicosia, in the course of which EOKA-Beta sharpshooters assassinated U.S. Ambassador Rodger P. Davies and his secretary. While six EOKA-Beta suspects were tried for this murder, only two of them were convicted, the rest having been released on legal technicalities, while the Greek Cypriot community regarded their sentences, respectively, of five and seven years' imprisonment as outrageously severe. Evidence emerged during the trial revealing that EOKA-Beta had penetrated the Greek Cypriot national guard as well as the civilian government while the lenient behavior of the Cypriot judiciary also suggested EOKA-Beta co-optation of the state. EOKA-Beta announced its dissolution in 1978, having failed in its goals and having lost the sponsorship of the Greek military junta that was overthrown following its failure to resist the Turkish invasion and partition of the island.

EPL. See Popular Liberation Army

ERP. People's Revolutionary Army (Ejército Revolucionario de Pueblo), one of the constituent groups of the Farabundo Martí National Liberation Front (See Farabundo Martí National Liberation Front).

ETA, or, *EUZKADI TA ASKATASUNA*. See Basque Fatherland and Liberty

EUROPEAN NATIONALIST FASCISTS. The *Faisceaux Nationaux Européens* (FNE) is a French neo-Fascist group that seeks to harass and intimidate Jews, North Africans, and black Africans in order to force them to leave France. This organization is the direct successor of FANE (Fédération d'Action Nationale Européene), the Federation for National European Action, a group founded in 1966 by French Fascists and anti-Semites. In 1980 anti-Semitic violence crested in France, with 122 incidents of arson and violence directed against minority group members as well as 66 threats and acts of violence. In September 1980 FANE was banned by the French government for its role in promoting two violent incidents. FANE members were suspected of bombing the Rue Copernic synagogue in Paris on 4 October 1980, which killed 4 and wounded 12, but this terrorist act turned out to have been the work of Palestinian terrorists. In spite of the ban on FANE, its members immediately reconstituted themselves as the European National Fascists (FNE). FNE installed as its head Robert Petit, director of the Vichy regime's "Center for the Study of the Jewish Question."

Following the spate of anti-Semitic incidents that forced the banning of FANE, the French authorities seemed to avoid investigating the activities of FNE. French Jewish organizations and the secretary-general of the French detectives union in 1980 believed that at least 150 national policemen were members of this, and similar, neo-Fascist groups. Some sources claimed that one-third of FNE's membership was made up of policemen. If true, this would represent an example of penetration and co-optation of the state by a subversive terrorist organization.

EUZKADI TA ASKATASUNA. See Basque Fatherland and Liberty

EXTRADITABLES. The Extraditables, one of the Medellín drug cartel's terrorist organizations, is aimed at pressuring the Colombian government to desist from its campaign to end cocaine production and smuggling in Colombia. The group was formed in reaction to the late 1989 Colombian government crackdown on the Medellín cartel and was intended to prevent the extradition of key drug kingpins to the United States.

By the end of 1989 the Extraditables had carried out 200 bombings, killing 261 and wounding over 1,200 people. On 27 November 1989, the group bombed in mid-flight an Avianca Airlines Boeing 727 flight, killing all 107 passengers and crew abroad, reportedly just to kill five police informants on board. On 6 December 1989, a truck bomb loaded with at least one-half ton of dynamite was exploded by the group outside the Bogotá police headquarters, killing over 60 and wounding over 250 people. On 15 December 1989, however, Colombian police ambushed and killed José Gonzalo Rodríguez Gacha, the major Medellín cartel leader at the heart of the Extraditables. The following month the Extraditables sued the government for peace, but Colombian officials refused to negotiate any deal.

On 13 June 1990 the mastermind behind the Extraditables' bombing campaign, Juan Jairo Arias Tascoon, was killed in a firefight with police. The other major figure involved in the group, Gustavo de Jesús Gaviria, was likewise killed fighting the police on 11 August 1990. Nonetheless, activities continued in the name of the group: On 28 June 1990 a Medellín police station was car bombed, killing 14 and wounding 30 people. On 18 October 1990, motorcycle-riding gunmen of the group killed High Court Justice Héctor Jiménez Rodríguez in Medellín.

Pablo Escobar Gaviria, another major drug lord and founder of the ''Death to Kidnappers'' death squad (See MAS) surrendered himself to Colombian authorities on 19 June 1991 on the condition that he be allowed to build his own luxurious prison and to maintain his own bodyguard. In spite of this purported surrender, Pablo Escobar continued trafficking in cocaine and murdering his rivals in defiance of the Colombian government. After his escape from captivity in late July 1992, Pablo Escobar was responsible for over 60 car bombings in Bogotá during 1993 in an effort to pressure the Colombian government to relax its pressures on him. On 2 December 1993 Pablo Escobar was tracked down and killed by Colombian troops which apparently has ended the reign of terror by the ''Extraditables'' of the Medillín drug cartel. While the rival Cali cartel has filled the place formerly occupied by the Medellín cartel in the cocaine trade, it so far has relied more on bribery to co-opt the Colombian government rather then having recourse to terrorism.

- F -

FAL. Fuerzas Armadas de Liberación (Armed Forces of Liberation), one of the constituent groups of the Farabundo Martí National Liberation Front (See Farabundo Martí National Liberation Front).

FALN. See Armed Forces of National Liberation

FANE. The Federation for National European Action (Fédération d'Action Nationale Européene) was the direct predecessor of FNE, (*Faisceaux Nationaux Europeens*), the European Nationalist Fascists. See European Nationalist Fascists

FARABUNDO MARTÍ LIBERATION FRONT (FMLN). The Farabundo Martí National Liberation Front is an umbrella group uniting several leftist guerrilla groups that sought to create a Marxist revolution within El Salvador following the Sandinista model in Nicaragua. The creation of this united front of all major leftist guerrilla groups was a condition imposed by Fidel Castro for Cuban sponsorship of the Salvadoran leftist insurgents. In addition to Cuban state sponsorship, the FMLN received arms, sanctuary, and other material assistance from the Sandinista government of Nicaragua prior to 25 February 1990 and afterward continued to receive arms sporadically from units of the Sandinista People's Army. The five groups joined in the FMLN are described separately in what follows:
1. The People's Liberation Forces (Fuerzas Populares de Liberación, FPL) founded in 1970 is the oldest of the armed guerrilla groups. The FPL had its stronghold in Chalatenango province in the mountains bordering Honduras. While the FPL had 1,500 to 2,000 regular guerrilla fighters, it also had "urban front" guerrilla fronts that were responsible for much of the antigovernment terrorism in El Salvador's cities following 1977, including intimidation of voters during the March 1978 municipal

elections, the machine-gun murders of 12 prominent citizens, including Carlos Alfaro Castillo, the chancellor of the National University, and Rubén Alfonso Rodríguez, a former president of the National Congress. On 28 November 1979, FPL kidnapped South African Ambassador Archibald Dunn, whom they later murdered. An urban front of this group was responsible for the first killing of an American official by an FMLN group when it assassinated Lt. Commander Schaufelberger, the Deputy Commander of the U.S. Advisory Group in El Salvador, on 25 May 1985. From April 1980 to November 1984, the FPL carried out seven attacks on U.S. targets, including three attacks on the U.S. Embassy, using light antitank rockets, and two assassinations of U.S. Embassy personnel. Apart from its urban terrorist campaign FPL has on occasion committed atrocities against civilians in rural areas, such as the massacre of 22 civilians in Santa Cruz Loma in 1985.

This group suffered from some internal quarreling, leading to the murder of the second-in-command, Melinda Anaya Montes (aka, "Commandante Anna María"), in the FMLN Managua office at the hands of other FPL members. This reportedly led the founder of the FPL, Cayetano Carpio (aka "Marcial") to take his own life on 6 April 1983.

2. The People's Revolutionary Army (Ejército Revolucionario de Pueblo, ERP), founded in 1972, is the strongest FMLN guerrilla organization, having 2,000 combatants. This group operated largely in Morazán province and other areas in eastern El Salvador but has very little involvement in political front organizations in the cities, having preferred a rural military strategy over political negotiations. Its leader, Joaquín Villalobos, is a brilliant but ruthless tactician. The ERP followed a policy of kidnapping and murdering local mayors and other functionaries of the Salvadoran government and has committed numerous atrocities against peasants suspected of collaboration with the government. As in the case of FPL,

instances of intramural terror have occurred in the ERP. The murder of ERP member Roque Dalton, a Salvadoran intellectual and world-renowned poet, at the hands of comrades within ERP for an alleged ideological offense created much scandal within the Salvadoran left and among their sympathizers. The excessive brutality and ideological rigidity of ERP under Villalobos's leadership led many observers to dub him the "Pol Pot of Central America."

While most of ERP's terrorism has been both repressive and revolutionary, directed internally at domestic targets, it has also struck at some international targets. On 4 February 1980, ERP gunmen attacked the Guatemalan embassy with automatic weapons fire. On 25 March 1980, ERP bombed the International Telephone and Telegraph office in San Salvador. On 16 September 1980, ERP fired five Chinese antitank rockets at the U.S. Embassy, causing damage but no injuries.

3. The Armed Forces of National Resistance (Fuerzas Armadas de la Resistencia Nacional, FARN) was formed in 1975 partly in reaction to ERP's excessive use of terrorism and brute force. By contrast FARN has concentrated not only on guerrilla operations with its 1,000 guerrillas but also on infiltrating and influencing the legal labor, students, and human rights organizations active within Salvadoran society. Virtually no major terrorist incidents have been attributed to this group. In addition to eschewing purely terrorist actions FARN differs from other members of the FMLN in stressing Salvadoran nationalism rather than Marxism in its political platform and program.

4. The Revolutionary Party of Central American Workers (Partido Revolucionario de los Trabajadores Centroamericanos, PRTC) actually began in Costa Rica in 1976 as a regional movement but is most active in El Salvador. Its armed wing is known as the Armed Forces of Revolutionary Popular Liberation, numbering some 500 combatants.

PRTC has compensated for its small numbers by some audacious terrorist actions, including the 19 June 1985 Zona Rosa massacre in which four off-duty U.S. Marine embassy guards, two private U.S. citizens, and seven Salvadoran civilians were machine-gunned to death at a sidewalk café in the Zona Rosa district of San Salvador. The perpetrator, Nidia Díaz, was captured but freed on 24 October 1985 in exchange for the kidnapped daughter of Salvadoran president José Napoleón Duarte.

5. The Armed Forces of Liberation FAL (Fuerzas Armadas de Liberación, FAL) is the armed wing of the Communist Party of El Salvador (PCES). While numerically small, having around 500 combatants, it was of great importance to the FMLN during the Salvadoran civil war due to its close connections with the Soviet and Cuban leadership. Its leader, Shafik Handal, served as the FMLN spokesman in the formerly Communist countries and also played a role in creating support networks in non-Communist countries, including the United States. Its urban guerrillas on 10 September 1985 kidnapped Inez Guadelope Duarte Durán, daughter of the then Salvadoran president José Napoleón Duarte. Both she and another kidnap victim, the Civil Aviation Director Colonel Omar Napoleón Avalos, were released along with 33 kidnapped mayors and municipal officials on 24 October 1985 in a prisoner exchange between the FMLN and the Salvadoran government.

While the Salvadoran transitional regime has often been criticized for its human rights abuses due its failure to suppress, or perhaps its direct role in, the operation of right-wing death squads (q.v.), the FMLN also was guilty of human rights violations in conducting its rural insurgency and urban terrorist campaigns. By 1986 the United Nations report on human rights in El Salvador noted that the FMLN was guilty of increasing human rights violations while the Salvadoran government's record had improved substantially.

Prior to 1980 the constituent groups of the FMLN believed

in the theory of prolonged popular warfare. With the Sandinista victory in Nicaragua in July 1979 the leftist guerrillas already active were encouraged to redouble their own efforts at revolution. On 15 October 1979, a reformist coup ousted the ineffective and corrupt President Romero and sought to implement badly needed social and economic reforms in order to forestall a Nicaraguan-style revolution in El Salvador. The leftist rebels, not to be deterred from their own goals, rejected conciliation with the new junta. The transitional government meanwhile had its own problems with rightist military and police officials who sought to preempt a leftist insurgency there by using death squads (q.v.) to kill off as many supporters of the guerrillas as possible.

The leftists unified their military command in November 1979 as a precondition to receiving Cuban aid. In May 1980, the Unified Revolutionary Directorate (DRU) was established in Havana to be the decision-making body for the entire FMLN. In January 1981, the FMLN attempted a "final offensive" against the major cities of El Salvador in which they were bested by a Salvadoran army resupplied with U.S. military aid. They retreated to the rural areas, and from 1982 until 1983 their numbers of combatants grew from 2,000 to 12,000 until they were engaging the Salvadoran army in battalion-sized engagements. At the same time, the FMLN was engaged in systemic sabotage of the economic infrastructure and intimidation of the rural population.

By 1985 the Salvadoran army had improved to the point that the FMLN was forced to go back to deploying its forces in smaller groups. Following November 1986 the leadership and rank and file of the FMLN began suffering declining morale. FMLN documents captured during that period indicated there was much internal criticism of the ERP and its strategy. In July 1987, the FMLN undertook to rebuild its forces within the cities in order to foment a popular uprising, a move reflected in increasing incidents of urban terrorism in the following year. The FMLN tried with little success to disrupt the 19 March 1989 elections, which were held in at least 90 percent of the country. Even the Revolutionary Democratic Front (FDR), the leftist coalition of parties sympathetic to the FMLN, broke with the FMLN over the question of participating in the elections and ran a candidate in those elections.

The FMLN attempted a second "final offensive" on 16 November 1989 with no greater success. Elsewhere the changes under way in the Soviet Union and Eastern Europe began to make Cuba, the Sandinistas, and the FMLN seem curiously anachronistic. With the election of Violeta Chamorro as president of Nicaragua on 25 February 1990, ending Sandinista domination of that country, future Nicaraguan aid was put into doubt. Negotiations resumed in May 1990 and continued in three rounds until a cease-fire was signed on 31 December 1991. During these negotiations a U.S. helicopter carrying three U.S. military advisers was shot down by FMLN forces on 2 January 1991. One crewman was critically injured and died later, but two survivors, Lt. Col. David Pickett and crew chief PFC Earnest Dawson, were murdered by the FMLN. This incident undermined international and regional moral support for the FMLN.

The FMLN and Salvadoran government agreed on 1 January 1992 to end the 12-year-long civil war in which at least 75,000 people had perished. One agreement reached on 25 September 1991 allowed the armed units of the FMLN to be incorporated under a separate command into the civilian Ministry of the Interior rather than under the Ministry of Defense, therefore allaying the guerrillas' fears for their personal security. While many acts of political violence have occurred since January 1992, many of these appear to be individual acts of revenge rather than part of any systematic terrorist campaign. Although the FMLN remains as an armed force until a mutually agreed upon deadline is reached for effective demilitarization, it remains essentially as a political grouping within El Salvador rather than as a guerrilla or terrorist force.

FARC. See Revolutionary Armed Forces of Colombia

FARN. *Fuerzas Armadas de la Resistencia Nacional* (Armed Forces of National Resistance), one of the constituent groups of the Farabundo Martí National Liberation Front (See Farabundo Martí National Liberation Front).

FATAH, AL. Fatah, the oldest of the Palestinian guerrilla groups founded in 1957, is currently the dominant member of the Palestine Liberation Organization (PLO, q.v.). The name *Fatah,* the Arabic word meaning "conquest", is also the reverse acronym of the name *Harakat al Tahrir al Filasti-niyya,* meaning "Palestinian Liberation Movement."

The current goals of Fatah are to seek establishment of an independent, secular Palestinian state on any part of "historic Palestine liberated from Zionist occupation" and to win recognition of the PLO as the sole legitimate representative of the Palestinian people. Prior to 1974 Fatah aimed to regain all of former mandatory Palestine but began to revise this goal gradually. In 1974, Fatah also declared its intention to cease carrying out terrorist operations outside of Israel and the occupied territories. In fact, certain Fatah-sponsored groups, such as Force 17 (q.v.) and the Hawari group (q.v.), continued terrorist operations internationally. By 15 November 1988, Fatah had persuaded the nineteenth Palestine National Council to declare its acceptance of the right of Israel to exist embodied in U.N. Resolutions 242 and 338 in exchange for Israeli withdrawal from the lands occupied in the 1967 war. On 13 September 1993, a peace accord between the PLO and Israel was signed by PLO Chairman, Yasir Arafat, and Israeli Prime Minister, Yitzhak Rabin, allowing mutual recognition and the eventual creation of an autonomous Palestinian government under PLO auspices within the West Bank and Gaza Strip.

Although Fatah formerly received support from both conservative and radical Arab states, it has lost the support it once enjoyed from Kuwait, Saudi Arabia, and the Persian Gulf emirates, because it openly sided with Iraq during Operation Desert Storm. While the Soviet Union and eastern bloc nations also formerly provided substantial aid following the collapse of communist governments in those countries, this source likewise has ended, leaving only China and North Korea, which continue to provide some support.

Fatah differs from other Palestinian guerrilla groups in insisting on self-determination for the Palestinian people apart from seeking the goal of Pan-Arab unity. Fatah also has sought to prevent itself, or the PLO, from becoming co-opted into the service of any Arab state. Since self-determination also implies self-initiative and independence of action, Fatah held that the Palestinians needed to undertake armed struggle themselves rather than trusting in the Arab states to deliver them.

Fatah's strong resistance against the Israeli army during the latter's March 1968 raid on the Fatah camp at Karameh, Jordan, boosted the group's prestige in the Palestinian community and encouraged enlistments of young Palestinians into Fatah's ranks. By July 1968 Fatah was admitted to the PLO in its fourth Palestinian National Council (PNC) meeting. At the fifth PNC meeting in February 1969, Fatah took control of the PLO and the history of the two organizations merged.

From 1969 to 1974 PLO-sponsored terrorism was carried out throughout the Middle East and non-Communist nations against Israeli, U.S., West European, and Arab targets. The government of Jordan was especially singled out for terrorist reprisal due to its crackdown and expulsion of the PLO in September 1970, following the confrontation between King Hussein and the PLO over the Popular Front for the Liberation of Palestine's hijacking of airplanes to Dawson's Field and holding over 400 civilian passengers as hostages. The most notorious Palestinian terrorist group during this period was Fatah's own Black September (q.v.), which was responsible for the massacre of the Israeli athletic team at the

Munich Summer Olympic games in 1972 as well as several other atrocities.

Beginning in 1974 Fatah declared its renunciation of terrorism outside of the borders of former mandatory Palestine, a declaratory policy not always followed by its own special operations groups, such as the Hawari (q.v.) group or Force 17 (q.v.). This renunciation was part of a revision within Fatah of its goals from seeking the liberation of all of Palestine and replacing Israel by a secular democratic state, to the creation of a separate Arab Palestinian state on any "liberated part of Palestine." This last phrase was understood to mean the West Bank and Gaza Strip following an Israeli withdrawal from those territories. While Fatah still believed armed struggle was necessary to achieve its goals, it came to view armed struggle as not sufficient in itself without parallel initiatives on the diplomatic front. This revisionism was anathema to the more radical leftists within the PLO, who then sought to sabotage Fatah's diplomatic initiatives with their own terrorist operations and who also tried to depose Yasir Arafat from the leadership of the PLO both by political and even military means.

After September 1970, Fatah and other PLO groups regrouped in Lebanon from which they staged raids into Israeli territory. In spite of securing increased quantities of more sophisticated weapons, including rockets, tanks, and antiaircraft artillery, the PLO forces have never been able to withstand the Israeli Defense Forces in conventional combat. The large Palestinian presence in southern Lebanon and the tendency of the non-Fatah PLO groups to meddle in Lebanon's internal politics helped precipitate the Lebanese civil war in 1975. This tied up Fatah and the rest of the PLO who at various times found themselves fighting the Christian Phalange (q.v.), the Shiite Amal (q.v.) militia, the Syrians, and at times even anti-Fatah Palestinians. The Camp David Accords, which excluded the PLO from any role in the peace negotiations, briefly united the PLO in its denunciations of Egypt and the United States, and opposition to the Camp

David agreement became a fixed feature of Fatah rhetoric and diplomacy.

The Israeli invasion of southern Lebanon and siege of Beirut in the summer of 1982 forced the PLO to remove its forces from Lebanon and to move its administrative offices to Tunis. Although Fatah troops were moved to Tunisia, Algeria, and South Yemen, they began infiltrating Lebanon again in 1983. An anti-Arafat revolt among Fatah troops instigated by Syria forced Arafat to leave Lebanon again in 1983. Following the murder by Fatah agents of three Israeli vacationers in Larnaca, Cyprus, on 25 September 1985, the Israeli air force retaliated with a bomb and missile attack on the PLO headquarters south of Tunis in which 60 Palestinians were killed and around 100 wounded. Fatah since then has dispersed its offices and personnel across several countries. One of Fatah's original founders, Khalil al Wazir, who was Yasir Arafat's second-in-command and chief of the Fatah terrorist operations unit responsible for the Larnaca murders (See Force 17), was assassinated by an Israeli commando team on 16 April 1988. The Israelis have claimed that Khalil al Wazir, known also as Abu Jihad, masterminded the triggering of the intifada (q.v.) uprising in addition to being "an arch-terrorist steeped in blood." Fatah lost another of its original founders and ranking members when an assassin of Abu Nidal's Fatah Revolutionary Council (q.v.) killed Salah Khalaf, along with three other PLO officials on 14 January 1991.

Following the eruption of the Palestinian intifada on 9 December 1987, Fatah and its opposition within the PLO set aside some of their differences. The nineteenth PNC meeting in Algiers on 15 November 1988 issued a declaration of independence on behalf of the Palestinians in the West Bank and Gaza Strip. In this conference the PLO formally adopted Fatah's long-standing declaratory policy renouncing terrorism outside of the occupied territories and Israel and also declared its acceptance of United Nations resolutions 242 and 338 contingent on Israel's withdrawal from the occupied territories and the establishment of a Palestinian state there. Although Yasir Arafat reiterated Fatah's and the PLO's renunciation of terrorism and recognition of Israel's right to exist before the U.N. General Assembly on 13 December 1988, in practice this declaration entailed no willingness to denounce terrorist acts committed in the name of the intifada nor subsequent attacks within Israel such as the Fatah-aligned Palestine Liberation Front's raid on the beaches of Tel Aviv on 30 May 1990. Al Fatah further eroded its diplomatic leverage and international goodwill for which it had strived so long by openly siding with Iraq in its August 1990 invasion of Kuwait and its defiance of the United Nations. Despite its repeated military failures and intramural frictions with other members of the PLO, Yasir Arafat's Fatah has maintained its dominant position within the PLO and still accounts for the bulk of the fighters available to the PLO. (See Black September, Force-17, Hawari Group, Palestine Liberation Organization)

FATAH REVOLUTIONARY COUNCIL. Also referred to by Western intelligence and law enforcement agencies as the Abu Nidal Organization, the Fatah Revolutionary Council (FRC) is a Palestinian terrorist group founded in 1974 and led by Sabri Khalil al Banna, known by his nom de guerre of Abu Nidal (''Father of the Struggle''). This group is quite possibly the most dangerous terrorist organization existing today and has been credited with over 90 major terrorist attacks killing or wounding over 900 people. The FRC is an umbrella group encompassing different groups, or at least using different names depending on the targets. The FRC is also known as the Arab Revolutionary Council but chooses to claim credit for its actions under the names of the Arab Revolutionary Brigades, the Revolutionary Organization of Socialist Muslims when claiming credit for attacks on British targets, Black June (q.v.) when claiming credit for attacks on Jordanian targets, the Black September Organization, and possibly the ''Peace Conquerors.'' Altogether these groups number several hundred. The use of these names helps to confuse opponents about Abu Nidal and his group; for example, witness the use of the "Fatah Revolutionary Council," which has no connection with Fatah, or the use of "Black September" after 1981 when the original organization of the same name had been disbanded seven years earlier.

A former member of Fatah (q.v.), Abu Nidal broke with both Fatah and the rest of the Palestine Liberation Organization (q.v.) in 1974 and formed the FRC as an alternative organization. The FRC seeks a total nationalist and social revolution not only to totally destroy Israel in favor of a Palestinian state but also to rid the Palestinians of those whom Abu Nidal regards as compromisers and reactionaries, and to create a total revolution throughout the Arab world. The FRC has used, and used up, a number of state sponsors, having been sponsored by Iraq from 1974 until 1983, then Syria until 1987, and since then Libya. While Libya may remain the chief sponsor, some reports indicated a cutoff of sponsorship in 1989. Such states have eventually found that the cost in international opprobrium for aiding and abetting Abu Nidal far exceeded the benefits obtained from sponsoring such a client. Yet a greater concern for them has been the irascibility and waywardness of Abu Nidal himself, who has remained beholden to no one and too apt to turn against his erstwhile sponsors.

Despite its radical revolutionary rhetoric, the FRC in recent years appears to be pursuing terrorism almost as an end in itself and has shown also an entrepreneurial willingness to hire itself out without regard to the politics of its patrons. While one-third of its resources came from Arab states, the FRC has also been able to derive another third of its income from extortion and another third from a consortium of businesses throughout the world, many of which may be legitimate by themselves but all of which function as a support network for FRC operations. In many respects the FRC is becoming more like an organized crime syndicate, which may perpetuate itself even after the demise of Abu Nidal regardless of what the future geopolitical complexion of the Middle East may be.

Among the more notorious acts of the FRC were the following: the attempted assassination of Israeli Ambassador to Britain, Shlomo Argov, on 3 June 1982 in the name of Black June (q.v.); the 27 December 1985 massacres of travelers at the Rome and Vienna airports, killing 18 people, including a child, and wounding 60 others; the 6 September 1986 attack on the Neve Shalom synagogue in Istanbul, in which two gunmen murdered and mutilated 21 people. As an example of the extreme waywardness and unpredictability of the FRC, the same group that directed a suicide car bomber to strike the Israeli embassy in Cyprus on 11 May 1988, in revenge for Israel's assassination of PLO official Wazir al Khalil, is itself suspected of having assassinated another PLO official, Salah Khalaf, along with three other PLO officials on 14 January 1991.

The FRC was identified as having committed 44 major terrorist acts in the period from 1980–1987, of which 11 were assassinations, 7 bombings, and 1 car bombing. In addition, using the name of the "Black September Organization," it carried out 17 more actions in the period from 1981–1987, of which 6 were assassinations, 4 bombings, and 1 car bombing. Using the name of the "Arab Revolutionary Brigades," it committed another 15 actions from 1982–1986, of which 6 were assassinations, 5 bombings, and 1 car bombing. Under the name of the "Revolutionary Movement of Socialist Muslims," it committed another 11 actions from 1984–1985, including 4 bombings, 3 kidnappings, and 2 assassinations. Using the Black June group it committed another five actions from 1981–1986, including two assassinations and one bombing. Reports indicated that during the latter part of 1988, Abu Nidal carried out a massive purge of his organization, killing a large number of former colleagues. If true, this may account for the relative inactivity of the FRC in recent years.

FEDAYEEN, alternate spelling, FIDAIYIN. Arabic plural of Fidai, "one who offers (self-) sacrifice," that is, one who offers himself sacrificially in a holy struggle. This name has been adopted by at least four different groups in the history of terrorism.

1. The Ismaili Fedayeen—In the eleventh and twelfth centuries Ismaili Shiite activists in southwest Asia organized corps of assassins willing to undertake attacks against Sunnite rulers in which the assassin was certain to be killed or captured. To counter the awe and respect these bold attacks created among the common people, apologists of the Abbaside dynasty targeted by the Ismailis gave out that the attackers were really "Hashshishin," those under the influence of hashish. This term became the source of the word "assassin." These Fedayeen continued to operate for over a century, using the mountainous region around Alamut in central Iran as their base of operations, until they were exterminated by the invading Mongol armies.

2. The Fidaiyan-i Islam—An Iranian terrorist group founded by the Shiite junior clergyman Navab Safavi in 1944 to kill Iranian intellectuals and politicians held to be responsible for the decline of Islam in Iran. The Fidaiyan began with the dramatic killing of the secularist historian Ahmad Kasravi in 1946 and then followed up with the killings of the Minister of Court Hazhir, Prime Minister Razmara, and attempted assassinations of Prime Minister Ala and Shah Muhammad Reza Pahlavi. The Iranian security police later smashed the Fidaiyan organization in 1956, executing its main members, including Navab Safavi. As late as 1965, however, the assassination of Prime Minister Alam was carried out by a self-proclaimed member of the Fidaiyan. Following the 1979 revolution in Iran, survivors of the group reconstituted themselves openly as a minor Islamic political party in Iran. Members of this group appear to have been behind the attempted assassination of Iraqi Vice President Tariq Aziz on 1 April 1980.

3. The Palestinian Fidaiyan—With the rise in Palestinian terrorist and guerrilla attacks on Israel and Israeli targets the term Fidaiyan came to be used by Palestinians to designate guerrilla fighters attacking Israel without being exclusively reserved for the fighters of any single Palestinian group. The organizations that sponsor Fidaiyan fighters dominate the PLO and are known as *tanzimat.*

4. The Fidaiyan-e Khalq-e Iran—The "People's Fidaiyan of Iran" was a Marxist guerrilla group that split from the Iranian Communist Party in 1963. Its members were mainly university students who received guerrilla training in PLO camps in Lebanon and South Yemen. On 8 February 1971, the Fidaiyan tried to start a guerrilla war against the Iranian government in the forested regions around Siahkhal in Gilan Province on the Caspian Sea but were crushed by regular army troops. The survivors of the Siahkhal affair tried then to organize urban guerrilla warfare but accomplished little until the revolution of 1978–1979 gave them opportunity to participate in street fighting and attacks on police and army barracks. Following the victory of the revolution the Fidaiyan's open following grew to include as many as 50,000 adherents. In the face of widespread popular support for the regime of the Ayatollah Khomeini (q.v.), the Fidaiyan temporized in the mistaken expectation that the situation would ripen in favor of another revolution along Marxist lines. This temporizing cost the Fidaiyan the support of disaffected Iranian middle-class students and intellectuals who were attracted instead to the rival Mujahideen-e Khalq (q.v.), which took a more forthright stand against the clerical regime.

Internal dissent over their relationship with the clerical regime led to a split into a minority faction that advocated armed struggle with the regime and a majority faction that continued to temporize. With the crackdown on the Mujahideen in June 1981, other armed leftist groups, such as the Fidaiyan, were crushed as well. Many surviving Fidaiyan joined other leftists in an abortive guerrilla campaign in the region of Amol near the Caspian Sea in which, in a curious replay of the Siahkhal affair of the previous decade, they were again crushed on 9 November 1981 by army troops and Islamic Revolutionary Guards.

FLN. See National Liberation Front of Algeria

FLQ. See Quebec Liberation Front

FNE. See European Nationalist Fascists

FORCE 17. Name of internal security unit of al Fatah (q.v.) formed in the early 1970s, charged with providing personal security for Yasir Arafat and other Fatah leaders, enforcing discipline within the Palestine Liberation Organization by arresting and punishing dissidents and criminals, and with undertaking active measures against non-Palestinians threatening PLO interests. Within the PLO, viewed as an extraterritorial government of the Palestinians, Force 17 can be considered a tool of state repression or terror while in its operations against non-Palestinians it may be regarded simply as an extension of Fatah. Force 17 was commanded by Khalil al Wazir until he was assassinated by an Israeli commando team on 16 April 1988.

During the early 1970s Force 17 would regulate the behavior of Palestinian guerrillas in Lebanon to prevent abuses against Lebanese nationals that might jeopardize PLO relations with the Lebanese government. On 17 April 1978, Force 17 arrested around 100 members of Abu Nidal's Fatah Revolutionary Council (q.v.), then backed by Iraq, in southern Lebanon in order to prevent them from disrupting a cease-fire with the Israeli Defense Forces. In August 1987 and May 1989, two Force 17 commanders were assassinated in feuding between Fatah loyalists and Syrian-backed dissidents.

Force 17's entry into externally directed terrorism dates

from 25 September 1985, when Fatah agents seized and killed three Israelis in Larnaca, Cyprus, whom they suspected to be Mossad agents. This occasioned Israel's retaliatory air raid on the PLO headquarters in Tunis on 1 October 1985 in which 60 Palestinians were killed and 100 wounded. Afterward Force 17 claimed responsibility for several attacks occurring within Israel: on 2 February 1986, a bus bombing in Jerusalem that injured six people; on 17 September 1986, throwing of explosives into the El Al offices in Tel Aviv; on 14 November 1986, a stabbing death of a Yeshivoth student in Jerusalem; on 28 June 1987, the bombing of a popular beach near Haifa, wounding a woman and child; and on 27 November 1987, the murder of two agents of Shin Bet, Israel's internal security service, who had their throats slashed. These actions bear close resemblance to the sorts of apparently random, spontaneous attacks occurring within Israel since the beginning of the intifada uprising on 9 December 1987. Israeli authorities have maintained that Khalil al Wazir was actually the mastermind behind the intifada.

FP-25. See Popular Forces of 25 April

FPL. Popular Liberation Forces (Fuerzas Populares de Liberación), one of the constituent groups of the Farabundo Martí National Liberation Front (See Farabundo Martí National Liberation Front).

FRANCIA. The Front d'Action Nouvelle Contre l'Indépendence et l'Autonomie (New Action Front Against Independence and Autonomy) was a nonstate group of French settlers on the island of Corsica with the limited aim of opposing the FNLC, the National Front for the Liberation of Corsica (q.v.). The group was formed in 1978 mainly of French settlers displaced from Algeria. In 1979 it conducted about 40 attacks against suspected FNLC members. In August 1980 a leader of FRANCIA, Yannick Leonelli, was arrested.

FREE SOUTH MOLUCCAN YOUTH ORGANIZATION. The Free South Moluccan Youth Organization, also called the South Moluccan Suicide Commando, was a nonstate-sponsored revolutionary nationalist group that used terrorism to force the Netherlands to pressure Indonesia to restore an independent South Moluccan homeland. During the Indonesian war for independence the South Moluccans, who had been converted to Christianity by the Dutch, fought on the side of the Netherlands on the understanding that they would afterward have their own independent state. An Indonesian victory prevented the Netherlands from fulfilling this promise and instead the South Moluccan allies of the Dutch were allowed to settle in the Netherlands as refugees. Most of the members of these groups came from a younger second generation of alienated South Moluccans who lacked any outside state sponsorship.

On 2 December 1975 some 7 Moluccan youths armed with automatic pistols seized a passenger train in Beilen, taking over 70 passengers hostage and killing one passenger and the train's engineer. The train was besieged by over 1,000 Dutch Marines and police. On the fourth day of the siege the terrorists killed another passenger after the Dutch government announced its refusal of the group's demands. In the face of the government's refusal to waiver and due to the severe cold in the unheated train cars, the terrorists surrendered on 14 December. During the siege, several passengers escaped while several others were released by their captors, particularly elderly or ill passengers.

On 4 December, seven other members of the same group seized the Indonesian consulate in Amsterdam, also taking as hostages several schoolchildren within a classroom in the building. Three consular employees escaped by lowering themselves from the second story, but a fourth fell to his death. By 19 December 1975, all the hostages in this siege were also released.

On 23 May 1977, another passenger train hijacking and

hostage seizure took place in Assen in which 13 Moluccans seized a train with 85 passengers. It lasted 19 days. In addition to calls for Moluccan independence, these terrorists also demanded the freeing of their comrades who had been tried and jailed for the Beilen incident. On 11 June, Dutch Marines stormed the train, killing all the terrorists as well as two passengers who had bolted when the shooting began. On the same day the Assen train was seized, 4 other members of the same group seized a primary school in Bovinsmilde, taking 105 children and 6 teachers hostage. All of the children and one sick teacher were released by 26 May. Dutch Marines stormed the school on 11 June, seizing the four terrorists and freeing the remaining teachers.

In July 1975 several Moluccans were convicted for conspiracy to kidnap Queen Juliana and other members of the Dutch royal family. These incidents provoked anti-Moluccan backlashes among the Dutch population while the killings of the terrorists also aggravated the anti-Dutch sentiments among the exiled Moluccan community.

- G -

GAL. See Anti-Terrorist Liberation Groups

GEORGE JACKSON BRIGADE. The George Jackson Brigade, active in the northwestern United States from the mid- to late 1970s, had revolutionary pretensions of being a militant left-wing organization, naming itself after a black militant killed at San Quentin prison during rioting on 21 August 1971. Its record of activities appeared more criminal and opportunistic than coherently revolutionary, consisting of several small-scale thefts and bombings in Oregon and Washington state.

GRAPO. See October First Antifascist Resistance Group

GREY WOLVES. The *Bozkurtlar* form the university student and youth wing of the National Action Party (NAP), a secular, Pan-Turkist party of the extreme right-wing of Turkish politics. Originally a student group organized in the late 1960s to oppose Marxist-Leninist students in the universities of Turkey, once the Grey Wolves were put under the direction of NAP leader Col. Alparslan Türkes in 1976 they turned into a right-wing death squad. By 1980 the group was reputed to have committed 694 political murders. Since Türkes became Deputy Prime Minister in a coalition government that included the NAP, the Grey Wolves may be regarded as having been a quasi-state-sponsored repressive group.

Türkes ran two commando-style training camps outside Ankara and Izmir for the Grey Wolves. The group also proselytized younger expatriate workers living in western Europe. Before being recruited by the Bulgarian secret police, Mehmet Ali Agca had once been a Grey Wolf member and had murdered a leftist Turkish newspaper editor, Abdi Ipekci, prior to his attempt to kill Pope John Paul II on 13 May 1981. With the imposition of military rule in Turkey in September 1980, the terrorist activities of the Grey Wolves were constrained with the crackdown on all paramilitary and political groups that followed. The group is estimated to have about 26,000 members in about 80 branches.

GUARDIANS OF THE ISLAMIC REVOLUTION. Name under which credit was taken for the 7 July 1980 bombings of the Rome offices of Snia-Technit Corporation and for the 2 October 1987 murder of an émigré Iranian dissident and his son in London. The group is ostensibly a pro-Iranian Shiite terrorist group and is believed to be responsible for the murders in 1988 of a former minister of the Shah's government and of a German banker close to the Iraqi war effort.

It is entirely possible that rather than being merely an Iranian-sponsored nonstate group that this group represents actually an extension of Iranian state terror and active measures beyond its borders, using Iranian intelligence and military personnel rather than an independent organization. In the case of the actual organization Hezbollah the group took care to prevent other persons or groups from falsely claiming credit in its nom de guerre of Islamic Jihad by issuing its communiqués only to certain news outlets, usually accompanied by some recent photographs of their hostages proving their identity.

In the case of a dummy organization, however, it would be easier for other groups to use that dummy organization's name without facing contradiction from that source. Thus persons claiming to be the "Guardians" claimed credit for the bombing of Pan Am flight 103 on 21 December 1988, which has been discounted by most experts. Curiously, persons claiming to represent Islamic Jihad also claimed credit for the 19 September 1989 bombing of a French UTA flight 772 over Niger in which 171 people perished. Currently it is believed both airplane bombings were conducted by Libyan state operatives who may have used the names of Iranian-associated organizations to divert attention from Libya's possible involvement.

GUATEMALAN NATIONAL REVOLUTIONARY UNION. URNG is an umbrella group uniting the three major leftist guerrilla groups seeking to create a Marxist revolution within Guatemala along lines similar to the Sandinista model in Nicaragua. These three groups are the Guerrilla Army of the Poor (EGP), the Rebel Armed Forces (FAR), and the Revolutionary Organization of the People in Arms (ORPA). This united front was a condition imposed by Fidel Castro for Cuban sponsorship of the Guatemalan leftist insurgents. In addition to Cuban state sponsorship, URNG has enjoyed the uses of sanctuaries in Mexico and of arms, safe haven, and other material assistance from the Sandinista government of Nicaragua prior to February 1990. While the three groups maintain an organizational unity, in fact, each operates in separate territories and each is sufficiently different from its fellows to merit separate descriptions:

1. The Rebel Armed Forces—The *Fuerzas Armadas Rebeldes* (FAR) was set up in 1962 by junior officers who had participated in a failed coup attempt in 1960 against a conservative government. FAR established itself in a rugged mountainous region in the extreme northeast of Guatemala, close to Belize. FAR was more of a nationalistic than Marxist group, but forged ties with leftists in order to fight more effectively. FAR conducted six major assassinations, including the killing of U.S. Ambassador John Gordon Mein in August 1968, the first time a U.S. ambassador had been murdered in the line of duty. In 1969, FAR moved some of its forces into Guatemala City, splitting the group's command. In March 1970, they murdered West German Ambassador Count Karl von Spreti. The same month they kidnapped the U.S. Labor Attaché, Sean Holly, who was released in a prisoner exchange. Guatemalan counterinsurgency efforts aided by the U.S. Army Special Forces pushed back FAR, which remained inactive from 1970 to 1975.

   In 1975, FAR activity resumed in Peten province with very little activity in the capital until 1979. On 29 June 1983, FAR kidnapped the sister of President Ríos Montt, who was released in exchange for imprisoned comrades. During this period the urban branch of FAR specialized in terrorist operations, concentrating on assassinations and kidnappings, while the branch in the northeast tried to fight the Guatemalan army, meanwhile sabotaging economic infrastructural projects and harassing oil exploration camps.

2. The Guerrilla Army of the Poor—The *Ejército Guerrillero de los Pobres* (EGP) was established in 1975 by a former FAR commander, César Montes, who revived the strategy of conducting simultaneous rural insurgency and urban terrorism. On 15 June 1978, an EGP truck bombing in the capital killed 17 military police, while four other

bombings were directed at the Argentinean, Uruguayan, and U.S. embassies, as well as the U.S. Chamber of Commerce office. On 31 March 1982, EGP also fired RPG-7 rocket-propelled grenades at the U.S. embassy. Rural operations were resumed in the northeast areas but also expanded to the northwestern regions bordering on Mexico while a new front was opened in a mountainous area just north of the capital. Much of the rural campaign involved burning of sugarcane fields to bankrupt the large landowners.

In a 10-year period, EGP committed 22 assassinations of prominent people, killing Colonel Elías Ramírez, a former counterinsurgency commander, the Nicaraguan ambassador in October 1978, and also the Army Chief of Staff, General David Barrios, in June 1979. EGP kidnapping victims included the Salvadoran Ambassador on 29 May 1977, and the foreign minister of Guatemala on 31 December 1977. In October 1979, the EGP kidnapped the president's nephew, who was released only after the government placed EGP political manifestos in paid advertisements in leading western newspapers.

César Montes initiated contacts with FAR and ORPA, and other antigovernment guerrillas, to promote forming a common front, which was the prelude to formation of URNG.

3. The Revolutionary Organization of the People in Arms—The *Organización Revolucionaria del Pueblo en Armas* (ORPA) is a Guatemalan leftist guerrilla group enjoying Cuban sponsorship and collaborating with two other major Guatemalan rebel groups within the framework of the Guatemalan National Revolutionary Union (URNG) in order to overthrow the Guatemalan government.

ORPA was formed in September 1979 in Solola department and, although smaller than the Rebel Armed Forces (FAR) or the Revolutionary Army of the Poor (EGP), it gained the reputation of being the most effective of the Guatemalan groups. In 1984, ORPA forces killed more than 120 Guatemalan army soldiers during a 10-day period. Most of ORPA's area of operations has been in the southwestern region of Guatemala, west of Guatemala City. The leader of the ORPA group is Rodrigo Asturias Amado, also called "Gaspar Ilom."

While ORPA was particularly effective in rural guerrilla warfare, and while most terrorist actions committed by URNG forces were usually carried out by FAR forces, one terrorist incident was clearly the work of ORPA. In November 1988, about 22 villagers were massacred by ORPA in the small town of El Aguacate. Until 1984 ORPA had largely been successful in its own propaganda work and co-optation of the Indian peasants.

Previous Guatemalan counterinsurgency efforts had played into URNG's hands due to the heavy-handed use of death squads and indiscriminate state terrorization of civilians in areas of rural insurgency. Following the 23 March 1982 coup raising Ríos Montt to power, the Guatemalan army undertook a more effective campaign to secure the support of the peasants with the result that the URNG lost much ground. Certain of these groups, such as ORPA, began to use the same retaliatory tactics against suspected civilian collaborators that previously had been the hallmark of Guatemala's state-sponsored right-wing death squads.

GUERRILLA FORCES OF LIBERATION. The Guerrilla Forces of Liberation is an obscure Puerto Rican independence group that claimed credit for a series of bombings that occurred in Puerto Rico on 25 May 1987, the day King Juan Carlos and Queen Sophia of Spain visited the island. Five pipe bombs exploded with minimal damage and no injuries. Three others were defused while another exploded en route to a demolition center. The caller claiming credit stated that the bombings were a protest against "colonialism." As the group was previously unknown, the "Guerrilla Forces of Liberation" may have been a nom de guerre for another known organization.

GUEVARA, ERNESTO "CHE". (b. 1928, d. 1967) A revolutionary, a guerrilla leader, and the close aide and friend of Fidel Castro, Che Guevara was also a theorist of revolutionary warfare who became idolized by sympathizers worldwide following his death at the hands of Bolivian counterinsurgency forces. His work *The Guerrilla War* advocated the use of terrorist violence to create intense fear, including the assassination and mutilation of local notables who refused to collaborate with the revolutionaries. Guevara left Cuba in 1965 to try to foment revolution in the Congo. In December 1966, he entered Bolivia where he tried unsuccessfully to launch a peasant revolt. On 10 October 1967, Guevara was captured and executed by U.S.-trained Bolivian counterinsurgency forces. Latin American revolutionaries have since then accepted Guevara's *Guerrilla War* as a basic textbook on revolutionary warfare.

GUILT TRANSFER. Guilt transfer refers to the ability of terrorists to distort public debate about the terrorists' political ends and particular demands by shifting public perception of the onus of responsibility from the terrorists themselves to others, either to their victims or the governments against which the terrorist actions are being directed. Guilt transfer is also achieved when public discussion shifts from the illegality or immorality of the terrorists' actions to discussion of the supposed historical and social "root causes" that compelled the terrorists to take such actions, as if the terrorists were themselves the victims and the targeted government their tormentor for having allowed the "root causes" to have occurred at all.

The Maze Prison hunger strikes in North Ireland during 1981 provide an example of guilt transfer. Ten convicted Irish Republican terrorists starved themselves to death in protest over the British government's refusal to grant them a special status as political prisoners as opposed to being classified as common criminals. Once the leader of the protestors, Robert "Bobby" Sands, died of starvation on 5 May 1981, a storm of protest rose in both Britain and the Republic of Ireland over the British government's alleged mistreatment of these prisoners. Although these prisoners had earlier decided to engage in a "dirty protest" of refusing to shave, bathe, or wear prison clothing, while also smearing the walls and floors of their cells with their own urine and feces, these self-imposed conditions were also cited by critics of the British government as evidence of mistreatment of the prisoners. Also terrorist attacks by the Provisional Irish Republican Army (q.v.) and other Irish Republican groups intensified, including several murders of the guards of Maze Prison.

The crisis of the American hostages held captive in Lebanon during the period from 1983–1991 provides another illustration. During the earliest phase of these kidnappings, the U.S. public's anger was directed against the shadowy kidnappers and their sponsors. Over time, however, as the U.S. public finally acknowledged the intransigence of the kidnappers and the inability of the United States to take military steps to free the hostages, its perceptions of where the onus of responsibility belonged shifted instead to the U.S. government, which was expected to "do something" even if this entailed some appeasement of the terrorists' demands. In time, the families and friends of the hostages formed political pressure groups to force such action by the U.S. government.

In the case of the victims of terrorism, guilt transfer means that the victims come to accept the terrorists' claims that they themselves, rather than their tormentors, are responsible for their misfortune. This enables the terrorists to secure the collaboration of their victims in making political statements or revealing information and also makes the demoralized victims less likely to resist the terrorists or attempt to escape.

GUSH EMUNIM. The "Bloc of the Faithful" is a Jewish fundamentalist group within Israel that seeks the forcible and permanent annexation of territories occupied by Israeli forces during the 1967 war. Founded in 1974, the Gush Emunim sought to force annexation by forming settlements on the West Bank and through inciting confrontations between Israelis and Palestinians that would force the Israeli state to expel the Arabs. On 13 September 1986, Gush Emunim members rigged explosive charges to the ignition of the car of the Palestinian mayor of Nablus, Bassam Shaka, who lost both his legs, and of Ramallah mayor, Karim Khalaf, who lost a foot. Gush Emunim activists also incited a Christian millennialist zealot from Australia to set fire to the Al Aqsa mosque. In June 1986, 12,000 members of Gush Emunim, and other Jewish fundamentalist groups, held demonstrations at the Temple Mount, the presumed site of the Second Temple, protesting Muslim control of the site. In clashes with Israeli police, 100 protestors were arrested.

Their ideology is a blend of ultranationalistic right-wing Zionism and pietistic millennialism, which leads them to hold that the redemption of Israel can only be accomplished once all the lands of the biblical kingdom of Israel are reincorporated into the land of Israel today. Therefore they reject all forms of peaceful accommodation with Arabs within the land of Israel.

- H -

HAMAS. Hamas, the Arabic acronym for the "Islamic Resistance Movement," (*Harakat al Muqawama al Islamiyya*) is a nonstate, revolutionary Palestinian group devoted to the complete eradication of the State of Israel and creation of an Islamic Palestinian state. Although Hamas is a separate organization from the PLO, it has sought to cooperate with other mainline Palestinian groups in conducting the intifada uprising, which began in December 1987. Unlike the PLO, which has always advocated a secular Palestinian state and which, since 1988, has indicated its willingness to accept a Palestinian state with a much reduced territory in coexistence with Israel, Hamas regards the entire territory of former mandatory Palestine as an "inviolable Islamic trust" and rejects the idea of a secular state altogether.

Hamas officially announced its existence with the publication of the "Covenant of the Islamic Resistance Movement" on 18 August 1988, but in fact it is continuous with the Ikhwan al Muslimin (Muslim Brotherhood) (q.v.) branch that established itself in Palestine in 1946 and that remained active in Gaza and the West Bank after the 1948 Arab-Israeli war. Until 1984 the Ikhwan had concentrated mainly on the education of Arab youth in Gaza and the West Bank and its politics seldom strayed beyond a belief in piecemeal Islamic reformism. On 17 September 1984, however, a leader of the Palestinian Ikhwan in the Gaza Strip, Sheikh Ahmad Yasin, and four other Ikhwan members were convicted of stockpiling automatic weapons and plotting to kill 300 prominent persons. Yasin is regarded now as the spiritual mentor of Hamas. In October and November 1987, the Ikhwan sometimes collaborated and other times competed with both the PLO and the Palestinian Islamic Jihad (q.v.) in creating demonstrations in the occupied territories that precipitated the intifada uprising.

The ideology of Hamas reflects not only the traditional fundamentalism of the Ikhwan but also the more radical beliefs of the Egyptian Ikhwan leader, Sayyid Qutb, as well as the contemporary beliefs of the Egyptian Munazzamat al Jihad (q.v.) group that assassinated Anwar Sadat. Although predominantly Sunnite in composition, there is evidence that Hamas takes inspiration from the tactical example of the Ayatollah Khomeini's Islamic revolution in Iran in rejecting piecemeal reformism and in its preference for direct popular uprising over either electoral campaigning or guerrilla warfare. Their Covenant defines the Palestinian struggle as being part of the Islamic religious duty of jihad incumbent on all Muslims under Israeli occupation. While the Hamas Covenant solemnly avows the Palestinian identity of the movement, and so disavows any right by the Arab governments to determine the fate of the Palestinians, it also places the Palestinian struggle in a Pan-Islamic context as an obligation demanding the moral and material support of all Muslims even outside of the Arab nations. Article 27 of the Hamas Covenant rejects the secular, nonconfessional platform of the PLO as reflecting the devious influences of "western missionaries, orientalists, and colonialists."

Hamas derives both its autonomy from secular Palestinian nationalists and its organizational strength from the Ikhwan's control over Muslim educational and religious foundations in the West Bank. During the period of Jordanian administration (1948–1988), the Ikhwan used the authority of the Jordanian Ministry of Religious Endowments to dominate the Arab schools and the appointments of all Friday Prayers leaders. The Ikhwan network also dominated the collection and disbursement of the religious tithes of the Muslim faithful. Over 50 percent of religious publications in the West Bank have been dominated by the Ikhwan. Following the cessation of Jordanian state support, the Ikhwan continued to draw on material support from other official and semiprivate Islamic religious organizations in Saudi Arabia and other Persian Gulf emirates. Hamas has rebuffed Iran's attempts to sponsor it through offers of financial and tactical aid.

A number of attacks have been carried out by individual Palestinian Hamas members, usually stabbings of individual Israelis. On 14 December 1990, two Hamas members stabbed to death three Israeli factory workers in Jaffa. Yet for a one-week period beginning 3 July 1992, Hamas clashed with followers of Yasir Arafat's Al Fatah group in the Gaza Strip in which one child was killed and over 150 people injured. Hamas opposed Fatah's participation in the October 1991 Arab-Israeli peace talks in Madrid and feared the PLO would accept newly elected Israeli Prime Minister Yitzhak Rabin's proposal for limited Palestinian autonomy on the West Bank.

HAWARI GROUP. The Hawari Group was the special operations group of the central security and intelligence apparatus of Yasir Arafat's al Fatah, the core group within the PLO. As such it shares the revolutionary goals of its parent group and is also a nonstate actor. Hawari takes its name from its leader, Colonel Hawari, a pseudonym for Abdullah Abdulhamid Labib. This group has been operating since 1985, after absorbing several former members of the Arab Organization of May 15 (q.v.), including Mohammad Rashid, believed responsible for the bombing of a Pan Am jet over Honolulu on 11 August 1982.

The group also operates under the name "Martyrs of Tal al Zaatar," and "Amn Araissi." In April 1985, Hawari bombed the Rome office of the Syrian state airline and in Geneva bombed a Libyan airlines office and a Syrian diplomat's car. In June 1985, Hawari bombed the Geneva railway station. On 2 April 1986, Hawari bombed TWA flight 840 en route from Cairo to Athens, killing four Americans. In August 1986, a Hawari terrorist team was captured in Morocco. In March 1987, French police arrested Hawari operatives and seized explosives and firearms, leading to Colonel Hawari's conviction and sentencing by a French court in absentia for bombing attacks committed in France and elsewhere during the 1980s. In May 1991, Col. Hawari was killed in an automobile accident while driving from Baghdad to Amman, making the future of the group problematic.

HEZBOLLAH. Hezbollah is the Shiite militia created by Iran in Lebanon during the summer of 1982. This state-sponsored group pursues the revolutionary goals of exporting Iran's Islamic revolution to Lebanon and creating an exclusively Islamic state there. The militia also seeks to expel Israeli and western forces from Lebanon and opposes the older Amal (q.v.) militia. The name "Hezbollah," meaning "Party of God," is taken from the Koran (Surat al Mujadilah, verse 22) as a term describing the true Muslim believers. It first began to be used to identity the mass followers of the Imam Khomeini in Iran, where the name was applied to organized mobs deployed by the Islamic Revolutionary Guards Corps (IRGC, q.v.) and the Islamic Republic Party against opponents of the Islamic Republic in Iran. Once the IRGC units arrived in Lebanon they gave the same name to the militias they organized there, as was confirmed by the confession of a Lebanese Hezbollah member arrested in Turkey on 10 April 1987.

Hezbollah was established by a contingent of 2,000 Islamic Revolutionary Guards dispatched to Lebanon in the summer of 1982, ostensibly to fight Israeli troops there. In fact, the IRGC unit remained in the Baalbak region and began organizing dissidents from Amal (q.v.). Iran consistently disavowed direct control over Hezbollah, and formal leadership lay in the hands of a Lebanese "Consultative Assembly" consisting of ranking Lebanese clergymen, such as Muhammad Hussein Fadlullah, and key laymen, such as Hussein Musawi. This Consultative Assembly met only infrequently from 1983 until 1987, usually in the presence of either the military attaché of the Iranian Embassy in Damascus or the Iranian chargé d'affaires in Beirut.

Using the nom de guerre "Islamic Jihad" Hezbollah conducted an impressive terrorist campaign against U.S. diplomats and civilians, and U.S., French, and Israeli military contingents in Lebanon. Its vehicle-bombings include the following major attacks: on 18 April 1983, the destruction of one wing of the U.S. Embassy in West Beirut, killing 61 persons, including the CIA station chief, and forcing the evacuation of the embassy to Christian-controlled East Beirut; on 23 October 1983, destruction of the U.S. Marine headquarters at Beirut Airport, killing 241 U.S. servicemen, and another attack on the French contingent's headquarters, killing 74 servicemen; on 4 November 1983, an attack on Israeli Defense Forces headquarters in Tyre, killing 30 servicemen; on 9 September 1984, the attempted bombing of the U.S. Embassy annex in East Beirut. Although the bomber was unable to destroy the diplomatic compound, the car bomb nonetheless killed 2 Americans and 21 bystanders; and on 10 March 1985, a car bomb attack on Israeli soldiers near Metulla, killing 12 persons.

Hezbollah masterminded the hijacking of Rome-bound TWA flight 847 on 14 June 1984 from Greece to Beirut where one U.S. serviceman found among the passengers was killed. Women and children were released after some time. The 39 remaining American men were held hostage until June 30. Amal assumed custody of these hostages from Hezbollah but refused to release them immediately until it received assurances that the United States would not retaliate against Lebanon for the hijacking. By doing this, Amal inadvertently confused the situation and ended up drawing most of the immediate blame upon itself for the hijacking, while Hezbollah obtained the main credit for obtaining the release of Shiite prisoners held in Israel's Atlit prison. The dissension created by this affair led to an outbreak of fighting between Hezbollah and Amal following the release of the remaining TWA 847 hostages. Syria, which had supported Hezbollah initially as a means of forcing the U.S. and French forces out of Lebanon, threw its weight behind Amal and began forcing Hezbollah units out of the Bekaa valley.

Following the withdrawal of U.S. and French multi-national units from Lebanon, Hezbollah apparently switched to hostage taking as its preferred tactic for ridding Lebanon of Western influence. In 1985 at least four Americans (not counting the TWA 847 passengers), one Swiss, two Britons, three Frenchmen, one Italian, four Soviets, and four Lebanese Jews were abducted. In 1986 some 15 foreigners were kidnapped and 10 other foreigners were taken in 1987. On 17 February 1988, U.S. Marine Lt. Col. William Higgins, on loan to United Nations peacekeeping forces in Lebanon, was kidnapped and later killed on 31 July 1989. Many of the kidnappings were followed by written messages accompanied by recent photographs of hostages to the Lebanese newspaper *Ash Shira',* claiming credit in the name of Islamic

Jihad. Another American, CIA station chief William Buckley, was also killed in captivity by Hezbollah. Revelations about the Reagan administration's arms sales to Iran in November 1986 further highlighted Iranian control over Hezbollah and prompted Hezbollah to take Church of England envoy Terry Waite hostage on 20 January 1987 as well.

Following the cessation of U.S. arms for hostages deals, Tehran found little future utility in continuing to have Hezbollah seize or hold hostages. The holding of the hostages remained the main reason for Iran's diplomatic isolation following the 1988 cease-fire in the Iran-Iraq war. The increase in U.S. influence in the Middle East as a result of Operation Desert Storm and the weakening of the position of Iran's Lebanese protégés in the face of increased Syrian support for Hezbollah's enemies in Lebanon may have forced both Iran and Hezbollah to release the remaining hostages before the end of 1991.

Predictions about the demise or eclipse of Hezbollah presuppose that the necessary condition of Iranian state sponsorship had been withdrawn. Following the death of Khomeini, however, the Iranian state had not succeeded in integrating the various clerical factions, some of which have had more influence over Hezbollah than the formal offices of the Iranian state. After the release of Western hostages in December 1991, Hezbollah again resumed car bombing attacks with the 17 March 1992 bombing of the Israeli embassy in Buenos Aires for which, once again, Islamic Jihad claimed credit.

HIJACKING. The forcible seizure of a ship, train, automobile, or airplane usually with the threat of bodily harm to the crew and/or passengers. In the 1960s, most instances of hijacking involving air carriers were cases of people seeking to escape to some other country. In that time, the United States experienced scores of hijackers attempting to divert domestic flights to Cuba. During the 1970s and 1980s, however, hijackings of airplanes were increasingly used to take the passengers as hostages with which to force the sovereign governments of the hostages to accede to the hijackers' political demands, or those of their state sponsors. By the beginning of the 1990s, total airplane hijackings since 1931, the year the first aerial hijacking occurred, were in excess of 700, with a total of over 500 passengers (including the hijackers and antihijacking police) and crew members killed by hijackers.

The problem of hijacking was compounded by the political offense doctrine, which allowed some states to grant immunity from prosecution, or from extradition, selectively to hijackers who claimed to be acting on political grounds or else who were political refugees seeking freedom. In April 1986, following the 1985 TWA flight 847 hijacking to Beirut Airport, the International Federation of Airline Pilots Associations put an embargo on Beirut Airport and have threatened to embargo other countries that tolerate hijacking. After the TWA 847 hijacking the United States began to apply a 1984 antiterrorist statute to prosecute hijackers who victimized American citizens, arresting Fawaz Younis in September 1988 for his role in a 11 June 1985 hijacking of a Jordanian airliner carrying some U.S. citizens.

Instances of nonaerial hijackings have included the Assen and Beilen train seizures by South Moluccan terrorists in 2 December 1975 and 23 May 1977 (See Free South Moluccan Organization) and the hijacking of the *Achille Lauro* cruise ship by Palestinian terrorists on 7 October 1985 (See Palestine Liberation Front). In each of these instances, hostages were murdered by the hijackers, showing that nonaerial hijackings could be just as deadly.

HOFFMANN MILITARY SPORTS GROUP. The *Wehrsportsgruppe Hoffmann* was a nonstate West German neo-Nazi group that engaged in paramilitary training and terrorist activities for the revolutionary aim of overthrowing the Federal Republic of Germany and restoring a right-wing nationalist authoritarian regime. The group was founded by

Karl-Heinz Hoffmann (b. 1937) in the latter 1970s. Since West German law forbids neo-Nazi parties or organizations from operating openly, the group represented itself as a club for engaging in military war games. The Sports Group stressed paramilitary training, racist ideology, anticommunism, and military romanticism.

The Sports Group is linked to terrorism proper first—through the activities of its own members within Germany, and second, through its ties to Palestinian terrorist groups. Hoffmann created a student branch of his organization called the University Circle of Tübingen Students. This group used to confront and beat up leftist students, often breaking up demonstrations against the apartheid policies of South Africa. The group also baited and attacked feminists and homosexuals.

In 1976, one Sports Group member tried to bomb the American Forces Network station in Munich. On 19 December 1980 a Sports Group member, Uwe Behrendt, murdered a Jewish publisher in Erlangen, Shlomo Levin, as well as Levin's female friend, and fled to the Middle East where he later committed suicide in 1982. While authorities could not prove that Hoffmann ordered Behrendt to commit this murder, this incident moved the West German Federal Office for Defense of the Constitution (Bundesamt für Verfassungsschutz) to ban officially the Sports Group as a neo-Nazi group on 30 January 1980.

Yet the most notorious incident associated with the Sports Group was the 26 September 1980 bombing of the Munich Oktoberfest, which killed at least 12 people and wounded over 217 others, including 7 U.S. citizens. While it now appears that the detonation of this bomb was an accident, perhaps because the timing mechanism malfunctioned, the bomb itself was produced by the Hoffmann group and the bearer of the bomb, one Gondolf Köhler, was a Sports Group member. Hoffmann was jailed on 27 September 1980 but was released the next day for lack of evidence that he was involved in the bombing.

Hoffmann and the Sports Group were also seeking ties

with Palestinian groups as an opportunity to provide training and operational experience to his cadres. In 1979, Hoffmann took 15 followers to Lebanon for training. In July 1980, Hoffmann visited Damascus to form ties with the PLO. Hoffmann not only left 20 more of his members in PLO camps but also struck a lucrative deal to ship used trucks and heavy equipment to the PLO. Hoffmann was again arrested in June 1981 in Frankfurt as he was ready to fly to Beirut. His followers who had undergone training in PLO camps were arrested on their return to Germany.

While the Sports Group has ceased to function as an organization, many of its members have continued to work in the neo-Nazi movement, which has continued to grow both in Germany and elsewhere, where a number of other neo-Nazi groups allow them the opportunity to continue quasi-legal or terrorist activities.

HUKS. The *Hukbalahap* (an acronym for *Hukbong Bayan Laban Sa Hapon,* meaning "People's Anti-Japanese Resistance Army") was a resistance army founded by the Communist Party of the Philippines in March 1942. Trained by Chinese Communist instructors sent by Mao Tse-tung and led by Luis Taroc, the Huks recruited extensively among the peasants and harassed the Japanese in guerrilla raids.

Following World War II, the Huks, who renamed their organization the *Hukbong Mapagpalaya ng Bayan,* "People's Liberation Army," attempted to set up a communist regime but were countered by U.S. forces. The Huks numbered around 10,000 active fighters at their height but lacked good weaponry. Consequently they relied more on terrorism than on conventional tactics, their most stunning attack being the ambush and murder of the widow of President Quezon in April 1949. In addition to undertaking a more thorough counterinsurgency effort, the administration of Ramon Magsaysay addressed many of the social and economic grievances of the peasant following of the Huks, who eventually disbanded in 1954.

HUSSEIN SUICIDE SQUAD. One of the pro-Iranian fundamentalist Shiite Muslim terrorist groups in Lebanon that became part of Hezbollah (q.v.).

- I -

IDENTITY CHRISTIANITY. The Identity Christianity doctrine is a synthesis of white supremacist doctrine, of xenophobic American populism, and of a post-millennialist version of Anglo-Israelitism that has become a major ideological inspiration for extreme right-wing terrorist groups operating in North America.

In the eighteenth century, Englishman Richard Brothers developed the Anglo-Israelite doctrine claiming that the true Israelites were not contemporary Jews but rather the northern European nations, and especially the British, who supposedly were descended from the northern "lost" tribes of Israel deported by the Assyrians in the eighth century B.C. This doctrine was modified by some Americans to identify North America rather than Britain as the new promised land. The modern form of Identity Christianity that grew out of Anglo-Israelitism was first propounded during the Depression era by a nondenominational preacher, Wesley Swift, who combined it with anti-Semitism and with extreme anti-Communism defined broadly enough to include socialists and most liberals. The modern doctrine asserts that nonwhites are descendants of "pre-Adamites" created only as prototypes of true humans and that Jews are the descendants of a sexual union between Eve and the tempting serpent that appeared in the Garden of Eden.

The post-millennialist component of Identity Christianity implies that the realization of God's Kingdom on earth requires the true believers (identified with white, Identity Christians) to struggle actively against the forces of darkness (identified with Jews, nonwhites, and communists.) What distinguishes Identity Christianity from evangelical Christian fundamentalism proper is that most evangelicals believe in premillennialism, which asserts instead that the realization of God's Kingdom on earth will proceed according to an inscrutable divine plan that can neither be helped nor hindered by human political efforts. Also most evangelicals regard modern Jews as the true descendants of the original Israelites and regard the creation of the State of Israel as a manifestation of God's gracious intervention in history fulfilling certain Biblical prophesies. By contrast, most Identity Christians regard the existence of the State of Israel as proof of a hidden, sinister conspiracy at work in the world, which they must fight.

The Identity Christian movement seems tailor-made to provide a unifying religious and political worldview for such groups as the various Ku Klux Klan, neo-Nazi, and right-wing survivalist groups as well as a theological justification for their hatemongering. Among those groups that are founded on variations of the Identity Christianity doctrine, or else that have adopted that doctrine, are the Aryan Nations (q.v.), the Order (q.v.), the Christian-Patriots Defense League (q.v.), and the Posse Comitatus (q.v). These groups have either directly participated in terrorist actions or else have condoned such actions by their members. Such terrorism usually involves attacks on Jews and other minority members or else attacks on officials of the U.S. federal government, which the Identity Christians refer to as the "Zionist Occupation Government," or simply as "ZOG." The Covenant, the Sword and the Arm of the Lord (q.v.) was another such group that ceased to exist with the arrest and recantation of its leader.

Not all white supremacists or extreme rightists necessarily profess Identity Christianity. Robert dePugh, founder of the Minutemen, was actually an avowed atheist. The leader of the Order (q.v.), Robert Mathews, who professed Identity Christianity, was secretly a worshiper of the Norse gods. Nonetheless such leaders have cynically used Identity Christianity as a means for attracting the support of disaffected white Christians who might otherwise be uninterested in the white supremacist political message. Viewed as a religious phenomenon Identity Christianity recalls the Marcionist doctrine of the early Christian era, an anti-Semitic interpretation of the New Testament that denied the validity of the Old Testament but that was rejected as heresy by orthodox Christian theologians. Viewed simply as a political phenomenon the Identity Christian movement is the closest thing to being an indigenous American fascist ideology having widespread appeal among politically disenchanted white populists.

INNER MACEDONIAN REVOLUTIONARY ORGANIZATION. IMRO was a state-sponsored Macedonian revolutionary nationalist group that undertook terrorist actions to create an independent Macedonian homeland. The group enjoyed Bulgarian state support from 1901 until 1912, when Bulgaria, Greece, and Serbia divided the former Turkish possession among themselves. IMRO was later supported by Hungary and Fascist Italy until World War II.

IMRO committed one of the earliest instances of seizing and holding a U.S. citizen as a hostage for political ends. In September 1901, an American Congregationalist missionary, Miss Ellen M. Stone, was kidnapped by IMRO and held for ransom. The Roosevelt administration considered, but rejected, the payment of the demanded ransom, which was instead provided by a $66,000 subscription raised privately by Stone's sponsoring missionary society and which was accepted by the Macedonian nationalists. Stone was freed in February 1902, while the proceeds of the ransom payment financed an abortive revolt against the Turks that was quickly crushed in August 1903.

In its later years IMRO changed from being a revolutionary terrorist group into an entrepreneurial terrorist organization that hired itself out to various regimes to commit assassinations on a contract basis.

INSURGENCY. One definition for insurgency is a struggle between a group lacking authority and the governing authorities in which the group lacking authority uses both political resources as well as violence to either destroy the legitimacy of the ruling group or else to change the terms by which legitimate power is held, and to establish their own alternative legitimacy (Bard E. O'Neill, 1990). Another criterion for distinguishing insurgencies from isolated guerrilla hit-and-run attacks or terrorist actions is whether the guerrillas have begun openly to control areas of land within a contested country. As such insurgency falls between the extremes of revolution, in which the major part of the society becomes involved in the change of regime and terrorism by individuals or groups lacking any nonterrorist complementary political program. Insurgents generally will use either conventional warfare or terrorist tactics as they perceive the situation warrants but may limit their terrorist actions as their political program requires. Using this definition, one may regard the Basque Fatherland and Liberty (q.v.) group as part of a Basque insurgency rather than as merely a terrorist group. The political goals of this group have directed their terrorist actions to attacking symbols of Spanish hegemony, and the Spanish security forces in particular, rather than Spanish civilians generally.

INTIFADA. The intifada (Arabic: "uprising, revolt") refers to the popular uprising against Israeli occupation among Palestinians on the West Bank and the Gaza Strip. This revolt began on 9 December 1987, with protests over an automobile accident in the Gaza Strip in which an Israeli motorist killed Palestinian pedestrians. While the early stages of the revolt involved youngsters taunting and throwing stones at Israeli troops, it eventually spread throughout the Palestinian population and involved organized demonstrations, civil disobedience, and boycotting of Israeli goods and services.

In spite of the apparent spontaneity of the outbreak of the intifada, the Palestine Liberation Organization (q.v.) and other non-PLO groups, such as Hamas (q.v.) and the Palestinian Islamic Jihad, have coordinated most of the leading events of the intifada. The majority of the activities carried out in the name of the intifada are not terrorist acts, while even such acts as stone-throwing or attacks on Israeli soldiers could arguably be viewed as political violence distinct from terrorism as such. Within the Palestinian community, however, reprisals, including murders, perpetrated against Palestinians viewed as Israeli collaborators or informers have become increasingly common with groups such as the "Black Panthers" on the West Bank killing those viewed as lacking zeal for their cause. Given al Fatah's governing role in the intifada through the Unified National Leadership (UNL), a PLO front group established to coordinate intifada activities, and its past record of using its covert operations and internal enforcement organ, Force-17 (q.v.), either within Israeli territory or against Palestinians viewed as enemies of al Fatah, there is a reasonable basis for viewing the bloodletting among Palestinians as systematic rather than random events constituting a terrorist campaign.

Most internationally voiced concerns about terrorism and the intifada have centered instead on alleged Israeli state terror being perpetrated against Palestinian demonstrators and activists. Israeli soldiers have sometimes retaliated against stone-throwing youths by breaking the arms of the offenders, while the Israeli government's bulldozing of homes of activists and deportation of selected Palestinian leaders of the intifada have led to denunciations of Israel both internationally and within the United States. In February 1989, the U.S. Department of State's annual report on human rights charged Israel with causing "many avoidable deaths and injuries" and with violations of Palestinians' human rights due to Israeli Defense Forces actions against Palestinian protestors.

Most of the intifada's activities have been confined to the territories occupied during the 1967 war. Other terrorist actions have occurred during the period of the intifada, including attacks on Israeli tourists in Egypt, attacks on Israelis within Israel by Arab migrant workers, and cross-border raids by Palestinians or other Arabs from Jordan into Israel. Similarly, during 1990 there have been attacks against Arabs carried out by Israeli civilians and soldiers, including an attack by a single Israeli gunman on 20 May 1990 outside Tel Aviv in which 7 Arabs were killed and 11 others wounded. Although such actions may not be part of the intifada proper, they are certainly related to the increased Israeli-Palestinian tensions resulting from the intifada.

INTIHARIOUN. ("Suicide Volunteers," from Arabic *intihar*, "suicide"), term used among Hezbollah (q.v.) militiamen for persons willing to undertake suicide attacks usually as drivers of vehicle bombs. The truck bomb attacks on the U.S. Embassy in Beirut (18 April 1983) and the U.S. Marine encampment at Beirut International Airport (23 October 1983) both involved *intihari* drivers, while credit for these attacks has been claimed by Islamic Jihad, a nom de guerre for Hezbollah. Although *intihari* attacks have been rationalized as a form of Islamic martyrdom, even Islamic clergymen supportive of Hezbollah, such as Muhammad Hussain Fadlullah, have pointed out that deliberate suicide is contrary to Islamic law whereas bona fide martyrdom involves death that is both unavoidable and unsought. Following the withdrawal of U.S. and French multinational units from Lebanon, Hezbollah apparently switched to hostage taking as its preferred tactic for ridding Lebanon of Western influence. Following the release of Western hostages in December 1991, Hezbollah again resumed car bomb attacks with the 17 March 1992 bombing of the Israeli embassy in Buenos Aires.

Intihari attacks are not a monopoly of Shiite militias. The Syrian Social Nationalist Party (q.v.) has developed and deployed its own corps of *intiharioun*, while in 1987 the PFLP-General Command deployed *intihari* hang-glider attacks against Israeli forces in Lebanon and settlements in Galilee. The Mujahideen-e Khalq (q.v.) have also used *intiharioun* to kill government officials and proregime clergymen in Iran.

IRAULTZA. Also known as the ''Basque Armed Revolutionary Workers' Organization,'' Iraultza is a Basque separatist organization dedicated to creating an independent and Marxist Basque state. Very little is known about the origins and composition of the organization or its relation to other Basque groups.

Iraultza does not leave written communiqués so all that is known about the organization comes from their telephoned messages, usually given as warnings shortly before their impending bomb attacks. The group opposes international investments in the Basque region. The group also opposes Spain's participation in NATO and was highly critical of the U.S. foreign policy of the Reagan administration. Despite its vocal anti-American sentiments, however, this group has never struck at, or threatened, U.S. diplomatic facilities or personnel.

Iraultza uses very small bombs that are usually exploded late at night in order to avoid injuring people. The only injury caused by an Iraultza bomb was due to a malfunction that failed to detonate the activated bomb at the right time, killing a construction worker who came across it the following day. Nonetheless, Iraultza has managed to inflict more bombings against U.S. business interests than any other European terrorist group. From May 1982 to the end of 1987, there were at least 31 bombings by this group, including 5 attacks on the offices of the Rank Xerox firm, 2 attacks on a Coca-Cola bottling plant, 6 attacks on banks, including branches of Citibank and Bank of America, and also on a theater showing the film *Red Dawn*. French business firms have also been favorite targets. All of these attacks have been confined to the Basque-inhabited areas of Spain. From 1987 to 1990 little was heard of this group, which appeared never to have more than 20 members. In March and April of 1991, Iraultza attempted three bombings, but three of its members were killed by a premature explosion.

IRGUN. The Organization for the Defense of the People (Irgun Zvai Leumi) was a nonstate Zionist paramilitary organization dedicated to the expulsion of British forces and the Arab population from Palestine in order to establish a Jewish state there. The Irgun was not simply a ''nonstate'' organization insofar as it was an illegal group from the viewpoint of the British mandatory regime but was also outside of the infrastructure of the Jewish Agency in Palestine, which already had the Haganah (Defense Organization) as its military wing, which became, respectively, the Israeli government and Israeli army upon independence. The Irgun was founded in 1937 by David Raziel, who was killed in 1941 helping the British quell a German-inspired revolt in Iraq. He was succeeded by Menachem Begin (b. 1913, d. 1990).

From 1944, Irgun and LEHI (q.v.) collaborated in attacking the British army and civil administration in Palestine. On 22 July 1946, the Irgun bombed the British administrative center in Palestine, located in the King David Hotel in Jerusalem, killing over 90 people, many of whom, ironically, turned out to be Jewish employees of the mandatory authority. On 9 April 1948, the Irgun attacked the Arab village of Deir Yassin located on the road connecting Jerusalem to Tel Aviv, killing all of its inhabitants except for two old women and a child. The news of this massacre in turn prompted many Palestinian Arabs to flee their homes when the first Arab-Israeli war broke out the following month. All told, the activities of the Irgun and LEHI caused the deaths of 373 people in Palestine. With the declaration of Israeli independence and the outbreak of war with the Arab states, most Irgun members joined the Israeli army.

IRISH NATIONAL LIBERATION ARMY. INLA is an Irish nationalist terrorist group that began as the military wing of the Irish Republican Socialist Party, itself a faction that broke with the Official IRA (See Irish Republican Army) in 1974. INLA aims to use armed struggle to force British troops out of northern Ireland, to force unification of the northern six counties with the rest of Ireland, and to over-throw the current Republic of Ireland in favor of a Marxist-Leninist revolutionary state, which would withdraw from the European Economic Community.

INLA terrorist activities have included not only bombings and shootings against British and Ulster officials, security forces, Protestant loyalists, and members of Protestant militias but also internecine bloodletting with both the official and provisional wings of the IRA as well as within INLA itself. The struggles with the older IRA groups lasted from 1974 until 1977, when INLA founder Seamus Costello was murdered by unknown persons.

On 30 March 1979, INLA killed Airey Neave, a British Conservative Party parliamentarian close to Prime Minister Margaret Thatcher and a vocal critic of Irish republican terrorists, by a bomb rigged within his car, which detonated within the underground parking garage of Westminster Hall. On 17 April 1979 INLA killed four members of the Royal Ulster Constabulary with a remote-control bomb, the most severe blow ever inflicted on the Ulster police until then. INLA then proceeded with a campaign of killing Ulster prison guards as well as British and Ulster undercover operatives. From November 1979 until September 1986, INLA carried out three successful bombings and at least two other attempts. The worst of these occurred on 6 December 1982, when the INLA bombed a nightclub in Ballykelly, killing 17 people (12 of them soldiers) and wounding 66 others. From January to June 1987, INLA reverted to internecine fighting, this time among its own members, killing at least 12 of its veterans before members of other republican groups negotiated a truce among the surviving INLA members.

INLA is much more openly Marxist-Leninist and more doctrinaire than the provisional or official branches of the IRA. INLA has cooperated with the West German Revolutionary Cells (q.v.) and French Direct Action (q.v.) leftist groups.

IRISH REPUBLICAN ARMY. The name of the IRA has been used loosely to refer to the Irish National Liberation Army (q.v.), the Official Irish Republican Army, the Provisional Irish Republican Army (q.v.), and other Irish republican or nationalist splinter groups. Historically the name was used first by James Connolly to designate the nationalist forces used in the Dublin Easter rebellion of 1916. Following the creation of the Irish Free State in 1922, the new Irish state disbanded the IRA and then proscribed it when militant nationalists opposed to the partition of Ireland refused to obey the Free State government.

The IRA began a bombing campaign in Great Britain during most of 1939 and the early part of 1940, striking over 50 targets in London, Manchester, Glasgow, and Birmingham. The Irish government banned the IRA in 1939, cooperating with the British in their suppression. During 1955 to 1962, the IRA unleashed a "border campaign" directed against the Royal Ulster Constabulary, which again was suppressed through official Anglo-Irish cooperation.

With the advent of the fiftieth anniversary of the Easter rebellion in 1967, militant Ulster Protestants increased harassment of Catholics in Northern Ireland. This prompted nationalist political organizers to form a Northern Ireland Civil Rights Association, which organized marches and protests even in Protestant neighborhoods. The IRA provided escorts for these marches but lacked sufficient arms to fend off arson attacks by militant Protestants against the homes and businesses of Catholics.

Disagreements within the IRA over its increasingly Marxist and political character led to the splitting off in 1969 of the more nationalistic Provisional Irish Republican Army (PIRA), which maintained that unification of Ireland by force even against the wishes of the Protestant majority in the north, not civil rights for Catholics in a separate Northern Ireland, was their main goal and that armed struggle rather than political negotiation was the main means to achieve this goal. By default the original organization from which PIRA split off became known as the Official Irish Republican Army (OIRA). OIRA and PIRA competed with each other and sometimes feuded in gun-battles with each other when each was not fighting the British army or Protestant paramilitary groups. In 1972, however, OIRA officially renounced armed struggle and eventually became known as the Workers' Party, competing openly in electoral politics in both Northern Ireland and the Republic of Ireland.

In reality the memberships of OIRA and PIRA were often overlapping. In an attempt to prevent OIRA members from using OIRA arms in PIRA operations, OIRA in effect expelled its more radical nationalist members in 1974. These radicals, who believed in armed struggle, in turn, formed the Irish National Liberation Army (INLA) (q.v.), a group at least as violent as PIRA but possessing also the extreme Marxist-Leninist ideology that had come to characterize OIRA.

The historical IRA had maintained a political front known as Sinn Fein (Irish for "Ourselves Alone"). With the reactivation of the IRA in 1969, the Sinn Fein party officially disavowed any connection with the IRA, a tactic that allowed the IRA a legal front and the option of resorting to negotiations if expedient. With the emergence of PIRA a Provisional Sinn Fein came into existence alongside the Sinn Fein associated with OIRA. Once OIRA renounced armed struggle, there was no longer the need for the pretense of a separate political front, and so since 1972 the name Sinn Fein now refers only to the political front of PIRA. INLA also had as its associated political front the Irish Republican Socialist Party. When organizers of this party found INLA, which they had viewed as their party's military wing, unwilling to submit itself to control by the party, they dissociated themselves from INLA, which then operated without any political front group.

Despite the historical discontinuity between the pre-1969 IRA and PIRA, most references to the IRA in public discussion and news reports deal mainly with PIRA. (See

Provisional Irish Republican Army, Irish National Liberation Army)

ISLAMIC AMAL. Islamic Amal is a splinter group that broke away from Amal (q.v.) proper in 1982. Islamic Amal was a nonstate group of more militant Amal militiamen who hearkened to Iran's call for Islamic revolution throughout the Middle East. They had grown disillusioned with the more secular and nationalistic leadership of Nabih Berri who had succeeded Imam Musa Sadr following the latter's disappearance in 1978.

In 1982 Hussein Musawi, a high-school teacher and member of the Amal Command Council, accused Berri of implicit collaboration with Israel during its invasion of Lebanon that summer. Musawi quit, or was expelled, from Amal but founded Islamic Amal in the vicinity of Baalbak, which had become a guerrilla training center run by Iran's Islamic Revolutionary Guards Corps (q.v.). Musawi was implicated in the 19 July 1982 kidnapping of David Dodge, the president of American University in Beirut, and in the October 1983 truck bombings of the French and U.S. multinational forces. In November 1983, Israel and France launched retaliatory air strikes on Musawi's Baalbak headquarters but without harming Musawi. He is related by marriage to Muhammad Ali Hamadi, one of the hijackers of TWA flight 847 later captured and imprisoned in Germany, and is the nephew of Sheikh Abbas Musawi, one of the leaders of Hezbollah killed by Israeli air attacks in 1992.

Musawi continued to speak in the name of Islamic Amal as late as 1986, but it is believed that Islamic Amal was incorporated wholesale into the framework of Hezbollah (q.v.) and that the fiction of Islamic Amal as a separate entity was kept alive as a form of disinformation to confuse Hezbollah's enemies.

ISLAMIC FRONT FOR THE LIBERATION OF BAHRAIN. This group is a nonstate group of Shiite

Bahrainis seeking to create an Islamic revolution in Bahrain under Iranian state sponsorship.

The Islamic Front for the Liberation of Bahrain was founded in March 1979 by Hujjatulislam Hadi al Mudarissi, a young Bahraini clergyman who had lived in Najaf, Iraq, as a member of Khomeini's entourage. His brother, Muhammad Taqi al Mudarissi, founded the Islamic Amal (q.v.) Party to promote an Islamic revolution in Iraq that was eventually merged into the Supreme Assembly for the Islamic Revolution of Iraq, the Tehran-based umbrella organization of Iraqi Shiite revolutionaries headed by the Al Dawa (q.v) Party of Iraq. Mudarissi was financed by two Iranian revolutionary foundations used to front subversive adventures abroad, namely the Foundation for the Oppressed and the Liberation Movements Office.

On 13 December 1981 the security police of Bahrain and Dubai arrested a total of 60 persons, 6 of them students in transit to Bahrain at Dubai International Airport, on charges of illegal possession of firearms and explosives, membership in a subversive organization, plotting to overthrow the government, and collaboration with a hostile foreign power. Thirteen other persons were later arrested in areas of Bahrain outside the capital of Manama. Substantial material evidence in addition to confessions of the arrested indicated that Iran had been the main principal behind the coup plot. Among the several arms caches seized police also found complete duplicate sets of Bahraini security police uniforms, which proved to be of Iranian manufacture.

Certain of those arrested revealed that they had undergone military training in Iran. Iran vehemently denied these charges but the Gulf Cooperation Council condemned Iran for its promotion of subversive activities among the Shiite Muslims of the Persian Gulf emirates.

ISLAMIC FUNDAMENTALISM. Islamic fundamentalism has been identified as the main ideological inspiration of the assassins of Anwar Sadat, the Hezbollah (q.v.) militia of

Lebanon, and of the Islamic Republic of Iran, which has engaged in state sponsorship of terrorism.

What non-Muslim Westerners have called "Islamic fundamentalism" Muslims prefer to call "al nihdhat al Islami," meaning "the Islamic movement," or better, "the Islamic resurgence." The term "Islamic fundamentalism" misleadingly suggests an analogy with Christian fundamentalism, which accepts a radical distinction between the "kingdom of God" and the kingdom(s) of this world. So-called fundamentalist Islam radically rejects such a separation of life into secular and religious domains, or any separation of politics and religion. The closest analogy in Western Christianity would be rather the prorevolutionary "liberation theology" (q.v.) of Latin America rather than the private pietism of mainstream American Protestant fundamentalism. Although using the term "Islamic resurgence" would be less misleading, the currency of the term "Islamic fundamentalism" will likely remain a linguistic fact of life in American English and therefore is used throughout this dictionary subject to the caveats outlined above regarding its proper meaning.

Central to Islamic fundamentalism is its insistence on reviving and comprehensively applying a unitary system of Islamic law covering all private and public affairs. This closed and comprehensive legal system stems from the Koran, an even larger body of traditions, authoritative commentaries, historic consensus, and judicial precedents. The various Islamic fundamentalist movements hold in common certain beliefs, which may be summarized as follows:

1. The Islamic laws have comprehensive solutions for all economic, social, diplomatic, criminal, and civil problems;
2. Islamic law is itself perfect, immutable, and organic, not to be abrogated in part or amended;
3. The current Islamic world, with its mixture of traditional Muslim and contemporary Western laws and institutions, and its division of the historic Islamic empire into several nation-states, represents a deviation from true Islam; and,

4. The religious duties of jihad, holy war, or of ''enjoining the good and forbidding the evil'' permit violence to rid Muslim lands of un-Islamic laws, institutions, rulers, foreign powers, and agents when other means fail.

Islamic fundamentalism is not a monolithic phenomenon but exists both in an ''official'' form and a ''populist'' form. The religious establishments within Saudi Arabia and the Persian Gulf emirates are officially fundamentalist in the sense outlined above but with the difference that they maintain that the true Islam is already being implemented in those countries. Such an Islamic fundamentalism is politically conservative and even counterrevolutionary. The opposing ''populist'' variety of Islamic fundamentalism comes also in two forms, namely, an *islahi* (reformist) version and a *salafi* (puritan) version. Reformist fundamentalists accept the notion of incrementalist reform of corrupt Muslim societies through educational efforts and such political participation or agitation as is permitted by the local Muslim government. Examples of such fundamentalists are to be found in the various Muslim Brotherhood groups (q.v.) that have operated as political parties and social welfare organizations in Egypt, the Sudan, Syria, Algeria, and other Muslim lands. The *salafi* fundamentalists reject such reformism as compromising with unbelief and insist instead on violent, revolutionary means to achieve the true Islamic state and society. An example of such fundamentalists was the Sunnite group that attacked and occupied the Masjid al Haram complex in Mecca on 20 November 1979. Nonetheless, even reformist fundamentalists have shown a willingness to resort to political violence and terrorism if they are frustrated in their attempts to work peacefully within the political system. The Muslim Brotherhood in Egypt in the Nasser period, the Brotherhood in Syria under Hafez al-Asad, and, more recently, the Islamic Salvation Front (q.v.) in Algeria and Islamic Tendency Movement (q.v.) in Tunisia have all resorted to political violence when denied the chance to reform those countries through political channels.

Most ''populist'' fundamentalists are hostile to the West, and to the United States in particular, for three main reasons: First, the United States is perceived as the main backer of the State of Israel, which is viewed as a Judaic and European imposition into the midst of the Muslim world. Second, the United States is viewed as the backer and supporter of those Muslim states that populist fundamentalists regard as apostate regimes. Third, the United States is the source of an attractive materialistic and individualistic culture that is incompatible with the traditional and community-centered ethos of an integral Islamic moral order. These perceived antagonisms will continue to provoke violent reactions, including terrorist attacks or threats against American citizens and U.S. interests in, or near, the Muslim world for the foreseeable future. Apart from antagonism toward the West and the United States, the incompatibility of Islamic fundamentalist aspirations with the conscious secularism of many Muslim states, especially the Pan-Arabist Bathist Syrian and Iraqi regimes, also portends terrorism by fundamentalists against such regimes as well as reciprocal state terror directed by those regimes against fundamentalists.

Although Islamic fundamentalism is perhaps the only remaining transnational ideological movement that challenges Western liberal democracy following the collapse of international communism, even among the *salafi* fundamentalists there is no monolithic ideological or organizational unity. Sectarian differences between Sunnite and Shiite fundamentalists, nationalistic differences between Arab and non-Arab nationals, and idiosyncratic antagonisms among and within groups or between individual leaders have vitiated efforts to create a cohesive Pan-Islamic movement. This was particularly evident in the case of the Iranian revolution in which the Shiite complexion of Iranian Islam and the historical animosity between Iranians and Arabs neutralized much of the appeal of that revolution even among fundamentalists in the Arab Sunnite countries. Nonetheless given the failure of attempts to implement socialism or Western-style democracy in the various Muslim countries and the repeated failures of Arab nationalist leaders to defeat Israel or the West, Islamic fundamentalism continues to grow in its appeal within Muslim countries as an indigenous moral-ethical and populist political ideology with which to answer the political and cultural challenges of the non-Muslim world.

ISLAMIC GUERRILLAS IN AMERICA. The Islamic Guerrillas in America is an obscure group of black American converts to Islam who believe in the revolutionary message of the Ayatollah Khomeini. They are believed to be sponsored by the Islamic Republic of Iran and used to repress Iranian dissidents living in the United States.

One assassination and an attempted assassination have been credited to the Islamic Guerrillas. On 22 July 1980, Ali Akbar Tabatabai, an outspoken Iranian critic of the Khomeini regime, was shot to death in Washington, D.C., by David Belfield, a black American convert to Islam also known as Daoud Salahuddin or Daoud Muhammad. Belfield fled to Iran where he was reported, in August 1986, to have been collaborating in Iranian efforts to convert black Americans to Khomeini's vision of Islamic revolution. On 31 July 1980, the residence of another Iranian dissident, one Shah Reis, was shot at in Los Angeles, an action also believed to have been done by the same gunman. The Islamic Guerrillas supposedly were formed and supported by a naturalized Iranian in Washington, D.C., who recruited its members mainly from black inmates of the District of Columbia prison system.

ISLAMIC JIHAD. The name *Al Jihad Al Islami*, meaning "Islamic holy struggle (or war)," has been used by at least three terrorist organizations:
  1. Hezbollah—The Iranian-sponsored Lebanese Shiite militia used the nom de guerre "Islamic Jihad," allowing its own Lebanese leaders and Iranian sponsors plausible deniability for the more heinous actions undertaken by

the group, such as the *intihari* suicide (See *Intiharioun*) vehicle-bombing attacks and the kidnapping and holding of foreigners and non-Muslim Lebanese as hostages. These actions are morally repugnant not merely to non-Muslim Westerners but also to most Lebanese Shiite Muslims, who regard both the kidnapping of innocents and the suicide committed by *intihari* bombers as violations of Islamic law. The "Open Letter of Hezbollah to the Oppressed in Lebanon and the World" published on 16 February 1985, however, identified the *intihari* bombers of Islamic Jihad with its own "martyrs." Subsequent statements by Hezbollah spiritual leader Muhammad Hussein Fadlullah and Islamic Amal leader Hussein Musawi denying knowledge of Islamic Jihad must be understood in the context of the Shiite practice of *taqiyah*, which permits dissimulation before nonbelievers on matters affecting the physical security and survival of the Shiite community.

2. Munazzamat al Jihad—Also known simply as "Jihad," this was the Sunnite Muslim fundamentalist group in Egypt responsible for the assassination of Anwar Sadat on 6 October 1981. This group was an offshoot of Tahrir al Islami (q.v.), itself an offshoot of the Muslim Brotherhood (q.v.). It is not directly connected with the Shiite militia Islamic Jihad of Lebanon (See Munazzamat al Jihad).

3. Islamic Jihad of Palestine—During the British Mandate in Palestine, the increase of Jewish settlers in the 1930s prompted an Arab backlash involving riots in Jerusalem and attacks on isolated Jewish settlements. The Arab riots were directed also against the British as protectors of the Zionist settlers. Muslim resistance to British control and Jewish settlement took the form of the guerrilla group known as Islamic Jihad formed in the 1920s by Sheikh Izzidin al Qasim who led attacks on both Jewish settlers and British mandatory authorities until he was finally killed by the British in 1936.

Islamic Jihad continued to exist underground during the

remaining mandate and into the period following the creation of the State of Israel. This organization has survived by adopting a cellular structure and a system of identifying members by six-digit numbers rather than names. Islamic Jihad remained distinct and aloof from the branch of the Muslim Brotherhood that entered Palestine from Egypt in 1946, which was more reformist than revolutionary in its orientation. By 1984, however, evidence surfaced of collaboration between members of Islamic Jihad and the Muslim Brotherhood. By 1987 this cooperation grew to include coordination with the more secular PLO in planning the protests in the occupied West bank and Gaza Strip that evolved into the intifada.

On 16 October 1986, two Palestinians made a grenade attack on a military swearing-in ceremony at the Wailing Wall in Jerusalem, killing 1 and wounding 68 others. This action was claimed by the Palestinian Islamic Jihad, although several other groups also claimed credit. On 4 February 1990, Palestinian Jihad members machine-gunned an Israeli tour bus en route to Cairo, killing 11 and wounding 17 others. On 28 May 1990, Islamic Jihad bombed a Jerusalem street, killing one and wounding nine passersby.

There has been no evidence of links between the largely Sunnite Islamic Jihad organization indigenous to Palestine and the Iranian-sponsored Hezbollah Shiite militia of Lebanon, which also uses ''Islamic Jihad'' as its nom de guerre. Islamic Jihad was the only Palestinian Islamic fundamentalist group that advocated the use of armed struggle against Israel prior to the outbreak of the intifada. Since then, however, Islamic Jihad has fully cooperated with the PLO-dominated Unified National Leadership (UNL). By contrast, the Hamas movement, having grown out of the Palestinian Muslim Brotherhood, has been much more inclined to compete with, and even fight against, more secular Palestinian groups active in the intifada. Since the Persian Gulf War in 1991 Islamic Jihad has been drawing closer to Iran while Hamas has grown aloof towards Iran.

4. Islamic Jihad for the Liberation of Palestine—Another nom de guerre of Hezbollah (q.v.) used when three American professors, Robert Polhill, Alan Steen, and Jesse Turner, and U.S. resident, Mithileshwar Singh, were kidnapped in Beirut on 24 January 1987. Singh was released on 3 October 1988; Polhill, on 22 April 1990; Turner on 22 October 1991; and Steen on 3 December 1991.

ISLAMIC JIHAD IN THE HIJAZ. Also known as Hezbollah in the Hijaz, this group and the Soldiers of Justice (q.v.) are both Iranian state-sponsored Shiite groups based in Lebanon that have the revolutionary goal of overthrowing the Saudi Arabian monarchy in favor of an Iranian-style Islamic Republic. The previously unheard of Islamic Jihad in the Hijaz group claimed credit on 7 January 1989 for the murder of Salah Abdullah al Maliki, the third secretary of the Saudi Arabian embassy in Bangkok, Thailand, who was shot while walking home on 4 January 1989. Their announced motive was to avenge the death of four of its members executed on 30 September 1988.

In this announcement the group identified itself as being, in effect, an extension of Islamic Jihad, also known as Hezbollah, a Shiite militia in Lebanon composed of Lebanese, Iraqi, and Kuwaiti Shiites under the tutelage of the Islamic Revolutionary Guards contingent in Lebanon. It is doubtful that the group has much of a grass roots organization in Saudi Arabia itself, much less in the Hijaz proper. Estimates of the Shiite population of Saudi Arabia range from 100,000 to 600,000 out of a population of perhaps 10 million largely Wahhabi Sunnite Muslims. Most of these Shiites live on the shores of the Persian Gulf in the eastern province of al Hasa. Due to a conscious policy of exclusion of Shiites from the western province of Hijaz practiced since Ottoman times until the present, there are virtually no Shiites living in the Hijaz.

Antiregime violence by pro-Khomeini Shiites in the Hijaz

has invariably been the work of Iranian or Kuwaiti Shiite pilgrims present in the Hijaz only for the Hajj rituals. The Islamic Republic of Iran had been engaged in agitational propaganda against the Saudi dynasty during the Hajj pilgrimages from 1979 until 31 July 1987 when Iranian-incited riots killed over 400 people in Mecca. The following day the official Islamic Republic News Agency of Iran announced that a new group, the "Hezbollah of the Hijaz," had vowed vengeance against the Saudi regime for the events in Mecca. The same day, an organized mob attacked the Saudi Embassy in Tehran causing the Saudi political attaché to fall from an upper story; he later died from his injuries. On 15 August 1987, a gas plant in Arabia was sabotaged. While the Iranian regime hailed this as the work of "Hezbollah in the Hijaz," the Saudis maintained it was not the work of native nationals. On 26 August 1987, Hezbollah in the Hijaz announced it intended to attack U.S. and Saudi interests to force the removal of "U.S. bases" from Arabia. On 3 September 1987, the Commander of the Islamic Revolutionary Guards Corps (IRGC, q.v.) announced that Hezbollah in the Hijaz was planning to attack U.S. and Saudi interests worldwide. Given that both the names "Hezbollah" and "Islamic Jihad" have been given to the same militia under IRGC direction within Lebanon, the role of the IRGC Commander in acting as a spokesman for Hezbollah in the Hijaz strongly indicates that the latter group was also under IRGC direction and most likely identical with the group that later identified itself as Islamic Jihad in the Hijaz.

In 1987, four indigenous Saudi Shiites who set fire to the Sadaf petrochemical plant in Jubayl in al Hasa province were arrested and executed by the Saudis. On 26 April 1988, Arabia severed diplomatic relations with Iran and greatly reduced the size of the Hajj pilgrimage contingent permitted to the Iranians. On 21 September 1989, Saudi Arabia executed 16 Kuwaitis for having carried out two bombings on behalf of Iran in the July 1988 Hajj season, from which Iranian participation had been largely excluded. Later on 30

September 1988, four more Saudi Shiites were executed for sabotage in the eastern province, which became the pretext for the murder of Maliki, the third secretary of the Saudi Arabian embassy in Thailand.

While the eastern province is far more valuable economically and far more vulnerable given the larger concentration of Shiites and the maritime proximity of Iran, the western province is far more valuable in the eyes of the Iranian regime as holding the two most holy cities in Islam, Mecca and Medina. Whoever rules over the Hijaz may claim the title of "Protector of the Two Holy Places," which implies a preeminence among Muslim rulers. Khomeini and other Shiite clergymen have resented Saudi possession of the Hijaz since this gives preeminence to a dynasty linked to the Wahhabi sect within Islam, which anathematized the Shiites as heretics and apostates and which sacked and destroyed Shiite shrines in Karbala, Iraq, and the Arabian Peninsula as well as killing Shiite pilgrims in the nineteenth and early twentieth centuries. Therefore the implied claim that Khomeini had indigenous followers within the Hijaz could serve to boost the prestige of Iran's credentials of Islamic leadership throughout the Muslim world.

The Islamic Jihad in the Hijaz group also claimed responsibility for the killing of a Saudi diplomat in Ankara, Turkey, on 21 October 1988, and the wounding of another in Karachi, Pakistan in December 1988. The Islamic Jihad in the Hijaz, like the Soldiers of Justice, probably represents operations being carried out by the same members of Hezbollah under Iranian auspices or else even involving the direct actions of Iranian special forces units.

ISLAMIC LIBERATION ORGANIZATION. Name used by Sunnite Muslims in Lebanon responsible for the 30 September 1985 abduction and hostage holding of four Soviet diplomats. Outside the Soviet Embassy in West Beirut, armed gunmen abducted the Soviet commercial attaché and Embassy second secretary at gunpoint while other gunmen abducted the cultural attaché and Embassy physician on another nearby street.

A group identifying itself as the Islamic Liberation Organization (ILO) contacted Agence France-Press and demanded that the Soviets pressure Syria to cease their offensive against the Sunnite Muslim Tawhid group in Tripoli, which had been besieged by the Syrians for the preceding two weeks. The group sent photographs of the recently abducted Soviet diplomats and threatened to kill them if their demands were not met. On 2 October, the ILO killed Arkady Katkov, the cultural attaché, who had been wounded trying to escape and whose wounds had developed gangrene. On 4 October, the Soviets evacuated their Embassy in response to an ILO threat to car bomb the premises.

The Soviets contacted Sunnite and Shiite community leaders to intercede with the ILO. On 30 October 1985, the three remaining hostages were released, the Syrian offensive against Tripoli having been played out in the intervening four weeks.

ISLAMIC REVOLUTIONARY GUARDS CORPS. The IRGC of the Islamic Republic of Iran is a state-run paramilitary organization charged by Article 150 of the 1979 Iranian Constitution with "defending the (Islamic) Revolution and safeguarding its achievements." Domestically, in addition to protecting the regime from possible coup attempts by the older branches of the Iranian armed forces, it has also served as an instrument of state terror and repression. In the war fronts of the Iran-Iraq war (1980–1988) and outside Iran, in Lebanon and the Persian Gulf, it serves a revolutionary purpose in assisting "Islamic liberation movements" to oppose conservative regimes and in attacking U.S., Israeli, and other Western interests.

The current IRGC was officially organized by decree of Ayatollah Khomeini on 5 May 1979, but had existed in rudimentary form just before the 1978–1979 revolution. Some Iranian Muslim student activists abroad had either served with Amal units in Lebanon or had undergone PLO guerrilla training there and elsewhere. With the ransacking of police and army armories during the Iranian revolution, various Shiite clerics armed their bodyguards and key lay followers who thereby became *pasdars,* or revolutionary guards. Given the lack of control over looted arsenals following the collapse of the Shah's government and given the presence of opportunistic armed leftist and rival Muslim groups, such as the Mujahideen-i Khalq (q.v.), the revolutionary regime saw fit to consolidate and better control a near-chaotic security situation. At the time of the May 1979 decree, there were only around 4,000 *pasdars.*

Many parallels have been noted between the development of the IRGC and Nazi paramilitary organizations. Like the first storm troopers the original *pasdars* were largely unemployed and uneducated street ruffians. Like the Waffen-SS the IRGC was originally intended to be a political militia with internal security duties, above all to counter any attempt at a military coup by officers in the regular armed forces having monarchist or secular nationalist sympathies. With the invasion of Iran by Iraq in September 1980, the IRGC changed into a more regular military force having a hierarchical command structure, logistical support, and heavy armaments. Also the numbers of IRGC swelled from about 25,000 at the outset of hostilities to around 350,000 as of 1986. With the intensification of intraregime rivalries between nationalists and fundamentalists, the IRGC was purged of leftist and more secularist elements until it stood solidly "in the line of the Imam" against perceived moderates such as Iranian President Bani Sadr deposed in June 1981. The IRGC played an essential role in organizing the street mobs of *hezbollahi*s, members of the "party of God," in a wave of regime terror against internal opponents and in collapsing the attempted insurgency of the Mujahideen-i Khalq in June 1981.

Beginning in February 1981, the IRGC was ordered by Khomeini to establish an "Islamic Liberation Movements" department. This unit established guerrilla training camps for Islamic activists from other Muslim countries outside Tehran and Qum and also dispatched IRGC units to Lebanon where training camps were established in the Bekaa valley where the Lebanese Hezbollah militia were organized. Officers and specialists of the regular Iranian armed forces special operations unit were induced to join the IRGC and apparently were instrumental in planning and supervising the truck bombings of the U.S. Embassy, U.S. Marines barracks, and French military forces headquarters in Lebanon during the period from April–October 1983.

In November 1982, the Islamic Republic sought to put the "revolutionary foundations," such as the IRGC, on a more regular footing with older, more bureaucratic offices of the government by giving each foundation its own ministry. Rivalries between the IRGC and the regular armed forces have been lessened, however, mainly by the experience of shared dangers and duties during the Iran-Iraq war. The factional rivalries of fundamentalist clergymen within the Iranian regime were reflected within the IRGC, as clannish and personalist ties between *pasdars* and clerical patrons continued to be felt in spite of extensive indoctrination of recruits, purging of undesirables, and ideological supervision by clerical political officers. According to the research of Kenneth Katzman, however, in the post-Khomeini period the IRGC has succeeded in quelling its internal factionalism and represents the strongest single institution within the Islamic Republic today.

ISLAMIC REVOLUTIONARY ORGANIZATION. Like the Islamic Jihad in the Hijaz (q.v.) and the Soldiers of Justice (q.v.), this appears to be an Iranian state-sponsored Shiite group based in Lebanon having the revolutionary goal of overthrowing the Saudi Arabian monarchy in favor of an Iranian-style Islamic Republic. The name of this group is used to claim responsibility for acts of sabotage carried out in the eastern oil-producing province of Saudi Arabia and has been used in Iranian Arabic-language broadcasts of anti-Saudi propaganda.

ISLAMIC SALVATION FRONT. Known also by its French acronym of FIS, the *Jabha al Islamiyyah li-Inqadh,* is a nonstate Islamic fundamentalist group that seeks to create an Islamic regime in Algeria under which religious and political affairs would both be governed by the Shariah, that is, the sacred law of Islam. It was the main underground Islamic fundamentalist party in Algeria at the time the National Liberation Front (q.v.) took steps towards democratization in 1989. Under Algeria's new national constitution, adopted on 23 February 1989, multiparty provincial and municipal elections were held on 12 June 1990, the first freely-contested elections since Algerian independence. The Islamic Salvation Front led by Abbasi Madani (b. 1931), the first new political party to be formed under the new electoral law, gained majorities in 32 of the 48 provincial governments and in 853 of the 1,539 municipalities. In the first round of parliamentary elections held on 26 December 1991, the Islamic Salvation Front won 188 of 231 races, although 199 seats required run-off elections.

Concerned over the apparent ascendence of the fundamentalists, secular nationalists within the government and armed forces staged an internal coup on 11 January 1992, forcing the resignation of President Chadhli Benjedid. The 5-member High State Council formed to govern the country cancelled the runoff parliamentary elections and outlawed the Islamic Salvation Front. An Islamic fundamentalist insurgent group, the Armed Islamic Movement, believed to be the armed wing of the Islamic Salvation Front, assassinated Algerian President Muhammad Boudiaf on 29 June 1992. He had headed the five-member junta that had assumed power. The Algerian government declared a 12-month state of emergency and proceeded with a crack-down on FIS, arresting over 7,000 supporters and killing about 270 before the end of 1992. FIS has retaliated not only with several armed attacks on Algerian officials and their security forces but also with attacks on non-Muslim residents of Algeria as well as unveiled women. Algeria has accused Iran of rendering moral and material support to the FIS in the current civil unrest.

ISLAMIC TENDENCY MOVEMENT. The *Nahdha* (literally, "resurgence"), or Islamic Renaissance Movement, is a nonstate Islamic fundamentalist group that seeks to replace existing secular governments in Tunisia with an Islamic regime under which religious and political affairs would both be governed by the Shariah, that is, the sacred law of Islam. The group enjoys the support of the Sudanese government, which is dominated by the National Islamic Front affiliated with the Muslim Brotherhood (q.v.), as well as Iran, which is providing military training for Nahdha members in Islamic Revolutionary Guard camps within the Sudan.

During the 1980s, this group emerged among university students and middle-class Tunisians who had been moved by the success of the Islamic revolution in Iran but also had been strongly influenced by the Muslim Brotherhood, which has maintained an underground presence in Tunisia since at least the 1950s. Much of the impetus for this movement comes also in reaction to the strongly secularist policies of Habib Bourgeiba, president from 1956 until he was deposed in 1987. Under Bourgeiba, French was preferred over Arabic as the language of government and commerce, the European workweek and calendar system remained in effect, Islamic prayers were banned from the national radio and television service, and members of Islamic groups such as Nahdha were persecuted by police harassment.

Nahdha activists undertook protests against the Tunisian tourism industry, accommodating 2 million Western tourists each year, as promoting the use of alcohol, libertine sex, and further erosion of Islamic values. On 15 May 1987, the Tunisian government accused Iran of promoting local fundamentalists through its diplomatic mission and of meddling in

Tunisian domestic politics. Several Iranian diplomats were declared persona non grata while Nahdha spokesmen denied any ties to Iran.

Following Bourgeiba's ouster in 1987 by Zayn al Abidin Bin Ali, the new president tried to identify his government more with Islam by relaxing the restrictions enforced by his predecessor. Nahdha was invited to participate as a legal political party but was forbidden to identify itself as an Islamic party. On 22 May 1991, Tunisian security forces arrested around 300 members of Nahdha, of which 100 were members of Tunisia's armed forces, including officers of the rank of major, for plotting to establish an Islamic regime through a military coup. Tunisian police arrested members of armed Nahdha groups in December 1991 following alleged coup conspiracies in September and early December 1991. Cooperation between Algeria and Tunisia in containing their Islamic fundamentalist movements led Algeria to expel the leader of the Nahdha movement, Rashid el Ghanoushi, who went to the Sudan. Diplomatic relations between the Sudan and Tunisia were all but severed in October 1991 in protest of the Sudan's renewing a diplomatic passport for Rashid el Ghanoushi.

- J -

JAPANESE RED ARMY. The JRA is a group of Japanese anarchistic leftists intent on igniting a worldwide revolution through terrorist actions enjoying foreign state sponsorship. The JRA has maintained cooperative ties since 1971 with the North Korean regime and the Libyan regime as well as having a long-term relationship with the Popular Front for the Liberation of Palestine (PFLP, q.v.). Since the JRA maintains its center and training camp in the Syrian-controlled part of the Bekaa valley in Lebanon, Syria may also be considered one of its state sponsors. The Japanese name for this "Red Army" is *Sekigun*, "Japanese Red

Army'' being *Nippon Sekigun*. Since May 1986, the JRA has been using the name ''Anti-Imperialist International Brigades'' as either a new cover or as a nom de guerre.

Similar in many ways to the German Red Army Faction (q.v.), the JRA has rationalized its terrorism in revolutionary leftist terms but appears to pursue terrorist violence as an end in itself rather than as a strategy to achieve revolution. The JRA can be considered ''leftist'' insofar as it seeks to smash capitalism, professes the superiority of a socialist state, and often uses Marxist jargon. Yet they must also be considered anarchistic insofar as they have limited their program to destroying the existing capitalist states rather than building the foundations of some successor socialist state. Often the JRA has claimed to seek the role of serving as a rallying point for similar anarchistic leftists in Japan, opposing Japanese and Western ''imperialism,'' and establishing a People's Republic in Japan. The venue of most of its actions are outside of Japan, however, and even when the JRA has used hostage taking or hijacking to force the Japanese government to release comrades imprisoned within Japan, such compliance tends to be a relatively low-visibility event. Therefore, it is unclear how the JRA terrorist program can expect to influence public opinion within Japan.

The JRA emerged from an internal purge of the Japanese Red Army Faction in 1970–1971, leading to the murders of several members. These murders led to a police crackdown in Japan, forcing many members of the JRA Faction to flee abroad. A JRA Faction liaison with the PFLP in Lebanon, Fusako Shigenobu, invited other fugitive members to join her there where the JRA was formed. Shigenubo remains the leader of the JRA.

From 1971 to 1991, the JRA accomplished 17 noteworthy actions and planned, or attempted, at least 9 major actions that were aborted. Of the 16 successful actions, 12 percent (=2) were armed attacks using knives, samurai swords, small-arms or automatic weapons; 17 percent (=3) were hijackings; 24 percent (=4) were bombings; 12 percent (=2) were hostage seizures; and 35 percent (=6) were rocket attacks. It should be noted that hijackings and hostage seizures occurred from 1971 to 1977 involving hand-held weapons and direct contact with victims. Such tactics seemed legitimated in Japanese culture by the martial Bushido tradition emphasizing personal valor in direct confrontation and actually helped boost the prestige of the group within Japan. Then there was a hiatus in JRA activity from late 1977 to mid-1986 after which the JRA began relying instead on bombings and rocket firings in which the JRA members would be quite remote from the target and could escape more easily. The change in tactics helps preserve in working order an organization that, given its own remoteness from Japan, has had difficulties recruiting new members. Also the JRA has been, and remains, a rather small group, numbering at most perhaps 25 members, whose identities have become fairly well known among police organizations throughout the world, making it more imperative for them to avoid capture.

The most notorious of the JRA actions was the massacre of 26 people at Israel's Lod Airport in 30 May 1972, carried out by three JRA gunmen on behalf of the PFLP. The sole surviving gunman, Kozo Okamoto, was imprisoned in Israel until 1985 when he was released in exchange for Israeli prisoners and allowed to fly to Libya where he was accorded a hero's welcome. On 4 August 1975, 10 JRA gunmen seized the U.S. Consulate in Kuala Lumpur and held 52 hostages, threatening to kill them if 7 imprisoned JRA members in Japan were not released. Only five of those JRA members released opted to leave, flying to Libya via Kuala Lumpur. On 14 May 1986, they detonated a car bomb outside of the Canadian embassy and launched rockets against the U.S. and Japanese embassies in Djakarta from a nearby hotel. Fingerprints found in the room with the launcher matched those of a known JRA member, although credit was taken in the name of the ''Anti-Imperialist International Brigade.'' This resumption of JRA activity occurred within a month following the U.S. retaliatory raid on Libya, a circumstance that along with JRA members' choice of Libya as a sanctuary tends to suggest Libyan state-sponsorship of this group. On 9 June 1987, a similar rocket attack coupled with a car bombing was made against the U.S. and British embassies in Rome, causing but minor damage. On 14 April 1988, the second anniversary of the Libya raid, the "Jihad Brigades" claimed credit for bombing a U.S. servicemen's club in Naples in which five people were killed, but the suspects seized in connection with this bombing were also JRA members. Two days earlier Yu Kikumura, a JRA member, was arrested in New Jersey in possession of three powerful bombs. It is believed that he was supposed to bomb some U.S. military facility at the same time as the Naples bombing to mark the second anniversay of the U.S. raid. On 8 January 1990, the JRA attacked the Imperial palaces in Kyoto and Tokyo simultaneously using homemade rockets.

The change in tactics from direct personal combat to the use of remotely triggered rockets and bombs has made future JRA attacks potentially much more lethal. Evidence gathered from arrests of JRA members has shown that the group has an extensive support network, generous finances, and an ability to move members freely throughout the world. Despite the recent collapse of world communism there is little to suggest that members of the JRA have renounced their terrorist program.

JEWISH DEFENSE LEAGUE. The JDL was a Jewish self-defense movement that began with the limited goals of protecting orthodox Jewish neighborhoods in New York City from depredations by young black and Puerto Rican hoodlums and to protest local instances of anti-Semitism. Eventually the JDL embraced a universal program of fighting for Jewish interests worldwide. The group was self-sustaining and lacked any support from mainstream Jewish organizations in the United States or from the State of Israel.

The JDL was founded in 1968 by Rabbi Meir Kahane, who

began to organize young Jewish men as vigilantes to protect Jews and Jewish businesses in the Williamsburg and Crown Heights areas of Brooklyn and elsewhere in the New York City area. Within a year the group had graduated from vigilantism and demonstrations against alleged anti-Semites to burglarizing the files of the PLO U.N. Mission and launching attacks on Soviet diplomatic, trade, and tourism offices and personnel. According to the FBI, the JDL was responsible for at least 37 terrorist acts in the United States in the period from 1968–1983, while the *International Terrorism: Attributes of Terrorist Events* (ITERATE) database developed on behalf of the United States Central Intelligence Agency by Edward F. Mickolus recorded 50 such incidents from 1968–1987, making the JDL second only to the Puerto Rican FALN (q.v.) as the major domestic terrorist group. Nonetheless the JDL is a legally incorporated political action group and has officially disavowed responsibility for any violent actions carried out by its members. Bombings accounted for 78 percent of all JDL terrorist activities; shootings accounted for 16 percent; while arson attacks, vandalism, kidnapping, threats, and verbal harassment accounted for the rest.

From 1969 to 1985 the JDL targeted mainly the representatives of governments perceived to be anti-Israeli or anti-Semitic, most of which were directed against Soviet targets. Thus the JDL bombed the San Francisco branch of the Iranian Bank Melli on 26 January 1981 and bombed the Iraqi U.N. Mission on 28 April 1982 to protest the mistreatment of Jews in those two countries. The JDL once bombed the office of impresario Sol Hurok, who helped arrange performances of Soviet ballet troupes in the United States, which caused the death of one employee. For the most part, these attacks seemed intended to intimidate but not to kill their victims. Beginning late in 1985, however, the targeting shifted to individuals suspected of being anti-Israeli or anti-Semitic, and the attack mode became much more lethal. On 11 October 1985, the Los Angeles offices of the Arab-American

Anti-Discrimination Committee (ADC) was bombed, killing the ADC director Alex Odeh, who had sought to rationalize the actions of the hijackers of the *Achille Lauro* on a local newscast the previous evening. On 15 August 1985, a sixty-one-year-old Waffen-SS veteran, Tsherim Soobzokov, was bombed at his Paterson, N.J., home and later died of his wounds. In such attacks an anonymous caller would claim the action in the name of the JDL, and afterward an official JDL spokesman would disavow the group's responsibility. In 1987 several JDL members were convicted on a variety of criminal charges, and since then there has been no record of JDL terrorist activity.

As the JDL was very much the personal creation of Rabbi Kahane, following his emigration to Israel in 1971 the group began to experience factionalism. The day immediately following the bombing murder of Alex Odeh, Kahane announced his resignation as JDL leader. Despite the national prominence of the JDL, this group had poor to acrimonious relations with more conventional Jewish political and social organizations, such as B'nai B'rith's Anti-Defamation League, which regarded the JDL as a marginal group and an embarrassment to the American Jewish community. Without the leadership of Rabbi Kahane, who was shot dead by an Egyptian fundamentalist on 5 November 1990 in New York, the prospects for a revival of the JDL appear dim.

While living in Israel, Kahane founded the Kach Party, an ultranationalist group favoring expulsion of the Arabs from both Israel and the occupied territories. Following his death another group, Kahane Chai (Kahane Lives), split off from the Kach group. Many former JDL members who followed Kahane's example in emigrating to Israel joined these groups, often living in settlements within the Occupied Territories. On 25 February 1994, a Kach Party member and former JDL activist, Dr. Baruch Goldstein, opened fire on Palestinian Arabs in the mosque built over the Tomb of the Patriarchs in Hebron, killing at least 29 and wounding scores more before he himself was killed. This incident led to anti-Israeli rioting throughout the occupied territories and stymied the peace negotiations underway between the PLO and Israel. On 13 March 1994, the Israeli government banned both the Kach and Kahane Chai groups in an effort to stem the furor caused by the massacre in Hebron.

JIHAD. The term *jihad* is an Arabic verbal noun derived from *jahada*, meaning "to struggle," that is, to struggle with something that is disagreeable or else against something that is wrong. While "holy war" is not a literal translation, it does summarize the essential idea of jihad. The Muslim jurists give the most general definition of jihad as the Muslim believers' exerting their abilities, talents, and power in struggling in the path of God using their resources of life, property, speech, and all available instruments to make the Word of God prevail in this world. Muslim jurists distinguish between a "greater jihad," which is the struggle against the world, the flesh, and the devil in the spiritual realm, and a "lesser jihad" consisting of open physical warfare with the enemies of Islam or of the Muslims. In the course of the revival of Islamic fundamentalism (q.v.) the doctrine of jihad has been invoked to justify resistance, including terrorist actions, to combat "un-Islamic" regimes, or purported external enemies of Islam, such as Israel and the United States.

The classical doctrine of jihad did not necessarily exclude its use to spread the Islamic religion by force of arms since the classical Muslim thinkers ibn Rushd and ibn Khaldun both accepted this interpretation. Most modern jurists, however, have preferred an interpretation of jihad comparable to that of purely defensive warfare. Islamic fundamentalists, such as Sayyid Qutb, other members of the Muslim Brotherhood (q.v.), and members of the Munazzamat al Jihad (q.v.) group that murdered Anwar Sadat, have maintained that the object of jihad was the full enactment of the sacred law of Islam, rather than defense or conquest as such, and that there was no reason to limit the role of jihad merely to defensive warfare.

The Muslim jurists make two other distinctions regarding jihad important to understanding its possible connection with terrorism. Ordinarily jihad is a collective, rather than a personal, obligation. If a Muslim nation undertakes jihad lawfully, the duty of waging jihad is discharged by the Muslim army and its commander on behalf of the entire Muslim community. The conditions under which this form of jihad may be lawfully initiated and exercised are remarkably similar to those governing the Judeo-Christian Just War doctrine: Jihad can be declared only by the competent religious-cum-secular authorities. Recourse to jihad is permissible only after all other diplomatic channels for redress of grievances have been exhausted. During jihad, noncombatant enemy civilians may not be attacked, killed, or taken prisoner nor may the Muslim army engage in random destruction of enemy property. Muslim soldiers and officers must observe proportionality in their defensive and retaliatory attacks. Such a definition of jihad quite rules out most of what might be considered terrorist actions.

In the case of an invasion of a Muslim land by non-Muslim forces, however, jihad ceases to be a collective obligation, becoming instead the personal obligation of every Muslim man, woman, and child, whether old or young, infirm or well. Given the disproportionate force enjoyed by the invading army over that possessed by the individual believer, upon whom waging jihad becomes religiously obligatory, a greater allowance may be extended to the individual, in effect exempting him or her from the usual limits placed on lawful warfare. Islamic fundamentalist groups like Hezbollah (q.v.) in Lebanon, Hamas (q.v.) in the occupied territories of the West Bank and Gaza Strip, or Munazzamat al Jihad (q.v.) in Egypt tend to view their nation as being occupied by an invading un-Islamic power, even in the case of a nominally Muslim government such as that of Sadat's Egypt. This in turn allows them to claim the right to wage jihad without the authorization of competent religious authorities and by means that may be described as terroristic.

Despite the religious technicalities that limit the correct application of the term jihad to only a few situations, the tendency of secular Pan-Arab nationalism to exploit Islamic religious symbols and sentiments whenever expedient has led Arab nationalists to misuse the term "jihad" to designate what actually have been wars on behalf of Arab nationalism rather than Islam proper. During the 1990–1991 Persian Gulf conflict, Iraqi President Saddam Hussein tried to rally Arab support for himself by describing his war as a "jihad" against the West and Israel. Saddam Hussein, however, lacked the moral and religious credentials of an authority competent to declare jihad nor could he invoke it credibly to defend Iraq's usurpation of another Muslim land. Interestingly during the entire course of the Iran-Iraq war, the Islamic Republic of Iran never described its war with Iraq in terms of jihad but only as a *jang-i difai al muqaddis*, that is, a "war of holy defense against aggression." Shiite fundamentalist Muslims have been less inclined to use the term jihad than their Sunni counterparts due to their belief that jihad proper can be declared only by one of their apostolic Imams.

JUNE SECOND MOVEMENT. This group was an anarchistic leftist group formed in West Berlin in 1971 that sought to resist the liberal democratic establishment in West Berlin through bombings, bank robberies, kidnappings, and murders. The group is named after the anniversary of Benno Ohnejorg's death, who was killed in a demonstration against the visiting Shah of Iran in Berlin on 2 June 1967.

The group bombed the British Yacht Club in Berlin on 2 February 1972, killing a German attendant. On 10 November 1974, members of this group shot and killed West Berlin Chief Justice Günter von Drenkmann in reprisal for the death by suicide of a June Second member in jail. On 27 February 1975, the group kidnapped the leader of the Berlin Christian Democrats, Peter Lorenz, who was released in exchange for the freeing of five anarchistic leftist terrorists who were allowed to leave for South Yemen.

The group was closely associated with the Red Army Faction (q.v.) and after the majority of its members had been arrested by the end of the 1970s, the remainder were absorbed into the RAF group.

JUSTICE COMMANDOS OF THE ARMENIAN GENO-CIDE. The JCAG is an Armenian nationalist revolutionary organization founded in 1975 seeking to re-establish an independent Armenian state within the territory occupied by the former Republic of Armenia during World War I within eastern Turkey. It has pursued this goal through attacks on Turkish diplomats and economic interests outside Turkey in the belief that Turkey bears responsibility for the slaughter of Armenians and the destruction of the Armenian Republic that occurred in 1915.

JCAG differs from the other major Armenian terrorist group, the Armenian Secret Army for the Liberation of Armenia (ASALA, q.v.) in two important respects: First, JCAG is primarily nationalistic rather than Marxist-Leninist. Therefore it has relied almost exclusively on private support from Armenian communities rather than state-sponsorship from countries hostile to Turkey. Second, the members of JCAG, being very Westernized nationalists, value Western and world public opinion highly and therefore take pains to avoid harming non-Turkish nationals mindful of the poten-tial harm such actions could render the Armenian cause. Nonetheless JCAG has conducted attacks on Turkish targets within the United States, making themselves felt there as a very serious terrorist threat to law and order.

An analysis of 29 noteworthy actions by JCAG in the period from 1975–1983 showed that 52 percent (=15) in-volved assassination of Turkish diplomats, 2 of them in the United States and another in Canada; 45 percent (=13) involved bombings and arsons of Turkish diplomatic, tour-ism, and commercial offices; while 3 percent (=1) repre-sented an unfulfilled threat against Turkish targets. JCAG terrorism within the United States took place entirely from

January 1982 to May 1982: On 29 January 1982, Kemal Arikan, consul general of Turkey in Los Angeles, was shot and killed as he was driving home. On 22 March 1982, the offices of Orhan Gunduz, honorary Turkish consul general in Boston, were firebombed and he himself was shot and killed on 4 May 1982. A conspiracy to bomb the home of the honorary consul general of Turkey in Philadelphia was foiled in October 1982. Since then nothing further has been heard of JCAG either in the United States or abroad, a curious fact that requires some explanation.

On 15 July 1983, the ASALA bombed Orly Airport near Paris, killing 7 and wounding over 60 bystanders. This event led to a crisis within ASALA as many members protested what they believed to be counterproductive violence against non-Turkish nationals. The dissenting faction became known as ASALA-Revolutionary Movement, to be distinguished from the mainline ASALA-Militant. Beginning also in July 1983, the name "Justice Commandos of the Armenian Genocide" dropped from use while actions similar to those of JCAG began to be claimed in the name of the "Armenian Revolutionary Army" (ARA). Many analysts believe that the JCAG merely changed its name to ARA and that it is essentially the same organization. It is also possible that members of ASALA-RM and JCAG may have amalgamated themselves into the new ARA. An analysis of 7 actions by ARA in 1983–1985 show that 43 percent (=3) of these involved assassinations; 14 percent (=2) involved hostage and siege situations; while one car bombing and an unfilled threat each accounted for 14 percent of ARA activities. While ARA made the same disclaimers as had JCAG that it intended no harm to non-Turkish bystanders in contrast to earlier JCAG operations, at least six non-Turkish nationals were killed as a result of these operations.

In fact, very little is known about the memberships of these groups, their internal structures, or their relations with possible sponsor states or with other terrorist groups. What little is known about the Armenian groups indicates that they have been involved in factional disputes and internecine fighting that has reduced their effective presence as terrorist groups since the mid-1980s.

- K -

KANAK SOCIALIST NATIONAL LIBERATION FRONT. The *Front de Libération Nationale Kanake Socialiste* (FLNKS) is a coalition of several proindependence political parties representing the interests of the Kanaks, that is, the Melanesian natives of New Caledonia, as opposed to the interests of settlers of French or other origins. The FLNKS coalition includes the Union Calédonienne, the oldest and largest Kanak party; the quasi-Marxist Parti de Libération Kanak (PALIKA); the socialist Union Progressiste Melanésienne; and the Front Uni de Libération Kanak (FULK) led by Yann Celene Uregei.

The agenda of FLNKS is revolutionary since attaining the twin goals of independence for New Caledonia and sovereignty for the indigenous Kanaks, who now make up only 44 percent of the archipelago, would entail civil war with the non-Kanak majority. So far terrorist actions by members of FLNKS have been sporadic and limited in their aims, being undertaken either to draw the attention of the French government and public to Kanak aspirations or else to block specific measures believed to threaten Kanak interests.

In late October 1981 three bombings occurred in Paris. The first on October 25 hit Fouquet's restaurant on the Champs-Élysées; the second on October 27 destroyed a car parked at Charles de Gaulle Airport; and the final bombing struck a cinema in downtown Paris. Injuries were sustained only in the last bombing, in which three persons, including a pregnant woman, were hurt. Credit for these attacks was taken by callers claiming to represent the ''Kanak Liberation Front'' or the ''Army for the Liberation of New Caledonia.'' Authorities suspected PALIKA was the responsible group.

In New Caledonia clashes and shooting incidents erupted between Kanaks and French settlers from 30 November to 6 December 1984, leaving 10 dead and 4 wounded. Following these incidents the head of the Union Calédonienne and chief leader of FLNKS, Jean-Marie Tjibaou, confirmed that 17 Kanaks had received paramilitary training in Libya. On 4 May 1987, FLNKS officially disavowed the pro-Libyan stand and statements of FULK leader Uregei who was in Tripoli at that time. Because pending French autonomy plans and regional elections threatened the hope of Kanak sovereignty, independence activists attacked French gendarmes on the small island of Ouvea on 24 April 1988, killing 4 gendarmes and holding the remaining 23 as hostages in a cave. When negotiations failed, French commandos stormed the cave on 5 May, killing 19 and capturing 8 of the Kanak militants. In addition the French soldiers manhandled noncombatant islanders and tortured their Kanak prisoners, three of whom died.

Following this incident Kanak youth from the FULK party attended the Thirteenth World Festival of Youth and Students held in Pyongyang, North Korea, in July 1989, eight of whom remained behind to attend a "training camp" that may have included terrorist tactical instruction. Apart from the potential importation of terrorism into New Caledonia from outside parties, such as Libya and North Korea, intramural tensions within the Kanak community also portend political violence or terrorism, as became evident in the assassination of the politically moderate Kanak leader Jean-Marie Tjibaou on 5 May 1989. Tjibaou went to Ouvea to attend the anniversary commemoration of the deaths of those Kanaks killed by French commandos a year before. Because Tjibaou's accompanying deputy, Yeiwene, was viewed by the Ouvea islanders as a pro-French traitor, both Yeiwene and Tjibaou were assassinated by relatives of those killed or tortured by the French commandos. As about 20 to 30 percent of the Kanak population has consistently favored retaining the union with France and as the Kanaks will lack the majority needed to carry the referendum on Caledonian independence scheduled for 1998, it seems likely that tensions between Kanaks and settlers and among the Kanaks themselves will worsen and so increase the potential for terrorist incidents.

KANSAI REVOLUTIONARY ARMY. Name of covert action group of Chukaku-Ha. (See Chukaku-Ha)

KHMER ROUGE. Originally founded under Vietnamese sponsorship in 1951, the Khmer Communist Party is a revolutionary group that sought to create a socialist state in Cambodia following the Maoist model of guerrilla warfare and cultural revolution. The name *Khmer Rouge* was a coinage of Prince Sihanouk, who alternatively fought and allied himself with the Khmer Rouge led by Pol Pot. After 10 years of fighting the governments of Prince Sihanouk until 1970 and of Lon Nol until 1975, the Khmer Rouge took the capital of Phnom Penh on 17 April 1975.

In an exercise of state terror scarcely matched in its scope and brazenness, the Khmer Rouge initiated a reign of terror and state repression in order to destroy totally pre-Kampuchean Cambodia and to create their ideal agricultural state. The Khmer Rouge depopulated the cities of Cambodia, which they renamed Kampuchea, forcing the urban population into agricultural communes where they were enslaved and brutalized. From 1975 to 1978, the Khmer Rouge systematically overworked and starved the subject population, selectively executing the educated and killing others even for minor breaches of rules. Approximately 1 million people perished under Khmer rule. With the 25 December 1978 invasion of Vietnamese forces lasting until 1989, the Khmer Rouge reverted once again to being a guerrilla army, continuing to terrorize and repress Cambodians in the regions it controlled.

The North Vietnamese and Khmer Rouge remained tactical allies until the fall of the pro-U.S. Lon Nol regime in

1975. By 1978 bitter warfare erupted between the Chinese-backed Khmer Rouge and the Soviet-backed Vietnamese. In 1980, Khieu Samphan replaced Pol Pot as leader and the Khmer Rouge began to receive tacit Thai aid in the form of sanctuary within border areas of Thailand while China supplied weapons, munitions, radios, and medical equipment. The Khmer Rouge fielded about 35,000 combatants and often exerted de facto rule within Cambodian refugee camps within Thailand. Despite the appalling human rights record of the Khmer Rouge, the United Nations and many of its members, including the United States, continued to recognize the Khmer Rouge as the legitimate government of "Democratic Kampuchea" in preference to the puppet regime established there by Vietnam. Following withdrawal of Vietnamese forces in 1989, a coalition government was established in which the Khmer Rouge was invited to participate as the price to be paid to avert the continuation of civil war. Under the United Nations-sponsored settlement concluded on 23 October 1991, the Khmer Rouge agreed to formally dissolve their Khmer Communist Party in December 1991 and to become coalition partners in a civilian government. Many Cambodians continued to fear that these concessions were merely short-term tactical accommodations by an unreconstructed Khmer Rouge not unlike their alliance of convenience with their former enemy Prince Sihanouk. In fact throughout 1992 and 1993 the Khmer Rouge has not ceased its activities as an armed, revolutionary party and has attacked the militias belonging to other coalition partners as well as firing upon members of the U.N. Transitional Authority in Cambodia.

KHOMEINI, RUHALLAH MUSAWI AL. (b. 1902 ?, d. 1989) Under Ayatollah Khomeini's leadership, Iran became a state sponsor of terrorism in the name of fighting the influence of the United States and Israel in both Iran and the remaining Middle East and also in the name of "exporting the Islamic revolution." Khomeini is also a leading theorist of Islamic fundamentalism (q.v.) and has had an impact on the aspirations and actions of Sunnite, as well as Shiite, Muslims worldwide.

Khomeini's involvement in politics began in 1942 with the publication of his *Kashf al Asrar,* "the revelation of secrets," in which he denounced the secularist programs of Reza Shah, who had been deposed by invading British and Soviet forces in late 1941. During 1963 Khomeini began agitation against Muhammad Reza Shah Pahlavi, the son of Reza Shah, who had begun to undertake a modernization and social reform program required by the Kennedy administration as a precondition for U.S. military aid to Iran. Khomeini attacked the status of forces agreement signed between Iran and the United States required for U.S. military aid as a "capitulationist" treaty violating Iranian sovereignty. These speeches led to nationwide rioting on 5 June 1963, in which at least 300 people were killed by security forces. Khomeini was arrested and exiled to Turkey in early 1964. A year later Khomeini moved to Najaf, a Shiite shrine city in Iraq, where he was able to gather some of his clerical and lay followers about him and where he kept in contact with supporters within Iran through contacts with Iranian pilgrims. During the period from 1964–1978, he developed a network of supporters within Iran and wrote his dissertation on Islamic government *Vilayat-i Faqih,* "The Governing Role of the Scholar of Religious Jurisprudence," which became the guiding theory for the theocracy he later established in Iran.

A vituperative attack on Khomeini published by the semi-official Iranian daily *Ittilaat* in November 1977 triggered protests in Tabriz in which police killed several demonstrators. This in turn led to a nationwide round of demonstrations linked to 40-day cycles of mourning for the "martyrs" in which all sources of opposition to the rule of the shah participated, including secular nationalists and leftists. Eventually the demonstrations developed into a national revolution to overthrow the shah in which Khomeini's network played a mobilizing and dominating role.

Following the collapse of the shah's government on 11 February 1979, a transitional period ensued in which liberal nationalists, leftists, and subnational secessionist groups sought to gain political advantages while Khomeini's Islamic fundamentalists sought to consolidate control over government institutions and through their own revolutionary foundations, such as the Islamic Revolutionary Guards Corps (IRGC, q.v.). When liberal nationalists within Iran's Constituent Assembly opposed codification of the principle of Vilayat-i Faqih within Iran's new constitution, Khomeini concluded that the United States was covertly involved in this, as well as in all other, manifestations of opposition to his rule within Iran.

The admission of the ailing deposed shah to the United States for medical treatment in late October 1979 provided Khomeini and his followers with the appropriate pretext to occupy the U.S. Embassy, which they regarded as "the den of espionage and fountainhead of all conspiracies," and to seize in excess of 100 hostages later reduced to 53 U.S. nationals. While the Embassy seizure has been regarded as a state-sponsored act of terrorism, the group of student followers of Khomeini and the accompanying IRGC members were not actually under the control of the nominal provisional government of Iran. Given Khomeini's later designation of this action as the "second (Iranian) revolution" it could also be regarded as a vanguardist coup d'état since it caused the discredited Bazargan provisional government to fall in favor of an Islamic Revolutionary Council more directly under the control of Khomeini. The hostage seizure and U.S. reaction to it precipitated an atmosphere of crisis within Iran, facilitating the mass mobilization of Iranian opinion around Khomeini and the consolidation of effective power in the hands of his supporters.

On 23 March 1980, Khomeini issued a general directive to the Iranian government to "export (the Islamic) revolution" to other Muslim countries. Conferences of Muslim laymen, clerics, and students from throughout the Islamic world were periodically held in Iran to rally support for Iran's revolution among foreign Muslims and to build contacts within other countries. On 5 February 1981, Khomeini decreed the creation of a Liberation Movements Department within the IRGC. The IRGC developed training bases for terrorists outside Tehran, Qum, and Mashhad, while the revolutionary Foundation for the Oppressed, comprising the domestic and overseas offices and assets of the former Pahlavi Foundation, provided a support network for groups operating abroad. In June 1981, Iran began sending IRGC units to the Bekaa valley in Lebanon where training bases for Lebanese Shiites were established and the pro-Iranian militia Hezbollah (q.v.) was established. On 13 December 1981, Bahrain uncovered and quashed an Iranian-sponsored plot to overthrow that country's government in favor of an Islamic republic. During 1983, the U.S. Embassy in West Beirut, the U.S. Marine encampment at Beirut International Airport, and the French and Israeli military headquarters in Lebanon were all car bombed by Hezbollah suicide volunteers. Similar bombings were attempted in Kuwait against the U.S. and French embassies. Beginning also in 1983 but increasing in 1984, Hezbollah undertook a campaign of kidnapping U.S. nationals in Lebanon as a means of removing Western influence from that country. Many of those hostages would be released only by December 1991. At Khomeini's insistence the Islamic Guidance Ministry of Iran on 26 May 1984 undertook a role in organizing an "independent brigade for carrying out irregular warfare in enemy territory," which included references to plans to incite anti-Saudi rioting during the Hajj pilgrimages in Mecca ceremonies. Such a riot on 31 July 1987 killed more than 400 people in Mecca.

While it has been argued that Iran undertook support of terrorism against, and subversion of, other Arab and Muslim governments in reaction to their support of Iraq during the Iran-Iraq war, such an apology ignores the fact that Saddam Hussein decided to invade Iran partly in reaction to Iranian agitation of Iraq's Shiites already under way, which included an assassination attempt against Iraqi Vice President Tariq Aziz on 1 April 1980 by Iranian agents. Likewise other Arab regimes supported Iraq because of their fear of the threat of Iranian-sponsored subversion against them.

In late 1988, Khomeini authorized the Iranian government to accept a U.N.-sponsored cease-fire with Iraq. This signaled no retreat from a willingness to use terrorism as an instrument of policy, however, for on 14 February 1989, Khomeini issued a declaration of *takfir* against British author Salman Rushdie, sentencing him to death on charges of blasphemy arising from the publication of his book *Satanic Verses*. Khomeini died on 3 June 1989, having presided for more than a decade over the development of an Islamic revolutionary society within Iran but without witnessing the creation of any sister Islamic Republic outside of Iran's borders.

Khomeini's own position on terrorism remained highly ambivalent. In his *Kashf al Asrar* and *Vilayat-i Faqih,* Khomeini appeared to endorse the traditional Shiite view that only defensive warfare, rather than jihad (q.v.) proper, is permitted in the absence of the apostolic Twelfth Imam. In questions 2826–2834 of his jurisprudential handbook *Risalih-i Taudhih al Masail,* "Treatise on the Clarification of Problematic Issues," Khomeini derives the right of defensive warfare and resistance to unjust rulers not from the Koranic injunctions regarding jihad but rather from the Koranic command to "enjoin the good and prohibit the bad." On 8 August 1984, while criticizing a Radio Tehran commentary that had praised the mining of the Red Sea, Khomeini declared the hijacking of ships and airplanes, the seizing of passengers as hostages, and the bombing of public places in which innocents might be killed or maimed as being "against the sentiments of world opinion, against Islam, and against common sense." Nonetheless this declaration was followed by Hezbollah's hijacking of TWA flight 847 on 14 June 1985 and by the al Dawa group's hijacking of Kuwaiti Airways flight 422 on 5 April 1988, in which both groups of hijackers were under Iranian sponsorship. On 7 January 1988, however, Khomeini publicly adopted the position that the Islamic Republic, for reasons of state, was permitted not only to act against the decrees of the Koran but even to compel Muslim believers to do so, a position that would permit the Islamic Republic or its sponsored groups to engage in any terrorist actions they deemed to be necessary. The religious scrupulosity reflected in Khomeini's earlier writings and speeches may have simply crumbled under the pressures of running a nation-state and conducting a war. To the end of his life Khomeini never renounced the Islamic Republic's right to use terrorism. That Khomeini's successor as *faqih*, Ayatollah Ali Khamenehi, has openly reaffirmed the death sentence passed against Salman Rushdie on each of the anniversaries of its promulgation only confirms the essential continuity of Tehran's terrorist policy in the post-Khomeini era.

KIDNAPPING. The deliberate seizure of a person, or persons, as hostages has become a major tactic of terrorists. Hostage taking can serve either purely revolutionary ends or may have entrepreneurial ends as well. Often the kidnapping of a prominent person, as in the case of the Red Brigade's kidnapping of former Italian premier Aldo Moro, or even the seizure of relatively unknown persons who have symbolic importance, such as the diplomats and staff of the U.S. Embassy in Tehran, can serve to gain the terrorists publicity and leverage for gaining political concessions from the state or society being attacked through the hostage seizure. Often, however, terrorists seize hostages as bargaining chips to obtain the release of imprisoned colleagues or else to exact ransom, which in turn may be used to finance other terrorist or political operations of the group. Hijacking may be considered a special case of kidnapping since it is the seizure of hostages on air or sea carriers that gives the terrorists political leverage rather than the mere fact of seizing a transportation carrier.

KU KLUX KLAN. The historic Ku Klux Klan was a white supremacist organization founded in 1865 by Confederate veterans of the Civil War. The name has continued to be used by a number of groups who adhere to the twin beliefs of the racial superiority of the white race and the need to safeguard that primacy by protecting its purity against desegregation, integration, and miscegenation. The distinguishing marks of the Klan are the burning cross and the hooded and white-sheeted garments of its members. Its typical tactics were nighttime raids in full regalia against blacks and others, in which they would beat, tar and feather, or lynch their victims.

For most of its history the Klan and its successor groups acted largely as a repressive group, seeking to counter the power of northerners in the south and to keep blacks socially and politically subordinate. Therefore the federal banning of the Klan in 1871 made little difference since many of the Klansmen's limited aims were achieved through the electoral laws passed by post-Reconstruction southern legislatures that effectively deprived their black citizens of civil rights. The latter-day Klan groups, however, have developed beyond having limited aims of repression to becoming right-wing revolutionary groups willing to undertake more ambitious terrorist activities, including forming alliances with neo-Nazi groups.

The original Ku Klux Klan targeted blacks and northern agents of Reconstruction. The revived Knights of the Ku Klux Klan in 1920 expanded its list of enemies in 1920 to include Roman Catholics, Jews, and, later in the 1930s, Communists as well. The Klan dwindled during the Depression and afterward until the Supreme Court decision in *Brown v. Topeka Board of Education* ordering desegregation of public schools in 1954. Since then there has been a rise in Klan memberships and activities proportionate to the advances in the Civil Rights movement. The revival of the Klan peaked in 1981 when the various Klan organizations together possessed about 11,500 members. The use of civil lawsuits by relatives of Klan victims greatly damaged some of these organizations and reduced their freedom of action. Three major Klan organizations have accounted for most Klan activities in recent years:

1. The *United Klans of America* (UKA), formerly headquartered in Tuscaloosa, Alabama, was the old guard of the Klan, being the most traditional, the oldest and the least active. While it once boasted the largest membership of the three Klan factions, UKA suffered a great reverse when Mrs. Beulah Donald, the mother of a UKA lynching victim, successfully sued UKA for $7 million in civil damages.

2. The *Invisible Empire* (IE) was established in 1975 as a breakaway group from the Knights of the Ku Klux Klan, which struck many Klansmen as being too overtly neo-Nazi. IE membership was open to white Roman Catholics. This organization suffered loss of membership when the founder of the IE, William Wilkinson, was exposed as an FBI informant. IE had 1,500 to 2,000 members nationwide when it was forced to file for reorganization under federal bankruptcy laws.

3. The *Knights of the Ku Klux Klan* (KKKK), named after the revived Klan of 1915, was established in 1975 by former neo-Nazi David Duke. This Klan group is the most recent and made up largely of people born after the Korean War. This organization has also proved itself most adept at using media relations and mass marketing techniques to sell its message and recruit members. Duke handed leadership of the KKKK to Don Black in 1980. The more revolutionary nature of the younger Klan groups is illustrated by Don Black's conspiracy, thwarted in April 1981, to carry out a coup d'état on the Caribbean island of Dominica, which he had planned to turn into a Klan safe haven. Following Black's arrest and conviction, the KKKK broke into two factions. Nonetheless this group has shown great adaptability, vitality, and ability to recruit new younger members.

Besides these three groups there are many splinter groups

and independent Klan organizations. In the latest phase of the third revival of the Klan (i.e., since 1954) the newer Klan groups have identified themselves closely with the Identity Christian movement and shown less hesitation in identifying themselves with neo-Nazi groups. These Klans have established paramilitary training camps throughout the country and certain of them have affiliated themselves with the Aryan Nations (q.v.) neo-Nazi group. Louis Ray Beam, Jr., Grand Dragon of the Texas Ku Klux Klan, became ''Ambassador at Large'' of the Aryan Nations and heir apparent of Aryan Nations leader Richard Butler. Another more graphic instance of the greater terrorist inclinations of younger Klan groups is shown by the role of Frazier Glenn Miller, former neo-Nazi and leader of the Carolina Knights of the Ku Klux Klan, in instigating the 3 November 1979 massacre of five leftist anti-Klan demonstrators in Greensboro, North Carolina.

Attempts to curtail Klan activities through criminal and civil lawsuits continue with a mixed record of success. Miller and members of his White Patriot Army (q.v.) were arrested in 1986 for conspiracy to murder Morris Dees, the anti-Klan activist lawyer who had encouraged Mrs. Beulah Donald to sue the UKA in 1987. Miller's trial revealed also his acceptance of $200,000 of stolen funds from the Order (q.v.) terrorists. An attempt, however, to convict Louis Beam and other white supremacists associated with the Aryan Nations and Klan groups on charges of sedition and violations of civil rights laws ended in acquittal of those defendants by the Federal District Court in Ft. Smith, Arkansas, in April 1988.

KURDISTAN WORKERS' PARTY. The PKK is a Marxist-Leninist Kurdish separatist group seeking to create a Marxist-Leninist and independent Kurdish homeland comprising the Kurdish-inhibited regions of Turkey, Iraq, and Iran. Several Kurdish leftist students who had met in a Dev Genç

(Revolutionary Youth) meeting in Ankara in 1974 founded the PKK on 27 November 1978 in Diyarbakir. The PKK conducts terrorist attacks on Turkish civilians and military personnel in the region claimed as "Kurdistan." The PKK received Syrian and Soviet state support, as well as the support of the Iraq-based Kurdish Democratic Party (KDP). The PKK also draws on support of expatriate Kurdish workers in Germany to obtain needed supplies, some of whom raise funds by narcotics trafficking in Europe. During the Iran-Iraq war the Iraqi government did not prevent the PKK from setting up bases in northern Iraq but also did not prevent the Turkish air force from launching retaliatory strikes against Kurdish bases in northern Iraq.

From 1978–1980 the PKK engaged in assassinating local landlords, robbing banks, and setting up "peoples courts" to rule the few villages they overran. During this time the PKK murdered 243 people. With the military crackdown beginning on 12 September 1980, Abdullah Ocalan, the PKK leader, fled to Syria. Shortly thereafter the Turkish military uncovered 100 rocket launchers smuggled by a PKK group from Syria. PKK fighters using Iraqi territory as a base attacked a Turkish army unit in May 1983, killing three soldiers. On 15 August 1984, the PKK took over the villages of Eruh and Semdinli, each 200 miles apart, and held each for one hour, departing before Turkish forces could arrive. On 22 October 1986, PKK fighters attacked the NATO air base at Mardin.

Whereas the preceding incidents involved probing attacks of more symbolic than material effect, the PKK proceeded with attacks directed largely against unprotected civilians. On 20 June 1987, the PKK massacred 30 Turkish villagers in Mardin province, including 16 women and 8 children. Another 30 civilians were murdered on 11 July 1987, also in Mardin province. In 1987 there were 13 similar attacks, some made in larger towns such as Diyarbakir. From August 1984 until September 1989, about 1,500 people died due to PKK violence. For the entire year of 1988, 315 people were killed, but in the first six months of 1989 alone 258 were killed, showing the steady increase in PKK activity. Once world attention began to focus on the situation of Kurdish refugees from Iraq during Operation Desert Storm, the PKK decided to step up its activities, causing the death figure to rise to 900 in 1991. On two occasions in August 1991 PKK kidnapped Western tourists in southeastern Turkey but in each case released them unharmed within the year.

PKK activity has centered on Mardin, Siirt, and Hakkari provinces, a triangular area bordering Iran and Iraq, which the PKK is trying to turn into a "liberated zone." The pattern of attack is always to hit, kill scores of Turks, or attack a government or military facility, and then leave before the Turkish army can arrive. This armed propaganda is meant to demonstrate the impotence of Turkish rule, to terrorize Turks, and to encourage Kurds to resist the government. The PKK suffered when Iraq began in 1987–1988 to suppress the Iraqi Kurds. This in turn forced the KDP to come to terms with Turkey in order to gain asylum for 60,000 of its own forces. These terms include discontinuing support for the PKK. The tactic of murdering Turkish civilians also alienated Turkish leftist terrorists (with the exception of Dev Sol) who had previously supported the PKK.

After 1988 the PKK desisted from its practice of massacring civilians and concentrated instead on hitting Turkish military outposts, police stations, and government offices. Heavy-handed counterinsurgency efforts by the Turkish military have exasperated the local Kurdish population in southeastern Turkey, causing many of them to accept the legitimacy of the PKK. Beginning in 1991, the PKK began striking at Turkish military targets outside of southeastern Turkey, killing 4 and wounding at least 12 in Adana, Istanbul, and Izmir. Estimates of PKK membership in 1987 put its fighting strength at 1,100 and noncombatant supporters at around 3,400. By mid-1989, another estimate put the fighting strength at 5,000.

- L -

LAUTARO YOUTH MOVEMENT. The MJL, also known as the Lautaro Faction, the United Popular Action Movement (MAPU/L), or the Lautaro Rebel Forces (FRPL) is a Chilean anti-government group that appeared following the Presidential election and transfer of power on 11 March 1989, ending the rule of General Augusto Pinochet. Although the MJL appears to have leftist leaders and uses leftist rhetoric, its following consists largely of alienated unemployed urban youth of slum areas and may represent more of an anarchist than leftist revolutionary group.

MJL attacks on police often involve deceptive calls for help or diversionary attacks used to lure solitary policemen to ambushes. MJL members also have engaged in bank robberies and attacks on Mormon missionary posts. On 24 January 1991, MJL members shot dead two policemen in Santiago. Following the release of a Chilean government report on the state terror of the Pinochet era, detailing over 2,000 slayings committed by the Chilean secret police, three police stations were bombed and six banks robbed. The perpetrators claimed to be leftists protesting the unwillingness of the Christian Democrat administration of President Patricio Aylwin to prosecute General Pinochet, who retained command of the Chilean armed forces following the installation of the democratically elected government on 11 March 1989, or others also responsible for the state terror.

On 15 March 1991, MJL members shot dead Héctor Sarmiento Hidalgo, chief investigator of Concepción, who had not been involved in the human rights abuses of the Pinochet era. Certain Chilean government officials believe that some of these attacks were actually instigated by Chilean right-wing agents-provocateurs seeking to create an antileftist backlash in favor of a renewed authoritarian military regime and to forestall serious investigations of human rights abuses under Pinochet. Three days following the 1 April 1991 slaying by unidentified gunmen of Senator

Jaime Guzmán, a former Pinochet confidant and adviser, the Chilean government announced a 150 percent increase in spending for the national police force and a 400 percent increase in spending for the government Department of Investigations.

Most of the MJL's activities have taken place in the Santiago area while little is known of their numerical strength or sponsorship by other domestic groups or foreign states.

LEBANESE ARMED REVOLUTIONARY FACTION. The *Factions Armées Revolutionnaires Libanaises* (FARL) formed in 1979 is a Lebanese revolutionary group seeking to create a Marxist-Leninist state in Lebanon. Although this group was one of the three groups that emerged from the breakup of the PFLP Special Operations Group upon the death of its leader, Wadi Haddad, in 1978 most of its members have been Lebanese Christians rather than Palestinians. FARL opposes the Phalange party (q.v.) as well as foreign supporters of the constitutional government of Lebanon, in particular, the United States, France, and Israel and also seeks to demonstrate its revolutionary affinity with the Palestinian cause by attacking Israeli targets outside of Lebanon. The group has collaborated with the French Direct Action (q.v.) and Italian Red Brigades (q.v.) groups and is suspected of having ties with Hezbollah (q.v.). FARL is believed to number only about 25 members and was led by Georges Ibrahim Abdullah (aliases: Salih al Masri, Abdul-Qadir Saadi), who joined the group after 1978 but who has been imprisoned since 1984.

FARL conducted at least 18 noteworthy actions from 1981 until 1987, including 4 assassinations, 2 assassination attempts, 4 separate bombings and 1 bombing campaign, 2 kidnappings, 1 armed attack, and 4 threats. On 18 January 1982, FARL shot dead the U.S. Army Attaché to Paris, Lt. Col. Charles Ray. On 3 April 1982, FARL machine-gunned to death an Israeli diplomat in Paris. Later a police raid on a

Direct Action hideout revealed the Sten gun used in this, and other, FARL attacks. On 15 February 1984, FARL claimed credit for the murder in Rome of U.S. citizen Leamon Hunt, the director of the multinational observer force in the Sinai. While the Red Brigades (q.v.) also claimed credit for killing Hunt, it appears that FARL collaborated with the Red Brigades in this action.

The capture of Georges Ibrahim Abdullah in 1984 led to a hiatus in FARL activities, except for the kidnapping and murder of a Frenchman in Lebanon and a series of threats against the French government if Abdullah were not released. During September 1986 FARL fulfilled some of its threats by carrying out a bombing campaign in Paris, in which ASALA (q.v.) and some pro-Iranian elements may have participated, killing 15 people and wounding over 150 others. Nonetheless French courts sentenced Abdullah to life imprisonment in 1987 for the murder of Lt. Col. Ray, and on other charges. Most of FARL's members returned to Lebanon that year and have been relatively inactive since then.

LEHI. The Fighters for the Freedom of Israel (*Lohame Herut Israel*), also known as the Stern Gang, was a breakaway faction from the Irgun (q.v.), which was dedicated to the same goals of ousting both the British forces and Arab population from Palestine in order to establish a Jewish state there. In 1940, Irgun members differed over the tactical question of observing a truce with Britain for the duration of the war with Germany, which the majority of Irgun believed to be necessary but which Abraham Stern (b. 1907, d. 1942) and others opposed.

The dissidents left Irgun, forming LEHI in 1940 to continue terrorizing British forces in Palestine during the war. Stern and his followers included among their targets moderate Jews opposed to the use of terrorism, killing at least 15 Jews and even contemplating an attack against the Jewish Agency in the event of winning independence. After the death of Stern in 1942, LEHI activities stayed in a lull until 1944. That year they assassinated Lord Moyne, the British minister for Middle Eastern affairs, in Cairo. The same year, LEHI and Irgun began cooperating in attacking British government offices and soldiers in Palestine.

In 1945, British authorities broke up most of LEHI, deporting many members while others joined other Jewish paramilitary organizations. LEHI members joined with Irgun in the 9 April 1948 attack upon the Arab village of Deir Yassin in which over 200 villagers perished. On 17 September 1948, LEHI members murdered the Swedish Count Folke Bernadotte and the French Colonel André Serot in the belief that their work as United Nations mediators would impede the full establishment of the Jewish state. Among the leaders of LEHI was Yitzhak Shamir, who later became prime minister of Israel.

LIBERATION THEOLOGY. Liberation theology is an attempt to reinterpret the Christian gospel as a creed of social, economic, and political liberation and to reconcile it with leftist revolutionary movements. This theology has spread predominantly among the Roman Catholic clergy of Latin America, although it is also being espoused by segments of older Protestant denominations represented within the World Council of Churches and has developed advocates among Roman Catholics and nonfundamentalist Protestants outside of Latin America. Of the various clerical orders the Society of Jesus has been most intimately connected with this movement, while the missionary religious order associated with Maryknoll has also undertaken advocacy of this worldview.

Many have concluded that liberation theology is little more than an amalgamation of Marxism and dependency theory with Christian theological window dressing and that its advocates are clearly partisans of Marxist-Leninist guerrilla and terrorist groups. Actually an examination of the writings of the leading theorists of liberation theology such as Paulo Fiere, Gustavo Gutierez, and Camillo Torres, shows that the doctrine owes much to the Catholic concept of corporal acts of mercy, to the view of the congruity and synergism of good works with faith, and to a postmillennialist view of church history. Together these elements suggest that the revelation of God's kingdom on earth requires active struggle against the forces of evil on the part of the faithful in a directly physical rather than merely spiritual sense. A Christian theologian holding such a view could easily view Marxist revolutionary and national liberation movements as objectively correct but devoid of correct spiritual intention. By propounding the theology of liberation and joining forces with the revolutionaries the spiritual and physical struggles against evil would be harmonized. A more cynical interpretation is also possible, namely that advocates of liberation theology hoped to buy themselves a place in any future Marxist revolutionary state(s) by joining themselves to leftist revolutionaries as religious propagandists and apologists of the revolution.

Following the Second Vatican Council the Catholic hierarchies encouraged more experimentation with, and adaptation of, Roman doctrine to new or local circumstances. In 1968, the Council of Latin-American Bishops in Medellín, Colombia, passed resolutions endorsing many of the tenets of liberation theology. Certain bishops, such as Archbishop Arnulfo Romero y Galdamez of El Salvador, became leading social critics of conservative or right-wing regimes while many secular priests and Jesuits became involved in establishing student Bible-study groups and "base communities," which many right-wing Latin Americans viewed as communist indoctrination classes and cellular organizations. Just as the former identification of Roman Catholicism with the Spanish colonial establishment embarrassed the church, eventually so too did certain aspects of Catholic clergymen's absorption in revolutionary politics. In Nicaragua under Sandinista rule the close association of certain priests with the Sandinista regime actually split the Catholic church there, pitting the proregime "people's church" against Archbishop Miguel Obando y Bravo and the clergymen faithful to him. Meantime in Guatemala the absorption of the Roman Catholic priests and educators in liberation theology left them unprepared and uncertain of how to deal with a growth in conversions of local Catholics to Protestant fundamentalist and pentecostal denominations that were decidedly conservative in their politics though clearly popular with a great and growing proportion of the Guatemalan population.

Following the elevation of Pope John Paul II, the Vatican took a decidedly hostile line toward liberation theology. On 6 August 1984, the Sacred Congregation of the Faith issued a "special instruction on liberation" made public on 3 September 1984. Among other things this document repudiated the emphasis of social-political liberation to the exclusion of its spiritual sense of liberation from sin, repudiated the use of revolutionary violence as a means to liberation, and declared the absolute incompatibility of Marxist analysis and practice with Christian doctrine and exhorted clergymen to set aside any involvement in revolutionary politics.

LIBERATION TIGERS OF TAMIL EELAM. The LTTE is a Tamil separatist group in Sri Lanka that seeks to create a separate state for the minority Tamils in the northern and eastern provinces of Sri Lanka, areas in which they outnumber the Sinhalese who form the majority of the Sri Lankan population. The LTTE enjoyed material and moral support from Tamil Nadu State in India but this support ended when the Indian government sent the Indian Peacekeeping Force upon official Sri Lankan request in 1987.

The LTTE engage in armed attacks on Sri Lankan security forces as well as terrorism against nonseparatist Tamils and members of rival Tamil radical groups. While the group was founded in 1972, it began its first terrorist attacks in 1975 when it claimed responsibility for killing the mayor of Jaffna. The separatist terror campaign began in earnest in 1977 with attacks directed against Tamil politicians who did not endorse the separatist cause. The LTTE's attacks on

Sinhalese security forces in July 1983 sparked ethnic violence between Tamils and Sinhalese throughout the island in which at least 387 people were killed. The expulsion of the moderate Tamil United Liberation Front (TULF) from Sri Lanka's parliament for its refusal to dissociate itself from separatist goals has left the LTTE as the foremost group championing the Tamil minority.

While the TULF was founded on 14 May 1972 its youth league attracted the core of younger, more militant Tamils who founded the Tamil New Tigers as a more activist clique within the youth league. On 5 May 1976, the Tamil New Tigers reconstituted themselves separately from the TULF as the Liberation Tigers of Tamil Eelam. LTTE set up training camps in jungles south of the Jaffna peninsula, recruiting young Tamil refugees forced from their homes by Sinhalese rioters. The Sri Lankan government unwittingly boosted recruitment into the various Tiger organizations by its practice of inflicting indiscriminate punishment on the Tamil community for specific acts of terrorism committed by Tiger groups. As a result, the LTTE was able to put about 10,000 men under arms. Training camps were later established in Tamil Nadu State in India whose state government provided active support to the LTTE while the Indian government passively acquiesced in this quasi-state sponsorship.

Up until the early 1980s, the LTTE financed itself from bank robberies in Sri Lanka. Since around 1982, the LTTE has tapped into a network of expatriate Tamil supporters not only in India but also in Europe and North America. In order to finance better its arms acquisitions and smuggling operations, it became active in the smuggling and distribution of Afghan heroin. By 1985, LTTE was responsible for the smuggling of 500 kilograms of heroin each year into Western Europe alone, fielding around 1,000 couriers at any given time. LTTE's arms and drug smuggling operations have brought it into contact and cooperation with the rightist Grey Wolves (q.v.) organization in Turkey as well as with Palestinian terrorist groups in Lebanon.

Approximately 25 different unrelated "Tiger" organizations have appeared since the LTTE began, but it has violently asserted its preeminence over them. This reflects the leadership style of Vellupillai Prabakharan, a low-caste youth who is the lone survivor of the original founders of the Tamil New Tigers, having killed off all his rivals within the LTTE. Prabakharan directed the LTTE to eliminate all rival Tiger groups in internecine battling from May 1986 to September 1987. By April 1989, the LTTE and the remnants of three other Tiger organizations formed an umbrella group, the Eelam National Liberation Front. While Prabakharan claims to seek a "socialist egalitarian" society in the envisioned Tamil state of Eelam he has a marked antipathy toward Marxist ideologues. His ruthless liquidation of rival Tiger leaders and groups as well as of ordinary Tamils unsympathetic to the separatist cause has led some observers to describe him as "implacably violent and as fascist a leader as South Asia has yet produced" (Austin and Gupta, 1988). Although Prabakharan is the leading personality among the Tamil separatists, he is not articulate and chooses to speak through a front man, Anton Balasingham.

The LTTE, unlike other Tiger groups, has not limited its attacks mainly to Sinhalese government and military targets but has directly terrorized Sinhalese civilians as well. On 3 May 1986, a bomb hidden aboard an Air Lanka Tristar in Colombo exploded while passengers were embarking, killing 17 and wounding 21 of the 111 who had embarked. Had the airplane not been delayed 15 minutes from its scheduled departure, all the passengers and crew would have perished. In April 1987, LTTE bombed the main bus terminal in Colombo, killing 106 and wounding 295 others, and carried out an ambush of four buses in the Trincomalee district, killing 107 civilians. LTTE fighters are also heedless of their own lives, often killing themselves by swallowing cyanide carried in ampules around their neck rather than allowing themselves to be captured and interrogated by Sinhalese forces.

With the failure of Sri Lankan forces to retake the Jaffna peninsula following the virtual collapse of Sri Lankan authority in the north of the island in 1987 and with the outcry of Indian public opinion against Sinhalese atrocities against Tamils, Sri Lanka agreed to allow Indian troops to land in Jaffna to restore order. The LTTE turned on its erstwhile Indian supporters and inflicted heavy casualties on Indian forces trying to capture Jaffna, killing 350 and wounding 1,100 Indian troops by 15 December 1987. These casualties amounted to 7 percent of India's total forces deployed in Sri Lanka, a rate of casualties twice that sustained in the wars fought with Pakistan. The campaign also cost India the life of former Prime Minister Rajiv Gandhi, who had ordered Indian troops into Sri Lanka. On 21 May 1991, while campaigning in the south of India, Gandhi was killed by an LTTE suicide bomber reportedly acting on orders from Prabakharan.

The LTTE continues to threaten the Sri Lankan government despite the presence of the Indian troops. On 2 March 1991, a LTTE car bomb in Colombo killed the Deputy Defense Minister of Sri Lanka along with over 50 bystanders, while another car bomb destroyed the Sri Lankan Military Operations Headquarters in June 1991.

LORENZO ZELAYA POPULAR REVOLUTIONARY FORCES. The *Fuerzas Revolucionarios Populares Lorenzo Zelaya* (FRP-LZ) was a Honduran guerrilla group seeking to overthrow the current Honduran government through a Marxist-Leninist revolution. It targeted U.S. diplomatic facilities and firms as well as those of Latin American countries whose policies supported U.S. initiatives against the Sandinista government of Nicaragua. FRP-LZ members claim to have received training in Nicaragua and Cuba. Most of their actions have been confined to Honduras, although they are said to have served as auxiliaries in the Sandinistas' internal war against the contras.

FRP-LZ was formed in 1978 but initiated its terrorist

career by its 30 October 1980 machine-gun attack on the U.S. Embassy in Tegucigalpa and bomb attack against the hilean Embassy. On 23 September 1981, they ambushed five members of a U.S. military training unit and bombed the second floor of the National Assembly building. On 21 April 1982, they made another machine-gun attack on the U.S. Embassy, targeting especially the Ambassador's suite and threw bombs at the Argentinean, Chilean, and Peruvian embassies. On 28 April 1982, four FRP-LZ members hijacked an airplane, which the Honduran government allowed to leave for Cuba on May 1 after the passengers held hostage were released. Other targets up through 1983 included IBM and Air Florida offices, two other U.S. subsidiary companies, one Salvadoran firm, the British Embassy, and the Guatemalan Consulate.

In 1983, the FRP-LZ leader, Efraín Duarte Salgado, was arrested and turned informer against his own group. FRP-LZ activities fell off after the loss of this leader, and with the arrest of two remaining leaders in 1987 the activities of the group ceased.

- M -

M-19. The "April 19th Movement" (Spanish: Movimiento 19 de Abril, M-19) is a Colombian insurgent group, enjoying occasional sponsorship from other non-Colombian terrorist groups and states, that has been pursuing both entrepreneurial and revolutionary agendas. Its revolutionary goal is to lead the Colombian people in a populist revolution against the "bourgeois" establishment in Colombia and to resist U.S. "imperialism," particularly in the form of U.S. economic penetration of Colombia. The group's ideology represents an eclectic blend of Marxist-Leninist ideas mixed with heady doses of populism and nationalism. Its entrepreneurial activities have included, first, kidnapping and extortion directed against foreign-affiliated companies to force them to finance M-19's projected revolution, and, second, collaboration with, and/or extortion of, Colombian drug traffickers also as a means of financing its revolution. As of late 1989, M-19 entered the Colombian electoral arena as a legal political party, but whether this represents a change in its revolutionary agenda or is merely tactical opportunism has yet to be seen.

M-19 has received help from Cuba, Nicaragua, and Libya, as well as training from Argentinean Montoneros and Uruguayan Tupamaros. Cuba trained 300 M-19 guerrillas in 1980. Both Cuba and Nicaragua supplied M-19 with arms in the early 1980s. M-19 has had contacts with the Ecuadoran Alfaro Vive Carajo group (q.v.) as well as other similar groups in Costa Rica, El Salvador, Guatemala, Peru, and Venezuela. In April 1984, M-19 announced it had formed ties with the Basque Fatherland and Liberty (q.v.) separatists. M-19 became a member of the Simón Bolívar Guerrilla Coordination board, organized under Revolutionary Armed Forces of Colombia (FARC) auspices in 1985, and later ran candidates in Colombian presidential elections in May 1990.

Although its activities began with a series of bank robberies in 1973, M-19 first announced its existence on 17 January 1974, when it stole the spurs and sword of Simón Bolívar from his former villa, now a Bogotá museum. It declared itself retroactively "founded" on 19 April 1970, the date of the electoral defeat of National Popular Alliance (ANAPO) presidential candidate Rojas Pinilla. Although M-19 was formed by ANAPO activists frustrated with what they regarded as the corrupt electoral system in Colombia, the ANAPO party apparatus disavowed any connection with M-19.

The terrorist activities of M-19 commenced with the February 1976 kidnapping and murder of trade unionist José Raquel Mercado whom they accused of being a CIA agent. In the next two years M-19 would kidnap for ransom over 400 victims. For nationalistic reasons M-19 has tended to target multinational companies and executives for extortion and kidnapping, including the Colombian branches of Sears and Texaco, rather than targeting purely Colombian enterprises. Beginning in 1977, M-19 also began sabotaging petroleum production facilities. By 1979, M-19 emerged as the most active of the guerrilla groups operating in Colombia.

In 1979 to show solidarity with the Sandinista cause M-19 kidnapped the Nicaraguan Ambassador, Barquero Montiel. In February 1980 M-19 captured 15 diplomats and 16 other hostages at the Embassy of the Dominican Republic, including the U.S. Ambassador, Diego Asencio, and held them 61 days in exchange for ransom and safe passage to Cuba. In January 1981, in an unsuccessful bid to force the U.S. Summer Linguistic Institute out of Colombia they kidnapped U.S. citizen and Institute employee Chester Bitterman whom they murdered on 7 March 1981. In April 1983, they bombed the Honduran Embassy, seriously wounding the Honduran Consul. In October 1985, they attempted to ambush the automobile of General Rafael Samudio Molina but failed. Likewise in December 1985, they botched an ambush set for the National Police Subdirector, General Guillermo Medino Sánchez, and again in June 1986 failed in an attempt to kill Minister of Government Jaime Castro as he was driving to his office. In May 1988, M-19 kidnapped former Conservative Party presidential candidate lvaro Gómez Hurtado, who was released two months later after a meeting between government officials and M-19 leaders at the papal nuncio's office in Bogotá. Also on 23 March 1988, M-19 struck the U.S. Embassy in Bogotá with a rocket, causing minimal damages and no injuries.

The most serious terrorist action of M-19 was the 6 November 1985 seizure of the Justice Ministry building in Bogotá in which they seized nearly 500 hostages, including members of the Supreme Court and of the Council of State. Colombian security forces attacked, killing at least 19 terrorists. In the course of this operation 11 Supreme Court Justices were killed along with 50 hostages and all of the terrorists.

The most questionable undertaking of M-19 has been its relations with Colombian drug traffickers. By 1982, evidence emerged linking Colombia drug trafficker Jaime Guillot Lara with M-19 as well as four close aides of Fidel Castro. In 1982, a Miami, Fl., U.S. Federal grand jury handed down indictments against Cuban officials for assisting Lara's smuggling operations in exchange for his providing funds and Cuban arms to M-19. Whether this was a case of M-19 extortion practiced on the drug traffickers or else a temporary tactical alliance between criminals and terrorists, in either case the relationship went sour. The drug traffickers founded their own death squad "Death to Kidnappers" (MAS, q.v.), which was directed in particular against M-19, apparently in retaliation for M-19 having kidnapped for ransom key members of the drug rings.

M-19 has around 1,000 members. It is made up of two fronts, a southern front in Putumayo Department and a western front in Caldas, Cauca, Valle de Cauca, Quinido, and Tolima Departments. These fronts are subdivided into "columns" for different municipalities. Its founders included former ANAPO Congressman Carlos Toleda Plata, who led M-19 until his capture in 1982, and Jaime Bateman Cayón, a former FARC member who remained M-19's principal military commander.

M-19 participated in the "national dialogue" between the Colombian government and other major leftist guerrilla groups and signed the truce of May 1984. By September 1989, M-19 had signed a series of accords with the Colombian government allowing it to participate legally as a political party. M-19 announced its intention to demobilize in exchange for pardons and guarantees of protection and finally surrendered its weapons to the government on 8 March 1990. Subsequently agents of drug traffickers killed M-19 Presidential candidate Carlos Pizarro León-Gómez on 26 April 1990.

MACHETEROS. The "Machete Wielders," otherwise known as the *Ejército Popular de Boricua* (Popular Army of Boricua), is a Puerto Rican separatist group that considers itself engaged in a war of independence against the United States. It is not known to have any external state sponsorship nor any known contact with other Latin American leftist insurgent groups outside Puerto Rico, although they are supported by the small Marxist-Leninist Puerto Rican Socialist Party led by José Mari Bras, who is believed to be close to Fidel Castro. Within the Puerto Rican community, however, the Macheteros have shown some coordination with another separatist group, the Organization of Volunteers for the Puerto Rican Revolution (OVPR, q.v.), and have claimed to carry out certain terrorist actions to express solidarity with members of the Armed Forces of National Liberation (FALN, q.v.) group imprisoned in the United States. Although the Macheteros use Marxist-Leninist jargon, the essence of their program appears to reduce to nothing more than the demand for total independence for Puerto Rico.

The Macheteros appear to be a relatively small but highly organized and carefully screened group that has eluded infiltration. It operates mainly within Puerto Rico, targeting primarily U.S. military facilities, U.S. military personnel, as well as the Puerto Rican police and operates mainly within Puerto Rico. Since 1978, the group has carried out a few very competently executed terrorist actions that can be considered armed propaganda. On 3 December 1979, they ambushed and machine-gunned a bus carrying U.S. Navy personnel, killing 2 sailors and seriously wounding 10 others. On 12 March 1980, in a similar ambush of a bus the Macheteros wounded one of the three ROTC instructors aboard. On 16 May 1982, they machine-gunned four U.S. sailors leaving a San Juan nightclub, killing one and wounding the others. On 6 November 1985, they shot and seriously wounded a U.S. Army recruiting officer as he was riding his motor scooter to work.

The most dramatic Machetero action was the sabotage of the Puerto Rican National Guard airfield at Muniz Air Base outside San Juan on 12 January 1981. Disguised in military uniforms 11 Macheteros penetrated the security fence and planted 21 bombs in 11 jet fighters, 8 of which were destroyed and 2 of which were damaged, causing in excess of $45 million in damages. The date selected was the birth anniversary of Eugenio María de Hostes, a Puerto Rican hero in the struggle for independence from Spain. The significance of the use of ''eleven'' in the number of men deployed and number of planes targeted was to express solidarity for 11 FALN members being tried for terrorist activities in the United States at that time. Similarly on 28 October 1986, they planted 10 bombs at military bases and facilities across the island, 3 of which exploded destroying 2 recruiting facilities. This action was undertaken to protest a supposed plan to train Nicaraguan contras in Puerto Rico. The group has also used rocket-propelled grenades in attacks on U.S. government office buildings in San Juan.

On 16 September 1983, the Macheteros conducted an operation on the U.S. mainland, robbing the Wells Fargo armored truck terminal in Hartford, Conn., of $7.2 million. While bank robberies in Puerto Rico had been a primary source of funds for the group, the evidence provided by this holdup allowed the FBI to arrest several Macheteros leaders in Puerto Rico on 30 August 1985. In spite of this crackdown, the Macheteros were responsible for 9 of the 10 terrorist attacks occuring in Puerto Rico in 1986, although 7 of these attacks failed to achieve their objective.

MANUEL RODRIGUEZ PATRIOTIC FRONT. The *Frente Patriótico Manuel Rodríguez* (MRPF) is the armed wing of the Chilean Communist Party, formed originally with the aim of overthrowing the Pinochet regime by urban guerrilla warfare, which has continued to seek the overthrow of the post-Pinochet democratic Chilean government. The group relies on bombings, assassinations directed at Chilean government and police targets, former Pinochet regime officials, and at the U.S. diplomatic and economic presence in Chile. Although the group first appeared only in 1983, it has access to impressive quantities of high-quality weapons and explosives and appears very well organized. Apparently it enjoyed material assistance from Cuba and other communist states.

In the period from 1983–1985, the MRPF conducted simultaneous bombing campaigns in the eight largest cities in Chile, including attacks on power substations, the U.S.-Chilean Cultural Institute in Valparaíso on 7 August 1984, and a car bombing outside the U.S. Embassy on 19 July 1985 that killed one passerby and wounded four others and two policemen. One of the 21 bombings conducted on 29 April 1986 involved a 15-kilogram bomb detonated outside the U.S. Ambassador's residence, which caused no injuries.

On 11 August 1986, Chilean security forces uncovered an arms stockpile at Corral Bay consisting in part of 338 M-16 rifles, 37 Soviet hand grenades, 315 Katyusha rockets, detonators, fuses, and 1,872 kilos of high-yield explosives, and 210,000 rounds of ammunition. A clandestine field clinic and an airstrip were also located near the arms stockpile. Twenty MRPF members were arrested in this raid. Chilean authorities claimed the arms were off-loaded from Soviet and Cuban fishing vessels and were intended for use in an offensive to be launched against the government in September 1987. On 7 September 1986, 21 MRPF gunmen attempted to kill General Pinochet with grenades and automatic weapons fire as his motorcade drove to his summer residence. Five guards were killed and another 11 were wounded while Pinochet suffered only a cut on his hand. On 10 September 1986, Chilean security forces found a 25-meter-long tunnel packed with 200 kilograms of explosives beneath a road over which General Pinochet had been due to travel the next day. During late 1986 and 1987, MRPF conducted numerous bombings of power pylons, once plunging much of Santiago and Valparaíso into a blackout just as General Pinochet was due to make a national radio and television address. On 28 December 1989, MRPF bombed the American-Chilean cultural center in Santiago to protest the U.S. invasion of Panama. On 21 March 1990, the MRPF wounded General Gustavo Leigh, former Air Force commander, in an assassination attempt. Leigh had been accused of overseeing death squad activities directed against Chilean leftists during the rule of General Augusto Pinochet.

The membership of MRPF is estimated between 500 and 1,000 and appears to be headquartered in Santiago. The MRPF has shown a greater willingness to strike at lower-ranking policemen and ordinary soldiers than did its leading rival, the Movement of the Revolutionary Left (MIR) and to risk indiscriminate killing of civilians and bystanders in its bombing campaign since MRPF uses higher-yield explosives than did MIR and makes greater use of car bombs. MRPF has also engaged in kidnapping industrialists for ransom and apparently once prepared a ''people's prison'' to house hostages. Unlike MIR, the MRPF also has seized radio stations several times in order to broadcast its own messages to the public.

Following the restoration of democratic rule in Chile in 1989, the MRPF has not desisted from attacks against the Chilean government and actually was the first group to launch a terrorist action with an antitank rocket attack on police posts in the southern towns of Los Quenes and Pichi-Pehuhuen on 21 October 1988. This has created division in the Chilean Communist Party, many of whose members believe that there is no rationale for such terrorist actions in the post-Pinochet period. The MRPF has rationalized its continuation of terrorism as a protest against the reluctance of the Aylwin administration to prosecute former Pinochet regime officials for human rights abuses.

MARIGHELLA, CARLOS. (b. 1912, d. 1969) Brazilian terrorist and theorist of terrorism best known for his tract, the *Minimanual of the Urban Terrorist,* written in June 1969, which has often been called a masterpiece on terrorist strategy. Specialists in political violence and terrorism have found little originality in its discussion of terrorist tactical doctrine and have found it also to be quite devoid of any discussion of the moral dimensions of terrorist action. None-theless this book has been avidly read by sympathizers and other would-be terrorists who have taken Marighella's pre-scriptions very much to heart. For instance, Marighella wrote in the *Minimanual* that no Marxist revolution would succeed in the United States until white college radicals joined forces with black prison inmates. Groups such as the Symbionese Liberation Army (q.v.) and the Revolutionary Armed Task Force (q.v.) proceeded to follow this precept quite literally. Because of the popularity of this work among revolutionary leftists, many Latin American and European countries have banned its publication and distribution.

As a former Executive Committee member of the Brazilian Communist Party who had become disillusioned with the ineffectiveness of political action, Marighella embraced the notion of "violence before politics" in 1967 when he left the Brazilian Communist Party and helped found a leftist terrorist group called the National Liberation Action. He was killed in a police ambush in November 1969, and the group he helped found was smashed by Brazilian security forces within a year of his death.

MARXIST-LENINIST ARMED PROPAGANDA UNIT. The Marxist-Leninist Armed Propaganda Unit (MLAPU) was a nonstate group seeking to overthrow the Turkish Republic in favor of a communist state. It was founded in Paris in 1973 by leftist Turkish students and the widow of Mahir Çayan, a Turkish leftist and founder of the Turkish People's Liberation Front (q.v.) killed by Turkish security forces in 1972. The group was one of several left-wing death squads and terrorist groups vying with right-wing extremist counterparts in the period of escalating internal political terrorism in Turkey in the late 1970s and early 1980s. MLAPU was also considered to be the most virulently anti-American of Turkish leftist groups.

In 1979, MLAPU killed seven U.S. citizens. On 2 January 1980, they machine-gunned the manager of the El Al Airlines office in Istanbul as he was driving home. On 16 April 1980, three MLAPU gunmen killed a U.S. Navy noncommissioned officer and his taxi driver. The three gunmen were pursued by police, one being killed in pursuit and the other two captured. On 15 November 1980, two other U.S. Air Force noncommissioned officers were shot at by MLAPU gunmen. One was killed, but the other escaped injury. The two gunmen were apprehended and later executed in 1985.

With the military coup of September 1980 and imposition of martial law, MLAPU, and other similar groups, were ruthlessly suppressed by the military. Many of those leftists already imprisoned, including the gunmen arrested for the incidents mentioned above, were executed under the military regime.

MAS. The "Death to Kidnappers" group (Spanish: Muerte a Secuestradores, MAS) is a nonstate death squad run by Colombian drug traffickers for the limited purpose of countering and containing their main enemies, namely Colombian leftist revolutionaries, politicians, and the Colombian state. The drug traffickers' alliances with leftist rebels against the government, or with right-wing elements in the security forces against leftist revolutionaries, have been purely tactical in nature and intended by the drug traffickers at preserving their relative autonomy in a fractured and weak Colombian state.

MAS was founded in December 1981 by drug traffickers Carlos Ledher Rivas and Jorge Luís Ochoa Vásquez. The leader of the Medellín drug cartel, Pablo Escobar Gaviria (d. 1993), was also believed to be among the patrons of MAS. This group was originally directed particularly against guerrilla groups, such as M-19, that had been kidnapping drug kingpins for ransom. Eventually it became a right-wing death squad that targeted leftist politicians, students, and other activists. MAS is believed to function as an umbrella organization for a number of right-wing paramilitary groups of which 128 could be identified by 1988.

Although there has been evidence of collusion in the early 1980s between drug traffickers and leftist guerrillas, who shared at least a common enemy in the Colombian government if not a common ideology, such a relationship was problematic at best, probably more on the level of mutual extortion than cooperation. By the late 1980s, the drug traffickers began attacking the leftists in earnest. On 11 October 1987, Jaime Pardo Neal, a leader of the Patriotic Union (UP) Party, the political front of the Revolutionary Armed Forces of Colombia (q.v.) (FARC), was killed by agents of a major drug trafficker. On 22 March 1990, traffickers also assassinated UP Presidential candidate Bernardo Jaramillo Ossa at Bogotá airport and on 26 April 1990 killed M-19 Presidential candidate Carlos Pizarro León-Gómez. Ironically both candidates had opposed extradition of narcotics traffickers to the United States.

MAS is also suspected of perpetrating the January 1989 killings of 12 members of a judicial commission investigating death squad activity in Colombia.

MAU MAU. The Mau Mau were gangs deployed by the Central Association of the Kikuyu tribesmen in Kenya originally to drive British settlers off Kikuyu lands but which became part of the overall anti-colonial Kenyan independence movement. The Mau Mau were active from September 1952 to October 1956, attacking and killing British settlers as well as burning their crops, slaughtering their cattle, and destroying the huts of African tenants on British farms.

Following the first attacks the British administration declared a state of emergency in October 1952 and imprisoned Jomo Kenyatta (b. 1897) in 1953 as the suspected leader of the Mau Mau. By the end of 1953, over 3,000 rebels had been killed and by the end of 1956 over 11,000 rebels had been killed while less than 100 of the British security forces had been killed. The vast majority of the 2,000 civilians killed were black Africans.

The power of the Mau Mau lay not so much in their

material strength, for they seldom had more than 500 firearms, but rather in the psychic hold that the Kikuyu leaders held over followers and supporters by means of magical oaths whose violation threatened supernatural terrors against the oath breaker. The Mau Mau obtained weapons by theft from the police while local Africans were forced to contribute funds to support the group.

The organization suffered a severe blow with the capture and defection of one key Kikuyu leader in 1954. The capture and execution of another key leader in October 1956 effectively destroyed the organization. Jomo Kenyatta was released from prison in 1961 and became prime minister of Kenya upon its independence in 1963.

MAXIMILIANO HERNÁNDEZ MARTÍNEZ ANTI-COMMUNIST BRIGADE. This was a quasi-state-sponsored group aimed at repressing leftists and even moderates who opposed the interests of the landowning oligarchy in El Salvador. Named for the Salvadoran military dictator who suppressed the *Matanza* peasant uprising of 1932, this group was one of several Salvadoran right-wing death squads (q.v.) that generally grew out of the "special units" maintained by Salvadoran security forces during the 1970s and that were used to kill off suspected "subversives." Many of the leaders and members of such groups were themselves members of the Salvadoran military and police even though such groups ceased to have legal status following the dissolution of the ORDEN (q.v.) paramilitary security force in the month after the coup of 15 October 1979. The major moving force behind the Maximiliano Hernández group was Roberto D'Aubuisson, formerly an officer of the Salvadoran intelligence agency who founded the White Warriors' Union (q.v.) death squad in 1976 and who later founded the Republican National Alliance (ARENA, q.v.) party.

The Maximiliano Hernández Martínez group is believed responsible for the 24 March 1980 assassination of Archbishop Oscar Arnulfo Romero y Galdamez, an outspoken critic of the Salvadoran government. On 27 November 1980, they kidnapped Enrique lvarez, head of the leftist Democratic Revolutionary Front (FDR), and four other leftist leaders whom they tortured and killed. From September to October 1983, they killed the highest ranking FDR official residing in San Salvador, 18 trade unionists, a few professors, and bombed the Jesuit residence at the Central American University. This group is also believed responsible for the killings and repression of many other less prominent leftists, centrists, human rights activists, religious activists, academics, and trade unionists.

MAY 1. The Revolutionary Organization of 1 May is a nonstate Greek leftist group that engages in terrorism for the limited purpose of opposing "U.S. imperialism," the Turkish presence in Cyprus, and government economic austerity measures. It has no known state sponsorship but appears to work in close concert with the November 17 (q.v.) and the ELA (q.v.) groups. It appears likely that both May 1 and November 17 evolved from the same core membership of ELA, which originally was formed with the revolutionary objective of overthrowing the Greek military junta. In the post-junta period, November 17, and these similar groups, appear more anarchistic in nature, lacking an overall objective but attaching themselves to revolutionary raisons d'être as these happen to appear.

May 1 appeared as part of a campaign against Greek jurists that demonstrated revolutionary solidarity with May 15 (q.v.) terrorist Mohammad Rashid, who was fighting extradition to the United States due to his role in the 11 August 1982 bombing of a U.S. air carrier. On 23 January 1989, the group assassinated in Athens a deputy public prosecutor of the Greek Supreme Court. Two other public prosecutors were killed by members of the May 1 or November 17 group (q.v.), which led two Supreme Court justices to resign. While Rashid was not extradited to the U.S., he was tried in October 1991, convicted in early 1992, and sentenced to a long prison term. During the Persian Gulf war May 1 and ELA mounted 5 bombing attacks on U.S. and British corporate offices in Athens. In mid-July 1991, May 1 and ELA joined November 17 in communiqués to Turkish terrorist groups, urging them to step up their attacks just prior to the visit of President Bush to both Greece and Turkey.

Little is known about the membership of these groups or their relations with other terrorist groups or political parties. Since their area of operations seems to be confined to Athens, it is assumed their total numbers are small (less than 100). While the ideology of the groups is marked by Marxist themes, there is also a very strong undercurrent of Greek nationalism and anti-Turkish sentiment, evinced in the step-up in terrorist operations whenever Greece, Turkey, and the U.S. seek to discuss the issue of Cyprus.

MAY 15. The Arab Organization of May 15, named for the anniversary of the first declaration of war by the Arab states against the newly declared State of Israel, is an obscure splinter group of the Popular Front for the Liberation of Palestine Special Operations Group.

May 15 carried out operations under its own name from 1978 to 1983, specializing in making sophisticated barometrically triggered bombs used to destroy civilian air carriers, including one Tokyo to Honolulu Pan Am flight on 11 August 1982, which exploded just before landing, killing one person. In the period from 1980–1982, May 15 carried out five bomb attacks against El Al offices, the Israeli embassy in Athens, a Jewish restaurant in West Berlin, and the Mount Royal hotel in London, killing 2 people and wounding 15. In April 1986, May 15 bombed a TWA flight killing four people. On 15 February 1984, a parcel bomb sent by May 15 exploded, maiming Iran's ambassador to Syria, Hujjatulislam Ali Akbar Muhtashami, who was intimately involved in overseeing the Hezbollah militia in Lebanon and whom May 15 regarded as a gratuitous meddler in intra-Arab affairs.

Very little is known about this organization. It appears that many of its members have joined other groups and that May 15 is no longer active.

MAY 19TH COMMUNIST COALITION. The May 19th Communist Coalition was an outreach umbrella organization created as a front for the Revolutionary Armed Task Force (RATF, q.v.), itself a merger of the remnants of the Weather Underground and Black Liberation Army. The name was taken from the common birth anniversary of Malcolm X and also of Ho Chi Minh. The organization also called itself the May 19th Communist Organization.

This front attempted to recruit other leftist revolutionaries or black prison inmates into the RATF or BLA organizations. The May 19th group also established contacts and fraternal ties with other terrorist groups, such as the New Afrikan Freedom Fighters (q.v.), the Puerto Rican FALN (q.v.) separatists, and even the PLO. The May 19th spokesperson, Judith A. Clark, represented the organization at a conference sponsored by the PLO in Beirut in September 1981.

In recruiting black inmates, May 19th cadres represented themselves to prison authorities and prisoners as offering free legal services and counsel for indigent prisoners. Once they gained access to potential recruits they would undertake "consciousness-raising" sessions to convert them to the revolutionary cause. Outside of the prisons the group maintained a network of communications and safe houses for the RATF. The group collapsed when the FBI arrested the core members of the RATF from May 1985 to February 1986, many of whom, like Judith A. Clark, were arrested on charges stemming from their participation in RATF criminal activities.

MINUTEMEN. Founded in 1961 by Robert dePugh, a Missouri manufacturer of pet and livestock vitamins and food supplements, the Minutemen were the predecessors of the Posse Comitatus (q.v.) and other right-wing extremist groups that advocated or practiced terrorism against alleged "communists and traitors." The name was taken from that of the Revolutionary War militiamen, and their ideology, which stressed extreme anticommunism and survivalism, took on a peculiar relevance during a period when fear of international communism and of nuclear war would be greatly aggravated by the Cuban missile crisis of October 1962. The anticommunist component of the group's ideology included attacks on the Internal Revenue Service and Federal Reserve System as being anti-American conspiracies while the Minutemen's tabloid *On Target* identified 20 Congressmen investigating right-wing movements as being "communists" and made veiled threats against their lives. Following the outbreak of racial rioting in the mid-1960s, the Minutemen advocated that whites undertake guerrilla warfare training in order to fight minority members in the event of racial warfare.

DePugh was imprisoned in 1968 on a conspiracy conviction arising from violations of federal firearms laws. He jumped bail in 1968 and survived in the wilderness of the Rockies and New Mexico desert until arrested in Truth or Consequences, New Mexico, in 1970. Following his release from prison in 1973 he wrote a manual on survival *Can You Survive? Guidelines for Resistance to Tyranny for You and Your Family* that became widely read and admired among other right-wing survivalists.

The Minutemen actually carried out very little in the way of terrorism, but this group served as the inspiration for other groups that have since then engaged in terrorist actions. The Posse Comitatus and Arizona Patriots absorbed many of the former Minutemen and much of the Minuteman ideology. The Christian-Patriots Defense League (q.v.) fused Minuteman ideology with Identity Christianity (q.v.).

MOGADISHU HIJACKING RESCUE. On 13 October 1977, some 4 terrorists of the Popular Front for the Liberation of Palestine (q.v.) hijacked a Lufthansa Boeing 737 flying from Majorca to Frankfurt carrying 86 passengers and 5 crew members. The hijackers not only had handguns and crude homemade hand grenades but also 60 pounds of plastic explosives and were demanding that the 10 main Red Army Faction (q.v.) terrorists be freed from West German jails, along with 2 Palestinians in Turkish jails, as well as demanding a ransom of $15 million. The hijackers had the plane fly to Rome, Cyprus, Bahrain, Dubai, Aden, and finally to Somalia.

Following the murder of the pilot in Aden by the hijackers' leader, the West German government resolved to deploy a 26-member Grenzschutzgruppe-9 unit to Mogadishu Airport to free the hostages. There on 18 October 1977, two members of the British elite antiterrorist Special Air Services accompanied the German team and blinded the terrorists with special magnesium-flash grenades for six seconds, allowing the Germans to storm the plane successfully. Only one of the terrorists survived while the remaining hostages were rescued. On hearing the news of the rescue three of the leading imprisoned Red Army Faction prisoners committed suicide while the Red Army Faction kidnappers holding West German businessman Hanns-Martin Schleyer murdered him in reprisal for the deaths of their comrades.

MONTONEROS. The *Movimiento Perónista Montonero* was a leftist Argentinean guerrilla group formed in 1970 to promote the populist and nationalistic policies of the exiled dictator, Juan Domingo Perón, and to facilitate his return to power. Although the group was not Marxist-Leninist it did seek a type of socialist revolution within Argentina coupled with a fight to rid Argentina of foreign economic penetration. Following Perón's return to power, once the Montoneros learned that Perón had embraced the more conservative wings of the Perónist movement they turned against him to pursue their own populist and socialist revolution.

Prior to the return of Perón the Montoneros sought and received help from Cuba. In the early 1970s they had contacts with other leftist insurgents in Latin America, such as Colombia's M-19 group, and within Argentina they had about 10,000 supporters. Following the break with Perón they made common cause with the Cuban-backed Armed Revolutionary Forces (FAR) as well as with Trotskyite groups in fighting the regime.

The Montoneros began their career by kidnapping and murdering the former president, Pedro Aramburu, on 29 May 1970. They financed themselves through numerous kidnappings of foreign executives for ransom during 1970–1973. From May until September 1973, they became, in effect, a state-sponsored group under the Perónista Campora administration. Tensions with the more right-wing Perónist groups erupted, however, in an armed clash between the factions on 20 June 1973 at Ezeiza Airport marring the homecoming ceremony planned to honor the returning Juan Perón. In this clash with rightist Perónists 13 people perished and over 100 were wounded. After Perón's re-election as Argentina's president in October 1973, the Montoneros grew disenchanted with his rightist policies. On 12 February 1974, several Montoneros were arrested in connection with a plot to assassinate Perón and his wife Isabel. On 1 May 1974, Perón broke with the Montoneros, whom he castigated in his May Day rally address as "treacherous and mercenary" elements.

Two weeks following Perón's death on 1 July 1974, the Montoneros unleashed their "popular war" against the Argentinean regime using arson, bombings, murder, and sabotage to try to provoke the military into a crackdown that would precipitate a popular revolution against right-wing oppression. This campaign began with the 15 July 1974 assassination of a former foreign minister. Again the group sought funds through kidnapping for ransom, netting $60 million alone in ransom for the Born brothers, sons of Argentina's wealthiest family, abducted on 19 September 1974. The government reacted to this by rigorously enforcing a law forbidding negotiations with, or payments to, terrorist groups. The rigorous enforcement of this law led the

Montoneros to kill executives of Fiat, Bendix, Chrysler, Ford, General Motors, and a West German pharmaceutical firm when they could not collect extortion payments from those companies. They also tried to kill a Goodyear executive and wounded three other foreign executives by bombs delivered hidden in flower bouquets.

On 16 September 1974, they conducted 40 bombings throughout Argentina targeting U.S. firms and banks. Other attacks on U.S. targets included the 8 September 1974 bomb attack on the U.S.I.S. office in Rosario; an attempted bombing of the U.S. Embassy on 19 September 1974; and the kidnapping and murder of U.S. consular official John Egan on 26 February 1975. On 20 September 1976, the Montoneros set fire to the new U.S. chancery building, causing $10,000 in damages. Attacks on the Argentine government included the 1 November 1974 bombing that killed Federal Police Chief Alberto Villar; the murder of General Jorge Cáceres Monie on 3 November 1975; and the murder of General Cesaro Cardozo on 18 June 1976. On 22 August 1975, the Montoneros bombed and sank a naval destroyer under construction, causing $70 million in damages.

The Montoneros succeeded at least in their immediate goal of provoking a violent right-wing crackdown. Ultimately, however, this crackdown led to the complete suppression of all leftist insurgent groups in the country. The Argentine military took control of all security forces and undertook its "dirty war" (q.v.) to kill all suspected leftists beginning in February 1975. By the end of 1976, 1,600 Montoneros had been killed and another 500 were killed in the first half of 1977. Following the flight of Montonero founder and leader Mario Firmenich to Rome in October 1977, along with a few of his lieutenants, Montonero activities continued only sporadically in Argentina and ended in 1979 when security forces killed Horacio Mendizábal, the chief Montonero leader who had remained active underground within Argentina. Finally in December 1981, Mario Firmenich called on surviving Montoneros to cease armed struggle in favor of political action, in effect signaling the end of the Montoneros as an active guerrilla and terrorist group. Firmenich returned in June 1987 to Argentina where he was tried for the terrorist offences of the Montoneros and sentenced to 30 years imprisonment. Firmenich received a presidential pardon on 29 December 1990, ironically along with General Jorge Videla who had conducted the ''dirty war'' campaign against leftist groups such as the Montoneros.

The Montoneros failed to perceive that the populist message of Juan Perón, as an eclectic hodgepodge combining leftist and rightist appeals designed to draw as broad a following as possible, could not be reduced simply to an unambiguous appeal for socialist revolution. Likewise the broad support the Montoneros received prior to the return of Perón was largely a function of public adulation of Perón, which extended to the Montoneros only insofar as they were perceived as his loyal followers. Thus when the Montoneros undertook their campaign in 1974, they overestimated the degree of popular support for themselves and their own ''authentic Perónism.''

MORAZANIST PATRIOTIC FRONT. The *Frente Patriótico Morazanista* (FPM) is a leftist guerrilla group, believed to be an arm of the outlawed Honduran Communist Party founded in 1979, that seeks primarily to drive out the U.S. military and diplomatic presence from Honduras. Whereas the Lorenzo Zelaya (q.v.) and Cinchonero (q.v.) groups had sought to create a leftist revolution following the Nicaraguan model in the early 1980s, the success of U.S.-trained Honduran counterinsurgency forces led many leftist survivors of those groups to conclude that the U.S. presence in Honduras would first have to be driven out before any revolution could succeed. Those groups and the FPM also enjoyed Cuban support and that of the former Sandinista government of Nicaragua. Given this Sandinista support and the use of Honduras as a staging area for contra forces fighting the

Nicaraguan government, the Morazanistas decided to concentrate on attacking U.S. advisers and military support personnel in Honduras.

On 8 August 1987, the FPM bombed a restaurant in Comayagua, north of Tegucigalpa, wounding five U.S. soldiers and six Honduran soldiers. On 17 July 1988, FPM made a machine-gun and grenade attack on U.S. soldiers leaving a discotheque in San Pedro Sula, wounding four of the nine soldiers who were part of a joint U.S.-Honduran task force stationed at the Honduran air force base in Palmerola. In December 1988, FPM claimed credit for bombing a Peace Corps office. In 1989, there were three other similar attacks on U.S. servicemen, including a 13 July 1989 bombing attack on nine U.S. Army military policemen outside the Lido Discotheque in the northern coastal city of La Ceiba. On 31 March 1990, three FPM snipers opened fire with automatic weapons on a U.S. Air Force bus en route from the coastal city of Tela to an inland military base, in which six soldiers were wounded. On 23 June 1991, the FPM launched an antitank rocket at the U.N. Observer Group office in Tegucigalpa causing damages.

Despite the group's effectiveness in making so many attacks and wounding so many U.S. and Honduran military personnel, it appears to be a small group. The regional peace efforts undertaken by the Central American nations and the replacement of the Sandinista regime in Nicaragua have not ended FPM activities.

MORO LIBERATION FRONT. The Moro Liberation Front, or Moro National Liberation Front (MLF), is a nonstate group of Muslim revolutionaries seeking autonomy for the Muslims in the islands of Mindanao and the Sulu Archipelago, a region covering about 13 provinces in the southern Philippines. The group has enjoyed the support of Libya's Muammar Qaddafi, the Chief Minister of the Malaysian state of Sabah, Tun Mustapha, and lately has begun to receive assistance from Iran. While not a material sponsor, the

Islamic Conference Organization, through its efforts at mediation between the MLF and Philippine government or among MLF factions, does confer moral support in backing the Moro guerrillas as an oppressed Muslim minority.

In 1972, Nur Misuari reorganized the Mindanao Independence Movement, which had been a relatively sedate political group, into a separatist and leftist revolutionary organization. In 1973, the MLF raised 15,000 fighters and captured most of Cotabato Province. In 1974, they captured Jolo Town and nearby Notre Dame College in the Sulu islands, which the Philippine armed forces were only able to recover after first leveling them with naval artillery and air force bombardments. The offensives of 1973 and 1974 apparently were timed to coincide with the Islamic Foreign Ministers' Conferences held in Benghazi in 1973 and then in Lahore the following year in order to force the Moro issue upon the agenda of these conferences and enlist the support of the Islamic Conference. On 7 April 1975, three MLF members hijacked a domestic Philippine Airlines flight, releasing the passengers in Manila, but holding the plane's crew and one of the Airline's executives hostage to guarantee safe passage to Libya. On arriving in Libya on 13 April 1975, they freed the hostages and were granted asylum by the Libyan government.

Although Nur Misuari succeeded in gaining the approbation and sympathy of the Muslim states, this in turn created a backlash within the Philippines. First, the resolve of the central government to crush the rebellion grew stronger. Second, Misuari's tactics and intransigent position alienated many Muslim supporters within the Philippines who thought the MLF would jeopardize their more attainable goals of gaining civic equality for Muslims and limited autonomy.

Misuari agreed to a 16-point accord with President Ferdinand Marcos in 1976, which established a cease-fire and provided for a referendum in April 1977 in the disputed 13 provinces. As Christians formed majorities in eight of these provinces the bid for Muslim autonomy was overwhelmingly rejected at the polls. The MLF never recovered from this moral defeat. Sporadic violations of the cease-fire occurred including the killings of Brigadier General Bautista and 34 unarmed soldiers in February 1977.

Internally the MLF splintered in rival factions with rivals of Misuari seeking some sort of accommodation with the Philippine government. Misuari continued to seek aid from Libya and later from Iran following its Islamic revolution, while the Marcos government succeeded in co-opting the local Muslim aristocracy as well as Misuari's rivals in the MLF. During the period from 1984–1986, when the central government was in some disarray due to the domestic revolution against Marcos, Misuari's followers made very limited gains in the south. Their new tactic, however, of kidnapping and holding foreigners as hostages alienated much of the international support they had previously enjoyed. In 1986 the new Philippine President Corazon Aquino signed a truce with the MLF, and violence substantially subsided afterward.

MOUNTAIN OFFICERS. The Mountain Officers is an obscure intrastate group of Guatemalan military officers that has sought the limited end of moving government policy further to the right through terrorist actions and threats. The group claimed responsibility for the bombing of a Mexicana Airlines office in 1988 in protest against the Mexican government's granting Guatemalan leftist guerrilla leaders safe passage and sanctuary. The right-wing group also made several death threats in spring 1988 against Mario Vinicio Cerezo Arevalo, the first democratically-elected civilian President of Guatemala since 1966.

MOVEMENT FOR THE LIBERATION OF BAHRAIN. The MLB is an Iranian state-sponsored group of Bahraini Shiite Muslims who aim at toppling the Al Khalifa dynasty in the Emirate of Bahrain and creating an Iranian-style Islamic Republic there. Following the abortive coup attempt of 13

December 1981 by the Iranian-sponsored Islamic Front for the Liberation of Bahrain (IFLB) that group had very limited success in trying to recruit more Bahrainis. While the IFLB turned more to contacting international human rights organizations and trying to accuse the Bahraini government of mistreatment of the arrested coup plotters, the Front had lost credibility as being an independent Islamic liberation movement.

The Movement for the Liberation of Bahrain, formed in 1983, essentially is a repackaging of the IFLB in a form more attractive for the recruitment of young Bahraini Shiites alienated from the current Sunnite government ruling the largely Shiite island-state. Its record so far has not been more impressive than that of its predecessor. In February 1984, the Bahraini coast guard intercepted a large shipment of Iranian arms before it landed. In late December 1987, one oil refinery engineer who had been recruited by Iran and trained to carry out a sabotage operation at Bahrain's one oil refinery was arrested.

MOVEMENT OF THE REVOLUTIONARY LEFT. The *Movimiento de la Izquierda Revolucionaria* (MIR) was a Chilean leftist guerrilla group and political party sponsored by Cuba that advocated revolution to establish a Marxist state in Chile. MIR also was given the use of radio facilities by Algeria and has received more limited support from other states close to Cuba such as Angola, Mozambique, and Nicaragua during the Sandinista period.

Founded in 1965 by leftist students at the University of Concepción, MIR became Castroite in 1967 and obtained Cuba's moral and material backing. Its current leader, Andrés Pascal Allende, a nephew of President Allende, runs MIR from its Havana headquarters. MIR benefitted from an amnesty under the Popular Unity government of President Salvador Gossens Allende (1970–1973) and was allowed to operate openly. MIR fought the military takeover the hardest of all the Chilean leftist groups even long after it became apparent that Allende was dead.

While MIR's recourse to political violence and terrorism could be rationalized in the context of the military coup of 11 September 1973 and subsequent violent repression of leftists in Chile, in fact its terrorist actions began as far back as 1967 when it began armed robberies, assaults, and murder as a part of its tactical repertoire. In spite of the wide opportunities for legal political participation under the government of Salvador Allende, MIR continued to act outside of the sphere of Chilean legality by organizing its own militias, carrying out illegal expropriations of farms and businesses, and assaulting members of rightist or rival leftist groups. The leaders of MIR reasoned that through such illegal acts they could compel Allende to advance beyond mere electoral politics, so forcing the establishment of a Marxist revolutionary state in Chile. In fact, Allende's reluctance to control MIR and the far-left wing of his Popular Unity government prompted the Chilean military to undertake the coup of 11 September 1973.

Following the killing of MIR's leader, Miguel Enríquez, in a shoot-out with security forces in 1974, Andrés Pascal Allende took command but was forced to flee Chile by 1976. From 1973 until 1983, MIR remained quiescent but with the wave of dissent that shook Chile beginning in 1983 was reinvigorated and re-established its political wing.

MIR has carried out several machine-gun attacks on police and security forces as well as bomb attacks on police stations during the 1980s. On 15 July 1980, MIR killers machine-gunned to death Lt. General Roger Vergara Campos, head of the Army Intelligence School, also killing his driver. During October and November 1983, MIR bombed four U.S.-affiliated firms. In June 1988, MIR bombed four banks in Santiago, causing serious damage but not harm to life or limb. MIR has tried to target higher-ranking functionaries of the Chilean government rather than ordinary policemen or soldiers and has been careful to avoid taking the lives of civilians or bystanders. MIR also has shunned targeting foreign nationals for assassination or kidnapping for ransom. Although MIR bombed four offices of U.S.-affiliated corporations in a 10-day period spanning October and November of 1983, as well as the bank bombings in June 1988, these bombings appeared intended to create maximum material damage rather than human injuries, which were minimal. Bombing attacks have also been directed at power lines, but MIR has generally abstained from using car bombings, unlike the rival Manuel Rodríguez Patriotic Front (q.v.).

At its height in 1973, MIR numbered some 10,000 members. Estimates of the total membership of the political and military branches of MIR put their strength between 100 and 500 members, although Andrés Pascal claimed MIR had at least 3,000 active members. MIR stockpiled its arms through infiltration and theft of Chilean arsenals as well as through Cuban support. In its bombings, MIR has used low-yield explosives generally available through thefts from mining operations. Despite the appearance of the Manuel Rodríguez Patriotic Front in 1983 as a dynamic rival, MIR remained the foremost underground revolutionary group within Chile as late as 1986. By 1987, however, it had split into two hostile factions and experienced a severe decline in membership and activities. Many MIR activists had left Chile by 1989, while in December 1989 Brazilian police cracked a kidnapping ring run by MIR in São Paulo used to finance its activities in Chile. Since that time the group appears to have remained inactive.

MUJAHIDEEN. The term mujahideen (Arabic plural of mujahid, "one who engages in struggle for the sake of God") is both a general designation for Muslim fighters engaged in jihad (q.v.) but also has been used as the name of various Muslim political and paramilitary groups.

1. Afghan Mujahideen - Following the Soviet invasion of Afghanistan in December 1979, those rebel groups that had been fighting the procommunist Kabul regime then undertook to resist and expel the Soviet troops. As they were

fighting what could be viewed as a jihad to rid Afghanistan of an infidel invading army, they became generally known as mujahideen.

The Afghan fighters actually belong to several different groups often divided along tribal and linguistic lines. Certain of these groups are primarily Islamic fundamentalist in character, such as the Hizb-i Islami (Islamic Party) of Gulbiddin Hikmatyar, which has received support from Iran, and the Harakat-i Inqilab-i Islami (Islamic Revolutionary Movement) led by Muhammad Nabi Muhammadi, which has received support from the Persian Gulf states. Other Afghan groups, such as the National Liberation Front and the National Islamic Front of Afghanistan, are umbrella organizations that have a more nationalistic than fundamentalist emphasis.

Following the 16 April 1992 collapse of the Najibullah regime, the more nationalistic mujahideen factions formed a new government that since then has been fighting the Islamic fundamentalist mujahideen led by Gulbiddin Hikmatyar, which have laid repeated sieges to, and made rocket attacks upon, districts and government buildings within Kabul.

2. Saziman-i Mujahideen-i Khalq-i Iran - The "People's Mujahideen Organization of Iran" is a nonstate Iranian revolutionary group that undertook armed struggle against the shah's regime in order to establish an Islamic state. The Iranian Mujahideen were mainly university students who formed an offshoot group from the Iran Liberation Movement, a group led by Mehdi Bazargan, which continued to exist as a token opposition group in Iran until banned on 18 October 1992.

The Mujahideen undertook armed struggle following an abortive revolt instigated by the Ayatollah Khomeini in 1963. The group became influenced by the syncretistic quasi-Islamic, quasi-Marxist teachings of the Iranian sociologist, Ali Shariati, who had been directly influenced by Frantz Fanon while studying in Paris. On 13 August 1972, they killed General Taheri, the police chief of Tehran, former warden of the Komiteh Prison in which Mujahideen members had been held and tortured and who had also crushed the civilian uprising in Qum during June 1963. On 2 June 1973, they killed U.S. Air Force colonels Turner and Sheafer in Tehran, and in August 1976 they killed three U.S. technicians associated with the U.S. military aid program to Iran. In 1975, however, the group split with a more secularist wing defecting to the Fedayan-i Khalq (q.v.).

While the group participated in the street fighting that brought down the Pahlavi monarchy in 1978–1979 Khomeini rejected their credentials as Islamic revolutionaries due to their refusal to accept his principle of leadership by the Shiite *ulama* (specialists of religious law) and also due to the Marxist content they had incorporated into their eclectic understanding of Islam. The Mujahideen allied themselves with the more liberal and nationalistic politicians led by President Abulhassan Bani-Sadr, who, however, was later deposed from the Iranian Presidency by Khomeini on 20 June 1981. Following Bani-Sadr's ouster, the Mujahideen carried out a terrorist campaign against the Khomeini regime. On 28 June 1981, the Islamic Republic Party headquarters was bombed, killing at least 72 high-ranking functionaries of the regime. A bomb that killed the next Iranian President Rajai and Prime Minister Bahonar on 30 August 1981 was also believed to be the work of the Mujahideen. The Islamic Republic retaliated with its own terror campaign against the Mujahideen and their known supporters. In the months that followed, the Mujahideen conducted suicide attacks in which individuals would approach Friday Prayers leaders and then detonate explosives hidden on their bodies, killing themselves and their victim. Often a motorcycle driver and passenger team would conduct drive-by machine-gun attacks on government offices. On 8 February 1981, Musa Khiabani, the operational head of the terrorist campaign within Iran, was tracked down and killed by Islamic Revolutionary Guards and the Mujahideen campaign within Iran sputtered into relative insignificance.

Although the Mujahideen had hoped in June 1981 to launch their own revolution against the clerical regime, they made two miscalculations. First, being themselves mainly members of the less traditional, more Western-oriented middle classes, the Mujahideen underestimated the depth of support Khomeini enjoyed among the masses of the more traditional lower classes of society. Second, because they undertook their campaign of antiregime terror during the middle of a national war of self-defense against an Iraqi invasion, their actions were arguably treasonable in spite of whatever the political failings of the regime may have been. In fact, the Mujahideen later accepted the sponsorship of the Iraqi regime, set up bases within Iraq, and deployed their own armed units under Iraqi command against Iranian troops in the warfronts, a move that cost them whatever support they had enjoyed among Iranian nationalists within Iran. The Mujahideen leader, Masud Rajavi, who had fled Iran with Bani-Sadr in 1981, briefly rallied exiled opposition groups in a National Council of Resistance. Over time, however, the Mujahideen degenerated into a cult of personality centered on Rajavi, which enforced a rigid ideological conformity on its membership and alienated the support of most of its allies and sympathizers.

3. Mujahideen-i Inqilab-i Islami - In March 1979, seven Islamic guerrilla groups that had fought against the Pahlavi regime before and during the Islamic revolution of Iran formed themselves into one militia group, the Mujahideen of the Islamic Revolution (MIR), a nonstate group enjoying Iranian state sponsorship that assisted the Islamic Republic of Iran in both its external revolutionary agenda and its internal repression of dissent. While some of its members had once been part of the People's Mujahideen of Iran (See above, subheading 2), the new group steadfastly avowed its belief in the leadership of the Shiite clergy, in particular the leadership of Khomeini.

This group was instrumental in the actual takeover of the U.S. Embassy on 4 November 1979. The most prominent member of the group was Behzad Nabavi, who served as one of the chief Iranian negotiators in ending the holding of the U.S. hostages and who later became Minister of Heavy Industries in the Islamic Republic. The MIR group were mainly laymen and, while they rejected the quasi-Marxism of the People's Mujahideen, they nonetheless favored the state capitalism and nationalization of basic industries and foreign trade that characterized the more radical wing of the Islamic Republic Party led by Prime Minister Hussein Musavi. The group split into factions, one aligned with the more radical hardliners of the Islamic Republic Party and others supporting the more pragmatic group led by Hujjatu-lislam Rafsanjani. When the infighting of the group became a scandal, Khomeini ordered the group dissolved on 6 October 1986.

MUNAZZAMAT AL JIHAD. Also known as "Tanzim al Jihad," or simply as "Jihad," this was the Sunnite Muslim funda-mentalist group in Egypt responsible for the assassination of Anwar Sadat on 6 October 1981. This group was an offshoot of Tahrir al Islami (q.v.), itself an offshoot of the Muslim Brotherhood (q.v.). It is not directly connected with the Shiite militia Islamic Jihad of Lebanon.

The Jihad group is an example of a *salafi* (puritan) Islamic fundamentalist group, believing it imperative for Muslim societies to return to a purely Islamic state similar to the city-state of Medina in the time of the Prophet Muhammad. Unlike the Egyptian Muslim Brotherhood, salafi fundamen-talists, such as Jihad, reject reformism and participation in electoral politics as means to purifying Islamic society, as being themselves part of the un-Islamic corruptions of contemporary Muslim civilization. That leaves jihad (q.v.), or holy war in the path of God, as the only means to restore true Islam. This group regarded Anwar Sadat as an apostate ruler due to his Westernization programs and to his role in shaping the Camp David peace accords with Israel, itself regarded by them as the absolute enemy of Islam. Therefore, as an enemy of Islam, the religious duty of jihad required them to fight and kill him. Sadat's assassins fully believed that once he was killed the majority of Egyptian Muslims would rise up and finish off the work of overthrowing what they held to be an apostate regime.

Following the assassination of Sadat by Jihad members led by Khalid Islambuli, an Egyptian Army officer and brother of Muhammad Islambuli, who was another Jihad member imprisoned earlier by the Egyptian government, Egyptian security forces arrested remnants of the assassins and other members of Jihad not directly involved. The five main principals were tried and later executed. Jihad activists in Asyut seized the local radio-TV station, several police stations, and the security forces local headquarters. Government forces retook Asyut in two days of heavy fighting, killing 188 of which 54 were government forces.

The leadership of Jihad consisted of Sheikh Umar Abdul Rahman (q.v.), a blind doctor of Islamic religious law at Asyut University, Muhammad Abdul Salam Faraj, the group's leading theoretician and publicist, and Aboud Abdul Latif Zumur, a lieutenant colonel in Egyptian military intelligence. At least 4 percent of Jihad members arrested before Sadat's assassination turned out to be members of the military, police, or intelligence services. In December 1986, about 30 Jihad members, including two Army majors, one captain, and one lieutenant, were arrested for setting up antigovernment combat training centers. In late February 1986, over 17,000 conscripts of the Central Security Police rioted in five provinces as well as Cairo, inflicting $500 million in damages on bars, nightclubs, and luxury hotels, all of which had been targeted by fundamentalist radicals, and looting police arsenals of their weapons.

MUNICH MASSACRE. On 5 September 1972, a group of Black September (q.v.) terrorists attacked the Israeli Munich Olympic Games team in the Olympic Village, killing 2 Israeli athletes outright and taking the remaining 9 Israeli athletes and coaches hostage. The 8 terrorists demanded the release of 234 prisoners in Israel, including Kozo Okamoto, the surviving Japanese Red Army member of the terrorist team that had struck Lod airport in May 1972. After 17 hours of negotiations between the terrorists and the West German government, which Israel had informed of its refusal of the terrorists' demands, the terrorists and their hostages were transferred in two helicopters to Fürstenfeldbruck airport outside Munich where, they were told, a Boeing 727 would take them to Cairo. Instead Bavarian police sharpshooters botched an attempt to kill the terrorists as they left the two helicopters. In the melee that ensued at about midnight on 6 September 1972, the terrorists shot their hostages dead and set the two helicopters on fire. Five of the terrorists died as well and their remaining wounded were captured and imprisoned. These, however, were later released in exchange for the release of a Lufthansa passenger plane seized by other Black September operatives on 29 October 1972.

The incompetence of the Bavarian police operation led West Germany to develop an elite antiterrorist squad, the Grenzschutzgruppe-9 (GSG-9), while the Israelis established the Wrath of God covert operations group that tracked down and killed those responsible for the operation.

MUSLIM BROTHERHOOD. The *Ikhwan al Muslimin* is a non-state Islamic fundamentalist group that seeks to replace existing secular governments in the Muslim world with Islamic regimes under which religious and political affairs would both be governed by the Shariah, that is, the sacred law of Islam. The name is applied to several territorial organizations, e.g., the Egyptian Muslim Brotherhood, the Syrian Muslim Brotherhood, and so on, that are formally independent of one another though all are historically derived from the original Ikhwan founded in Egypt by Hassan al Banna (b. 1903, d. 1949) in 1928. In lands whose governments are either sympathetic or at least not hostile to the Ikhwan, the local organization tends to define its aims and methods in terms of *islah*, reformism, whereas in countries whose governments are hostile the Ikhwan tends to define its mission in Islamic revolutionary terms. Terrorism has been used by the Ikhwan only instrumentally, in order to achieve their agenda when electoral means or other forms of political participation have been denied to them. Although individual territorial Ikhwan organizations have sought the support of other Muslim governments, whether of religious regimes such as Saudi Arabia or of secular regimes such as Bathist Iraq, these amount to little more than tactical alliances with what the Ikhwan may regard as its own strategic enemies.

Banna, a primary schoolteacher in Ismailia, founded the Ikhwan to educate young men in the values of Islam and to protect them from seduction by Western values. A brilliant organizer, Banna quickly developed the group into a nationwide network. By 1933, the headquarters were moved to Cairo, and by 1940, the Ikhwan had 500 branches. The political strength of the Ikhwan aroused the fear and jealousy of the ruling Waqf party, which threw Banna into prison briefly in 1941. In 1942, Banna ordered the formation of the secret apparatus of ''spiritual messengers'' skilled in the ''art of death.'' By 1946, the Ikhwan had 5,000 branches comprising at least 500,000 members as well as 40,000 employed in its secret apparatus. Members of the Ikhwan were to be found even among the teaching faculty of Al Azhar University, which remains the most esteemed Islamic theological school in the Sunnite Muslim world and from which students of 22 different Muslim countries brought back home the message of the Ikhwan and began to create new branches of the organization abroad.

During the period from 1946–1947, the Ikhwan clashed with Waqf supporters in street riots, which led to the December 1948 ban on the organization. That same month the Egyptian prime minister was assassinated by Ikhwan members. In reprisal, government agents murdered Banna by February 1949. From 1950 to 1954, the Ikhwan collaborated with the Egyptian Free Officers in overthrowing King Farouk. Conflict then broke out between the Islamic fundamentalist Ikhwan and the secular, modernizing military junta under Gamal Abdel Nasser. With the failure of the 23 October 1954 Ikhwan-inspired assassination attempt against Nasser, a ban on the Ikhwan and crackdown ensued in which 6 Ikhwan leaders were hanged and 4,000 followers arrested.

Following Nasser's death, his successor, Anwar Sadat, pardoned the remaining imprisoned Ikhwan members, allowed the return of those who had fled Egypt in 1954, and allowed limited participation of the Ikhwan in elections. Sadat hoped to co-opt the Ikhwan in order to bolster his image among the Egyptian public as a believing, religious president. In fact, by 1978 the Ikhwan had infiltrated and co-opted the majority of the 1,000 legal Islamic associations chartered in Egypt and had become the largest legal source of opposition to Sadat's free trade and investment policies as well as to his policy of seeking a separate peace agreement with Israel. Sadat erred also in believing that by indulging a chastised Ikhwan, he could thereby split and weaken the Islamic fundamentalist opposition.

Although the Ikhwan and the more radical, illegal Islamic fundamentalist groups, such as Munazzamat al Jihad (q.v.) and Takfir wal Higrah (q.v.), maintained an appearance of mutual disapproval and rivalry, in fact, according to research by American University in Cairo sociologist Saadeddin Ibrahim, the Ikhwan functions very much as the generator of these more radical groups and as their legal front organization as circumstances require. In this light, Sadat's assassination less than a month after his 3 September 1981 crackdown on the Ikhwan appears less coincidental as does also the fact that the same radical groups that did not hesitate to murder a former Minister of Religious Affairs or Sadat himself have never attacked or killed members of the Ikhwan despite their appearance of rejecting the Ikhwan for having allowed itself to be co-opted by the same abhorred regime. By the late 1980s, the Ikhwan was Egypt's leading opposition party, while the other illegal fundamentalist groups had between 70,000 and 100,000 adherents.

As the Ikhwan propagated and reproduced itself in other Arab lands, it has shown remarkable adaptation to local circumstances, becoming a political party wherever electoral competition promised power, such as Egypt or pre-1963 Syria, or becoming charitable and educational societies where political competition was more constrained, such as in Jordan or the emirates of the Arabian peninsula. In Tunisia the Ikhwan renamed itself the Hizb al Islami, the Islamic Party, the direct precursor of the Islamic Tendency Movement (q.v.). In Algeria the Ikhwan called itself the Ahl al Dawa, People of the Call (to faith), which has created the Islamic Salvation Front. In the Gaza Strip and West Bank the Palestinian branch of the Ikhwan formed the Islamic Resistance Movement, known also as Hamas (q.v.), which has played a major role in the intifada (q.v.).

In Syria, where the Ikhwan have been banned since the Bathist coup of 1963, the Ikhwan has attempted to carry out an armed insurgency with occasional major terrorist acts, which have been retaliated against by massive acts of Syrian state repression. Following the military defeat of Syria in the 1967 war with Israel, Ikhwan members from the Syrian cities of Homs, Aleppo, and Hama underwent military training in Al Fatah (q.v.) camps in Jordan, which marked the transformation of the Syrian Ikhwan from a party to a paramilitary movement. Following Syrian president Hafez al-Asad's decision in 1976 to enter the Lebanese civil war on the side of the Maronite Christian forces and against the Palestinians, the Ikhwan decided to undertake jihad against the Syrian regime. In February 1978 the Ikhwan assassinated key Bathist officials and attacked Rifaat al-Asad, the president's younger brother, who headed the national security forces. On 16 June 1979, the Ikhwan began to strike at police stations, Bathist party offices, and government and military facilities, beginning with a massacre of military cadets at the Aleppo Artillery School. The Ikhwan also began to assassinate

Soviet civilian and military advisers and Sunni clergymen who supported the regime.

In April 1980, al-Asad launched a crackdown on the front organizations that supported the Ikhwan and arrested 5,000 supporters. On 25 June 1980, the Ikhwan attempted to assassinate al-Asad. In reprisal the Syrian regime summarily executed as many as 300 imprisoned Ikhwan leaders and passed a decree on 7 July 1980 making membership in, or association with, the Ikhwan a capital offense. On 11 August 1980, the regime summarily executed all 80 apartment dwellers from a complex that had harbored an Ikhwan sniper. The Ikhwan had goaded the regime into such repressive measures in the hope that the Syrian people would then rise up against regime repression, but the severity of the state terror had the opposite effect of quelling all open support for the Ikhwan.

The Ikhwan ceased activities for one year in order to reassess strategy and tactics. They published a manifesto, "the Declaration and Programme of the Islamic Revolution in Syria," and sought Iranian support. Iran, which had a tactical alliance with Syria against its current wartime enemy Iraq, declined its support. The Ikhwan then turned to Iraq for support and obtained light arms and shoulder-held rockets as well as the use of Iraqi radio facilities. On 28 November 1981, a massive car bombing killed 64 people in downtown Damascus, an action blamed on the Ikhwan by Syria but for which the Ikhwan denied responsibility. Iraqi agents had conducted similar operations in Tehran even before the outbreak of the Iran-Iraq war. In February 1982, the Ikhwan launched its offensive in Hama in which they defeated the Syrian Third Armored Division. The Iraq-based radio called on the Syrian people to rise up and join the insurgency. Al-Asad responded with 12,000 soldiers who cordoned off Hama, a city of 200,000 people, and began to level it over a two-week period by tank fire, artillery, and helicopter gunship fire. The Syrian army lost 1,000 men while as many as 25,000 civilians perished.

The Syrian Ikhwan have never regained their strength

since this defeat. While they had 30,000 members before the 7 July 1980 decree banning membership in the group on pain of death, their numbers fell afterward to less than 5,000.

The various Ikhwan organizations have had histories of using assassination, military attacks, and arson or bombing of bars, nightclubs, or hotels as means to force Muslim states to heed their agenda when they have otherwise been repressed by those governments or else denied full political participation. In the period from 1990–1991, while Muslim states such as Jordan, Algeria, and Tunisia have allowed greater scope to electoral and parliamentary processes, the Ikhwan-generated Islamic political parties have scored impressive electoral victories. In this regard one should note that political violence and terrorist actions have erupted in Algeria and Tunisia only after the secular governments there have taken steps to nullify the electoral gains of such groups. In the same period the various Ikhwan organizations have sought more coordination and mutual assistance. Following the Tunisian government's crackdown on the Islamic Tendency Movement, the government of the Sudan, now dominated by Ikhwan members, gave the leader of the Tunisian group refuge. The Ikhwan-dominated Sudanese government has also allowed Iranian Islamic Revolutionary Guards (q.v.) and Lebanese Hezbollah (q.v.) to set up training bases in Sudan while the Islamic Republic of Iran has declared its support for the Ikhwan-based political parties in Algeria and Tunisia, which were denied electoral victories in 1991.

- N -

NAR. See Armed Revolutionary Nucleus.

NARCO-TERRORISM. Narco-terrorism refers actually to two different phenomena: first, a form of revolutionary terrorism in which insurgents or terrorists use the production of narcotics to finance their revolutionary activities or else as a means of undermining the social fabric of the United States; second, a form of entrepreneurial terrorism in which the drug traffickers themselves use terrorism in order to keep governments, police forces, or guerrilla groups from interfering with their operations or profits.

Evidence of the entrepreneurial narco-terrorism is quite striking, with the Medellín drug cartel sponsoring the "Death to Kidnappers" group (See MAS) as well as the "Extraditables," (q.v.). These groups assassinated 3 Colombian presidential candidates and have carried out several car bombings and also have bombed at least one domestic Colombian airplane flight, in order to force the Colombian government to desist from its antidrug campaign. Evidence of guerrilla involvement with drug trafficking can be found in Colombia, Peru, and Thailand where guerrilla insurgents control areas of drug crop cultivation or smuggling.

Demonstrating that guerrillas aid and abet drug trafficking in order to corrupt North American society is not quite so straightforward. The simplest explanation consistent with the known facts would seem to be that guerrillas will use whatever resources are available to them, whether extortion or kidnapping or drug trafficking, to finance their revolutionary agenda. Similarly, certain of the Afghan Mujahideen groups have participated in the manufacture and smuggling of heroin derived from Afghani opium but did so without regard for their own Islamic scruples against narcotics and without regard for the ultimate markets of these drugs, which were more likely to be found in the West than in the Soviet Union. While this line of reasoning suggests that narco-terrorism by guerrilla groups need not be truly revolutionary in its intent, the terrorism researcher Rachel Ehrenfeld has documented several instances of what are purported to be narco-terrorism as a form of revolutionary terrorism meant to undermine capitalist societies.

NARODNAYA VOLYA. The Russian *People's Will* group was among the earliest self-consciously revolutionary terrorist groups of the modern era. They sought to assassinate high-ranking Tsarist officials to bring about a social and political revolution in Russia. This group also embraced the idea of using suicide-bombing attacks if necessary to achieve their goals but were also very careful to avoid killing innocent bystanders unnecessarily. Narodnaya Volya theorist Gerasin Romanenko argued the moral superiority of terrorism over mass revolution on the grounds that terrorism avoided the massive bloodshed certain to accompany any mass uprising. Narodnaya Volya also argued that terrorism was impermissible in democratic countries as political activists there had nonviolent means to seek social progress or redress of social wrongs.

From 1878 to 1881, this group assassinated the governor-general of St. Petersburg and also the head of the internal security branch of the Tsarist secret police. The group actually made five assassination attempts against Tsar Alexander II before finally succeeding in a sixth attempt on 1 March 1881. Shortly afterward most of the 50 or so members of the group were arrested and the principal leaders hanged in public.

NATIONAL FRONT. A political party of British fascists founded in 1967 with the aims of opposing nonwhite immigration to Britain, opposing leftists and Jews, and seeking to create a racialist and corporatist state in Britain through a combination of political violence and electoral competition. From 1972 to 1977, the ranks of followers of the National Front expanded greatly due to British backlash against a heightened increase in black Caribbean, East Indian, and African immigration from former colonial possessions to Britain. In the 1974 general election, the Front averaged 3.1 percent of the vote and by 1977 gained 5 percent of the votes in Greater London's local council elections.

The Front achieved its mobilization of racist votes partly through its strategy of holding marches through predominantly nonwhite urban districts. Youths from Skinhead gangs (q.v.) would use these occasions to bait nonwhites and commit acts of vandalism. These marches also attracted radical leftist counterdemonstrators. Racial riots often broke out as well as clashes between the rightists and leftists.

While the National Front became the largest and most successful of Britain's fascist groups, personal rivalries and disagreements over the group's fundamental strategy rendered it largely ineffective. In 1979, the National Front leader Martin Webster (b. 1943) was convicted of inciting racial hatred, while a former Front chairman, Kenneth Matthews (b. 1935), was sentenced to six years in prison for attempted arson of a leftist newspaper office.

NATIONAL FRONT FOR THE LIBERATION OF COR-SICA (FNLC). The FNLC, a nonstate sponsored terrorist group seeking Corsican independence from France, has been active at least since May 1976 when it began a bombing campaign in mainland France and in Corsica. Most of its mainland targets have been French governmental offices, banks, or tourist offices connected with Air France, while in Corsica properties belonging to non-Corsicans have been targeted as well. FNLC conducted 6 bombings in Paris on 23 April 1980; 4 bombings in 1981, including an attack causing heavy damages upon the Palais de Justice in Paris; 2 bombings in Corsica in 1982; 20 bombings in Paris in 1983; and 16 bombings in 1984, hitting targets in Paris, Marseilles, and Toulon. In 1985 alone, FNLC was responsible for 96 of the 142 incidents of domestic terrorism in France. In its bomb attacks, the FNLC has been careful to avoid human casualties, its first known casualties having been caused in 1980 after 4 years of operations. Following the 1 May 1986 FNLC raid on the Cargese Holiday Camp on Corsica, 2 people were killed and 3 wounded when the camp owner tried to defuse the bomb the FNLC had left behind. In a previous case, on 22 March 1986, masked FNLC gunmen robbing a tourist resort in southern Corsica evacuated the 20 tourists from the facilities before bombing them so that none of their victims would be hurt. On 11 December 1989, the FNLC destroyed some 40 holiday homes on Corsica under construction for French buyers.

Apart from these bombings the FNLC made one machine-gun attack on French policemen guarding the Iranian Embassy on 14 May 1980, apparently in retaliation for the sentencing of seven Corsican separatists that day. On 23 April 1983, French police uncovered two FNLC arms caches and discovered an FNLC counterfeiting operation.

The FNLC is not known to have any foreign state sponsorship and little more is known about its political agenda apart from the demand of independence for Corsica.

NATIONAL LIBERATION ARMY. *Ejército de Liberación Nacional* (ELN) is the name of at least two major revolutionary guerrilla groups in Latin America.

1. The Colombian National Liberation Army is a Castroite revolutionary group enjoying Cuban state sponsorship. Its main distinction from other Colombian guerrilla groups has been its steadfast refusal to participate in the national reconciliation negotiations ongoing between the Colombian government and other major leftist insurgent groups since March 1984 or to participate in open electoral politics. The ELN has around 1,000 members and consists of several operationally independent fronts, some of which have turned into separate factions. One of these fronts, the Frente Simón Bolívar, eventually came to oppose the intransigence of the main leadership of the ELN.

The ELN was established on 4 July 1964 by leftist students disillusioned with the Communist Party of Colombia (PCC) and more attracted to the Cuban Revolution. Throughout its history, ELN has had poor relations with the Communist Party of Colombia which in turn formed its own guerrilla organization, the Revolutionary Armed Forces of Colombia (q.v.)(FARC) largely to counter the ELN initiative.

Although ELN began with Cuban material and moral

support, in 1968 due to Soviet pressure on Cuba to cease support for Colombian guerrilla groups, ELN experienced a hiatus in activity and its membership fell to around 80. In 1969, it began to finance itself through a series of kidnappings for ransom and by bank robberies. From 1969 until 1973, ELN was considered the most effective of Colombia's guerrilla groups until military anti-insurgency efforts destroyed its support network in the cities. Following 1975, ELN re-emerged and by the late 1980s numbered around 500 to 1,000 combatants. Since 1988, it has become the most active terrorist group in Colombia. ELN's main area of activity has been in the eastern plains of Colombia.

Some of ELN's more noteworthy actions include the following: On 6 October 1975, ELN killed the inspector general of the Army, Ramón Arturo Rincón Quiñones. On 21 January 1976, they bombed the Spanish Embassy in Bogotá. During July 1983, ELN conducted a bombing campaign called "Operation Free Central America" in which the Salvadoran Consulate in Medellín and police stations in Aranjuez were struck. On 23 November 1983, ELN kidnapped Dr. Jaime Betancur Cuartes, the brother of the Colombian president. This action, as well as ELN reluctance to undertake peace talks with the government, drew forth a rebuke from Fidel Castro, who persuaded ELN to release Dr. Cuartes three weeks after his capture.

Although ELN gained publicity from having recruited the Catholic priest Fr. Camilo Torres Restrepo, a member of a prominent Colombian family who was killed in guerrilla warfare in 1966, and although another priest, Fr. Manuel Pérez Martínez, became an ELN leader, there is no evidence that the group's secular ideology owes any of its inspiration to liberation theology (q.v.) whose emergence it antedates by several years. Actually ELN has been active in targeting religious groups or figures of whatever denomination that they view as being politically conservative or aligned with U.S. "imperialism." In October 1987, in addition to bombing a naval facility in Barrancabermeja, ELN bombed three

Mormon churches in Boyaca. In October 1989, ELN killed the Catholic bishop of Aracua.

ELN has tried to destroy systematically the economic infrastructure of Colombia. In December 1986, they attacked U.S.-associated oil production facilities, destroying machinery and stealing explosives. During January to August 1987, ELN bombed petroleum pipelines, attacked oil exploration and drilling camps, as well as other U.S.-Colombian targets. These attacks serve the twofold purpose of protesting the foreign presence in the Colombian economy and of depriving the government of economic viability. Attacks on the petroleum-producing facilities cost the Colombian government $400 million in 1988 alone. In June 1989, an ELN bombing of the pipeline terminal in Covenas, Sucre Department, temporarily halted oil exports from that port.

Although ELN remains one of the most active of Colombian guerrilla groups in the late 1980s, its relative prominence owes more to the reduced activity of the other major leftist groups, which have chosen to take advantage of the truce of May 1984 and to participate in the open political arena.

2. The Bolivian National Liberation Army is an umbrella group embracing the Nestor Paz Zamora Commando (q.v.) and other minor Bolivian leftist groups. The original Bolivian ELN was the group founded and led by Ernesto Che Guevara in Bolivia from November 1966 to October 1967, which was routed and destroyed by Bolivian troops trained by U.S. counterinsurgency advisers. Little is known of the current ELN apart from the activities of the Nestor Paz Zamora Commando. The tactics and rhetoric of the group suggest that, like the original ELN, the current one may be a foreign-directed group imported into Bolivia rather than a true domestic phenomenon. In this case the Tupac Amaru Revolutionary Movement (q.v.) appears to be the primary sponsor of the ELN. On 10 October 1990, the twenty-third anniversary of the announcement of Che Guevara's death, the Nestor Paz Zamora group bombed the U.S. Embassy

Marine guards residence in La Paz. Numerous threats were made against the U.S. Embassy through 1991 in the name of the ELN, while a fake bomb was found in an elevator in the U.S. Embassy in April 1991.

NATIONAL LIBERATION FRONT OF ALGERIA. The *Front de Libération National* (FLN) was an Algerian nationalist party that engaged in guerrilla warfare and terrorist attacks on the French colonial government to obtain independence for Algerian Arabs. Founded on 1 November 1954, the FLN fought both an urban guerrilla terrorist campaign in Algiers and dominated large areas outside the cities. The FLN also conducted assassinations of pro-colonial Algerian Arabs and a bombing campaign within France during August-September 1958. Egypt and Syria provided funds and arms while Tunisia and Morocco also provided sanctuaries and bases after those states had achieved independence in 1956.

France reacted to FLN activities with massive reprisals and systematic torture of Arab suspects, which further alienated Algerian Arabs from colonial rule. About 1,200 FLN urban guerrillas contested French control of Algiers in the "battle of Algiers" for the first eight months of 1957. The French crushed this insurrection ruthlessly, but at the cost of alienating the noncombatant Arab population. By 1958, around 87,000 Algerians, 10,000 of them noncombatants, had been killed as opposed to 8,700 French, of which 1,500 were civilians. After assuming power, President Charles de Gaulle decided in 1959 to hold negotiations with the FLN to grant Algerian Arabs self-rule and eventual independence. This prompted a strong reaction from the French settlers in Algeria and certain military officers who formed the OAS (q.v.), or Secret Army Organization, which terrorized both Arab Algerians and the French government with bombings and assassinations both in France and Algeria.

France agreed on 5 July 1962 to put Algeria independence to a referendum vote in September 1962 in which 91 percent voted for independence. The FLN became the single official state party. Internal divisions led to purges within the FLN, which adopted secularist and socialist policies. During the FLN's domination, Algeria has provided sanctuary, facilities, and training bases to various terrorist or insurgent groups, such as the Basque Fatherland and Liberty (q.v.) group, the Chilean Movement of the Revolutionary Left (MIR, q.v.), the French Canadian FLQ (q.v.), and Polisario, as well as financial and moral support for the PLO.

The FLN ceased to be the only legal party with the adoption of a new national constitution on 23 February 1989 allowing a multiparty system. In the first freely contested elections held in Algeria since independence, however, the FLN was defeated in provincial and municipal elections on 12 June 1990 by the Islamic Salvation Front, an Islamic fundamentalist party. In the first round of parliamentary elections on 26 December 1991, the Islamic Salvation Front won 188 seats. Remnants of the FLN within the government and armed forces staged an internal coup on 11 January 1992, forcing the resignation of President Chadhli Benjedid, and cancelled the runoff parliamentary elections, so denying the fundamentalists a national electoral victory. Currently, the remnants of the FLN within the secular Algerian government are facing an Islamic fundamentalist insurgent group, the Armed Islamic Movement, believed to be the armed wing of the Islamic Salvation Front, which assassinated Algerian President Muhammad Boudiaf on 29 June 1992.

NATIONAL SALVATION FRONT. The NSF is a coalition of Palestinian groups opposed to the 11 February 1985 Amman accords with Jordan agreed to by Yasir Arafat and much of the Palestine National Council. These accords would have allowed some political solution to the Palestinian problem with less than full sovereignty or total territorial integrity of pre-1948 Palestine. The Front was formed on 25 March 1985 in Damascus with the Popular Front for the Liberation of Palestine (q.v.), the National Alliance, and the Palestine Liberation Front, and several other groups opposed to Arafat.

Syria and Libya, supporters of the rejectionist elements within the PLO, gave their support to the NSF as an organization that could challenge Arafat's leadership and legitimacy within the Palestinian community.

From the viewpoint of Syria's President Al-Asad the presence of Syrian-sponsored groups within the NSF, such as Saiqa and the Fatah-Provisional Command, made the NSF appear to be a potential vehicle for Syrian policy. Also the NSF served to divide and weaken the PLO, allowing Syria to dominate Lebanon more easily. These calculations went awry with the outbreak of the "war of the camps" on 19 May 1985, when members of Amal (q.v.), a Syrian-sponsored Shiite militia, clashed with Palestinian militia members guarding the PLO refugee camps. In the off-again, on-again fighting that lasted until 7 April 1987, over 2,500 people were killed.

The upshot of the war of the camps was that the NSF chose to side with Fatah in defending the Palestinian camps against Amal while Amal itself was weakened. Rather than becoming a vassal of Syria, the NSF was largely dominated by the PFLP while the groups beholden to Syria within the NSF played only a marginal role.

NATIONAL SOCIALIST LIBERATION FRONT. The National Socialist Liberation Front (NSLF) is the most violent of the U.S. neo-Nazi groups that advocates terrorism and armed revolution to overthrow the United States government. After the 25 August 1967 assassination of George Lincoln Rockwell, founder and leader of the American Nazi Party, Rockwell's successor, Matthias Koehl changed the party name to the National Socialist White People's Party (NSWPP) and undertook other changes that angered Rockwell loyalists. Karl Hand, Jr. and other neo-Nazis who did not accept Matthias Koehl as Rockwell's successor broke away from the NSWPP in 1969 to form their own American Nazi party. The NSLF made the older American Nazi party organization the first object of its attacks but later, in the 1970s, turned its energies to attacking leftist organizations, such as the now defunct Socialist Workers' Party. The NSLF is believed responsible for a number of bombing attacks against leftist organizations in southern California conducted in the 1970s, including the 4 February 1975 fragmentation bomb attack on the Los Angeles headquarters of the Socialist Workers Party, causing severe injuries to all present.

The group is headquartered in Metaire, Louisiana, and recruits its members heavily from the state and federal prisons, pressure cookers of the sort of racial hatreds and tensions that provide both the fertile ground for neo-Nazi ideology and those recruits having the skills needed for an organization dedicated to the use of violence and terrorism to achieve its white supremacist goals.

NAXALITES. Naxalites were mainly Indian university students of middle-class origin who rejected parliamentary democracy and sought to create a Chinese-style communist revolution in India beginning with guerrilla warfare and a peasant insurgency. This name, which actually has been applied to several Maoist groups active in northern India and West Bengal in the 1960s and 1970s, is derived from the West Bengal village of Naxalbara where these leftists incited a short-lived peasant revolt in 1967. Beginning in 1969, they promoted an ''annihilation campaign'' directed at landlords, moneylenders, and local policemen against whom the rural peasantry had substantial grievances. When the Naxalite ''Red Terror'' campaign was carried into Calcutta in 1970, the Indian government responded with its own wave of repression in the period from 1970–1972. Thousands more were arrested during the state of emergency declared in 1975. Many of these were shortly released under an amnesty declared by the Janata government in 1977, which had succeeded Indira Gandhi's government. Naxalite violence resumed briefly with two bombings of the Soviet Trade Mission in Calcutta in April 1978; it then diminished during the 1980s, however, being restricted mainly to West Bengal and other rural regions of India.

While the Naxalite movement has often been compared with anarchistic leftist terrorist groups that appeared in the same period, such as the Red Army Faction (q.v.) or Direct Action (q.v.), unlike those groups the Naxalites did succeed in mobilizing a class-based constituency of oppressed rural peasants and in instigating an insurgency that went beyond the actions merely of a vanguardist group. In this respect, the Naxalites were more comparable to the Sendero Luminoso (q.v.) of Peru, which has similarly mobilized Peruvian Indian communities, although the Naxalites apparently lacked the cohesive leadership and disciplined following that Sendero achieved.

NECHAYEV, SERGEY G. (b. 1847, d. 1882) Russian revolutionary and author of the *Catechism of the Revolutionist,* written in 1869, which provided the portrait of the ideal terrorist willing to sacrifice everything in devotion to the revolutionary cause. In the *Catechism,* Nechayev advocated the assassination of moderate political leaders so that the remaining hardliners would resort to severe repression that would in turn either alienate the public or move them to join the revolutionaries, a line of thought echoed in the writings of Marighella and several other revolutionary terrorists. Nechayev caused a comrade to be killed as part of an internal purge in his own circle of revolutionaries. This discredited Nechayev in the eyes of other revolutionaries while he himself was convicted for the murder and sent to prison where he died of tuberculosis.

NEO-NAZIS. Neo-Nazism is an attempt to revive, rehabilitate, or romanticize the political movement or ideology of the Third Reich. Neo-Nazi groups usually advocate overthrowing a constitutional democratic order in favor of a racialist, totalitarian state and rationalize the use of political violence and terrorism to achieve this goal. Two essential Nazi doctrines are, first, the belief in the superiority of an imagined Indo-European racial stock that alone is believed to have advanced human civilization, and, second, the belief in the absolute evil and malice of the Jews, viewed as the corrupters of European civilization.

A number of groups have appeared both within Germany and in other countries that idolize the memory of Adolf Hitler and seek to reproduce his racist and ultranationalistic movement in some form. Such groups are outlawed in Germany under its post-World War II constitutional law as is the display of Nazi memorials and symbols. The West German Federal Office for Defense of the Constitution (Bundesamt für Verfassungsschutz) is charged with investigating and banning groups that seek to revive Nazism. Accordingly many of them assume the guise of student clubs or sporting clubs and usually do not openly display swastikas or pictures of Adolf Hitler. In Germany such groups included the Action-Front of National Socialists (q.v.), the National Democratic Party, the Hoffmann Military Sports Group (q.v.), all of which are now banned or defunct, though such groups tend to reappear under different names and guises. By 1983, there were an estimated 1,400 known neo-Nazis in West Germany of whom 850 were organized into groups. Following the reunification of Germany in 1990, the visibility of neo-Nazism in Germany increased dramatically with a marked increase in attacks upon Eastern European immigrants and Romanian gypsies. During August 1992, over 800 neo-Nazis convereged on the Baltic port of Rostock and attacked foreign refugees with fire bombs, gunfire and clubs. German neo-Nazis engaged in 4,500 such attacks on foreigners causing 17 deaths and over 100 injured in 1992 alone.

In other countries neo-Fascist organizations have developed that may not openly identify with Nazism but have a similar ideology and political program and whose membership contains many neo-Nazis. In Great Britain the National Front (q.v.) is an example, while in France the European Nationalist Fascists (FNE, q.v.) is another, whose members include former functionaries of the Vichy regime of Nazi-occupied France.

In the United States the American Nazi party of George Lincoln Rockwell was the most prominent and earliest neo-Nazi group. Its name was changed to the National Socialist White People's Party after Rockwell's assassination and later to the New Order. The National Socialist Liberation Front (q.v.) is a more militant group that broke away from the National Socialist White People's Party. The National Alliance of William Pierce, a Rockwell disciple, is another neo-Nazi group. The Order (q.v.), also called the Bruder Schweigen, was a neo-Nazi group that grew out of the Aryan Nations movement.

Those groups that adhere to the Identity Christianity (q.v.) doctrine often share beliefs and attitudes virtually identical to those of the neo-Nazis. Such groups include the Aryan Nations (q.v.), the Christian-Patriot Defense League (q.v.), the Covenant, the Sword and the Arm of the Lord (CSA, q.v.), the Ku Klux Klan (q.v.), and the White Patriot Army (q.v.). Very often members of these organizations have been formerly members of neo-Nazi groups, or else continue to hold membership in such groups, or else will join some neo-Nazi group in preference to, or in addition to, membership in these other organizations.

Neo-Nazi groups have tried to coordinate their moves with similar groups both within the United States and elsewhere. The Order donated many of the proceeds of their armored truck robberies to a number of neo-Nazi groups and figures in the United States. German neo-Nazi groups used to receive financial support and printed materials from American neo-Nazis, such as Gary Lauck. Neo-Nazis have also sought sponsorship from states and groups known to be hostile to Israel. Manfred Roeder, formerly a leader of the neo-Nazi *Deutsche Aktionsgruppen*, met once with Yasir Arafat's deputy, Khalil al Wazir, and even tried to solicit aid from Iran, but without success. The Hoffman Military Sports Group established a cooperative arrangement with al Fatah, sending Sports Group members to train in PLO camps.

Another phenomenon closely tied to neo-Nazism has been

the Skinhead (q.v.) movement. Just as the original Nazis recruited many of their original Stormtroopers from the hoodlums and youth gangs of Berlin and other German cities, so too neo-Nazi groups in the U.S. such as the White Aryan Resistance, are recruiting Skinheads. Similar phenomena have been witnessed in Britain, where soccer club rowdies as well as Skinheads would spontaneously join in National Front demonstrations or assaults on Asian or African immigrants, as well as in Germany where soccer clubs also will join with neo-Nazis in assaulting minority members, feminists, or homosexuals. Although Nazism, and Fascism generally, are regarded by believers in the liberal democratic tradition as discredited movements, the existence and apparent vitality of so many neo-Nazi groups throughout the Western world indicates the continuing appeal of this ideology.

NESTOR PAZ ZAMORA COMMANDO. The CNPZ describes itself as a unit of a National Liberation Army (q.v.), named after the group of the same name founded and led by Ernesto Che Guevara in the 1960s. The CNPZ seeks to overthrow the democratic Bolivian government in favor of a Cuban-style revolutionary Marxist state. The tactics of the group strongly suggest external aid from the Tupac Amaru Revolutionary Movement (q.v.) of Peru, itself a beneficiary of Cuban state support.

The CNPZ undertook its first action with the kidnapping of Jorge Lonsdale, the president of the Bolivian subsidiary of Coca-Cola, on 11 June 1990 who was held for $500,000 ransom. Lonsdale was killed on 5 December 1990 during a police raid and attempted hostage rescue. On 10 October 1990, the CNPZ bombed the U.S. Embassy Marine Guard residence in La Paz, severely damaging the building. This bombing was accompanied by a machine-gun attack that killed one Bolivian guard and wounded another.

The CNPZ is named after a former Roman Catholic seminary student who became a leftist guerrilla after the

capture and execution of Che Guevara in 1967. Nestor Paz
Zamora and his group perished in 1970, reportedly of
starvation and exposure while trying to fight the Bolivian
army. Ironically Nestor Paz Zamora was the brother of Jaime
Paz Zamora, elected president of Bolivia in 1989, who also
had been a Roman Catholic seminary student and leftist
opponent of the Bolivian government.

While the CNPZ is supposed to be only one group within
the umbrella organization of the National Liberation Army
(ELN), there is little information available about other
members of that umbrella group. The CNPZ is thought to
have about 100 members and may constitute the bulk of the
ELN. After the murder of Jorge Lonsdale, it was learned that
his killer was actually an Italian, Michael (Miguel) North-
fuster, while another of the guerrillas slain in the rescue
attempt turned out to be a Peruvian. The Tupac Amaru group
is believed to have expanded its operations into Bolivia
primarily to expand its fund-raising extortionary activities
there and possibly sponsors and controls the CNPZ group.

NEW AFRIKAN FREEDOM FIGHTERS. The New Afrikan
Freedom Fighters (NAFF) is a leftist black American group
that aims to undertake armed revolution to create an independent black homeland within the United States. This group is
an offshoot of the Republic of New Afrika, a black nationalist political group that advocates that black Americans
establish their own independent black homeland in the
southeastern United States.

On 18 October 1984, nine NAFF members were arrested
in New York City for conspiracy to rob an armored car and to
assist in the prison escape of Nathaniel Burns (aka, Donald
Weems), who was convicted for his participation in the
October 1981 Brinks armored car attack by the Revolutionary Armed Task Force (q.v.). FBI investigations revealed
that these NAFF members had stockpiled weapons and
explosives to be used in the breakout attempt. Evidence
emerged that NAFF had broken itself up into independent

cells to carry out robberies and terrorist actions while connecting themselves to front organizations for support.

The NAFF activists are based in New York City and differ from the Republic of New Afrika activists in their commitment to aid in the creation of a socialist republic in what is now South Africa. The Republic of New Afrika seeks, in addition to creating an independent black homeland in North America, reparations from the U.S. government of $10,000 for each black American for past injustices. Another subgroup of the Republic of New Afrika is the New Afrikan People's Organization, which seeks to create a socialist republic in the future independent homeland but which believes armed struggle is necessary to achieve this goal.

NEW PEOPLE'S ARMY. The Communist Party of the Philippines, Marxist-Leninist (CPP-ML) founded the NPA in 1969 as its armed wing to carry out protracted armed struggle to overthrow the current constitutional government in favor of a "people's democratic state." Chinese sponsorship of the NPA ended in 1976, and following some retrenchment, the group began to grow again by 1982, financing itself through extortion and arming itself by raids on police and army units. While the NPA is the armed wing of the outlawed CPP-ML, it has established its own legal political front, the National Democratic Front, which operates openly in Manila. The head of the CPP-ML, Jose Maria Sison, currently resides in the Netherlands. The membership of the NPA is estimated to have 18,000 to 20,000 members and a much larger support network.

While originally a rural guerrilla insurgency following Maoist precepts of guerrilla warfare, in recent years the NPA has involved itself increasingly in urban operations and in entrepreneurial terrorism in targeting foreign investors and contract workers for extortion or else for kidnapping to gain ransom. The more purely revolutionary terrorism of the group is seen in the operations of its death squads, called "Sparrow Squads," who murder Filipino politicians, military figures, policemen, government collaborators, and even members of the news media who dare criticize the NPA. These actions are meant to drive foreign investment out and to provoke the government to undertake repressive measures that would discredit it with the Filipino population. Prior to the 1992 closing of Clark Air Force Base and the Subic Bay U.S. Naval facility, the Sparrows had also targeted U.S. servicemen. Within those parts of central and northern Luzon island where the NPA controls rural areas and villages as well as within the ranks of NPA members and supporters, the organization also practices its own repressive terrorism, having imprisoned, tortured, or executed some 1,000 of their own ranks in recent years.

Since 1987 there has been a marked upswing in NPA terrorism. The growth and success of the group is in part due to the neglect of the countryside and corruption experienced during the Marcos regime as well as the difficulties of the Aquino administration in presiding over the transition to a democratic order. The marked increase in NPA terrorism since 1987 may be due to the NPA exploiting a unique historic opportunity afforded by the instability accompanying the transition from dictatorship to democracy. Such an explanation may account for increased NPA terrorism directed at others but does not so readily explain the upswing in the NPA's internal purges and disciplining of its own members. This increased internally directed terrorism may be an attempt to quell dissent within the NPA ranks over the proper goal and strategy of the NPA in the post-Marcos era.

From 1974 to 1991, the NPA conducted at least 56 noteworthy actions of which 41 percent (=23) were assassinations; 14 percent (=8) were bombings and arson; 9 percent (=5) were kidnappings; 7 percent (=4) were armed attacks; while the remaining 28 percent (=16) were threats not followed by any fulfilling action. Four kidnappings were for ransom, while a kidnapping of a South Korean contractor on 10 November 1987 was undertaken to force the Philippine Army to remove units from a certain region. Certain of the bombings and arson attacks against foreign-owned farms and factories also may have been retaliation for refusal to pay extortion money.

Except for the shooting deaths of three servicemen at Subic Bay on 13 April 1974 and a few sniping and mortar attacks on the Voice of America transmitting station in the Tinang area, there had been virtually no attacks on Americans until 28 October 1987 when two U.S. servicemen, one retired U.S. serviceman, and a Filipino retired from the U.S. armed forces were gunned down by Sparrow Squads. On 15 April 1987, the NPA had announced that it would deploy the Sparrow Squads to kill U.S. military personnel or diplomats involved in the Philippines counterinsurgency program, but none of those killed on 28 October fit that description. On 21 April 1989, Sparrows shot dead U.S. Army Colonel James Rowe while he was driving to work in Manila. On 26 September 1989, the NPA murdered two U.S. Defense Department civilian workers outside Clark Air Force Base. On 6 March 1990, an American rancher was murdered for refusing to pay the NPA extortion money. On 13 May 1990, two U.S. Air Force airmen were shot dead by NPA gunmen near Clark Air Force Base.

During 1991, the Philippine government captured over 80 ranking members of the CPP-ML and the NPA, including Romulo Kintanar, head of the NPA General Command. These arrests and the successful convictions of the murderers of Colonel Rowe set back the terrorist operations of the NPA for most of that year. Despite these setbacks, the NPA has shown itself to be one of the few leftist insurgencies that is still actively growing, despite the demise of communism throughout the rest of the world, and through its urban terrorism it continues to pose a significant threat to the stability of the current democratic government in the Philippines.

NEW WORLD LIBERATION FRONT. The New World Liberation Front (NWLF) was a nonstate Californian leftist group active in the 1970s that engaged in bombings for the limited purpose of protesting against corporate power. The NWLF declared that it sought relief for poor people and "to demonstrate that, in unity through armed struggle, poor people can and will win." The Front later also declared its support for Puerto Rican separatists. Its membership consisted of two men with several hangers-on.

The Front was founded in 1973 in the San Francisco Bay area and began its career in 1974 with a series of bombings against the International Telephone and Telegraph company to protest that firm's alleged involvement in the coup toppling the Allende government in Chile. The NWLF continued its bombings with numerous attacks against other public utilities and private firms, including General Motors, Standard Oil, Pacific Gas and Electric Company, and the Union Oil Company. By 1979, the NWLF had carried out almost 100 bombings in the San Francisco Bay area.

Like many other left-wing groups, such as the United Freedom Front or Armed Resistance Unit, the NWLF tended to pick symbolic targets for bombings, to target property rather than human life, and to use the terrorist event as "armed propaganda" for specific issues or causes rather than as direct military tactics to achieve revolution. Therefore the NWLF used to give frequent press conferences through its front, the People's Information Relay No. 1 (PIR-1). In September 1979, however, the two men who had founded the group quarreled, leading one to murder the other for which crime he was arrested, so ending the NWLF.

NEW WORLD OF ISLAM. This is a Muslim group made up of only black Americans seeking to create a black nationalist separate homeland in the southeastern United States. Since 1978, members of this group have been involved in bank robberies in the northeastern states, 21 of which have been staged in the New York and New Jersey metropolitan areas alone. In May 1985, the group issued a threat that its members would "execute" any police officer they encountered.

NOVEMBER 17. The Revolutionary Organization of 17 November (*Epanastatiki Organosi 17 Noemvri*) is a nonstate Greek leftist group that engages in terrorism to force Greece out of NATO, force the U.S. military presence out of Greece, and to oppose imperialism and capitalism. It has no known state sponsorship but appears to work in close concert with the May 1 (q.v.) and the Revolutionary Popular Struggle (ELA, q.v.) groups, all of which operate within the Athens area. It appears likely that both May 1 and November 17 evolved from the same core membership of ELA, which originally was formed with the revolutionary objective of overthrowing the Greek military junta. In the postjunta period, November 17, and these similar groups, appear more anarchistic in nature, no longer having one governing objective but attaching themselves to revolutionary raisons d'être as these happen to appear.

While both ELA and May 1 have bombed U.S. targets, November 17 differed from them in having assassinated, or attempting to assassinate, U.S. diplomats and Armed Forces servicemen in Greece. On 23 December 1975, November 17 assassinated CIA station chief Richard Welch. On 15 November 1983, they murdered a U.S. military attaché, Capt. George Tsantes (USN), and his driver. An assassination attempt was made against Master Sergeant Robert Judd on 3 April 1984. Judd took evasive action when he spotted two riders on a motorcycle approaching his car and was only slightly wounded. November 17 has assassinated two Greek police officials, two Greek businessmen, and has wounded one other Greek businessman. On 21 January 1988, they botched an attempted assassination of a DEA agent outside his Athens home. An unusual circumstance in all these cases has been that November 17 hit teams all use the same pistol, making verification of November 17 shootings certain. On 18 January 1989, they shot and wounded a Greek Supreme Court deputy prosecutor, and, on 26 September 1989, they killed a member of the Greek parliament. On 7 October 1991, they shot dead a Turkish embassy press attaché.

Beginning in April 1987, November 17 twice has tried to bomb U.S. military shuttle buses using remotely detonated bombs, injuring 18 people on 24 April 1987 and another 10 on 10 August 1987 but causing no deaths. Previously on 26 November 1985, a similar bombing had been directed at a Greek police van, in which 12 were injured and 1 was killed. On 5 October 1987, November 17 and ELA both claimed credit for bombing four Greek government offices. On 28 June 1988, November 17 killed the U.S. military attaché with a car bomb and likewise killed a former Greek minister of public order on 4 May 1989. On 10 June 1990, November 17 claimed credit for firing a bazooka at the Athens Procter & Gamble office, which caused no injury. A similar rocket attack narrowly missed a Greek businessman's car on 20 November 1990. November 17 used a remote-triggered bomb to kill U.S. Air Force Sergeant Ronald Stewart as he left his apartment on 12 March 1991. On 16 July 1991, November 17 used a remote-triggered car bomb to wound the Turkish chargé d'affaires and two other Turkish embassy workers.

The November 17 group is assumed to be quite small, having perhaps no more than 25 members. Nonetheless it has proved itself to be professional and highly successful in carrying out the relatively few operations it has conducted. To date, no November 17 member has ever been arrested and very little is known about the organization.

- O -

OAS. The ''Secret Army Organization'' was an intrastate terrorist group formed by French colonists and French military officers opposed to French President Charles de Gaulle's negotiations with the National Liberation Front (q.v.) leading to Algerian independence. Led by four French generals, French troops and settlers opposing independence initially attempted a coup d'état in Algiers on 22 April 1961, which succeeded in seizing the city but collapsed on 26 April when other French troops remained loyal to the government. The disgruntled settlers and military officers then formed the OAS and embarked on a campaign of terror both in France and Algeria against Algerian Arabs and Frenchmen favoring independence. The initial aim was to sabotage the negotiations and force a crackdown on the Algerian Arabs. Failing in this, their aim became instead to exact vengeance upon de Gaulle.

The OAS began using plastic explosives in a massive bombing campaign. On 13 May 1961, one bombing in Paris wounded 10. On 16 June 1961, a bombing against the home of the French Ambassador to the United States wounded five. In the period from 22–25 January 1962 3 bombings occurred, one at the Foreign Ministry in Paris killing 1 person and wounding 13 others. Following the negotiated cease-fire, a car bombing on 2 May 1962 killed 62 Arabs in Algiers. This led to a wave of anti-French terrorism in Algeria, forcing many European residents to flee that country.

On 22 August 1962, the OAS made an assassination attempt against de Gaulle and others who had negotiated Algerian independence. The mayor of the French town of Evian, which had hosted the independence talks, was killed in a bombing. From March 1963 to August 1965, the OAS made at least another eight assassination attempts against de Gaulle, while at least three other plots were quashed in the planning stages. The French government responded with a crackdown, eventually imprisoning around 4,000 OAS activists.

OCTOBER FIRST ANTIFASCIST RESISTANCE GROUP. The *Grupo de Resistencia Antifascista, Primero de Octubre* (GRAPO) is a communist splinter group seeking to overthrow the Spanish state in favor of a Marxist state. GRAPO opposes Spanish membership in NATO and the U.S. presence in Spain. GRAPO has no known state sponsors but once had ties with Direct Action (q.v.) and the Red Brigades (q.v.).

GRAPO emerged in 1975 as the military component of the Communist Party of Spain-Reconstituted, an illegal splinter group with Maoist tendencies that emerged out of the legal Spanish Communist Party. GRAPO is the second major terrorist group in Spain, the other being Basque Fatherland and Liberty (ETA, q.v.). GRAPO finances itself through kidnapping for ransom, bank robberies, and exacting extortion payments from individuals and businesses.

From 1975 to 1991, GRAPO carried out 46 noteworthy actions, which can be summarized as follows: Bombings accounted for 52 percent (=24) of these, killing at least 8 and wounding at least 46; 15 percent (=7) involved assassinations; another 15 percent (=7) involved kidnapping for ransom; 9 percent (=4) involved hostage seizures; and another 9 percent (=4) involved armed attacks.

Bombing attacks have targeted foreign businesses, mainly U.S. and French firms, Spanish government offices, and the U.S. Cultural Center in Madrid. Assassinations have killed senior Spanish military officers, the director of penal institutions, the president of the Seville Association of Businessmen, as well as Civil Guardsmen and ordinary police.

More recently GRAPO bombed the Madrid Stock Exchange, the Constitutional Court, and the Economics Ministry on 17 September 1990, wounding six people. GRAPO claimed credit for having bombed parts of the NATO oil pipeline in Spain and also claimed to have bombed a railroad line outside of Madrid. GRAPO leader Juan Carlos Delgado de Codex had been killed in a shoot-out with police in 1979, and by 1991 some 20 GRAPO activists were arrested and fewer than a dozen were suspected to be remaining at large then.

OMEGA 7. Omega-7 was a nonstate Cuban émigré group with the revolutionary goal of overthrowing the Castro regime in Cuba. In the period from 1968–1983, over 56 anti-Castro groups claimed credit for 155 terrorist acts. Of these, only Alpha-66, Brigade 2506, the Cuban Nationalist Movement, Cuban Liberation Front, and Omega-7 were of much consequence. Of these, only Omega-7 remained active into the 1980s. From 1980 to 1982, Omega-7 carried out at least 18 major terrorist acts, which included 10 bombings or attempted bombings, 4 arson attacks, 2 attacks on firms doing business with Cuba, 1 car bombing, and the assassination of a Cuban U.N. diplomat in a drive-by shooting on 12 September 1980.

Together with other similar Cuban émigré organizations, Omega-7 sought to sabotage Cuban governmental economic interests and diplomatic offices abroad, to intimidate private businesses having trade with Cuba, to attack Cubans in the United States considered to be "Communist sympathizers" as well as non-Cuban sympathizers of the Castro regime, and to discourage the tourist trade from patronizing Cuba. The longer-range goal was to raise and train an émigré Cuban army to overthrow the Castro regime. In 1978, Omega-7 twice firebombed the Cuban mission to the United Nations. On 25 March 1980, they planted a car bomb under the car of the Cuban Ambassador to the United Nations, which was disarmed.

Omega-7 used the émigré Cuban community in the United States as a base of support, sometimes extorting contributions from the émigrés. By 1981, the other major Cuban exile groups had resigned themselves to the prospect of Castro remaining in power and the Cuban émigré community lost interest in the cause of Omega-7. Omega-7 then resorted to drug smuggling and trafficking to finance itself. The increasingly criminal character of the group alienated members of the Cuban community and created internal dissension within Omega-7. In 1982, six key leaders were arrested, and in July 1983, the group's founder and leader, Eduardo Arocena, was arrested. During his arraignment, his role as an FBI informant within his own organization was revealed, which effectively destroyed the organization.

OPEC SIEGE, VIENNA. On 21 December 1975, five terrorists led by Ilyich Ramírez Sánchez, also called "Carlos," attacked the OPEC Secretariat office in Vienna, killing 1 secretariat worker and 2 guards and then taking 11 oil ministers and about 60 others hostage. Although the attackers called themselves "the Arab Revolution," the group consisted largely of German members of the Red Army Faction (q.v.) and the Venezuelan Carlos. The terrorists demanded $5 million in ransom and may have received as much as $50 million from Iran and Saudi Arabia.

After 36 hours of negotiations, the Austrian government allowed the terrorists and 42 of their hostages to leave Austria on a DC-9 that landed first in Algeria, where a wounded West German terrorist was taken off the plane, then to Libya where their ransom money was off-loaded and transferred to a South Yemenese bank, and then back to Algeria where the terrorists surrendered and the hostages were released.

Apparently the motive of the terrorists was primarily extortion. Carlos disappeared from public view thereafter but was arrested in the Sudan on 15 August 1994.

ORDEN. ORDEN was a state-sponsored right-wing Salvadoran death squad. ORDEN, short for "Organización Democrática Nacional," was originally founded in 1968 as a state-sponsored rural militia organized by General José Alberto Medrano. Recruits in the Army Reserve made up most of the ORDEN ranks and were trained by the National Guard. Units of the militia were established in all villages until by 1978 it had around 100,000 members. Within 10 years it had degenerated into a death squad, killing not only leftist guerrillas, but also union organizers, political moderates, religious workers, and human rights activists. ORDEN particularly targeted members of the Christian Democratic Party and politically moderate rural mayors. Guerrillas of the People's Liberation Forces, which in 1980 formed an anti-government leftist guerrilla front known as the Farabundo Martí Liberation Front (FMLN, q.v.), undertook an insurgency in 1978 during which they began to kill known members of ORDEN.

In November 1979, following the coup that overthrew President Romero, ORDEN was officially disbanded. In spite of this, many members of El Salvador's military and security forces continued to collaborate with members of the banned organization, and rightist death squad activities increased and grew more brutal until January 1981 when the defeat of the FMLN's "final offensive" brought a subsidence in the cycles of violence. The violence was directed not simply at FMLN guerrillas but also at government workers seeking to implement agrarian land reforms.

Although ORDEN itself officially ceased to exist, it supplied recruits to the "White Warriors' Union" (q.v.) founded in 1977 by a protégé of Medrano, Roberto D'Aubuisson, who later led the rightist Republican National Alliance Party (ARENA, q.v.), also suspected of sponsoring death squad activities. On 23 March 1985, General Medrano was killed by assassins belonging to the Clara Elizabeth Ramírez Front (q.v.), a renegade FMLN splinter-group.

ORDER. The Order was a nonstate U.S. white supremacist paramilitary group with the aim of overthrowing the United States government, which they call the "Zionist Occupation Government" (ZOG). The Order is among a number of white racist groups affiliated with the Aryan Nations (q.v.) led by Richard Butler, himself a minister of the Identity Christianity (q.v.) movement. The group was headquartered in Metaline Falls, Wash., and numbered around 24 known members. The Order was also known among its members as the "Bruder Schweigen," while it identified its territorial domain around the Metaline Falls area as the "White American Bastion."

The Order was founded in 1983 by Robert Mathews (b. 1953, d. 1984), a right-wing enthusiast and organizer, who patterned the group on a fictional group of the same name found in the *Turner Diaries,* a novel about an apocalyptic race war in a future America. The group sought to finance the various right-wing organizations associated with the Aryan Nations by counterfeiting operations and robberies of banks and armored trucks. A series of successful holdups culminated in the 19 July 1984 holdup of a Brinks armored car outside Ukiah, Calif., netting around $3.6 million, the largest heist of its kind until then. The Order had also embarked on a scheme of assassinating those whom it believed to be influential within the "ZOG." They had considered, but dismissed, the idea of conducting a suicide attack to kill the Baron de Rothschild, who was to visit Seattle, and settled instead on killing a controversial and acerbic Jewish radio talk-show host in Denver, Alan Berg, who had insulted white supremacists on his program. Berg was murdered by the Order at his home on 18 June 1984. Other Order activities included a robbery on 16 March 1984 of a Continental armored car in Seattle, another Continental armored car robbery coupled with the diversionary bombing of a pornographic film theater in Seattle on 23 April 1984, and the bombing of the Ahavath Israel synagogue in Boise, Idaho, on 29 April 1984.

Robert Mathews was killed in a shoot-out with the FBI on Whidbey Island in Washington state on 8 December 1984. Most of the remaining Order members were eventually arrested and tried in the Seattle U.S. District Court on racketeering and conspiracy charges arising from the robberies and on civil rights violation charges connected with the murder of Alan Berg. While evidence from this trial clearly connected the Order with the Aryan Nations and other white supremacist groups, a subsequent trial of leaders of these other white supremacist groups on sedition and conspiracy charges before a federal court in Ft. Smith, Ark., held February-April 1988 failed to obtain any convictions.

The Order did not totally perish with Mathews for a successor organization, the "Bruder Schweigen Strike Force II" emerged among Aryan Nations members in Hayden Falls, Idaho, whose members were involved in counterfeiting and six bombings during 1986.

ORGANIZATION FOR THE ARMED ARAB STRUGGLE. The OAAS is a group founded and run by the Venezuelan Ilyich

Ramírez Sánchez, better known as "Carlos (q.v.)," and accordingly the group is known also as the "Carlos Apparat." While the group generally carries out actions in support of Arab revolutionary causes, it appears to be primarily an entrepreneurial rather than an ideological group, that is, it works for Arab regimes or groups on a contract basis. It can also be viewed as entrepreneurial since it helps to aggrandize the reputation or myth of Carlos, its founder, as a master terrorist. This group is very small and seems to be supported by Libya and Syria.

Carlos was a leader within the Popular Front for the Liberation of Palestine-Special Operations Group (PFLP-SOG) and directed the 21 December 1975 seizure of the OPEC Secretariat in Vienna in which several oil ministers were seized for ransom. Following this action Carlos dropped from public view. He is believed to have become a contractual consultant to various Arab regimes and Middle Eastern terrorist groups, particularly the three groups that emerged from the breakup of the PFLP-SOG in 1978, namely, the May 15 Organization (q.v.), the Lebanese Armed Revolutionary Faction (q.v.), and the PFLP-Special Command (q.v.).

The OAAS emerged in 1983 with a series of attacks on French targets both in Lebanon and in Europe, including an August 1983 bombing of the French Cultural Center in West Berlin, two bombings in December 1983 of railroad facilities in France, and a January 1984 bombing of another French Cultural Center in Tripoli, Lebanon. Following this last bombing, no further actions were claimed in the name of the OAAS.

Carlos eventually was arrested in the Sudan by French police on 15 August 1994.

ORGANIZATION OF THE OPPRESSED OF THE EARTH. One of several noms de guerre of the Lebanese Shiite Muslim group, Hezbollah (q.v.), which is an Islamic fundamentalist revolutionary organization under Iranian state sponsorship. Hezbollah employed this name in the 14 June 1985 hijacking of TWA 847 in which U.S. Navy diver Robert Dean Stethem was murdered. This name was also used in taking credit for the 17 February 1988 kidnapping and subsequent 31 July 1989 killing of U.S. Marines Corps Lt. Col. William R. Higgins, commander of the United Nations Truce Supervisory Observer Group in Lebanon.

OVPR. The Organization of Volunteers for the Puerto Rican Revolution is a Puerto Rican "political-military" group dedicated to winning independence through armed revolution. This group is closely associated with the Macheteros (q.v.), having conducted its first operation jointly with them in a 3 December 1979 ambush and machine-gun attack upon a U.S. Navy shuttle bus, killing 2 sailors and seriously wounding 10 others. Also on 25 January 1985, they shared credit with the Macheteros in a rocket-grenade attack on a U.S. courthouse in San Juan. On 6 November 1985, they shot and seriously wounded a U.S. Army recruiting officer as he was riding his motor scooter to work.

In April 1986, OVPR terrorists murdered a former undercover agent of the Puerto Rican police, Alejandro González Maleve, and vowed to murder nine other policemen who were implicated in the killing of young Puerto Rican separatists. The OVPR has also made other bombing attacks within Puerto Rico but has not so far ventured to make attacks within the U.S. proper. (See Macheteros)

- P -

PALESTINE LIBERATION FRONT. The PLF refers to three current groups that originally were one PLF group that had split from the Popular Front for the Liberation of Palestine-General Command (q.v.). Like the PFLP-GC, the PLF factions seek the total destruction of Israel and establishment of a Palestinian state in its place by armed struggle. They also seek infiltration operations into Israel to carry out terrorist actions and try to capture Israeli hostages in order to exchange them for imprisoned Arabs. Also these groups, like the PFLP-GC, have shown resourcefulness in devising new ways to infiltrate Israel, having tried to use hot-air balloons in addition to hang gliders. As the PLF formed in 1976 was anti-Syrian, it found a natural sponsor in Iraq. Iraq, Libya, and Syria each back one of the three PLF fronts today while Fatah supports the Abu Abbas faction also supported by Iraq.

The original PLF was founded in 1961 by Ahmad Jibril, which coordinated itself with al Fatah (q.v.) in 1965. In December 1967, this group, along with the Arab Nationalist Movement and the "Heroes of the Return" group formed the Popular Front for the Liberation of Palestine (q.v.) headed by Dr. George Habash. Disgusted by the PFLP's preoccupation with ideological matters, Ahmad Jibril formed his own splinter group, the PFLP-General Command. The current PLF broke away from the PFLP-GC in 1977 due to dissent over Ahmad Jibril's support for Syria's intervention in Lebanon. The new PLF was recognized by PLO Chairman Yasir Arafat as a new PLO member in April 1977 as well as being recognized by the Rejection Front as one of its own members. In 1981, the group obtained seats on the Palestine National Council while its founder, Muhammad Abu Abbas, gained a seat on the PLO Executive Committee in 1984.

The PLF has been marked by acrimony with its parent group and among its own members. Fighting broke out between PLF and PFLP-GC members in the Sidon refugee camps in February 1978. In August 1978, the apartment building containing the PLF headquarters was blown up, killing at least 100 residents, an action likely done by the PFLP-GC. In late 1983, the PLF split when founder Muhammad Abu Abbas decided the group was growing too subservient to Syria. He and his followers left for Tunis in order to align themselves closer with Arafat's al Fatah. The PLF faction left in Damascus was headed by Talat Yaqub but itself split when Abdal Fatah Ghanim tried unsuccessfully to seize power over the PLF in January 1984. The Yaqub faction remained in Damascus while Ghanim and his followers established their rival PLF office in Libya. Following the *Achille Lauro* fiasco in 7 October 1985, for which Abu Abbas and his followers were responsible, the Tunisian government asked the Abu Abbas group to leave. This group is now headquartered in Baghdad, Iraq. Prior to the breakup of the PLF it numbered no more than 250 members, and currently all three factions are estimated to have at most 50 members.

A summary of the more significant PLF actions follows: Seven major actions in the period 1978–1983 all involved attempts to take hostages and all but one involved attempts to infiltrate Israel. Only three of the six infiltration attempts succeeded while in only one case did the terrorists succeed in seizing hostages, but in no case did they win the release of any Arab prisoners. In April 1979, four PLF members landed on a beach near Nahariyah, Israel, on a mission to seize hostages. Three Israeli civilians were killed by the terrorists, two of whom were killed and the other two captured.

On 7 October 1985, Abu Abbas and four PLF members hijacked the *Achille Lauro*, an Italian cruise ship. In reality the five had been intending to infiltrate Israel where the ship was due to dock, but when a cabin steward discovered the five cleaning their weapons, they then decided to hijack the ship and use the passengers as hostages. In the course of the hijacking, they murdered an elderly Jewish American, Leon Klinghoffer, who was an invalid, and threw his body, wheelchair and all, into the sea. Eventually the hijackers negotiated with the Egyptian government for safe passage in return for the lives of the remaining hostages. Although U.S. fighter planes forced the Egyptian airplane to land at a NATO air base in Signolla, Sicily, the Italians claimed jurisdiction over the five terrorists and released Abu Abbas who possessed an Iraqi diplomatic passport. The other four were tried and convicted by Italian courts on charges arising from the hijacking, and Abu Abbas was also convicted in absentia. Nonetheless the U.S. military action forcing a civilian plane to land and attempted arrest of the terrorists outside U.S. territory, the Egyptians' allowing the terrorists safe passage, and the Italians allowing Abu Abbas to escape, all occasioned mutual acrimony between the United States and its allies but also underscored the need for international cooperation in order to address the challenge of international terrorism. This furor led Tunisia to request the PLF to move elsewhere, so Abu Abbas moved his offices to Baghdad, Iraq.

On 30 May 1990 the Abu Abbas faction of the PLF, with Libyan support, made a seaborne attack on Tel Aviv beaches that was quashed by the Israeli Defense Forces. Four of the PLF terrorists were killed and 12 captured. This raid occurred in the eighteenth month of talks between the United States and the PLO. While Yasir Arafat disavowed any PLO connection with the raid, he also would not publicly condemn the raid nor expel Abu Abbas from the PLO Executive Committee. This in turn prompted a suspension by the United States of its dialogue with the PLO at that time. In the past rejectionist groups, such as the PFLP, the PFLP-GC, and the PLF had regularly defied al Fatah and sought to sabotage its efforts at diplomacy by staging such raids, and this may have been the intended aim behind this raid as well. In 1991, however, Abu Abbas resigned his membership in the PLO Executive Committee.

PALESTINE LIBERATION ORGANIZATION. The PLO is the umbrella organization comprising the major Palestinian political and guerrilla groups that defines itself, and is recognized by all Arab governments, as being "the sole, legitimate representative of the Palestinian people."

1. Goals and Nature of the PLO

When founded in 1964 its nominal leader, Ahmad al Shuqairy, had declared that the purpose of the PLO was "to drive the Jews into the sea.'' Currently the PLO asserts that it seeks an independent Palestinian homeland on any liberated part of "historic Palestine" and will recognize the right of the State of Israel to exist in exchange for that homeland. In either case, it is a revolutionary irredentist and nationalistic group that has, until recently, used terrorism and armed struggle as a means to achieve an independent Palestinian national state. While some constituent members of the PLO, such as the Popular Front for the Liberation of Palestine and other groups, have listed a Pan-Arab revolutionary movement, or a Marxist-Leninist revolution, or even a world revolutionary movement as among the goals of the Palestinians, such views are often idiosyncratic to these groups rather than representative of the PLO as a whole. Fatah, which has maintained the largest share of seats on the PLO Executive Committee, has not linked the issue of Palestinian national rights to the goal of Pan-Arab unity or to a specific social-economic order or program.

2. Relationship of PLO to Arab Sponsors

The original PLO was a creation of the Arab League founded on 28 May 1964, when the first Palestinian National Council met. Its complete subservience to the Arab states at that time was reflected in the fact that its National Charter made no mention of seeking to create an independent Palestinian state. Members of Fatah (q.v.), the oldest Palestinian guerrilla group, basically ignored the PLO at that time, regarding it as irrelevant to their own preparations for armed struggle against Israel. Following the 1967 war that discredited the Arab regimes sponsoring the PLO, Fatah and other similar guerrilla groups entered the PLO and seized control in February 1969 when the head of Fatah, Yasir Arafat, was elected Chairman of the PLO Executive Committee.

While the PLO since then has been willing to accept material aid from the various Arab states, it has jealously guarded its own claims of legitimacy apart from any other regime and of independence in decision making, on several occasions defying the wishes of several of its sponsors.

These quarrels led to the PLO's expulsion from Jordan in 1970 and once again in 1986, its partial expulsion from Lebanon in 1982 and the denial of use of Syrian territory for launching raids into Israel from 1983 onward. Since 1982, Tunisia has hosted the administrative offices and personnel of the PLO but required Abu Abbas's Palestine Liberation Front (q.v.) to leave Tunisia following the scandal of the *Achille Lauro* hijacking.

The Arab League recognized the PLO as sole representative of the Palestinians in 1974, therefore denying Jordan any right to negotiate unilaterally with Israel over the fate of the West Bank. In 1976, the Arab League accepted the PLO as a full member. While the PLO received contributions from member states of the Arab League, it has also relied on taxes levied upon the Palestinian diaspora. The various constituent member organizations of the PLO have each cultivated their own sponsors and resources as well. While the PLO has received contributions and other material assistance from various Arab states, this does not necessarily imply influence over the PLO by individual states. Saudi Arabia and the Persian Gulf emirates have distrusted the revolutionary and secular program of the PLO and have viewed Palestinians living within their borders as potential fifth columnists. For such regimes, contributions to the PLO were no doubt partly expressions of support for Pan-Arab ideals but may also have been viewed by those regimes as protection money against possible Palestinian terrorism or revolutionary activity within their borders. Following Operation Desert Storm many of these regimes curtailed contributions to the PLO after it openly sided with Iraq in its invasion of Kuwait.

3. Development of PLO Policy on Terrorism

The original PLO had as its military wing the Palestine Liberation Army (PLA), which consisted of Palestinian contingents under Egyptian, Syrian, and Jordanian command. These were trained to fight conventional warfare rather than guerrilla or terrorist operations and in practice answered to the orders of their host countries rather than to the PLO. When it became apparent after 1967 that the independent guerrilla groups were attracting large numbers of recruits, the PLA developed its own guerrilla unit, the Popular Liberation Forces, which lapsed into obscurity in a few years.

Following the takeover of the PLO by Fatah and other guerrilla groups, the PLA continued to remain under the nominal command of the PLO, while the PLO has relied more on the forces of its constituent guerrilla groups to carry out terrorist attacks or insurgent warfare against Israel or against other foes of the hour. Fatah guerrilla operations began after 1 January 1965. From 1969 to 1974, PLO-sponsored terrorism was carried out throughout the Middle East and non-Communist nations against Israeli, U.S., West European, and Arab targets, the government of Jordan having been targeted after September 1970. The most notorious Palestinian terrorist group during this period was Black September (q.v.), which was responsible for the massacre of the Israeli athletic team at the Munich Summer Olympic games in 1972.

Beginning in 1974, Fatah declared its renunciation of terrorism outside of the borders of former mandatory Palestine, a declaratory policy not always followed by Fatah-sponsored groups, such as the Hawari (q.v.) group or Force 17 (q.v.). This renunciation was part of a revision within Fatah of its goals from a liberation of the whole of Palestine, in which Israel would be replaced by a secular democratic state, to the creation of a separate Arab Palestinian state on any liberated part of Palestine, which was understood to mean the West Bank and Gaza Strip following an Israeli withdrawal from those territories. While Fatah still believed armed struggle was necessary to achieve its goals, it came to view armed struggle as insufficient if not joined with initiatives on a diplomatic front. This revisionism was anathema to the more radical leftist groups within the PLO, such as the Popular Front for the Liberation of Palestine (q.v.), which in turn sponsored the creation of a Rejection

Front (q.v.) of like-minded PLO members whose members boycotted the PLO Executive Committee from 1974 to 1978 while retaining their seats within the Palestinian National Council. A practical consequence of this internal division was that the PFLP and other Rejection Front members stepped up their terrorist attacks on Israel and on targets outside Israel in order to discredit Fatah's claim to speak for the PLO and to sabotage whatever diplomatic initiatives Fatah might seek.

Fatah's diplomatic initiatives paid off in 1974 with the seventh Arab League summit meeting in Rabat, Morocco, declaring the PLO to be the sole, legitimate representative of the Palestinians, followed that same year by the United Nations General Assembly declaring the PLO also to be the Palestinians' representative and granting the PLO observer status in the General Assembly. The Rejection Front's approach in winning national rights for the Palestinians was put to the test with the outbreak of the Lebanese civil war in 1975 and Syrian intervention from 1976 onward, in which certain Syrian-sponsored Palestinian groups fought against Fatah. The conflict split the PFLP-General Command, a Rejection Front member, whose factions actually fought each other. Despite a Fatah ban on attacks against Israeli targets within the southern "security zone" declared by Israel, anti-Fatah groups continued their operations there. When another anti-Fatah group, Black June (q.v.), attempted to assassinate Israel's ambassador to London in 1982, this occasioned Israel's invasion of Lebanon and siege of Beirut, which culminated in the expulsion of the PLO administrative apparatus from Lebanon and most of its fighters as well. Seeking to block the return of al Fatah fighters, after 1983 Syria further incited Palestinian forces against each other and encouraged division even within Fatah. This resulted in the emergence of a splinter group under the leadership of Abu Musa, a former deputy commander of Fatah, that fought alongside Syrian troops against Fatah loyalists. The rift between the Fatah loyalists and anti-Arafat factions was narrowed when Syria began backing the Shiite Amal militia's campaign against the Palestinian refugee camps when both sides largely drew together to fend off Amal's fighters.

While the PFLP and like-minded groups agreed with certain of the grievances and criticisms of Arafat expressed by the Abu Musa faction, they grew more anxious for the integrity of the PLO and its independence from the control of Arab governments. The outbreak of the Palestinian intifada (uprising) on the West Bank and Gaza Strip changed the focus of terrorist or insurgent activity from outside to within the borders of mandatory Palestine. On 15 November 1988, the eighteenth Palestinian National Council declared an independent Palestinian state in the occupied territories and tied PLO acceptance of United Nations resolutions 242 and 338 to Israeli withdrawal from the occupied territories. The PLO as a whole formally adopted Fatah's long-standing declaratory policy of abstaining from terrorism outside the occupied territories and Israel, making cessation of terrorism within those areas dependent also on an Israeli withdrawal from the occupied territories. Following 14 December 1988, the United States engaged in a diplomatic dialogue with the PLO, which was discontinued following a Palestine Liberation Front raid on a Tel Aviv beach on 30 May 1990.

With the 13 September 1993 peace accord concluded with Israel, the PLO has in principle renounced further insurgent or terrorist activity within Israel proper or the occupied territories.

4. Notes on Composition and Structure of the PLO

The PLO has developed legislative, executive, and quasi-judicial and police functions very much along the lines of a government-in-exile. The Palestine National Council (PNC) is the highest decision-making body, having met in 19 sessions attended by delegates representing the various guerrilla groups, the Palestinian "popular organizations," as well as a number of independents who represent geographic locations. This Council determines overall policy and elects members of the PLO Executive Committee, a 15-member group that actually runs the PLO from day to day, headed by the Chairman of the PLO Executive Committee. In 1973, the PLO Executive Committee created a PLO Central Council to serve as a sounding board of policy during the long periods between PNC sessions. This device has allowed groups such as George Habash's Popular Front for the Liberation of Palestine the opportunity to be consulted on policy matters even while they were grandstanding their differences with Fatah and Yasir Arafat by boycotting sessions of the Executive Committee. The Palestine Armed Struggle Command is a PLO military police used to patrol the refugee camps and to control guerrillas.

The PLO has developed a social welfare bureaucracy, a collection of archives, a research center, and the rudiments of a foreign service. With this governmental infrastructure, the recognition by other nations of the Palestinians as a national community, and the capacity to maintain diplomatic relations, all the PLO lacks for making a full claim to statehood is an independent territory to govern.

The guerrilla organizations, known as *tanzimat*, play roles similar to political parties in a parliamentary system. The dominant group since 1969 has remained Fatah, which may be considered the nationalist right wing of the PLO. The groups Black September (q.v.) and Force 17 (q.v.) were Fatah subgroups created to carry out covert operations and do not have independent status in the PLO. The second most influential group is George Habash's Popular Front for the Liberation of Palestine (PFLP, q.v.), which represents the Pan-Arabist Marxist-Leninist left wing of the PLO. The central position is held by the Democratic Front for the Liberation of Palestine (DFLP, q.v.). Al Saiqa (q.v.) is the second oldest guerrilla group within the PLO and has usually followed al Fatah's lead, although it is also highly influenced by Syria's sponsorship. The Arab Liberation Front (ALF, q.v.) is more partial toward the PFLP and is highly influenced by its Iraqi sponsorship. The Palestine Liberation Front (PLF, q.v.) has alternated between supporting the

PFLP and Fatah and is currently very much influenced by Iraq. The Popular Struggle Front (PSF, q.v.) had quit the PLO in 1974 because of disagreement with Fatah's policies but rejoined it in 1991. It is highly influenced by Syria. The Palestine Communist Party entered the PLO in 1982 on a par with the *tanzimat*, despite lacking an armed wing, because of its ability to mobilize mass action in the West Bank due to its deeply rooted political infrastructure there.

Fatah is estimated to have 6,000 to 8,000 members; the PFLP about 800 to 1,000 members; the DFLP about 500 members; Al Saiqa about 2,000 members; ALF about 500 members; PLF about 50 members; and PSF about 300 members.

Abu Nidal's Fatah Revolutionary Council (q.v.) has never been part of the PLO or Fatah even though Abu Nidal was a member of Fatah until 1974. Abu Nidal is under a death sentence by the PLO for having assassinated PLO officials and having tried to assassinate Yasir Arafat. The PFLP-General Command (q.v.) of Ahmad Jibril was expelled from the PLO in 1983. The PFLP Special Operations Group was a breakaway group of the PFLP and has been defunct since the death of its leader in 1978. The Lebanese Armed Revolutionary Faction (FARL, q.v.), the May 15 Organization (q.v.), and the PFLP-Special Command (q.v.) were all offshoots of the PFLP-Special Operations Group and have never been part of the PLO. The Islamic Resistance Movement, also known as Hamas (q.v.), is an offshoot of the Muslim Brotherhood and, like the Islamic Jihad of Palestine group, has never been a part of the PLO. It should be noted, however, that individual members of these latter organizations may have overlapping memberships in PLO groups.

PAN AM FLIGHT 103 BOMBING. On 21 December 1988, Pan Am flight 103, a Boeing 747 flying from London to New York, exploded at about 30,000 feet over Scotland. All 259 aboard perished, while 11 people in the Scottish village of Lockerbie were killed by the falling debris of the aircraft.

Reconstruction of the bomb from the debris that was scattered over a large area of southwestern Scotland revealed the use of a bomb made with Semtex explosive concealed in a Toshiba radio-cassette player identical to bombs manufactured by the PFLP-General Command (q.v.) group of Ahmad Jibril that had been seized by West German police in a raid on a PFLP-GC cell on 26 October 1989. Knowing from this the type of timing device used in the bomb, investigators determined that the bomb had been intended to explode once the airplane was over the Atlantic Ocean. A delay in departure of 25 minutes at London's Heathrow Airport caused the plane to explode instead over land, which made reconstructing the bomb and identification of its source possible. Forensic analysis of the luggage in which the bomb was placed revealed that the bomb had been loaded into the plane in Frankfurt and that the original source of the luggage was Malta.

While investigators had been certain that the bomb was manufactured by the PFLP-GC, an entrepreneurial terrorist group having ties with Iran, Libya, and Syria, this alone did not establish directly that the same group had itself planted the bomb nor did it reveal which state had sponsored the bombing. Originally credit for the bombing was claimed by telephone in the name of the "Guardians of the Islamic Revolution" (q.v.), causing suspicion to center on Iran, which was seen as having a sufficient motive in avenging the deaths of 290 passengers and crew killed when the U.S.S. *Vincennes* shot down Iran Air flight 655 on 3 July 1988 by mistake. The Maltese origin of the luggage, however, also suggested Libyan sponsorship. Following further investigations, the United States issued indictments on 14 November 1991 against two Libyan officials, charging the Libyan government with sponsorship of the bombing. In its April 1992 report on global terrorism, the U.S. State Department published evidence linking the Libyan regime with the bombing while Muammar Qaddafi has refused to extradite the two officials named in those indictments.

PATRIOTIC PEOPLE'S MOVEMENT. The PPM is a left-wing Sinhalese organization whose terrorist activities have the limited aim of sabotaging the 1987 Indian-Sri Lankan military accord. Activities included intimidation against Sri Lankan supporters of the agreement that allowed Indian troops into Sri Lanka in order to quell the Tamil separatist groups. A PPM campaign of threats against voters during the 1988 presidential elections may well have brought about the electoral victory of Ranasinghe Premadasa.

PEOPLE'S REVOLUTIONARY ARMY. The *Ejército Revolucionario de Pueblo* (ERP) was the armed wing of the Workers Revolutionary Army of Argentina, a Trotskyite political party. This group sought to launch a social revolution in the 1970s to overthrow the military regime in Argentina. Although doctrinally Trotskyite the ERP went to Cuba in the early 1970s to establish links with the Castroite regime. In Havana many of ERP's main cadres conferred with their compatriot Ernesto Che Guevara. During that time ERP also collaborated with leftist Perónist groups and had some contact also with the Sandinistas.

As part of their short-term tactics ERP sought to embarrass and stymie the Argentine military regime, to force foreign investors to bear the costs of the revolution through kidnapping and extortion, and to win popular support by forcing foreign firms to engage in highly publicized distributions of goods and services to the urban poor in exchange for the lives of their local executives whom ERP held hostage. In these actions they imitated the Tupamaros (q.v.) of Uruguay, and some analysts believe many Tupamaros had made their way into the ERP following their suppression in Uruguay.

During the 1970s, ERP became the most effective and boldest Latin American guerrilla group, in large part due to the charismatic leadership of Roberto Santucho. ERP organized itself into cells to carry out urban terrorist operations and viewed itself as the ''army of the masses.'' Beginning in 1970, ERP was mainly active in the urban areas of Buenos

Aires, Cordoba, Santa Fe, and Tucuman. By 1975, it had expanded its operations from purely urban terrorism to include rural guerrilla operations spread throughout many of Argentina's provinces; by October 1977, however, ERP had been eradicated from all areas except metropolitan Buenos Aires.

A brief history of ERP operations follows: Founded in 1969, ERP initiated its career by a series of bank robberies in Rosario during 1970. During 1972, ERP discovered the more lucrative expedient of kidnapping foreign businessmen for ransom while targeting members of the military government for assassination. On 10 April 1972, the ERP killed both General Juan Carlos Sánchez in Rosario and also Dr. Oberdan Sallustro, president of the Argentine branch of Fiat, whom they had kidnapped two weeks before. On 30 April 1972, ERP assassinated Rear Admiral Hermes Quijada.

In the two years following 1973, ERP changed its tactics from urban terrorism to carrying out open military assaults upon various garrisons and small towns in order to build up their material strength and to begin creating an ERP-controlled zone in the mountainous areas. These attacks culminated in the 23 December 1975 attack upon the barracks and armory of Monte Chingolo. On 19 July 1976, the leader of the ERP, Roberto Santucho, was killed in Buenos Aires along with his deputy commander, after which the fortunes of the group declined. Within a year the insurgency had been smashed.

Remnants went into exile and formed a leftist hit team for hire calling themselves "Red Action." On 17 September 1980, seven members of Red Action assassinated the exiled Nicaraguan dictator Anastasio Somoza Debayle along with members of his entourage as they drove through Asunción, Paraguay. Red Action was foiled in a kidnapping attempt in Mexico in 1981 and several of its members were captured.

PHALANGE. The Lebanese Phalangist Party, also known by its Arabic name as the *Kataib,* is a right-wing Lebanese militia with the aims of preserving the dominant political and social position of Maronite Christians within Lebanon, repressing other confessional or political groups that may challenge Maronite supremacy, and preserving the independence and territorial integrity of Lebanon from Syrian, Palestinian, or other claims. The Phalange was organized in the 1930s as an imitation of other Phalangist groups in Spain and Italy, which were Fascist paramilitary political parties. By the 1970s the relative growth of the non-Maronite groups in Lebanon and the transformation of southern Lebanon into a bastion for al Fatah guerrillas made Maronite supremacy in Lebanese politics untenable and led to the outbreak of civil war on 13 April 1975. Unable to match the combined strength of the Palestinian and non-Maronite forces, the Phalangists invited the Syrians to intervene, which occurred on 1 June 1976. Syria since then has shifted its sponsorship to other groups, such as the Shiite and Druze militias, and back again to the Phalange in an effort to maintain Syrian dominance in Lebanon.

The Phalangists have been supported by the United States as a group that has been generally pro-Western and also by Israel since the enmity between the Phalange and PLO disposes the Phalange to act as a tactical ally of Israel. Following the Israeli invasion of Lebanon and siege of Beirut, the Phalangists undertook a two-day-long massacre of the Palestinian inhabitants of the Shatila and Sabra refugee camps on 16 September 1982 to avenge the bombing attack that killed their leader, Bashir Gemayel, two days earlier. At least 800 people perished, most of them unarmed civilians.

PISHMERGA. A Kurdish word meaning ''(one who puts himself) in front of death,'' *pishmerga* is a generic term used to refer to Kurdish guerrilla fighters among the Kurdish Workers' Party (q.v.), Kurdish Democratic Party, and other Kurdish armed groups, whether of leftist or nationalistic complexion. Like the Arabic term Fidai (plural, Fidaiyin; also spelled, Fedayeen) meaning ''one who offers (self-) sacrifice,'' the term has been so generally appropriated by various and often opposing Kurdish groups that, by itself, it gives little clear identification of which group a particular *pishmerga* may represent.

POPULAR FORCES OF 25 APRIL. The *Forças Populares do 25 Abril* (FP-25) is a Portuguese communist terrorist group formed in 1980 dedicated to overthrowing the current Portuguese government in favor of some sort of revolutionary Marxist state. It also opposes Portugal's participation in NATO and is anti-American. The group is not known to have any ties with sponsoring states or other terrorist groups, although it has been speculated that FP-25 has collaborated with Basque Fatherland and Liberty (q.v.) and the Red Army Faction (q.v.) and that it has received some support from Libya. The name refers to the 25 April 1975 military coup that ended the former right-wing regime. FP-25 also used the names ''Autonomous Revolutionary Groups'' and the ''Armed Revolutionary Organization.''

An analysis of 40 incidents in the period from 1980–1986 shows that 65 percent (=26) were bombings, including firebombings; 13 percent (=5) were armed attacks involving mortars and antitank rockets; 9 percent (=4) were assassinations; while the remaining 13 percent (=5) were miscellaneous actions such as a prison breakout, a kidnapping, some robberies, and the like.

On 28 October 1984, FP-25 tried to fire two antitank rockets at the U.S. Embassy but failed due to a malfunction in the launching mechanism. On 25 November 1984, the ninth anniversary of the failed communist coup attempt, they fired four mortar rounds at the U.S. Embassy, hitting two vehicles. On 9 December 1984, they fired four mortar rounds at NATO's Iberian Atlantic Command headquarters outside Lisbon, damaging some buildings and one car. On 28 January 1985, they fired three mortar rounds at six NATO ships at anchor in Lisbon harbor, failing to hit any of them.

During 1984, the Portuguese counterterrorism units managed to arrest 56 members. In July 1985, however, the key prosecution witness, a defecting FP-25 member, was murdered before he could testify, and in September 1985, 10 imprisoned members managed to escape. In the following year, the group made another attempt to bomb the U.S. Embassy and to bombard the NATO Iberian Atlantic Command with mortars but without success. In September 1986, the group calling itself the ''Armed Revolutionary Organization'' appeared, which authorities believed to be the FP-25 group under a new name.

POPULAR FRONT FOR THE LIBERATION OF PALESTINE (PFLP). Founded on 11 December 1967, the PFLP is the main rival of Fatah (q.v.) within the Palestinian Liberation Organization (q.v.). Led by Dr. George Habash, the PFLP stresses Pan-Arabism, considering the Palestinian struggle as only one part of a broader revolution against both imperialism and reactionary politics within the Arab world. The organization has between 800 and 1,000 members and operates in Lebanon, Israel, and the occupied territories, the remaining Middle East, and Europe. It receives most of its funds and weapons from Libya and Syria.

The PFLP is a self-proclaimed Marxist organization and, unlike al Fatah, has not restrained itself from intervening in the politics of Arab host countries. PFLP intrigues and challenges to the Jordanian regime led eventually to the ouster of the PLO from Jordanian territory beginning in September 1970. Once the PLO relocated its forces in Lebanon, the PFLP alliance with leftist militias in Lebanon against the right-wing Phalange helped precipitate the Lebanese civil war in 1975, dragging the entire PLO into the conflict. While Fatah has tried since 1974 to limit its terrorist attacks to Israeli targets within the borders of former mandatory Palestine, and to avoid involving itself in extraneous politics or revolutionary movements, by contrast the PFLP has tried to carry out joint operations with revolutionary leftist terrorist groups in Europe and elsewhere, among them the Japanese Red Army (q.v.), the Red Army Faction (q.v.), the Revolutionary Cells (q.v.), and the Nicaraguan Sandinistas (q.v.). Due to its own commitment to a secular Arab nationalism, the PFLP eschews support for Islamic fundamentalist movements generally and disowns any identification of the Palestinian struggle with notions of a religious jihad.

The PFLP has opposed al Fatah for the latter's increasing emphasis on diplomacy rather than armed struggle and also opposes al Fatah's willingness to settle for a "mini-state" in Gaza and the West Bank rather than the whole of former mandatory Palestine. In 1974, the PFLP established the Rejection Front to oppose the participation of the PLO in any negotiated settlement. The PFLP-General Command (q.v.), the Arab Liberation Front (q.v.), the Palestine Liberation Front (q.v.), and the Popular Struggle Front (q.v.) all joined this opposition group. Opposition to the Camp David Accords drew these groups back closer to al Fatah, and the PFLP rejoined the PLO executive committee in 1981 after having boycotted it. Upset over a Fatah-sponsored accommodation reached between the PLO and King Hussein of Jordan in 1985, the PFLP set up the National Salvation Front (NSF, q.v.) composed of other groups opposed to al Fatah's diplomatic approach. The PFLP broke ranks with the NSF, however, to rejoin the mainstream PLO in the eighteenth Palestine National Council meeting in Algiers in 1987. The PFLP finally acceded to al Fatah's diplomatic approach and renunciation of terrorism outside the occupied territories and Israel in the nineteenth Palestine National Council meeting held 12–15 November 1988 in Algiers.

From 1968 until 1987, the PFLP engaged in at least 81 major actions, including 38 bombings, one of them an aerial bombing, and 5 attempted bombings; 10 hijackings and 1 failed attempt; 11 armed attacks, including 1 maritime rocket attack and a dinghy landing attempt scuttled by the Israeli navy; 9 kidnapping or hostage situations; 3 assassinations and 1 attempted assassination; and 3 threats. The actual record is confused by the tendency of PFLP splinter groups, like Wadi Haddad's PFLP-Special Operations Group and the Arab Nationalist Youth Organization, to claim their actions in the name of the PFLP. Among the PFLP's more notorious actions were the following: On 6 September 1970, the PFLP simultaneously hijacked three airliners to Dawson's Field, north of Amman, Jordan, in which over 400 passengers and crew were held hostage for three weeks to force the release of imprisoned terrorists elsewhere. While this operation was a terrorist tour de force, it also backfired since it completely exasperated King Hussein who dispatched his armed forces to rescue the hostages and expel the Palestinians. On 30 May 1972, acting at the behest of the PFLP three Japanese Red Army (q.v.) members carried out a massacre at Lod Airport, killing 28 people and wounding 76 others. On 27 June 1976, the PFLP together with members of the Red Army Faction (q.v.) hijacked an Air France Tel Aviv-to-Paris flight to Entebbe, Uganda, where 240 passengers were held hostage until rescued by Israeli commandos on 1 July 1976. Likewise PFLP and Red Army Faction terrorists hijacked a Lufthansa plane to Mogadishu, Somalia, on 13 October 1977 in order to force the German government to release the German terrorists Andreas Baader and Ulrike Meinhof, but these hijackers also were foiled on 18 October 1977 by West German GSG-9 commandos.

The brutality of these operations, which were directed very deliberately at innocent civilians, drew forth so much international condemnation and caused such embarrassment to the backers of the PFLP that by the end of the 1970s the PFLP came around to the al Fatah proposition that terrorist actions should be confined to Israeli targets within the boundaries of Israel and the occupied territories. It is worth noting that Dr. George Habash remains highly esteemed throughout the Palestinian community and is considered a figure of integrity as well as the outstanding representative of the more radical Pan-Arabist position within the PLO. Therefore his decision to acquiesce in, or else to resist, the

PLO's renunciation of terrorism outside Israel and the occupied territories carries great weight and may have far-reaching consequences.

POPULAR FRONT FOR THE LIBERATION OF PALESTINE-GENERAL COMMAND. The PFLP-GC led by Ahmad Jibril split away from the Popular Front for the Liberation of Palestine (PFLP) in October 1968 when Jibril became disenchanted with PFLP leader George Habash's preoccupation with ideological issues. While this group seeks the total destruction of Israel and establishment of a Palestinian state in its place, its leader, Ahmad Jibril, appears quite ready to hire out the services of the group on an entrepreneurial basis without regard for the politics of his patrons. The group joined the Rejection Front in 1974 but was expelled from it in 1977. It was also expelled from the PLO in 1983. Since then it has continued to be sponsored by Libya and Syria although lately it has also been drawing closer to Iran as well.

The Palestinian Ahmad Jibril was a former captain in the Syrian Army and head of the original Arab Liberation Front, which had helped to form the PFLP in 1967. While agreeing with Habash's principle of pursuing armed struggle and rejecting negotiated settlement of the Arab-Israeli conflict, Jibril has always been more interested in perfecting the mechanics of armed attacks. Because of its wayward tendency to promote factionalism within the PLO, this group was excluded from the PLO in 1983. Although the PFLP-GC has excellent operational capabilities and an impressive record of actions for so small a group (about 500 members) it has become a marginal actor within the politics of the Palestinian resistance. Internal dissension led to the splitting off of an anti-Syrian faction, the (second) Palestine Liberation Front (q.v.), in 1976.

The PFLP-GC imparts good commando training and uses some sophisticated and exotic hardware, such as SA-7 antiaircraft missiles, heavy artillery, ultralight aircraft, and hang gliders. It has carried out numerous cross-border assaults as well as operations in Israel's declared "security zone" in southern Lebanon. Commandos are prepared for "suicide" missions in which they are ready to kill themselves rather than be captured. In November 1987, a PFLP-GC member infiltrated Israel by crossing the security zone in a powered hang glider and succeeded in killing six Israeli soldiers and wounding seven others before being killed himself.

A favorite tactic of this group has been to seize Israeli civilians or soldiers as hostages in order to force the release of Arab prisoners by Israel. On 11 April 1974, three PFLP-GC members seized an apartment building in Kiryat Shemona, demanding the release of 100 Arab prisoners by Israel. The three killed 18 hostages and wounded 16 before killing themselves by setting off explosive charges wrapped around their belts when Israeli soldiers stormed the building. In the case of 4 Israeli soldiers captured in Lebanon, the PFLP-GC was able to negotiate their exchange for Arab prisoners, once in March 1979, exchanging one Israeli Defense Forces (IDF) soldier held one year for 76 Arab prisoners and again in May 1985, exchanging 3 IDF soldiers held since September 1982 for 1,150 Arab prisoners.

On 26 October 1988, West German police raided a PFLP-GC cell in Frankfurt arresting 14 members and seizing a number of weapons, Semtex explosives, and bomb detonators. Evidence obtained there linked one of those captured, Hafiz Qassim Dalkamoni, who is also a member of the PFLP-GC Central Committee, with two bombings of U.S. troop trains in Germany in 1987 and 1988. Following the 21 December 1988 aerial bombing of Pan Am flight 103 (q.v) over Lockerbie, Scotland, the PFLP-GC came under suspicion as having been the agent responsible for the action when it was learned that the bomb that destroyed Pan Am 103 was very similar to those assembled by this one PFLP-GC cell. While the bomb may have been assembled by the PFLP-GC, this alone did not mean this group itself planted the bomb on the doomed airplane, and suspicion for that act was later shifted instead to Libyan state agencies.

POPULAR FRONT FOR THE LIBERATION OF PALESTINE-SPECIAL COMMAND (PFLP-SC). One of three splinter groups that emerged from the Special Operations Unit of the Popular Front for the Liberation of Palestine, which fell apart after the death of its leader, Wadi Haddad, in 1978. The other two groups were the now defunct May 15 (q.v.) group and the Lebanese Armed Revolutionary Faction (FARL, q.v.). All three groups were critical of the diplomatic approach taken by more moderate Palestinian groups since 1982.

Formed in 1979, the PFLP-SC operated mainly in western Europe and the Middle East, claiming credit for various brutal terrorist attacks. In April 1985, the PFLP-SC bombed a restaurant in Torrejón, Spain, killing 18 Spanish civilians. This group has enjoyed Libyan and Syrian state support and is believed to have ties with ASALA (q.v.), Abu Nidal's Fatah Revolutionary Council (q.v.), and FARL. The size of the group was estimated at about 50 members.

POPULAR LIBERATION ARMY. The *Ejército Popular de Liberación* (EPL) is a Maoist revolutionary group that seeks to overthrow the Colombian state through prolonged popular warfare. The EPL is a rural guerrilla movement founded in 1967 as the armed wing of the Communist Party of Colombia-Marxist-Leninist, a Maoist political splinter group that broke away from the pro-Moscow Communist Party of Colombia (PCC) in July 1965. Although EPL claimed to look to Peking for leadership, sponsorship by the People's Republic was more in the form of moral than material support, including propaganda leaflets printed in China. During the post-Mao Tse-tung era, EPL continued to espouse the Maoist line, which has secured it a loyal following among a small circle of leftist intellectuals and academics.

The numbers of EPL guerrillas have been variously estimated at 350 or as high as 600 to 800 members. EPL operates four fronts in the Antioquía, Cordoba, and Risaralda departments. The deaths of key leaders in the 1970s led to internal dissent resulting in an unstable strategic approach and consequent tactical weakness. An example of this instability can be seen in EPL's equivocation in choosing to abide by the May 1984 government-sponsored truce, which it did not sign. This understanding abruptly ended when the leader of EPL, Ernesto Rojas, was killed in 1985.

During the late 1970s, the EPL engaged in sabotage, bank robberies, kidnappings, and bombings. Many of its military clashes have been with members of the Revolutionary Armed Forces of Colombia (q.v.)(FARC), the armed wing of the pro-Moscow PCC. In December 1982, the EPL kidnapped a Colombian land magnate for a $2 million ransom. In March 1984, they killed eight peasants accused of being Army informants as well as killing the mayor of a small town in northwestern Colombia. In November 1985, EPL ended its tacit compliance with the May 1984 cease-fire by attacking a town in northeastern Colombia in which four people were killed. In December 1985, EPL kidnapped two U.S. citizens working for Bechtel Corporation, one of whom died in captivity the following May while the other was later released. In June 1986, EPL bombed the Colombian-Soviet Friendship Institute in Medellín as retaliation for attacks by FARC against EPL forces. The same month, EPL also bombed the residence of the Honduran consul in Medellín, who was seriously wounded.

In early 1987, the EPL turned the Uraba region into one of its more active theaters in Colombia and has maintained an urban support infrastructure in Bogotá, Cali, Convención, Medellín, Pereira, Popayan, and Tierra Alta.

POPULAR RESISTANCE FRONT. Argentine leftist group responsible for 23 January 1989 attack upon the Third Mechanized Infantry Regiment base at La Trablada in the southwestern outskirts of Buenos Aires. The group was composed of remnants of the People's Revolutionary Army (q.v., ERP) and led by Enrique Haroldo Gorriaran Merlo (b. 1942), the second in command of the ERP. Gorriaran was among the ERP remnants who formed the Red Action assassination squad that murdered Anastasio Somoza in Paraguay in September 1980.

The group, numbering some 69 men and women, crashed the gates of the base, seized several recruits as hostages, took over six buildings, and fought a group of officers for three hours until police, along with army tank and artillery units, attacked the base, retaking it after 24 hours of fighting. In all, 28 attackers, 9 soldiers, and 2 policemen were killed. About 14 persons surrendered, 4 of whom were soldiers who had been held hostage. During the fighting Gorriaran escaped. This incident greatly shocked the Argentine public, who believed that the leftist groups had been wiped out during the "dirty war" (q.v.) during the military junta of General Videla.

On 1 February 1989, the Popular Resistance Front published a communiqué in a Uruguayan leftist paper claiming responsibility and stating that its motive was to deter a military plot to launch a coup d'état against the Alfonsín government. The communiqué identified the group as being composed of members of the All for the Fatherland Movement, founded in 1988, composed of remnants of the ERP under Gorriaran's leadership.

POPULAR STRUGGLE FRONT. The PSF, also called the Palestine Popular Struggle Front, is a Palestinian terrorist group that broke away from the PLO (q.v.) in 1974 but later rejoined it in 1991. The PSF joined the Rejection Front in 1975 and the National Salvation Front (q.v.) in 1985 to oppose an accord reached between the PLO and King Hussein of Jordan regarding a possible future settlement of the Arab-Israeli conflict. In common with other members of the Rejection Front (q.v.), the PSF rejects any accommodation with Israel in forming a Palestinian homeland out of the occupied territories, vowing instead total destruction of Israel and, until recently, opposing the PLO. The PSF is based in Damascus, Syria, with most of its forces in the Bekaa valley of Lebanon and is believed to be under Syrian sponsorship while also enjoying Libyan support.

On 28 June 1975, the PSF kidnapped U.S. Army Colonel Ernest R. Morgan in Beirut, Lebanon. The PSF passed him to the PFLP-GC (q.v.), another Rejection Front member. Eventually the PLO, which regarded the kidnapping as an unnecessary and dangerous provocation to the United States, pressured the PFLP-GC to release Col. Morgan. The PSF also has carried out guerrilla attacks within Israel, bombing the Ain Fashha resort in May 1975, bombing a tourist bus in Jerusalem in March 1979, and carrying out a rocket attack against the northern Israeli town of Metullah. This latter attack occasioned an Israeli air force bombing raid against PSF bases near Bar Ilyas in the Bekaa valley and in Shamlan near Beirut.

The PSF numbers around 300 members and has been led by Dr. Samir Ghosheh since 1974. In addition to documented attacks the group has made some claims for other attacks on Israel that have never been confirmed.

POSSE COMITATUS. Posse Comitatus (Latin for ''power of the county'') is a nonstate, revolutionary antitax protest group in the United States. The group openly advocates the limited ends of eliminating state and federal individual income taxes, abolition of the power of judicial review by the federal judiciary, abolition of the Federal Reserve System, and the restoration of the gold standard. Closer scrutiny of the organization reveals a more revolutionary agenda of replacing the current federalist system, which the group considers to be ''communist and unconstitutional,'' with supremacy of government at the county level. These goals proceed from an eccentric interpretation of the Posse Comitatus Act of 1878 and a belief in the superiority of the ''organic Constitution'' consisting only of those Articles and Amendments in force prior to the Civil War. The group's ideology views the current monetary, fiscal, and banking systems to be part of an anti-Christian conspiracy to defraud and enslave ordinary white Christians. Although the Posse Comitatus is not an Identity Christian or neo-Nazi movement, its views are

congruent with the anti-Semitic and white supremacist beliefs held by Identity Christian and other right-wing extremist groups with which Posse Comitatus has established
cooperation.

Posse Comitatus was formed by former neo-Nazi Henry
Lamont Beach in 1969 from remnants of the Minutemen
organization, which had fallen apart following the conviction
of its founder Robert dePugh on federal firearms violations.
During the 1970s, Posse chapters spread throughout every
state, instructing members in stratagems to avoid paying
taxes legally as well as more questionable methods such as
resorting to unrecorded barter transactions. Posse members
also used to file harassment suits against IRS officials and
law enforcement officers to obstruct these officials from
performing their duties. Posse also tried to create unchartered
barter-and-bullion based ''banks'' for its members as an
alternative to the existing banking system.

Following the crackdown initiated under the IRS Illegal
Tax Protestor Program begun in 1980, Posse tactics grew
more violent. In May 1983, Gordon Kahl, a North Dakota
farmer and Posse member already once jailed on conviction
for tax resistance, killed two federal marshals who sought to
serve subpoenas on him. On 3 June 1983, Kahl died in a
shoot-out with state and federal agents in an Arkansas cabin.
On 20 August 1986, a pipe bomb intended for U.S. Federal
District Court Judge Paul Benson was intercepted in Fargo,
N.D. Benson had sentenced Kahl and other Posse members
previously for tax resistance.

The Posse has produced at least one major splinter group,
namely the Arizona Patriots. Members of this group were
indicted in December 1986 of plotting to bomb the western
regional office of the IRS in Ogden, Utah using a vehicle
packed with explosives; to bomb several targets in Los
Angeles including the FBI office, the Simon Wiesenthal
Center, and two offices of the Jewish Defense League as well
as a synagogue in Phoenix.

Due to their distrust of the Federal government Posse

members have taken pains to avoid creating ''paper trails'' and have kept outsiders ignorant of the structure and leadership of their organization. Members avoid the use of standard identification cards, such as driver's licenses and Social Security cards. By the mid-1980s membership was variously estimated between 1,000 and 3,000 nationwide, but Wisconsin Posse leaders claimed to have over 2,000 members in their chapter alone. The Posse finds a major portion of potential recruits from midwestern farmers who have suffered as a result of unfavorable market conditions and bank foreclosures on mortgaged farms. One Louis Harris poll commissioned by the B'nai B'rith Anti-Defamation League of rural residents of Iowa and Nebraska in February 1986 found that 25 percent of this sample of midwesterners followed the activities of Posse Comitatus even if they were not openly affiliated with it and essentially accepted its core beliefs.

PRIMA LINEA. The ''Front Line'' (PL) group were Italian leftist terrorists active from November 1976 until 1981, second only to the Red Brigades as a major terrorist threat. Like the Red Brigades or the Red Army Faction, they rationalized their terrorism in revolutionary leftist terms but appeared to pursue terrorist violence as an end in itself rather than as a strategy to achieve revolution. While they did not appear to have state sponsorship, the group did collaborate with Direct Action (q.v.) and the Red Brigades (q.v.).

In ideology and organization, PL greatly resembled the Red Brigades perhaps because one of its leaders, Corrado Alunni, was also a leading Red Brigades figure. PL differed from the Red Brigades, however, in maintaining open contacts with the Italian left rather than going underground. Its initial act was an attack against the Fiat plant in Turin on 29 November 1976. By the end of 1978, PL had carried out 25 operations. In January 1979, PL murdered Milan Assistant Attorney General, Emilio Alessandrini. Like the Red Brigades, PL also specialized in ''kneecapping,'' that is, shooting captured victims in the knees, as it did in the case of the Italian manager of the Chemical Bank of New York in Milan who was shot 4 times in the legs on 11 May 1978, and also to 10 hostages in the Turin School of Industrial Management on 11 December 1979. After 1980, PL began concentrating more on assassinations, particularly judges and jurors who had convicted leftist terrorists.

The group originated in Turin and spread to Florence, Milan, and Naples. Due to the police crackdown following the kidnapping and murder of former prime minister Aldo Moro in early 1978 at the hands of the Red Brigades, Italian police were able to identify about 165 members of PL who were largely apprehended by October 1982, so ending the organization.

PROVISIONAL IRISH REPUBLICAN ARMY. The PIRA is the main Irish nationalist paramilitary and terrorist organization seeking to re-unite the six counties of Northern Ireland with the rest of Ireland into an ''Irish Socialist Republic'' primarily by revolutionary armed struggle rather than through political or diplomatic means. As PIRA's members are quite outnumbered by the Northern Irish police together with regular British forces and security forces in Northern Ireland, PIRA has resorted heavily to terrorism aimed at inflicting maximum casualties and has targeted civilians as well as military personnel.

PIRA began in 1969 with covert aid, including arms, from the Irish Republic during the Fianna Fail government of Prime Minister Jack Lynch. Later Irish governments desisted from covert support and took steps to intercept arms destined for PIRA being shipped through Irish territory. Libya has provided arms and financial help intermittently, having shipped 5 tons of arms from Tripoli on the *Claudia*, which were seized by the Irish Navy on 28 March 1973. This shipment was followed by a shipment of 150 tons of Libyan weapons, including Czech-made Semtex explosives, aboard the *Eskund*, seized by French customs and police on 1

November 1987. Iran and Algeria also have given aid to PIRA. Contacts were also made by PIRA with the Basque Fatherland and Liberty (q.v.) group as well as the Popular Front for the Liberation of Palestine (q.v.) and the Revolutionary Cells (q.v.) found in Germany. Most of PIRA's resources come from within the Irish community, however, through extortion and protection payments among the Irish in the six counties, bank robberies both in Northern Ireland and the Republic, and through appeals for donations from people of Catholic Irish descent living in the United States and elsewhere, often through front organizations such as NORAID (the Irish Northern Aid Organization). On 29 September 1984, the Irish Navy seized seven tons of arms on the trawler *Marita Ann* off-loaded from a ship that had transported them from the United States.

PIRA emerged on 29 December 1969 when dissidents in the existing Irish Republican Army formed their own ''Provisional'' Army Council, against the Army Council ruling body of the existing IRA, issuing statements to the press declaring their positions. In essence the ''Provos'' objected to the older IRA's increasing tendency to set aside armed struggle in favor of electoral and diplomatic measures. Moreover they believed the older IRA leadership was sacrificing Irish nationalism to Marxist-Leninist ideology, which struck little responsive chord with the largely Catholic nationalist population. Ironically PIRA would later itself experience similar defections in 1974 to another group to emerge out of the older IRA, namely, the Irish National Liberation Army (INLA, q.v.), and again in 1984–1985 when it appeared that PIRA was itself becoming more of a political than a military organization. In fact, PIRA has pursued an ''armalite and ballot box'' strategy of using political front organizations, such as the Sinn Fein, to seek electoral gains as tactics parallel with, but secondary to, its reliance on armed struggle.

PIRA terrorism has several objectives: It is intended to raise to unacceptable levels the economic and political costs to Britain of maintaining troops in Northern Ireland. It is intended to provoke British and Northern Irish military and police forces to violate the human and civil rights of PIRA suspects or ordinary Catholics in the hope that such abuses in turn will outrage Britain's domestic civil libertarians and excite international condemnation. It is meant also to mobilize forcibly into the struggle the Northern Irish Catholics over whom PIRA asserts its jurisdiction. This has entailed summary punishments against Catholics who themselves do not agree with the PIRA political program or who are suspected of cooperating with Northern Irish and British authorities, by means of "kneecappings," summary executions, and threats against family members. In recent years, PIRA has developed the tactic of using detected informers as suicide car bomb drivers against Northern Irish police and British troops. The suicide driver is usually a married man with family who is told that his family will be murdered if he does not cooperate. Such a suicide car bomber killed himself and five soldiers in an attack on a Londonderry checkpoint on 24 October 1990.

The primary targets of PIRA have been British Army troops, Northern Irish security forces, judicial officials, prison wardens and guards, and members of Ulster Protestant political parties and militias. Most attacks have been carried out in Northern Ireland with some attacks against British targets in the Irish Republic and many more attacks in England. PIRA has also carried its attacks into Europe against British Army personnel in Germany and the Netherlands. PIRA uses various handguns, automatic weapons, grenades, light antitank weapons, mortars, and bombs of various homemade manufacture including car bombs. From 1969 to 1982, PIRA had been legally implicated through convictions of its members of 2,269 murders, 7,521 bombings that killed 608 people, and at least 1,000 kneecappings. By the end of 1990 the total deaths caused by PIRA had reached a total of 2,781.

A few of the more notable actions of PIRA include the

following: On 21 July 1972, "Bloody Friday," PIRA conducted 22 bombings in Belfast, killing 11 and wounding
about 100. During September 1973, PIRA bombed the
London Stock Exchange, the House of Commons, the Bank
of England, the London subway, and several shopping areas.
On 21 November 1974, PIRA bombed 2 pubs in Birmingham, England, killing 21 and wounding around 120. On 21
July 1976, PIRA assassinated Christopher Ewart-Briggs,
British Ambassador to Ireland, by destroying his vehicle
with a land mine. On 27 August 1979, PIRA assassinated
Louis, Earl Mountbatten by bombing his yacht, which also
killed three others with him. On 20 July 1982, PIRA set off
two radio-controlled bombs in London, the first striking a
passing detachment of the Queen's Household Calvary
traveling through Hyde Park, killing four soldiers, and the
other bomb killing seven members of the Royal Green
Jackets, a military band, in Regent's Park. On 17 December
1983, PIRA car bombed Harrod's department store in London, killing 5 (including 1 American) and wounding 80
others. On 12 October 1984, PIRA bombed the hotel holding
the British Conservative Party conference in Brighton, England, killing 1 Cabinet member and 3 others and wounding
32 others. Prime Minister Thatcher would have been killed if
she had not moved into a different room just minutes before
the bomb detonated. On 8 November 1987, PIRA bombed a
Remembrance Day ceremony in Enniskillen, County Fer-
managh, killing 11 people and wounding 63 others. In
addition, PIRA has conducted five major attacks on British
Army bases in Europe. In 1990, PIRA began to carry out
more attacks in England, including two shootings and two
bombings, one of which killed Conservative Member of
Parliament Ian Gow on 30 July 1990. On 7 February 1991,
PIRA carried out a mortar attack against the British Prime
Minister's office-residence at No. 10 Downing Street while
Prime Minister Major was consulting there with senior
members of his cabinet. During 1991, PIRA also carried out
numerous bombings throughout Britain, including a 2,000-

pound bomb that was exploded outside a police station in Northern Ireland.

The PIRA terror campaign has led to unintended results that may have made its goal of unification of Ireland more remote. First, the bitterness of the terrorist war being waged by PIRA and other nationalist/republican groups, by the Ulster Protestant militias, and by the British forces has exacerbated the communal and sectarian tensions to the extent that the majority of Ulster Protestants may prefer to opt for a separate Ulster republic rather than consent to unification with the south should Britain decide to withdraw from Northern Ireland. Second, the terror campaign against British targets in England, and particularly the attacks on the prime minister and members of Parliament, has hardened official British attitudes toward the Irish nationalists and republicans and strengthened their resolve not to retreat from Northern Ireland. Third, the terror campaign has transformed the nationalist struggle from being a mass movement centered around civil rights to becoming an insidious war of covert operations and counterintelligence in which ordinary civilians play little active role and which has stifled open political participation.

While the original IRA conceived itself to be a true army, and organized itself accordingly with general orders and a hierarchical command structure, PIRA was forced to adopt a cellular structure in the 1970s to prevent the penetration and subversion of the organization by British agents. Beginning in 1981, the British resorted to the ''supergrass'' tactic of turning a captured terrorist, facing substantial charges, into a prosecution witness with immunity from prosecution for his own crimes if he would denounce several of his erstwhile colleagues. This system used trials without juries and the uncorroborated testimony of one witness to effect scores of convictions. While many of these convictions have been overturned on appeal, the tactic sowed much distrust and internal discord within the affected republican and loyalist terrorist groups and hampered their efficiency.

Although previous IRA terrorist campaigns, such as that which erupted in the Irish civil war of 1922–1923 or the "Border Campaign" of 1956–1962, eventually spent themselves out there is one important difference between those former campaigns and the present, ongoing one. In the prior cases the IRA had targeted the government of the Republic of Ireland as well as the government of Northern Ireland with the result that authorities on both sides of the border cooperated in suppressing IRA terrorism. With the formation of PIRA, a tacit accord appeared to exist between the Irish Republic and PIRA to the effect that PIRA would not target the Irish Republic so long as the Republic did not cooperate with the Northern Irish authorities in their efforts to stem nationalist republican terrorists. General Order No. 8 of the PIRA official handbook, "the Green Book," prohibits PIRA members from "any military action against 26 County [sic] forces under any circumstances whatsoever." Although the Irish Republic began in the mid-1970s to intercept arms shipments destined for PIRA and attempted to dissuade the Libyan government from supporting PIRA, the various Irish governments have avoided vigorous prosecution and internment of PIRA activists within the Republic. So long as PIRA enjoyed effective sanctuary and a base of operations within the Republic there was no reason to expect PIRA terrorism in Northern Ireland and elsewhere to diminish. The impact of the late 1994 truce remains to be seen.

PRTC. Partido Revolucionario de los Trabajadores Centroamericanos (Revolutionary Party of Central American Workers), one of the constituent groups of the Farabundo Martí National Liberation Front. (See Farabundo Martí National Liberation Front)

- Q -

QADDAFI, MUAMMAR. (b. 1941) Leader of the coup d'état that overthrew King Idris of Libya on 1 September 1969,

Colonel Muammar Qaddafi has been the president of the Libyan Arab Republic, also called by Qaddafi the Libyan People's Arab Socialist Jamahariyyah. Qaddafi is of Bedouin extraction and is a devout Muslim.

As a youth he greatly admired Egyptian leader Gamal Abdel Nasser and so Qaddafi's pronounced anti-Western sentiments appear to spring from his ardent Pan-Arabism and hatred of Israel. Accordingly he ordered the U.S. military forces out of Libya in 1970, cancelled the British-Libyan military accord in 1972, nationalized U.S. oil companies holdings in Libya, and played an instrumental role within OPEC in raising producer oil prices. Qaddafi's involvement with sponsorship of terrorist groups began in the same period with aid to Black September (q.v.) in its attack on the Saudi Arabian Embassy in Khartoum on 1 March 1973 and in its attack on Athens airport on 5 August 1973. Libya also supported the terrorists responsible for the OPEC Secretariat siege in December 1975, allowing them to unload their ransoms in Libya and later permitting them sanctuary there. The Venezuelan terrorist Ilyich Ramírez Sánchez, also called "Carlos," who led the OPEC siege, disappeared from public view at that time.

In 1975, Qaddafi broke off relations with the PLO and began to back the renegade Fatah Revolutionary Council led by Abu Nidal (q.v.). Consequently Qaddafi is suspected of complicity in the December 1985 hijacking of an Egyptair airliner to Luqua airport in Malta and the massacre of holiday travelers at Rome and Vienna airports on 27 December 1985.

Qaddafi clashed with the United States over the question of Libyan claims to sovereignty over the Gulf of Sidra. U.S. naval exercises in those waters led to clashes between Libyan and U.S. forces in March 1986. The United States held Libya responsible for the 5 April 1986 bombing of the La Belle discotheque in West Berlin, a favorite nightclub of U.S. servicemen. In retaliation, the U.S. Air Force conducted bombing raids on Benghazi and Tripoli, striking one of Qaddafi's residences and apparently killing one of his foster children. Qaddafi became uncharacteristically reticent after this incident. This did not portend any renunciation of terrorism, however. On 14 April 1988, the ''Jihad Brigades,'' a unit of the Japanese Red Army acting under Libyan sponsorship, carried out a retaliatory bombing against a USO club in Naples, killing five patrons. On 14 November 1991, the United States issued indictments against Libyan officials, charging the Libyan government with sponsorship of the bombing of Pan Am flight 103 on 21 November 1988, and the U.S. State Department published evidence in its April 1992 report on global terrorism linking the Qaddafi regime with the bombing. Qaddafi has refused to extradite the two officials named in those indictments.

Both Britain and the United States have also had concerns over Libyan state terrorism against anti-Qaddafi Libyans living as permanent residents or students in those countries. During 1980 Libyan agents murdered at least 10 anti-Qaddafi dissidents in Britain and Western Europe. Later such agents also tried to hire assassins to kill dissidents within the United States. On 17 April 1984, during anti-Qaddafi demonstrations outside the Libyan Embassy in St. James Square, London, members of the Libyan ''People's Bureau'' opened fire with automatic weapons on the crowds outside, wounding 11 Libyan protestors and killing a young British policewoman. Both Britain and the United States have retaliated for such incidents by expelling the Libyan diplomats involved in such behavior.

QUEBEC LIBERATION FRONT. The *Front de Libération du Québec* (FLQ) was a French Canadian group seeking independence for the province of Quebec from the rest of Canada along with creation of a socialist regime there. From 1962 to 1980, the FLQ was the single largest source of political violence in Canada, accounting for 50 percent (= 166 incidents) of all domestic terrorism in Canada, most of which occurred before 1972. Most incidents involved bombings of

Canadian federal buildings, firebombings of Canadian police stations, businesses in Quebec owned by American and Canadian Anglophones, and military installations, but eventually progressing to kidnapping and murder. The group enjoyed moral and limited material support from Cuba and Algeria.

The FLQ was founded in February 1963 by three Quebec separatists disgruntled with existing separatist organizations. On 21 June 1970, the group botched an attempt to kidnap the U.S. consul general in Montreal. On 5 October 1970, they kidnapped James Cross, the British trade commissioner in Canada, whom they released on 3 December 1970. On 10 October 1970, they kidnapped Pierre Laporte, Quebec's minister of labor. The Canadian government imposed the War Measures Act on 16 October 1970, suspending ordinary civil liberties and allowing police and military forces extraordinary powers to apprehend around 500 suspects and to conduct searches without warrants. The kidnappers murdered Laporte on 17 October 1970, and his body was found the following day in the trunk of a car. The four kidnappers eventually negotiated safe passage to Cuba in exchange for the life of James Cross.

The murder of Laporte greatly shocked English Canadian and Québécois public opinion and created a backlash against the FLQ even in Quebec. The outrage against the FLQ was heightened by the separatist Parti Québécois's impressive gains in recent elections, having secured 23 percent of the provincial election votes in 1970, which made the recourse to terrorism seem pointless and counterproductive. The War Measures Act expired in January 1971, but ordinary police powers resulted in a dozen arrests of key FLQ members that year. FLQ theoretician Pierre Vallières surfaced in December 1971, publicly repudiating the FLQ and calling on FLQ members to desist from terrorism. The FLQ was dormant from then until the electoral victory of the Parti Québécois in provincial elections in 1976 by which time most former FLQ members had opted to seek separatism through the Parti Québécois.

QUTB, SAYYID. (b. 1906, d. 1966) Egyptian Muslim theologian, social thinker and activist, and leader within the Muslim Brotherhood (q.v.). Sayyid Qutb exercised a cardinal influence on the development of Islamic fundamentalism (q.v.) through his writings and directly influenced the theory and practice of such fundamentalist groups as the various branches of the Muslim Brotherhood, the Munazzamat al Jihad (q.v.) group, and others who have used Qutb's doctrine of jihad (q.v.) to justify terrorist actions against ''apostate'' Muslim governments and rulers as well as against perceived external enemies of Islam.

In his seminal work *Maalim fi al Tariq*, ''Milestones,'' Qutb advanced the argument that since the main object of jihad was enforcing full enactment of the Islamic code of sacred law, rather than defense of Muslim lands or conquest of non-Muslims as such, there was no reason for Muslims to abstain from initiating military force in order to advance Islam in the world. Qutb's works also identified Westernizing and secular nationalist Muslim political leaders as agents of a revived *jahiliyyah* (pre-Islamic heathenism) who therefore were to be counted among those enemies of Islam who could be lawfully attacked at will by true believers. The Munazzamat al Jihad group incorporated Qutb's thoughts into their doctrine and enacted them with the assassination of Anwar Sadat on 6 October 1981.

Sayyid Qutb joined the Muslim Brotherhood in 1951 but was imprisoned in 1954 due to a crackdown on the Brotherhood following an unsuccessful assassination plot against Nasser. Qutb was released in the 1960s but was directly implicated in another assassination plot against Nasser in 1965 and executed the following year.

- R -

RED ARMY FACTION. The RAF, formerly known as the ''Baader-Meinhof Gang,'' is a group of German anarchistic, leftist terrorists active from 11 May 1972 to the present. The RAF, Direct Action (q.v.), the Red Brigades (q.v.), the Communist Combatant Cells (q.v.), and Prima Linea (q.v.) rationalized their terrorism in revolutionary leftist terms but appeared to pursue terrorist violence as an end in itself rather than as a strategy to achieve revolution. These groups can be considered "leftist" insofar as they despised capitalism, believed in the superiority of a socialist state, and often spoke in Marxist jargon. They were also anarchistic insofar as they limited their purposes to destroying the existing capitalist states rather than building the foundations of some successor socialist state. While RAF did not originally appear to have state sponsorship, evidence has been found in East German government files following the reunification of Germany showing that in the preceding 10 years the German Democratic Republic provided logistical support, sanctuary, and training to the RAF. In the period from 15–30 June 1990, East German police arrested 10 fugitive RAF members who had been given asylum by the formerly Communist regime. Even in the formative Baader-Meinhof period, however, the group was clearly dependent on the PFLP for initial training, which itself received Soviet and other Eastern Bloc assistance. The RAF did collaborate with Direct Action and the Communist Combatant Cells, both now defunct, and currently appears to collaborate with GRAPO (q.v.).

This group was formed out of the student unrest and leftist activism of 1968 when Andreas Baader (b. 1943), imprisoned in 1968 for firebombing a Frankfurt department store, escaped on 14 May 1970 with the help of Ulrike Meinhof (b. 1934), a left-wing journalist. Together with another comrade they went to the Middle East where they underwent terrorist training in camps run by the PFLP (q.v.). On their return they engaged in shootings, bombings, and abductions before being arrested in 1972. The continuing terrorist activities of the rest of the Baader-Meinhof Gang were directed to freeing the two imprisoned leaders. On 27 June 1976, RAF members together with members of the Popular Front for the Liberation of Palestine (q.v.) hijacked an Air France Paris-to-Tel Aviv flight to Entebbe, Uganda, where 240 passengers were held hostage until rescued by Israeli commandos on 1 July 1976, an operation in which all seven hijackers were killed along with approximately 20 Ugandan soldiers. PFLP terrorists hijacked a Lufthansa plane to Mogadishu, Somalia, on 13 October 1977, in order to force the German government to release Baader and Meinhof. When the hijackers were foiled on 17 October 1977 by West German GSG-9 commandos, Baader and Meinhof committed suicide. Since that time, the surviving group has called itself the Red Army Faction.

An analysis of 53 noteworthy actions committed by RAF from 1972 to 1991 shows that 55 percent (=29) of these involved bombings; 15 percent (=8) involved assassinations; and 8 percent (=4) involved armed attacks. Only one notable instance of hostage-taking is noted, namely the kidnapping of Hanns-Martin Schleyer on 5 September 1977, and two hijackings, namely the 13 October 1977 Lufthansa hijacking to Mogadishu, in which the RAF played a minor role. Hostage taking and hijacking each contribute 2 and 4 percent, respectively, to the total of the RAF activities. Sabotage actions account for another 11 percent while other actions (unfulfilled threats, arms smuggling, and so on) accounted for 5 percent.

Bombing targets have included a U.S. Officers' Club in Frankfurt (11 May 1972); an attempted bombing-assassination of NATO Commander Gen. Alexander Haig (25 June 1979); U.S. Air Force headquarters in Ramstein (31 August 1981); and the Rhein-Main Air Force Base car-bombing attack carried out jointly with Direct Action (8 August 1985). Assassinations have included the killing of German Supreme Court President Günter von Drenkmann (9 November 1974); German Federal Prosecutor Siegfried Buback (7 April 1977); Deutsche Bank Chairman Alfred Herrhausen (30 November 1989); an attempt on Interior Ministry State Secretary Hans Neusel (27 July 1990); and Detlev Rohwedder, a West German businessman involved in the liquidation and sale of former East German state enterprises (1 April 1991).

The RAF is the oldest of the groups described above as "anarchistic, leftist terrorists," which seek to destroy the capitalist state without any strategy to help build a successor socialist state. Currently the RAF also appears to be the last of this kind of terrorist organization. Given the recent revelations of its dependence on the defunct German Democratic Republic as a state sponsor, the future of RAF is problematic. The 13 February 1991 assault on the U.S. embassy in Bonn involving 250 rounds of small-arms fire in protest against Operation Desert Storm suggests that RAF could return to the Middle East for any needed support, where a number of anti-U.S. Middle Eastern states or groups might be willing to assume covert sponsorship of such a group.

Although this group is estimated to have only 10 to 20 actual fighters, it has succeeded in creating a support network that involves hundreds of Germans, many of whom are well-educated professionals. RAF has also succeeded in perpetuating itself through two generations of leadership, which indicates a higher potential for organizational survival.

RED ARMY FOR THE LIBERATION OF CATALONIA. The Ejército Rojo Catalán de Liberación (ERCA) is believed to be a Marxist-Leninist offshoot of the Terra Lliure (q.v.) Catalan separatist movement. As such it shares with Terra Lliure the goal of reconstituting an independent Catalan homeland in Catalonia, which would embrace also the Spanish provinces of Valencia and the Baleric Isles as well as the French province of Roussillon.

During 1987, ERCA bombed several U.S. targets in Barcelona. On May 13, the General Electric office was bombed, causing no injuries. On October 14, the U.S. Consulate General was bombed, injuring eight Spaniards. On December 26, a youth lobbed two grenades of Danish manufacture into a USO club, killing one U.S. serviceman, and wounding five other servicemen as well as three by-standers.

RED BRIGADES. The "Brigate Rosse" (BR) was a group of Italian anarchistic, leftist terrorists founded in 1970 and active from 18 April 1974 until 23 April 1988. The BR, Direct Action (q.v.), the Red Army Faction (q.v.), the Communist Combatant Cells (q.v.), and Prima Linea (q.v.) rationalized their terrorism in revolutionary leftist terms but appeared to pursue terrorist violence as an end in itself rather than as a strategy to achieve revolution. These groups can be considered "leftist" insofar as they despised capitalism, believed in the superiority of a socialist state, and often spoke in Marxist jargon. They were also anarchistic insofar as they limited their purposes to destroying the existing capitalist states rather than building the foundations of some successor socialist state. While the BR did not appear to have state sponsorship, the group had contacts in the mid-1970s with Uruguayan Tupamaros (q.v.), later collaborated with Direct Action and the Red Army Faction, and cultivated links with Palestinian terrorist groups, in particular the Lebanese Armed Revolutionary Faction (FARL, q.v.). Currently it appears some fugitive BR members have joined forces with GRAPO (q.v.).

The BR viewed itself as the vanguard for a proletarian party that would spontaneously appear once the group had paved the way by destroying the "SIM," the Italian acronym for "Imperialist State of Multinationals" and by raising the revolutionary consciousness of the working classes through acts of armed propaganda. Founded in 1970, the BR struck at the Italian state through assassination and "kneecappings" of judges, prosecutors, and jurors and also through attacks on the Christian Democratic party. About 75 percent of BR's attacks, however, were directed at businesses, with threats of arson, kidnapping, kneecapping, or murder if protection money was not paid. The BR seldom made use of bombing, except on 3 May 1979 in attacking the Christian Democrat party headquarters in Rome, unlike the Red Army Faction or Direct Action, although it used firebombs to initiate arsons.

During the period from 1974–1988, there were at least 50 noteworthy attacks committed by the BR, 47 assassinations, 19 cases of kneecapping of victims, and 13 kidnappings. Four kidnap ransoms alone netted the BR around $6 million. Like the Red Army Faction, the BR undertook many of their kidnappings and attacks on behalf of imprisoned comrades, either to pressure the judicial system to release them or else to take revenge on jurists and police involved in their capture and convictions. The waves of assassinations of jurists eventually caused Italian magistrates to go on strike in July 1980 in protest over their lack of security. During 1978–1980, called by Italians the "years of lead," hardly a day went by without an armed attack, political murder, kidnapping, or other terrorist actions due to the Brigades, similar leftist groups and imitators, as well as Italian neo-Fascists.

Three events stand out in the history of the Brigades: Inspired by the Red Army Faction's kidnapping of Hanns-Martin Schleyer, the BR kidnapped the head of the Christian Democrat party and former prime minister, Aldo Moro, on 16 March 1978, killing five of his bodyguards. Moro was killed 55 days later. While the BR viewed this as a great victory Italian society at large viewed it with revulsion and the Italian government empowered its security forces to suspend certain civil liberties in order to crack down on the Brigades and similar groups. On 17 December 1981, BR kidnapped Brigadier General James Dozier, U.S. Army, in Verona, who was rescued by Italian counterterrorist police in Padua on 28 January 1982.

The decision to kidnap a senior NATO officer had been inspired partly through a desire to show solidarity with the PLO by striking at an "imperialist" target. The BR connection with Palestinian terrorists was more obvious when they assassinated an American, Leamon Hunt, the director of the multinational observer team charged with overseeing the peace accord between Egypt and Israel on 15 February 1984, apparently with weapons provided by FARL (q.v.) agents. Following this murder, the BR carried out another three assassinations of prominent persons as well as an attempted assassination. In the first week of September 1989, Italian police arrested several brigadists after which BR activity appeared to cease.

RED GUERRILLA RESISTANCE. The Red Guerrilla Resistance (RGR) was a nonstate U.S. leftist group that engaged in bombings during the mid-1980s for the limited purpose of protesting U.S. and Israeli "imperialism," militarism, and South African apartheid. All of the bombings carried out in the name of this group occurred in New York City. On 5 April 1984, the RGR bombed the Israeli Aircraft Industries plant. On 26 September 1984, the group bombed the South African Consulate. On 23 February 1985, it bombed the New York City Police Benevolent Association offices. Some analysts believe that the Red Guerrilla Resistance was another nom de guerre of the May 19 Communist Coalition (q.v.).

RED HAND COMMANDOS. The Red Hand Commandos were an Ulster Protestant terrorist militia established in 1972 by John McKeague after his expulsion from the Ulster Defense Association (q.v.). This group and the Ulster Volunteer Force, with which it worked in tandem, functioned as anti-Catholic death squads in the Belfast area and were banned by the British government in 1973. In April 1975, the Commandos bombed a pub in a Catholic district killing six. The Red Hand Commandos were also suspected in the 17 May 1974 bombings of downtown Dublin and Monaghan, killing 30 and wounding 151.

McKeague was unsuccessfully prosecuted under the Stormont parliament's Incitement to Religious Hatred Law. Shortly after his acquittal in January 1982, McKeague was killed by militants of the Irish National Liberation Army (q.v.).

REJECTION FRONT. In 1974, the Popular Front for the Liberation of Palestine (PFLP) established the Front Rejecting Capitulationist Solutions to oppose the participation of the PLO in any negotiated settlement of the Arab-Israeli conflict. The PFLP-General Command (q.v.), the Arab Liberation Front (q.v.), the Palestine Liberation Front (q.v.), and the Popular Struggle Front (q.v.) also joined this opposition group. Given the acquiescence of the PFLP and several of these other groups with the resolutions of the Nineteenth meeting of the Palestine National Council on 15 November 1988 recognizing U.N. Resolutions 242 and 338 as the basis for a Middle East settlement, the Rejection Front must be regarded as defunct.

RENAMO (MNR). The Mozambique National Resistance (*Resistência Nacional Moçambicana*) is a Mozambican insurgent group formerly sponsored by Rhodesia and South Africa. Members of this group are largely anti-Marxist Mozambicans, both native Africans and Portuguese colonials, as well as disaffected former FRELIMO (Mozambican Liberation Front) members who are seeking to change the regime. The South African sponsors of RENAMO viewed it primarily as a means of pressuring Mozambique to stop giving sanctuary and support to the Umkhonto we Sizwe (q.v.) guerrillas fighting South Africa, who were associated with the African National Congress (ANC, q.v.).

When Mozambique was granted independence by Portugal on 25 June 1975, the new Marxist Mozambican government began giving aid and sanctuary to Zimbabwe African National Union guerrillas fighting the Ian Smith regime. Rhodesia countered by sponsoring the creation of the MNR in 1976, which recruited both native African and Portuguese colonial Mozambicans to attack the anti-Rhodesian guerrillas in their bases within Mozambique. Beginning in 1978, the MNR began attacking the economic infrastructure of Mozambique as well as seeking to destabilize the FRELIMO regime. After the transition of power in 1980 that created the new state of Zimbabwe from the former colony of Rhodesia, the MNR found a new sponsor in South Africa that also wished to pressure Mozambique to stop supporting the ANC-backed guerrillas. In 1982, the MNR changed its name to RENAMO and spread its area of operations into Zimbabwe, Malawi, and Zambia. From having started with a few thousand in 1976, RENAMO expanded to in excess of 20,000 guerrillas by the end of the 1980s. It enjoyed safe haven in South Africa as well as logistical support but neighboring states, such as Malawi, Tanzania, and Zimbabwe, countered by stationing some of their troops within Mozambique.

RENAMO's campaign has been marked by calculated, consistent, and extreme brutality directed toward noncombatants. An analysis of 47 noteworthy incidents from 1979 to 1987 showed that 51 percent involved kidnappings; 15 percent involved assassinations; and 4 percent involved bombings. The remaining 30 percent involved armed attacks and sabotage operations. Kidnappings have generally involved foreign nationals, such as aid and development workers, relief workers, and missionaries, some of whom have been killed in captivity, have died of disease or malnutrition, and four of whom have disappeared. African nationals of Mozambique and neighboring lands have also been, in effect, enslaved by RENAMO for use as human porters. In August 1979, the MNR murdered five Soviet advisers and in June 1982 murdered a Portuguese engineer. On 14 October 1983, RENAMO derailed a train and then murdered dozens of passengers. In July 1987, RENAMO carried out a massacre at Homoine, killing over 400 civilians. RENAMO has also engaged in mutilation of its victims.

By 1990, as the South African government gradually came to terms with the ANC, its support for RENAMO came to an end. RENAMO had meanwhile built up a support network in Europe and elsewhere among private individuals and groups. During 1991, negotiations between RENAMO and the Mozambican government were under way and hostilities there had been partly suspended. Although a RENAMO leader, Afonso Dhlakama, and Mozambique's President Joaquim Chissano signed a cease-fire in Rome in October 1992, sporadic fighting has continued between RENAMO and government forces.

REVOLUTION. A transformation of the political system of a society in which the majority of the people in the affected society withdraw their recognition of the legitimacy of the pre-revolutionary political system in favor of the system that replaces it. Revolution differs from a coup d'état insofar as a coup need only replace the main personalities governing the state without otherwise changing the state system. Revolutions usually involve some political violence, even in those using nonviolent civil disobedience, since even then the protagonists of the regime usually will violently resist being overthrown.

Throughout this dictionary, groups are described as having revolutionary goals even if their aim is secession or independence for a nationalist homeland rather than the political transformation of the entire society or economic-social order. In the case of the Irish Republican Army, their goals include the unification of the northern and southern counties of Ireland and total separation of a united Ireland from Great Britain. The IRA intends to destroy the legitimacy of the Northern Irish government but also to cause the British to acquiesce in the redefinition of the British state as well. Similarly the transformation of an authoritarian and bureaucratic Iranian state under the shah to a theocratic state under the rule of Shiite clergymen must also be counted as a revolution even if such a transformation does not meet historicist expectations of some linear scheme of tentative progress. There is no a priori reason to designate only leftist groups as being ''revolutionary'' while designating all rightist groups as ''counterrevolutionary.''

REVOLUTIONARY ARMED FORCES OF COLOMBIA. The *Fuerzas Armadas Revolucionarias de Colombia* (FARC) is a nonstate guerrilla group dedicated to creating a Marxist-Leninist revolution in Colombia. FARC is considered to be the best equipped, best-trained, and most effective guerrilla group in South America. Its main areas of operations have been the rural areas of the departments of Antioquía, Tolima, Magdalena, Boyaca, Caqueta, Huila, Cauca, Santander, Valle del Cauca, Cundinamarca, and Meta. Its headquarters are located in La Uribe in Meta department.

FARC's origins go back to 1958 when Colombian Communist Party (PCC) Central Committee member Manuel Marulanda Velez and Rigoberto Losada (d. 1992) founded FARC as an independent guerrilla group. In 1966 the PCC adopted FARC as its military wing. This move was taken in reaction to the creation of the Castroite National Liberation Army (ELN, q.v.) in 1964. In the period from 1966–1968, FARC numbered some 500 combatants. The normalization of relations between the Soviet Union and Colombia weakened FARC, which could no longer count on external aid.

Its members have been drawn mainly from the middle-class intelligentsia. FARC has undercut its appeal by its tactic of kidnapping and killing peasants who do not cooperate with it. During the early 1970s, FARC began financing itself through kidnapping for ransom of foreign nationals and wealthy Colombians and through extortion of foreign-affiliated businesses. During this resurgence, FARC organized itself into operationally independent units known as ''fronts,'' having five fronts by 1978, which increased to 27 fronts by 1987 and to 40 fronts by 1988. One of these fronts, the Ricardo Franco Front (q.v.), broke with the main body of FARC over the question of seeking a negotiated settlement with the government and became an independent terrorist organization.

The group has attacked both Colombian domestic and U.S.-affiliated targets. In February 1977, they kidnapped a U.S. Peace Corps volunteer in La Macrena who was released three years later only after payment of a $250,000 ransom. In August 1980, they kidnapped a U.S. banana grower in central

Colombia, who was released three months later after payment of a $125,000 ransom. In April and August 1983, two U.S. citizens residing in La Meta department were also kidnapped and released only on payments of ransom.

In May 1984, FARC, along with EPL, and M-19, signed a cease-fire with the Colombian government that did not require members of these groups to surrender their weapons. Various FARC fronts, as well as the Ricardo Franco Front, which broke away from FARC in March 1984, continued terrorist killings, extortionism, and kidnappings, as well as attacking military units:

During February 1985, eight U.S. businesses were bombed in Medellín, including IBM, General Telephone and Electronics, Union Carbide, and Xerox. In the course of these nighttime bombings, one person was killed and another wounded. The Medellín bombings may have been the work of the Ricardo Franco Front, which did not feel obligated to follow other FARC fronts in honoring the truce. In August 1985, FARC reportedly kidnapped 4 engineers and 30 workers of a construction company in Huila department following the firm's refusal to submit to a $80,000 extortion demand. In November 1986, a mass grave was discovered in Turbo containing the remains of about 100 men, women, and children thought to have been killed by the FARC. In December 1987, 50 FARC members attacked Gaitania using automatic weapons, grenades, and antitank rockets, killing two policemen and wounding five.

While some have seen this continuation of violence by FARC fronts as evidence of duplicity on the part of FARC, another explanation equally consistent with these facts is that the decentralized command structure of FARC and the continuing violence between government troops, drug traffickers, and leftist groups creates a situation in which hostilities and settling of old scores are likely to continue.

In late 1985, FARC established the Simón Bolívar Guerrilla Coordination board, an umbrella organization for all leftist insurgents in Colombia that succeeded the National

Guerrilla Coordination group from which FARC had been excluded. In 1985, it also created the Patriotic Union (UP) as a political front organization.

FARC has had a problematic relationship with Colombian cocaine traffickers. FARC's protection of trafficker's interests in exchange for cash can be understood as another form of extortion, especially since drug traffickers later began to sponsor their own terrorist attacks not only against the Colombian government but also against leftist politicians associated with FARC through its Simón Bolívar Guerrilla Coordination board front: On 11 October 1987, UP member and former presidential candidate Jaime Pardo Neal was killed by agents of José Gonzalo Rodríguez Gacha, a major drug trafficker. On 22 March 1990 traffickers also assassinated UP presidential candidate Bernardo Jaramillo Ossa at Bogotá airport.

REVOLUTIONARY ARMED TASK FORCE. The Revolutionary Armed Task Force (RATF) was a nonstate U.S. leftist terrorist group that sought to force changes in U.S. foreign policy through armed propaganda and "consciousness-raising" of the general U.S. public. Sometime in 1979, or shortly thereafter, remnants of the once exclusively black Black Liberation Army (BLA) merged with the mainly white Weather Underground to form the Revolutionary Armed Task Force. This new group attempted in turn to create an outreach umbrella organization, known as the May 19 Communist Coalition (q.v.), for recruiting other leftists or black prison inmates into the RATF or BLA organizations. The May 19 group established contact and fraternal ties with other revolutionary or nationalistic groups, such as the New Afrikan Freedom Fighters (q.v.), the Puerto Rican FALN (q.v.) separatists, and even the PLO. The RATF financed itself through bank robberies while its bombing campaign targeted offices of corporations doing business with South Africa, such as IBM, as well as U.S. Federal government offices. The group used a number of aliases, such as the

United Freedom Fighters (not to be confused with the United Freedom Front), the Revolutionary Fighting Group, the Armed Resistance Unit, and the Red Guerrilla Resistance.

From its robberies conducted from 1979 to 1981, the RATF netted around $1 million. Members of one RATF cell that was raided in May 1985 had carried out since 1982 at least 16 bombings in the New York and Washington, D.C., areas (including the November 1983 bombing of the U.S. Senate) and, at the time the cell was raided, had been planning 12 more bombings of Federal facilities in or near Washington, D.C., including the U.S. Naval Academy and the Old Executive Office Building.

A summary of the more noteworthy terrorist actions of RATF follows: On 20 October 1981, the RATF tried to rob a Brinks armored car outside Nyack, N.Y. but succeeded only in killing one Brinks guard and two policemen. During December 1981, RATF bombed the South African Airways freight offices at John F. Kennedy Airport and an IBM office in Harrison, N.Y. In January 1984, the "Revolutionary Fighting Group" bombed the New York FBI office. On 6 November 1983, the "Armed Resistance Unit" bombed the cloakroom of the U.S. Senate, which the group stated was retaliation for the U.S. invasion of Grenada the preceding month.

The arrest of several key members of the RATF destroyed the effectiveness of the remaining organization and greatly demoralized other leftist terrorist groups. In the abortive Brinks robbery attempt, the police captured five of the terrorists, including Kathy Boudin, a Weather Underground terrorist on the FBI's most wanted list for over 10 years. In May 1985, the FBI arrested Marilyn Jean Buck, a member of the cell responsible for the bombing of the U.S. Senate. By February 1986, the FBI had arrested all but one of the 35 people responsible for the Brinks holdup attempt. With the capture of these persons, authorities also seized papers, including detailed plans and forged travel documents, that exposed the internal workings of the organization, its ties to other leftist, ethnic, or nationalist groups, and revealing the identities of its core membership of 50 people. These raids essentially ended the career of the Revolutionary Armed Task Force.

REVOLUTIONARY CELLS. The *Revolutionäre Zellen* (RZ) is a group of German anarchistic, leftist terrorists active from 12 June 1974 to the present. The RZ has generally held itself aloof from the Red Army Faction and from groups like the Red Brigades or Direct Action. There has been some evidence of contact with the Popular Front for the Liberation of Palestine (PFLP, q.v.) and the Irish National Liberation Army (INLA, q.v.) but no firm evidence of direct foreign state sponsorship.

While the RZ sprung from the same social grouping of disgruntled leftist university students and shared the same desire to smash capitalist society as did the RAF, it differed in rejecting the elitism inherent in the RAF's approach with its vision of itself as the revolutionary vanguard and its authoritarian control over its members. By contrast, the RZ seeks to bring down capitalist society by multiplying cells of militants who continually engage in small-scale vandalism and harassment locally. The reasoning was that a multitude of cells would be harder for the state to target than one conspicuous armed group while the cumulative effect of *Spaßguerilla*, or small-scale terrorism, would prove no less deadly to the state. By advocating these radical anarchistic ideas in their journal *Revolutionäre Zorn* (Revolutionary Wrath), the RZ hopes to generate a wider generalized state of autonomous antiauthoritarian violence among disaffected individuals outside the ranks of the RZ. Apart from this different operational approach, RZ, like RAF, appeared to pursue terrorist violence as an end in itself rather than as a coherent strategy to produce a new social and political system.

From 12 June 1974 to the present, there have been at least 50 noteworthy incidents for which the RZ were responsible.

A breakdown of them shows that 76 percent (=38) involved bombings, usually directed at NATO military bases or commercial offices, but usually with minimal injuries; 18 percent (=9) involved hoaxes, threats, or vicious pranks; 14 percent (=7) involved arson and firebombings; 6 percent (=3) involved "kneecapping" a victim; and 2 percent (=1) involved murder although it appeared that the intent had been to kneecap rather than to kill their victim. This was the case involving the shooting death of Heinz Karry, economics minister of Hesse, on 11 May 1981. Other kneecapping incidents occurred on 28 October 1986 and 6 February 1987, both occurring in Berlin and in government offices. The overall pattern is one of low-intensity and generally non-lethal violence and harassment. RZ members have engaged in telephone harassment of victims and have resorted to pranks such as mailing victims packages containing human feces or a pig's head.

Actually such a statistical approach can only give a qualitative sampling of RZ violence rather than a precise quantitative measure for RZ does not necessarily seek credit for every action it commits and it is also not possible to distinguish between violence committed by RZ itself from similar violence committed by emulators. Since 1980, West Germany has experienced roughly 200 petty bombings and acts of arson each year, which fit the RZ pattern. By 1987, the RZ was credited by West German police with having caused over 200 million deutsche marks of damage. Estimates of the membership in the early 1980s held that there were 50 to l00 cells with together some 300 to 500 members. As early as 1978, the German Federal Office of Criminal Investigations (BKA) rated the RZ as "currently the strongest terrorist formation," an assessment that has not changed since then.

REVOLUTIONARY POPULAR STRUGGLE. The Greek "Epanastatikos Laikos Agonas" (ELA) is a shadowy leftist terrorist group formed in 1973 to oppose the former military junta in Greece. Actual terrorist activities began only in the postjunta period in which it has sought the limited aims of forcing Greece out of NATO and removal of U.S. troops from Greece.

During its existence, ELA has engaged in bombings causing property damage but no human casualties so far. From 1975 to 1987, ELA bombed at least 8 U.S. targets, usually military targets of little strategic value, such as NCO clubs or commissaries, or U.S. diplomatic properties, such as the U.S. Information Agency office in Athens, or offices of private American firms, such as the American Express office in Athens. In October 1987, ELA members had a shootout with Greek police in which one terrorist was killed and two others arrested. The Greek police believe ELA has connections with the November 17 (q.v.) group and appears to work in tandem with the May 1 group (q.v.). While ELA often declares its solidarity with other groups, little is known about either its own members or its connections with other leftist terrorist groups.

REX CINEMA ARSON AND MASSACRE. On 2 August 1978, the Rex Cinema theater of Abadan, Iran, was set ablaze during a showing of an evening film resulting in over 300 deaths, which until that time was one of the worst terrorist incidents in the modern history of Iran and of the Middle East generally. This event occurred during the early stages of the Iranian revolution when Islamic fundamentalists had been regularly carrying out arson attacks against movie theaters believed to offer features offensive to Islamic sentiments. When previous arsons of this kind had taken place, however, the arsonists would order the theater to be cleared or would strike when the theater was already emptied after hours.

The shah's regime, quite naturally, blamed the arson on its fundamentalist opponents. Islamic fundamentalists accused the monarchical regime of having staged the arson in order to discredit the fundamentalists. The evidence supporting the view that fundamentalists were responsible is increased by the circumstance that the film showing occurred on the anniversary of the martyrdom of Imam Ali, an anniversary in the Islamic religious calendar on which devout Shiites regard indulgence even in ordinarily innocent pleasures to be blasphemous. The other circumstance was that the theater owner, in order to prevent non-ticket buyers from sneaking into the theater, had chained the fire escape doors shut contrary to the municipal fire code. The explanation seemingly most consistent with these known facts would be that fundamentalist arsonists set out to torch the theater but set the blaze before learning that all of the exit doors were locked shut and very likely perished in the blaze themselves. Investigations into the event after the revolution were inconclusive in determining the identities and motives of the perpetrators.

RICARDO FRANCO FRONT (RFF). The Frente Ricardo Franco is a Colombian revolutionary guerrilla group not enjoying any state sponsorship. Formerly it was a front of the Revolutionary Armed Forces of Colombia (q.v.)(FARC) but severed its ties with the main body of FARC in 1984 due to its members' disagreement with FARC signing the March 1984 peace accord with the Colombian government. RFF has the same original goals as FARC, namely, creating a Marxist-Leninist revolution in Colombia. It has, however, the additional goals of undercutting FARC's attempts to gain political advantages from the 1984 agreement and to sabotage the national reconciliation process. Sporadic clashes have occurred between RFF and FARC forces ever since the schism occurred.

The Ricardo Franco Front has the strongest anti-U.S. stance of all leftist groups in Colombia and, during 1984 to 1985, it repeatedly targeted U.S. diplomatic and commercial facilities. In order to embarrass FARC and to sabotage the government's reconciliation scheme, RFF undertook joint actions in 1985 with the National Liberation Army (ELN, q.v.), the one major group rejecting the truce proposals and procedures, as well as with M-19 guerrillas.

In May 1984, RFF bombed a Honduran airline office, killing two and wounding eleven people, and also bombed a U.S. diplomatic office. In January 1985 RFF bombed the Colombian Labor Ministry and the following month conducted eight bombings against U.S. companies in Medellín, killing one person and wounding another. Deploying 150 guerrillas, RFF tried to occupy the upper-class suburb of Cuba near Bogotá in spring 1985, attempting 26 bombings throughout the city. In June 1985, RFF kidnapped an official of the State Oil Company for a $105,000 ransom but killed him only five days later. In September 1985, RFF fought for 10 days alongside M-19 guerrillas, afterward consolidating their joint positions in Tolima Department. During the same month, RFF made numerous attacks against the U.S. Embassy, other diplomatic missions, and also offices of multinational corporations and, in one case, used two small children to plant a bomb at the gates of the U.S. Embassy, which was deactivated without harm to life or limb.

In December 1985 an internal purge within RFF led to the mass executions and burials of around 100 RFF dissidents. Colombian security forces discovered and revealed these graves, which led other major leftist groups, such as M-19, to break off relations with RFF. Since being thus publicly discredited, the Ricardo Franco Front has ceased to conduct effective guerrilla operations and apparently has declined from being a political-military group to little more than a criminal gang. Its current membership is estimated at little more than 100.

RODERIGO FRANCO COMMAND. The Roderigo Franco Command is a Peruvian death squad linked to the right-wing of the American Popular Revolutionary Alliance (APRA) party. The Command emerged after 1987 when the Aprista politician Roderigo Franco was murdered by Sendero Luminoso (q.v.) and was originally intended for use against Senderistas. The scope of its attacks broadened to include a defense attorney representing Senderistas, murdered on 28 July 1988, and eventually included even conservative critics of APRA. During November 1988, the Command carried out bombings and threats in Lima, including an attack on two journalists, one of whom died.

EL RUKN(S). El Rukn (Arabic: ''the pillar'') is a Chicago-based criminal gang, a strictly entrepreneurial terrorist group, founded in 1968 by Jeff Fort and was originally known as the ''Blackstone Rangers.'' Although gang members affect Muslim names and refer to some of their meeting places as ''temples,'' there is no evidence that the group represents a bona fide Islamic group or sect, and it is believed to have affected the pretense of being a religious organization in order to mask its drug-trafficking and extortionary activities. Members of this gang have provided bodyguard services to Louis Farrakhan as well as martial arts training to members of Farrakhan's Nation of Islam, a black nationalist Islamic sect, which is also based in Chicago.

In 1986, El Rukn contacted a Libyan representative in the United States and obtained Libyan agreement in principle to sponsor terrorist actions by El Rukn in the United States in exchange for Libyan financial rewards. This plot was uncovered by FBI agents in August 1986 when police raids of a Rukn meeting place uncovered automatic weapons, pistols, hand grenades, and an M-72 rocket launcher. Wiretaps revealed that El Rukn members offered to carry out bombings of U.S. government offices and to shoot down a domestic commercial airliner on behalf of Libya in exchange for $2.5 million. In November 1987, five El Rukn members were convicted on weapons violations and conspiracy charges. None of the testimony in this trial revealed any ideological or sectarian sympathies between El Rukn and the Libyan regime.

The leader of El Rukn, Jeff Fort, was serving a sentence in a Texas prison for cocaine trafficking charges during the time of El Rukn contacts with Libya. The active membership of El Rukn is estimated in the range of 350 to 1,000.

- S -

AL SAIQA. Al Saiqa (Arabic: "Thunderbolt") is a Syrian state-sponsored Palestinian splinter group and militia with the revolutionary objective of destroying Israel to create a Palestinian state. The group was created in 1968 to allow Syria more influence over the Palestinian movement. While Saiqa has declared itself to be a member of the Rejection Front (q.v.) within the PLO, other Palestinian groups have recognized that Saiqa's positions directly reflect those of the Syrian government.

Saiqa numbers around 2,000 members, and its operations unit bears the name "Eagles of the Palestinian Revolution." This group has operated as a pro-Syrian militia during the Lebanese civil war. In the "Chopin Express" affair, Saiqa took three Jewish hostages in Vienna in September 1973 and forced Austrian Chancellor Bruno Kreisky to close down a transit facility for Soviet Jews emigrating to Israel. In response to the 1979 Camp David negotiations between Israel and Egypt, Saiqa was directed to occupy the Egyptian Embassy in Ankara in July 1979. In this attack two guards were killed and 20 hostages held. Saiqa also struck at the northern city of Tiberias within Israel and bombed Jewish students in two attacks in Paris.

Saiqa lacks both an original political program and broad popular support among the Palestinians. Its future would apparently depend on the foreign policy options that the Syrian regime will choose to pursue in the wake of the loss of Soviet military aid essential to Syria's role as a player in the Arab-Israeli conflict.

SAM MELVILLE-JONATHAN JACKSON UNIT. This was a nonstate U.S. leftist group that conducted bombing attacks in Massachusetts during the late 1970s. The name of the original group was taken from Sam Melville, a white leftist killed in the Attica Prison uprising in 1971, and from

Jonathan Jackson, a black radical killed in a shoot-out with California police in 1970.

With the arrests of five United Freedom Front (q.v.) terrorists in November 1984 and two more in April 1985, it was learned that the United Freedom Front was essentially the same organization as the earlier Sam Melville-Jonathan Jackson Unit. The tactics of each used bombing attacks on properties either of U.S. military organizations or else of defense-related industries and were designed to draw public attention to their protests against specific U.S. foreign or military policies rather than to seek revolution as such.

SANDINISTAS. The *Frente Sandinista de Liberación Nacional* (FSLN) is a Marxist-Leninist political party that overthrew the dictatorship of Anastasio Somoza Debayle in 1979 and attempted to create a Marxist-Leninist state in Nicaragua from 1979 to 1990. Before its rise to power, the FSLN maintained ties with the Popular Front for the Liberation of Palestine (q.v.) and afterward established close ties with Libya and Iran, both known to be state sponsors of terrorism. The FSLN enjoyed the support of Cuba and also Costa Rica prior to gaining power. Following the revolution, the United States became the foremost donor of financial aid to Nicaragua until mid-1981 when it became apparent that the Sandinistas had become involved in supporting the communist insurgency in El Salvador. Afterward the Soviet Union and Cuba remained the primary sponsors of the FSLN, while Libya also lent military aid.

The National Liberation Front was founded on 23 July 1960 in Honduras by Carlos Fonseca, Silvio Mayorga, and Tomás Borge Martínez. The name "Sandinista" was added to the name in 1962 to honor Augusto César Sandino, the nationalist general who had fought the U.S. Marines in the 1920s before being killed by National Guard chief Anastasio Somoza García in 1934. The FSLN made sporadic attempts at starting a rural insurgency in the 1960s and early 1970s without much success. On 27 December 1974, 13 FSLN members intending to take U.S. Ambassador Turner Shelton hostage crashed a Christmas party given in his honor only to find he had left. Nonetheless they seized 25 hostages including the Nicaraguan Foreign Minister as well as several businessmen and cronies of Anastasio Somoza Debayle. Negotiations through Archbishop Miguel Obando y Bravo gained the release of the hostages in exchange for safe passage to Cuba, $1 million in cash, and the release of 14 imprisoned Sandinistas.

Disagreements among the Sandinistas in 1975–1977 led to their breakup into three factions, one led by Jaime Wheelock Roman, another led by Tomás Borge, and another led by the Ortega brothers. The Ortegas' insurrectional strategy, involving the use of spectacular acts of armed propaganda to spur broad-based urban insurrections, was to succeed in 1977–1979 in overthrowing Somoza. On 10 January 1978, unknown assassins shot and killed Pedro Joaquín Chamorro, editor of *La Prensa* and longtime Somoza critic. This sparked off massive demonstrations against Somoza, who was believed responsible for Chamorro's killing. In this atmosphere, the FSLN insurrectionists were able to win support from Nicaraguan liberals, social democrats, and small businessmen. On 22 August 1978, Edén Pastora Gómez led 24 other FSLN commandos in storming the Nicaraguan Chamber of Deputies and seizing 1,500 hostages who were released in exchange for safe passage to Panama, the release of 59 prisoners, including Tomás Borge, $500,000 ransom, and the broadcast of a call to insurrection in the name of the FSLN. In the abortive insurrection that followed, during September 1978 fewer than 1,500 FSLN guerrillas fought 14,000 National Guardsmen and about 5,000 people were killed and 16,000 wounded, most of whom were civilians.

As Fidel Castro required vanguard unification as a condition for Cuban aid, accordingly on 7 March 1979 the three FSLN factions were united under a Combined National Directorate (DNC) composed of nine members, three from each faction. Apart from Cuban support, the FSLN received arms and political support from Venezuela, Panama, and Costa Rica, which not only allowed the FSLN sanctuary and staging areas in its territory but also helped to create Radio Sandino through which the FSLN coordinated the broad-based popular uprising. A combination of rioting in the cities, labor and business strikes, and FSLN attacks on an increasingly demoralized National Guard led to Somoza's resignation and flight from the country on 17 July 1979 and the takeover of Managua by the FSLN on 19 July 1979.

1. FSLN Terrorism Prior to 1979:

During the 1960s and early 1970s members of the FSLN collaborated with guerrilla and terrorist groups outside of Nicaragua, particularly the Guatemalan Rebel Armed Forces with whom FSLN cadres fought in Guatemala from July to October 1966. In September 1970 two FSLN members took part in separate hijackings led by the PFLP, one of which led to the capture of Leila Khalid when the hijackers were foiled while the other succeeded in taking a British BOAC plane to Dawson's Field in Jordan. On 21 October 1970, Carlos Aguero hijacked a Costa Rican plane and held four United Fruit officials hostage to gain the release of imprisoned Sandinistas. Apart from the attempt to kidnap the U.S. ambassador, the FSLN also bombed the U.S. military mission in Managua on 11 April 1977.

Up until 1979, the FSLN committed 64 noteworthy actions, of which 31 were armed attacks initiated by the FSLN; 15 were robberies of banks and businesses; 6 were assassinations; 5 were hijackings, of which 2 were unsuccessful; 2 were bombings; 2 were major hostage-taking incidents, namely the "Christmas Party" raid and the seizure of the Chamber of Deputies. Two instances of arson occurred as well as one bazooka attack against Anastasio Somoza's private bunker. Except for the robberies and hijackings, the FSLN appeared to target principally National Guard units and functionaries of the Somoza regime and otherwise avoided random killings of civilians. The two hostage takings resulted in the deaths of 15 guards and military policemen but only 1 civilian death.

2. Post-Revolutionary Repression:

Following the victory of the revolution, the FSLN created the party-controlled Sandinista Popular Army to form the core of the new armed forces. The police were similarly restructured to become instruments of party rule, and block watch committees known as Sandinista Defense Committees were created. Under Tomás Borge the Ministry of the Interior by mid-1985 had at least 186 Cuban advisers and instructors as well as 15 advisers and technicians from East Germany, Bulgaria, North Korea, and the Soviet Union, who proceeded to create a state intelligence and security organization typical of communist societies.

The General Directorate for State Security (DGSE) of the Interior Ministry also would mobilize members of the Sandinista "mass organizations," namely, Sandinista youth groups, women's groups, office workers, into mobs that became known as the *turbas divinas* (q.v).

Nicaraguan human rights groups and high-level Sandinista defectors have testifed that from 1979–1981 the DGSE was responsible for at least 114 summary executions of political opponents. The Nicaraguan Permanent Commission on Human Rights, which had amply documented human rights abuses under Somoza, counted 785 cases of disappearances of persons arrested by Sandinista authorities from July 1979 to September 1980. The FSLN adopted a heavy-handed relocation policy toward the Miskito, Sumo, and Rama Indians of the Atlantic coastal area. Thousands fled to Honduras where many Indian men joined the contras and eventually formed their own contra command. Within the cities, the FSLN persecuted some small religious groups, such as Jehovah's Witnesses, Mormons, and Pentecostals, as well as Roman Catholic priests suspected of being antiregime.

3. Sponsorship of International Terrorism:

Immediately after seizing power, the FSLN became a state

sponsor, along with Cuba, of the Farabundo Martí National Liberation Front (FMLN, q.v.) of El Salvador. On 2 January 1981, during the Salvadoran rebels' "final offensive," CIA aerial surveillance revealed direct FSLN logistical support for the transshipment of U.S.-made arms captured in Vietnam to Cuba, from Cuba to Nicaragua, and there to the Salvadoran rebels. On 9 March 1981, a presidential finding authorized CIA covert action to interdict the arms shipments, which led to U.S. support for the contras. On 1 April 1981, the U.S. ended foreign aid to Nicaragua, which had received at least $118 million in U.S. aid since the overthrow of Somoza. The FSLN support for the FMLN in the latter's effort to destroy the transitional government of El Salvador gave the Reagan administration the leverage needed to persuade a skeptical U.S. Congress to support the contras against the FSLN. Throughout the FSLN period, Nicaragua continued to be a transshipment point for Cuban and Soviet aid to the FMLN but also was used as a safe haven for the FMLN, which maintained many of its offices in Managua.

The FSLN also gave moral and material support to the Tupac Amaru Revolutionary Movement (q.v.) of Peru, the Cinchoneros Popular Liberation Movement (q.v.) and the Lorenzo Zelaya Popular Revolutionary Forces (q.v.) of Honduras, the Basque Fatherland and Liberty (ETA, q.v.) movement, the Guatemalan National Revolutionary Union (q.v.), the M-19 (q.v.) group of Colombia, and the Movement of the Revolutionary Left (q.v.) of Chile. The FSLN also gave safe haven to fugitives of the Italian Red Brigades and the Red Army Faction (Baader-Meinhof Gang), as well as refuge to remnants of the Uruguayan Tupamaros (q.v.) and Argentinean Montoneros (q.v.). The presence of Montoneros there in turn led Argentina to send military advisers and aid to help organize the contras in Honduras.

On 17 September 1980, the exiled Nicaraguan dictator Anastasio Somoza Debayle was murdered along with members of his entourage as they drove through Asunción, Paraguay. His assassins were members of an Argentinean group, the People's Revolutionary Army, which had long-standing relations with the Sandinistas even prior to their gaining power.

Nicaragua undertook training and outfitting of Marxist rebels also in Honduras and Costa Rica quite soon after taking power. The Honduran police raided a safehouse of the Morazanist Front for the Liberation of Honduras in Tegucigalpa on 27 November 1981 and captured documents indicating the formation of the terrorist group under FSLN direction and that it had received funds and explosives from Nicaraguan authorities. During July-August 1982, the main power station in Tegucigalpa was sabotaged and several U.S.-affiliated businesses bombed. A Salvadoran arrested in this case indicated the explosives had been supplied by the Nicaraguans along with arms for Honduran rebels. On 27 July 1982, Costa Rica declared three Nicaraguan diplomats persona non grata for their role in supplying explosives and instructions to a Colombian terrorist responsible for the 3 July 1982 bombing of the Honduran National Airlines.

In an address to the Sandinista Trade Union on 13 December 1987, Daniel Ortega stated that in the event the FSLN ever lost an election it would turn over the government, but not effective power, to whomever won. Although the Sandinistas lost the 25 February 1990 election to Violetta Chamorro, the FSLN retained the Sandinista Popular Army under its own command and sporadically continued to transfer arms to the FMLN guerrillas prior to the end of the insurgency in El Salvador. Therefore it is possible that the current non-FSLN government of Nicaragua represents a weak state effectively co-opted by the Sandinistas.

SENDERO LUMINOSO (SL). The ''Shining Path'' is a Maoist guerrilla movement that seeks to create a total Marxist-Leninist revolution within Peru and an ethnic Indian state by the turn of the century. It differs from other leftist insurgencies in Latin America in neither having accepted assistance from other leftist Latin American states, such as Cuba or

Nicaragua under the Sandinistas, nor associating itself fraternally with Marxist regimes or movements elsewhere. In part this may be due to the extremely dogmatic and authoritarian nature of the Senderista leadership, which would preclude much collaboration with other leftist groups. While there was some evidence of former limited contacts with the Colombian M-19 and the now defunct Alfaro Vive Carajo group of Ecuador, the Sendero Luminoso is preeminently a home-grown, inward-looking, and highly xenophobic phenomenon. It has attacked Soviet, Cuban, Chinese, and North Korean targets along with U.S. and other Western targets.

SL is also the most brutal and violent of the existing leftist insurgencies in Latin America and makes the most effective use of terrorism as part of its overall strategy. Insofar as Sendero Luminoso has established de facto control over its "liberated zones" in the interior Andean plateau and uses terror to maintain control over the subject population, it may be said to use terror to achieve quasi-state repression as well as its revolutionary goals.

Sendero Luminoso was founded in 1969 by Manuel Rubén Abimael Guzman Reynoso, also known as "Comrade Gonzalo," who is regarded by his followers and himself as the "fourth sword of revolution" after Marx, Lenin, and Mao Tse-tung. Guzman was a philosophy teacher at Huamanga University, primarily a teachers' training college, in the interior city of Ayachuco. After Guzman became personnel director of the university in 1971, he systematically built up a faculty who supported his own version of revolutionary Marxism. Also responsible for the first-year course of teachers' instruction, Guzman and his fellow faculty indoctrinated the student teachers who in turn have indoctrinated an entire generation of schoolchildren in remote towns and villages throughout the Andean interior of Peru. Guzman is said to have remarked that it made more sense to educate children into revolutionary Marxism than to indoctrinate adults since children did not need to be politically re-educated. Guzman carried out his program of recruitment, indoctrination, and outreach into the rural communities for 10 years before SL embarked on actual revolution.

Guzman exercises a highly personalistic and charismatic control over his followers, who accept ''Comrade Gonzalo's'' word as law and obey his promptings without equivocation. Dissenters within the SL have been summarily expelled or executed. Guzman and the other Senderista leaders have shown little inclination to collaborate with other leftists much less to enter into any dialogue with the regime they are fighting.

Apart from its highly dogmatic Marxist component, SL doctrine also incorporates within itself an Indian, nativist component that feeds off the resentments of the Indian and mixed-blood Peruvian population, who have been largely excluded from political participation and deprived of basic benefits by the Peruvian ruling elites. Originally SL was known as the ''Revolutionary Student Front for the Shining Path of Mariátegui,'' the reference being to José Carlos Mariátegui, one of the founders of the Peruvian Communist Party. Mariátegui had claimed in his writings that Peruvian socialism had to be built on the communalism of the pre-Columbian Peruvian Inca Indian civilizations and attributed most of the social injustices in Peru to the European-imposed feudal and capitalist culture. While many leftist groups elsewhere in Latin America have usually treated the Indian communities with disdain, SL pioneered an extensive outreach to the native communities in which SL activists would learn Quechua and other Indian tongues, and go to live among the Indians in order to gain their trust.

SL began its terrorist campaign on 17 May 1980 just as democratic rule was being restored to Peru, attacking polling places in the villages around Ayacucho. By the end of 1970, SL had conducted between 300 and 400 operations and, until June 1986, averaged between 30 and 40 operations per month. It has about 5,000 well-armed militants but avoids direct engagements with the Peruvian military. In its terrorist activities, SL relies on five-member cells, at least one member of which is always a woman. SL finances itself through robberies, extortion, and a "war tax" levied on coca producers and smugglers in the "liberated zones."

In its rural campaign, SL activists typically will move into a village and hold mock trials of local officials or landowners who would then be executed in some gruesome manner and their mutilated remains left exposed as a lesson to others. Five-member councils rule the villages and administer summary justice. In areas where peasants were once terrorized by Colombian smugglers and coca buyers, SL has intervened to promote a measure of equity on behalf of the coca-growing peasants and also to extort "war taxes" from the coca buyers. Economic infrastructure and investment projects promoted by the Peruvian government have been bombed, a favorite target being the power pylons that supply the major cities.

While SL originally conducted only rural operations on the theory that "encirclement of the cities" would consummate a successful rural guerrilla war, it began a parallel campaign in the cities prompted by the appearance of a rival urban guerrilla organization, the Tupac Amaru Revolutionary Movement (q.v.), in 1984. In its urban campaign SL has also sought out high-visibility targets, specializing in the assassination of members of the prominent American Popular Revolutionary Alliance Party or of high-ranking members of the counterinsurgency forces. On 14 August 1990, SL drove a car bomb into the presidential palace in Lima, exploding it and causing extensive damage to the building, although the newly elected President Alberto Fujimori was unhurt. More recently, when SL decreed a strike in Lima on 14 February 1992, Maria Elena Moyano, the deputy mayor of the Villa El Salvador district and outspoken critic of the Senderistas, defied the ban by organizing a peace march. The next day she was murdered by Senderistas and her body blown up with dynamite. On 16 July 1992, marking the end of the first 100 days of Fujimori's emergency rule, SL exploded two car bombs in Lima's wealthiest district, killing

18 and wounding 140 others, while around 100 SL fighters struck police stations throughout Lima. SL has not hesitated to attack and kill foreign aid workers, diplomats, priests, missionaries, and family members of targeted victims.

Around 25,000 people have perished and $22 billion in damages and lost revenues have been suffered due to the SL insurgency. Since overcoming its setback in the urban campaign caused by the penetration of its Lima cells in 1986, SL has shown increasing organizational sophistication, relying more on front organizations called "generated organisms" to penetrate and co-opt other leftist groups and to gather more potential recruits. It has set up legal aid and educational institutions in the slums surrounding Lima and uses the newspaper *El Diario* as its unofficial mouthpiece.

Originally the ineptitude of the Peruvian counterinsurgency program helped to boost recruitment into SL due to the military's tendency to exact retaliation upon Indians and "mixed bloods" generally when it could not find the actual SL perpetrators of an action. Beginning in the mid-1980s the Peruvian military began to rethink its intelligence requirements and started to have some success in penetrating the Senderista organization. By November 1989, however, the Peruvian military recaptured the Upper Huallaga Valley. In 1991, on assuming office President Fujimori made the insurgency the top priority of his administration, and on 13 September 1992, Peruvian security forces captured Guzman and his top lieutenants during a strategy-planning session in Lima.

The Shining Path represents something of an enigma. It emerged just after the leftist military regime of General Velasco had completed Peru's most extensive land reform and at the very time Peruvian democracy had been restored, a time when some Peruvian leftists had begun to despair of armed revolution. The success of SL in destroying Peru's fragile economy may well have contributed to the collapse of the presidency of the once highly popular Alan García. Its threat to the state prompted the assumption of unconstitutional powers by President Fujimori on 8 April 1992. During a time when communism has been collapsing in the Soviet Union and eastern Europe and revolutionary Marxism apparently discredited, the Shining Path has begun to attract support from die-hard leftists throughout the world just as previous generations of revolutionary leftists used to embrace the Sandinista revolution or the Cuban revolution. International support groups known as "Peru People's Movements" have sprung up in Europe while Maoist groups, such as the Communist Party of Turkey-Marxist Leninist and the Revolutionary Communist Party, U.S.A., have embraced the Shining Path movement, together forming a Revolutionary Internationalist Movement that includes other pro-Senderista Maoist parties in Germany, Sweden, France, Switzerland, and Mexico. These ties are being actively cultivated by Senderista representatives living abroad who claim political refugee status. Senderista activities have straddled the border with Bolivia while pro-Senderista factions have appeared in Ecuador, Colombia, Argentina, and Chile. The capture of Abimael Guzman would seem to curtail SL's prospects both within Peru as well as limiting the development of any international Senderista movement, though most observers believe that SL has developed sufficient resources to survive even the loss of its charismatic leader.

SKINHEADS. Skinheads are young white males usually organized in gangs who shave their heads, wear "Doc Marten" steel-toed boots, and listen to punk music bands playing violent and oftentimes racist lyrics. Like many other youth phenomena, Skinheads grew more by imitation than conscious propagation, originating in Britain in the 1960s and spreading by the 1980s to continental Europe, North America, Australia, and New Zealand. While not all Skinheads are necessarily racist, most Skinhead gangs have engaged in harassment and sporadic violence aimed at Asiatics, blacks, Hispanics, homosexuals, and Jews.

Viewed in isolation, most incidents of Skinhead violence could be classified as entrepreneurial, being aimed at the perpetrators' gratification from bullying minority scapegoats or at the gains of petty robberies. Yet insofar as the Skinhead gangs have been increasingly courted by, and drawn into, the white supremacist and neo-Nazi movements, such violence has increasingly taken on the motivations and tactics of right-wing revolutionary terrorism.

Tom Metzger, the former Grand Dragon of the California branch of the Knights of the Ku Klux Klan (q.v.), left the Klan in 1980 to form a neo-Nazi group called the White Aryan Resistance (WAR), based in San Diego. His son, John Metzger, heads the group's youth auxiliary known as the Aryan Youth Movement (AYM). The younger Metzger displaced a local Skinhead leader in San Diego in May 1987 and began to co-opt other Skinhead gangs nationwide through AYM chapters established on 20 U.S. college campuses. Following the November 1988 murder of an Ethiopian in Portland, Ore., who was beaten to death by Skinheads wielding baseball bats, the victim's family filed a civil lawsuit against the Metzgers and WAR for having encouraged the Skinhead youths in question to commit racial violence.

Allied with AYM is the neo-Nazi "American Front," which controls many Skinheads in the San Francisco Bay area. In June 1985, CASH, the "Chicago Area Skinheads," participated in a local neo-Nazi organization's demonstration and had contact with Robert Miles, a former Ku Klux Klan leader and currently one of the leading proponents of the Identity Christianity movement.

The numbers of Skinheads nationwide stand around 3,000 with gangs active in at least 31 states. Numbers of gangs and memberships of individual gangs fluctuate greatly due to the mobility and lack of permanent residences for most Skinheads. Moreover, as police pressure has increased against them, many Skinheads have started to grow their hair out again, making their identification more difficult. With their induction into white supremacist political terrorism, Skin-heads are now recruiting youngsters more actively. The appeal of the Skinhead movement is not confined to young-sters from depressed economic backgrounds, since many come from middle-class, and even affluent, homes. Rather a more striking commonality among Skinheads is a broken home with absent father, which has also been commonly observed among the members of black urban gangs.

SOLDIERS OF JUSTICE. An Iranian state-sponsored Shiite group based in Lebanon that has the revolutionary goal of overthrowing the Saudi Arabian monarchy in favor of an Iranian-style Islamic Republic. The group is based in Leba-non and is composed of Shiite Muslims from Lebanon and Saudi Arabia. The group is thought to have been formed under the tutelage of the Iranian Islamic Revolutionary Guards contingent present in that country.

In December 1988, Soldiers of Justice gunmen wounded an official at the Saudi Arabian embassy in Karachi, Paki-stan. They claimed credit for killing a Saudi diplomat in Bangkok, Thailand, on 4 January 1989, an action also claimed by the Islamic Jihad in the Hijaz organization (q.v.). The Islamic Republic of Iran had been engaged in agitational propaganda against the Saudi dynasty during the Hajj pil-grimages from 1979 until 31 July 1987 when rioting killed 400 people in Mecca. On 26 April 1988, Saudi Arabia severed diplomatic relations with Iran and greatly reduced the size of the Hajj pilgrimage contingent permitted to the Iranians.

One explanation for the appearance and activities of the Soldiers of Justice is that such groups were being sponsored by hard-liners within Iran opposed to the apparent concilia-tory foreign policy of the Rafsanjani government toward conservative Arab regimes in the period following the death of Khomeini. Such terrorist actions would be intended to sabotage any rapprochement between Iran and Saudi Arabia.

STATE CO-OPTATION. Discussion of terrorism ordinarily involves two main types: first, state terrorism either in the form of internal repression, use of active measures and surrogate groups outside the state's national boundaries; or second, revolutionary terrorism by groups fighting a given regime whether in a domestic or an international arena. Both extremes ordinarily assume that the sponsoring state, or else the state being attacked, is strong relative to its antagonists. In much of the Third World, however, and in certain other nations, the state may be so weak that nonstate groups can effectively usurp control over state bodies or agencies, making the penetrated state agency, in effect, a surrogate actor for the penetrating group. In such cases where the state organs are being used to perpetrate terrorism, it would be misleading to speak of state-sponsored terror since both society and the state as a whole are being attacked or usurped.

In the case of El Salvador during the 1980s, the transitional regime that seized power on 15 October 1979 tried to dissolve government-run death squads such as the ORDEN militia. Nonetheless, Salvadoran oligarchs opposed to the government's proposed land reforms enlisted the aid of military and police security personnel who maintained several death squad organizations in spite of official government policy. In the case of Northern Ireland, the Ulster Defense Regiment, an official militia group, became dominated by sectarian Protestant Ulstermen, including members of the proscribed Ulster Freedom Fighters and the legal Ulster Defense Association, who then exploited access to Ulster police files and weapons in order to pursue their own vendettas against the Irish Republican groups and nationalist population. In the case of the Islamic Republic of Iran, it appeared that radical Islamic fundamentalist factions within the Iranian government had a greater role in influencing the actions of the students holding the U.S. Embassy hostages than did the president of Iran, or the Iranian interior and foreign ministries. Each of these is an example of state co-optation.

The reality of state co-optation presents U.S. policymakers with dilemmas in dealing with co-opted states. While the perpetration of internal terror or external terrorism by agencies nominally under the control of the weak state would ordinarily call for punishment of that state as the responsible party, in effect this often plays into the hands of the penetrating groups, who only gain if the state is further weakened. Failing to respond to such terrorism, however, also would have the effect of emboldening the penetrating group to continue its terrorist abuses.

STATE TERROR. National states can engage in terrorism through state sponsorship of nonstate groups to carry out operations against enemies beyond its boundaries or else by creation of their own special operations units to carry out terrorist activities as covert actions abroad. National governments can also direct terrorism against their own citizens or subject peoples in order to subdue political opposition, which may be called state terror to distinguish it from state sponsorship of terrorism outside of its borders. In its cruder forms, state terror can involve the use of death squads (q.v.), torture, or genocide. In more developed and systematized forms, state terror makes extensive use of secret police and informers, some pretense of judicial procedures, and repression involving loss of employment, internal exile, or imprisonment in labor camps. The Soviet Union eventually developed the additional refinement of committing dissidents to psychiatric hospitals for indefinite "treatment."

Ordinarily such state terror has been viewed by the United States government as being mainly a human rights problem and as an internal affair of the offending state rather than as a national security threat on the order of nonterritorial or international terrorism. Even so, public revulsion over open and notorious state terror often has compelled the U.S. government to join in international censure as well as diplomatic and economic sanctions against offending states, as it did in imposing sanctions against South Africa for its apartheid policies.

State terror, however, has also been directed against émigrés involving state or state-sponsored actors operating outside the borders of the offending state. For example, during 1980 Libyan agents murdered at least 10 anti-Qaddafi dissidents in Britain and Western Europe. Later such agents also tried to hire assassins to kill dissidents within the United States. On 17 April 1984, during anti-Qaddafi demonstrations outside the Libyan Embassy in St. James Square, London, members of the Libyan "People's Bureau" opened fire with automatic weapons on the crowds outside, wounding 11 Libyan protestors and killing a young British policewoman. Such extraterritorial state terror not only violates the sovereignty of other nations as well as the human rights of their victims, but also threatens the national security of those nations and the rights of their citizens who could equally be targeted by virtue of personal or business association with targeted émigrés.

STERN GANG. See LEHI

STOCKHOLM SYNDROME. Named after a three-day hostage-holding incident in the Stockholm Kreditbank in August 1973 after which it was observed that the former hostages had developed affection and protective attitudes toward their former captors. Psychologists have also termed it "protective affiliation" and "traumatic bonding," and have explained it as a reaction to feelings of helplessness and total dependence on one's captors and an emotional transference that makes the captive view his or her own well-being as depending on the happiness and well-being of their captors whom they begin to love as well as to fear. Although this was observed in the case of the Stockholm hostages and in the case of the Iranian hostages of the Arab terrorists who occupied the Iranian Embassy in London in 1980, it is a phenomenon long understood by students and practitioners of brainwashing and interrogation techniques. One of the dangers of this syndrome is that former hostages will find themselves unable or unwilling to provide police with information needed to arrest former captors or to provide testimony needed to prosecute apprehended hostage takers.

SUDANESE PEOPLE'S LIBERATION ARMY. The SPLA is a guerrilla group comprising non-Muslim tribal peoples living in the southern parts of the Sudan who oppose the policies of the central government, promoting the use of Arabic at the expense of native languages and imposing an Islamic fundamentalist regime upon the nation. Christians and animists, who make up about one-third of the Sudan's population, have repeatedly accused the Sudanese government of deliberate discrimination and genocidal policies against them. They had already fought an insurgency from 1954 until 1972, at which time regional autonomy had been granted to them. Fighting resumed in 1983 when the SPLA was formed in reaction to the central government's attempt to impose Islamic law on the entire nation.

The SPLA began its career during the rule of Jafar Nimeiry (1969–1985), a pro-Western president who began to implement Islamic law to build himself support among Islamic fundamentalists and to offset criticism of his pro-Western stance. During this time the SPLA found support from Muammar Qaddafi, one of Nimeiry's enemies. Under President General Bashir, the National Islamic Front, a group affiliated with the Muslim Brotherhood (q.v.), intensified the government's Islamic fundamentalist policies. During the period from 1983–1987, the SPLA committed 11 noteworthy terrorist incidents. Seven (64%) of these involved kidnappings of Western foreigners, usually aid workers, technicians, or missionaries. In most cases kidnap victims were released within a matter of a month or less. On 15 November 1983, however, the SPLA decided to hold 11 kidnapped technicians as hostages. On 2 February 1984, the SPLA attacked a barge carrying foreign technicians building a canal for the Sudanese government, killing 3 and wounding 7 others. On 16 August 1986, the SPLA downed a domestic Sudanese air carrier with a SAM-7 missile, killing all 57 passengers and 3 crewmen.

Since 1990, the National Islamic Front has begun building its own militia, the People's Defense Force, under the supervision of Iranian Islamic Revolutionary Guards Corps advisors. This force is currently being deployed against the southern rebels.

SUPERGRASS SYSTEM. Beginning in 1981, British authorities in Northern Ireland resorted to the general tactic of turning a captured terrorist, facing substantial charges, into a prosecution witness with immunity from prosecution for his own crimes if he would denounce, and testify in court against, several of his erstwhile colleagues. Although both the Irish Republican terrorist groups and the Ulster Protestant militiamen had harsh codes of silence and enacted severe punishments, including executions, against persons regarded as willing informers, these terrorist organizations had also begun to attract scores of quasi-criminal recruits motivated more by the gains of extortion from belonging to these groups rather than by ideology. When arrested, such mercenary recruits could be turned much more easily than was the case with the more ideologically committed terrorists captured in the early years of the renewed Irish troubles.

This system has used trials without juries and the uncorroborated testimony of one witness to effect scores of convictions. While many of these convictions have been overturned on appeal, the tactic has sowed much distrust, mutual recriminations, and internal discord within the affected Republican and Loyalist terrorist groups and so hampered their efficiency.

SYMBIONESE LIBERATION ARMY. The SLA was a revolutionary leftist group in California that won notoriety with its kidnapping on 4 February 1974 of Patricia Hearst, daughter of newspaper publisher William R. Hearst, Jr. The SLA brainwashed Ms. Hearst who then, assuming the revolutionary sobriquet of "Tanya," became an active participant in their bank robberies and bombings. A nationwide dragnet for Ms. Hearst and the SLA led police to an SLA safe house in Los Angeles where six SLA members, including their leader Nancy Ling Perry, perished on 17 May 1974 when police gunfire caused their safe house to burn to the ground. Patricia Hearst was later arrested in September 1975 and then tried and convicted for her role in one of the group's bank robberies. Very little is known about what connections, if any, the SLA had with other contemporary leftist groups.

SYRIAN SOCIAL NATIONALIST PARTY. The SSNP is a Lebanese militia dedicated to the incorporation of Lebanon into "Greater Syria," encompassing all of Syria, Jordan, Israel, much of Iraq and Turkey, and the island of Cyprus. The SSNP began as a right-wing political party in the 1930s, modeled on the German Nazi party whose core members were largely derived from Antiochian Orthodox Christian backgrounds. Suppressed by the Lebanese government after an unsuccessful coup attempt in 1961, it eventually evolved into a militia under Syrian state sponsorship with an anti-Israeli and anti-Western agenda similar to Palestinian terrorist groups under Syrian control.

The SSNP has undertaken many terrorist attacks in recent years, including the bombing of the Phalangists' Beirut headquarters, killing President-elect Bashir Gemayel on 14 September 1982. The SSNP has also specialized in car bombing attacks against Israeli targets in southern Lebanon. The SSNP recruits young Arab women, often pregnant out of wedlock, whom they indoctrinate to become suicide bombers. The Syrian state broadcasting service often aired videotaped political testaments of such bombers the day after they accomplished their mission. By 1987 the Israeli Defense Forces had come to view the SSNP suicide car bombers as much more lethal than the Hezbollah suicide car bombers.

The SSNP is also believed to be responsible for the bombing of a TWA flight to Athens in April 1982.

- T -

TAHRIR AL ISLAMI, AL. The *Hizb al Tahrir al Islami* (Islamic Liberation Party) was an Islamic fundamentalist group that developed out of the Muslim Brotherhood (q.v.). With the suppression of the Muslim Brotherhood within Egypt following the failed assassination attempt upon Nasser in 1954, thousands of the Brotherhood fled Egypt for other Arab lands. In Amman, the Muslim Brotherhood became a strong presence in the University of Jordan among both students and faculty. Sheikh Takieddin Nabhani (d. 1978), a former judge of the Islamic law court of Haifa, who settled in Nablus under Jordanian control following the 1948 war, founded the Islamic Liberation Party, which came to include many members of the Muslim Brotherhood in Jordan. This party went beyond the Muslim Brotherhood in teaching the necessity of seizing state power, eliminating rival parties, and imposing observance of the sacred law of Islam by force.

After Nasser's death in 1970, the new Egyptian president Anwar Sadat released those Muslim Brothers still imprisoned within Egypt and allowed exiled Egyptian members of the Brotherhood to return to Egypt. A Jordanian of Palestinian origin named Salih Siriya formed cells of the Islamic Liberation Party in Cairo, recruiting around 140 members. On 18 April 1974, Siriya and 20 armed followers took over the Egyptian Military Technical College in the Heliopolis suburb of Cairo, killing 11 and wounding 27 people. The group apparently wanted to assassinate Sadat, who had been scheduled to visit the college, as a first step in fomenting a popular Islamic uprising. Siriya had visited Libyan leader Muammar Qaddafi in June 1973 and received funds in order to overthrow Sadat. In 1976, Siriya and his chief aid were executed for their role in this uprising.

TAKFIR. The Islamic judicial act of declaring someone, or something, to be a *kaffir*, one who deliberately rejects the true faith. Under traditional Islamic law the penalty for deliberate apostasy is death. The Sunnite and Shiite doctors of religious law reserved for themselves the right to issue religious decrees of *takfir* against those Muslims they deemed to be apostates or enemies of Islam. Such a declaration announced the religious permissibility, and even the duty of the faithful Muslim with means and opportunity, to execute the death penalty against the excommunicated person. When the head of a Muslim state is thus anathematized, the decree authorizes a coup d'état or revolution to remove the impious ruler.

The use of *takfir* has come into prominence twice in the recent history of terrorism. Using an interpretation of *takfir* developed by the medieval Muslim scholar Ibn Tamiyyah, Sheikh Umar Abdul Rahman, the religious leader of the Egyptian Munazzamat al Jihad (q.v.) group, issued a decree of *takfir* against Anwar al Sadat in 1980. Jihad activists accordingly assassinated Sadat on 6 October 1981. On 14 February 1989, the Ayatollah Khomeini issued a decree of *takfir* against the Indian-born British author Salman Rushdie for the writing and publication of *Satanic Verses*, a novel deemed to libel the character of the Prophet Muhammad and to insult Islam. Khomeini's *takfir* was later expanded in scope to include the American publishers and distributors of *Satanic Verses* as well as any who gave Rushdie comfort and aid. Reading or possessing the offensive work was also proscribed and the Iranian government offered a bounty to anyone, Muslim or non-Muslim, who would enforce the decree against Rushdie. This was unusual because ordinarily decrees of *takfir* are not issued against persons or institutions that were never previously Muslim, while obeying such a decree was also neither expected nor demanded of non-Muslims.

On 29 March 1989, Abdallah Ahdal, the rector of a mosque in Brussels was murdered for refusing to endorse

Khomeini's *takfir*. On 3 July 1991, Ettore Capriolo, the Italian translator of Rushdie's book was stabbed in Milan. On 12 July 1991, Hitoshi Igarashi, the Japanese translator of the book was stabbed to death in Tokyo. On 11 October 1993, William Nygnaard, the Norwegian publisher of the book, was shot three times in the back outside his home in Oslo but survived. Several incidents occurred in the United States and Britain of arson against bookstores carrying the anathematized book. Also, whereas ordinarily the decree of *takfir* would be automatically nullified by the open and sincere repentance of the excommunicated person, Khomeini specified that the *takfir* against Rushdie was irrevocable since his offense was deemed unpardonable.

TAKFIR WAL HIGRAH. The Jamaat al Muslimin (Muslim Society) is a Sunnite Muslim puritan offshoot of the Muslim Brotherhood (q.v.) that advocated total rejection of the contemporary Egyptian social and political system in favor of a fundamentalist state. The more familiar name of ''Atonement and Flight'' (more literally, ''Anathema and Exodus'') was given to it by Egyptian security organs as more descriptive of its beliefs and practices. Its leader, Shukri Ahmad Mustafa, demanded that members renounce what he regarded as deviations from pure Islam and that they try to remove themselves physically from the midst of an apostate society by living in the desert or in more traditional towns not ''corrupted'' by the Westernization occurring under the free trade and investment policies of Anwar Sadat.

Members of this group took advantage of antigovernment food riots on 18–19 January 1977 to ransack and burn the nightclubs and casinos that had sprung up as a result of the open-door policies of Sadat. After a government crackdown on all groups critical of Anwar Sadat, whether leftist or fundamentalist, about 60 members of this group were imprisoned. Accordingly on 3 July 1977, Mustafa and some followers kidnapped a former minister of religious affairs, Sheikh Muhammad Hussayn Dhahabi, and demanded the release of their brethren. The government refused their demands. After Dhahabi's body was found on July 7, Egyptian security forces cracked down on the society, with 6 people killed and 57 wounded in the fighting that ensued. Eventually about 620 members of the group were arrested, including Mustafa and four other key leaders who were tried and executed in March 1978.

The group had around 5,000 total adherents, many of whom lived in the Upper Egyptian city of Asyut, a stronghold of fundamentalism. While some aid came to the group from Libya, most of the group's resources came from expatriate Egyptians sympathetic to the group. In October 1981, the organization claimed responsibility for the murder of Anwar Sadat, which actually was accomplished by a different fundamentalist group, namely Munazzamat al Jihad (q.v.).

TAMIL TIGERS. Name used by over 25 different Tamil guerrilla organizations fighting the Sinhalese-dominated government of Sri Lanka. The youth league of the Tamil United Liberation Front (TULF) political party, founded on 14 May 1972, attracted younger, more militant Tamils who founded the Tamil New Tigers as a more activist clique within the youth league. On 5 May 1976, the Tamil New Tigers reconstituted themselves separately from the TULF as the Liberation Tigers of Tamil Eelam (LTTE, q.v.). Approximately 25 different unrelated "Tiger" organizations have appeared since the LTTE began. The LTTE and its rival Tamil Tiger groups engaged in internecine battling from May 1986 to September 1987. By April 1989, the LTTE and the remnants of three other Tiger organizations formed an umbrella group, the Eelam National Liberation Front. The LTTE and other Tamil Tiger groups had enjoyed the state sponsorship of Tamil Nadu State in India but such support ended after the Tamil Tiger groups began attacking Indian Army forces sent to Sri Lanka to restore order. See Liberation Tigers of Tamil Eelam.

TERRA LLIURE. ''Free Land'' (TL) was a left-wing Catalan group with the goal of reconstituting an independent Catalan homeland in Catalonia that would embrace also the Spanish provinces of Valencia and the Balearic Isles as well as the French province of Roussillon. While formed in the 1970s, it undertook a terrorist campaign in May 1981, shooting a professor of Spanish in Barcelona in the legs. That year it also exploded small bombs in foreign-owned banks and travel agencies in the cities of Alicante, Barcelona, Tarragona, and Valencia until December 1981 when Spanish police arrested some TL members.

On 25 July 1987, the last day to file personal income tax returns in Spain, TL bombed the Finance Ministry office in the Basque province town of Igualada. Five policemen were wounded along with the local tax commissioner and two civilians. TL has also claimed credit for the 1987 bombings in Barcelona of the U.S. Consulate General and a USO club for which credit was also claimed by the Red Army for the Liberation of Catalonia (q.v.), a radical TL splinter group. In July 1991, the group was reported to have renounced the use of terrorism.

TERRORISM, DEFINED. No consensus exists on the proper definition of terrorism. In part this is because ''terrorism'' is not simply a denotative label but also a label of reprobation so that partisans of a given party or political tendency will hesitate to apply it to those groups that they champion, while applying it quite freely to groups of whose politics they disapprove, even when the actions being committed by the two sets of groups are substantially comparable. The other difficulty is that nearly all conventional military or insurgent forces will occasionally engage in actions, whether by design or accident, that may be plausibly described as terrorist. At what point, then, should a combatant group cease to be counted merely as a belligerent and begin to be counted as a terrorist group? The approach used in this dictionary has been to regard as terrorists those groups that will ordinarily attack noncombatants or nonmilitary targets as freely as military targets. Likewise, their choice of tactics reveals whether or not they distinguish between combatants and noncombatants. Antiaircraft artillery can be used either against warplanes or civilian planes, but using car bombs almost always entails the risk of noncombatant deaths and injuries.

To distinguish terrorism from mere criminal violence, it is not sufficient to define it as "politically motivated violence," since other forms of nonterrorist violence, such as insurgencies and mob violence, can also be politically inspired. The specific quality defining terrorism is that it seeks deliberately to create terror in its victims whereas other forms of violence have as their primary object inflicting harm on objects or persons with terror being only a by-product. Terrorists cultivate fear in their victims and audiences not as an end in itself nor merely to torment their direct victims but rather to create terror in others who are the "audience" of the terrorists. Terrorists seek to force their "audience" to pay them attention and to respond in some manner. Therefore one definition of terrorism that has been proposed reads roughly as follows:

> Terrorism is the use of violence to create terror in others who are not the direct object of violence in order to cause them to act in certain ways. [H.H.A. Cooper, *Evaluating the Terrorist Threat: Principles of Applied Risk Assessment,* 1974]

International Terrorism - A fundamental distinction is often made between domestic, or territorial, terrorism and international terrorism: Domestic terrorism is limited to given countries or regions and is usually part of an internal insurgency or revolutionary war. International terrorism is nonterritorial in that it is not limited to any one region. For instance, in El Salvador, following the failure of the Farabundo Martí National Liberation front to overthrow the Salvadoran government in its ill-fated "final offensive" in 1981, the FMLN retreated to the jungles and then undertook a campaign of bombing the economic infrastructure and

murdering local officials or notables close to the government. In this case, the bombings can be viewed as a rational
tactic for crippling the economic resources of the government, while killing many of the Salvadorans could be
rationalized on the grounds of their being functionaries of the
government. This case is to be contrasted with the campaign
of bombings in England carried out by members of the
Provisional Irish Republican Army (PIRA) in the 1970s and
1980s. The English civilians who were killed were usually
quite unconnected with Northern Ireland, and the resulting
damages inflicted no direct blows on PIRA's enemies,
namely the British government, Unionist politicians, or the
Ulster Protestant militia groups. The object of such attacks
was rather to create terror and consternation among the
British public in order to incite them to put pressure on the
British government to withdraw their troops from Northern
Ireland and to allow the Irish to resolve the question of the
future fate of the northern six counties on their own.

Domestic and international terrorism often differ in that the
former usually can be readily identified with some insurgent
group that seeks formal recognition in the international community. In the latter case, more often the acting group is
sponsored by governments that wish to maintain a plausible
deniability of having any connection with the group, since acts
of violence against noncombatant civilians in another sovereign jurisdiction are nothing less than acts of war. Another
distinction is that while those responsible for acts of territorial
terrorism often are seeking recognition as legitimate governments or as new nation-states, such as the Basque separatists in
northern Spain or PIRA members in Northern Ireland, in many
cases of international terrorists the reverse is often the case,
namely, that they are seeking to attack the nation-state system
for tactical or ideological reasons.

Some key characteristics of international terrorism include
the following:

1) It is a form of psychological warfare intended to create
reactions on the part of its audience. It seeks out civilian vic-

tims rather than military targets since this creates greater terror in its audience. Viewers are supposed to be forced to think, ''but for God's grace there go I!'' [H.H.A. Cooper, 1974]

2) It is a form of communication. Besides communicating terror, such acts are forms of armed propaganda that force a captive audience to listen to political demands and threats. The object is to get people to think, ''Let us hear them out to see what they want,'' and then to get them to the point of agreeing to capitulate to certain demands. [Brian Jenkins, *International Terrorism: A New Mode of Conflict*, 1974] For instance, the continued holding of Terry Anderson and other hostages by the Lebanese Hezbollah group brought some of the hostages' relatives to try to bring pressure on the U.S. government to make concessions to gain their release.

3) It is also a form of criminality but not ''mere criminality.'' It would be a mistake to equate the robberies and murders committed by terrorists with those committed by common hoodlums for the former are instrumental in serving political ends beyond the mere crimes themselves. On the other hand, when the political nature of the act is made clear, there is the danger of the captive audience mentally capitulating to the act of armed propaganda and accepting the terrorists' claims that they are mere freedom fighters and that their actions are justified by their allegedly noble aims.

4) International terrorism is really a form of protracted warfare being carried out for political aims, often with the sponsorship of hostile governments.

Such political warfare is a form of low-intensity conflict that exploits the ambivalence of the Western nation-states toward such forms of conflict, falling between the extremes of declared conventional warfare and official diplomatic peace. This warfare is very cost-effective for the sponsoring regime but very costly to the targeted countries, where businesses are forced to spend much on protecting their executives and whose citizens are frightened away from traveling abroad. Such warfare allows nations deficient in conventional military strength to use sophisticated technology to strike at their enemies easily, as was shown by the bombing of Pan Am flight 103 over Scotland on 21 December 1988, by a small radio bomb.

The ambivalent nature of international terrorism creates policy ambivalence on the part of its victims: If it is considered "mere criminality," then it should be treated as a police matter, requiring minimal use of force. But if it is viewed as a military matter, then maximal force ought to be used. And if it is viewed as a political matter, then attempted negotiation, compromise, and capitulation would be in order. In short, terrorism is able to thrive on the very ambiguity that shrouds its nature.

TERRORIST STATES. The United States government currently lists Cuba, Iran, Iraq, Libya, North Korea, the Sudan, and Syria as state sponsors of terrorism, also called "terrorist states." This list is maintained and updated pursuant to Section 6 (j) of the Export Administration Act of 1979 according to factual findings certified by the U.S. Department of State each year. Testimony and evidence are reviewed to determine whether such governments are continuing to provide terrorists safe haven, travel documents, arms, training, and technical expertise and also whether such governments themselves directly engage in terrorism as tools of domestic and foreign policies. A lower level of support consists not so much of active cooperation with terrorists but rather a passive tolerance by governments in which they choose to allow terrorists to reside in, or travel through, or carry out logistical and recruitment efforts without official hindrance within their sovereign jurisdictions.

In August 1993 the U.S. Department of State added the Sudan to the list of state sponsors of terrorism. While there was no evidence that the government of the Sudan directly sponsored terrorism it had nonetheless given sanctuary to members of international terrorist groups, including the Abu Nidal organization, Hezbollah and various Egyptian fundamentalist groups.

TONTON MACOUTES. The "Volunteers for National Security" is a state-sponsored repressive organization created by the dictator François "Papa Doc" Duvalier in 1957 to eliminate his enemies and quell open dissent among the people of Haiti. Its more common name, the "Tonton Macoute" is Creole, meaning "Uncle Knapsack." Originally it was a personal presidential bodyguard and became an alternative militia to counter possible coups by the Haitian military and ultimately became an instrument of mass repression.

After Jean-Claude "Baby Doc" Duvalier was deposed from the Haitian presidency in 1985, the Tonton Macoutes were officially disbanded. In reality, the organization continues to exist underground and apparently found another patron in President Henri Namphy. On 11 September 1988, soldiers and Tonton Macoute members stormed the St. John Bosco Church in Port-au-Prince, killing 9 worshipers and wounding 77 and setting fire to the church. The parish priest, Jean Bertrand Aristide, was a vocal critic of the Namphy government, but the tactic backfired, as it prompted more clashes between citizens and the Tonton Macoutes leading General Prosper Avril to depose Namphy by a military coup on September 17. Yet Avril himself did not appear willing to suppress or prosecute the Tonton Macoutes, and he, too, was forced to resign on 10 March 1990. Jean-Bertrand Aristide, elected president on 16 December 1990, promised to prosecute the Tonton Macoutes but was himself ousted by a coup staged by Army officers having ties to the Tonton Macoute on 30 September 1991.

TUPAC AMARU REVOLUTIONARY MOVEMENT. The *Movimiento Revolucionario Tupac Amaru* (MRTA) is a Marxist urban guerrilla group that seeks to create a socialist revolution within Peru following the Cuban and Nicaraguan models. It is the main rival of Sendero Luminoso (q.v.) group within Peru from which it differs in rejecting the xenophobia and ideological isolationism of the latter group, stressing instead its fraternal unity with other Marxist national liberation movements and regimes. MRTA uses terrorism primarily for "armed propaganda" both to delegitimize the Peruvian regime and to force the U.S. diplomatic and commercial presence out of Peru.

MRTA was formed by leftist university students, many of whom went into exile in Cuba and the Soviet Union when Peru was under military rule during the 1970s. The group therefore reflects a more Castroite and internationalist perspective than does the Sendero Luminoso. MRTA was aided by Cuba and the former Sandinista government of Nicaragua and was suspected of receiving aid from Libya. MRTA also once had contacts with the Colombian M-19 group and is believed to collaborate with the Manuel Rodríguez Patriotic Front in Chile and with the reconstituted National Liberation Army (q.v., See also, Nestor Paz Zamora Commando) of Bolivia. The MRTA takes its name from an earlier national, anticolonial, and revolutionary hero, namely the Inca pretender "Tupac Amaru," who led Peru's Indian peasants in an abortive anticolonial revolt two centuries ago. Although Tupac Amaru based his revolt on an appeal to Indian nativist resentment against Spaniard domination, there is little evidence that MRTA makes any systematic appeal to Indian nativism as does its rival, Sendero Luminoso.

Although formed in 1983, MRTA became active in 1984. Of 51 confirmed MRTA terrorist actions conducted from 1984–1991, 37 (72%) involved bombings, 4 (8%) involved armed attacks using automatic weapons or light artillery, 3 (6%) involved car bombings, while 7 (14%) involved takeovers of radio stations, news agency offices, or churches to force publication of their propaganda. At least 9 (21%) of these attacks were directed at U.S. diplomatic property and persons, giving MRTA the distinction of making the most attacks on U.S. diplomatic facilities of any group in Latin America.

On 28 September 1984, 3 MRTA gunmen machine-gunned the exterior of the U.S. Embassy. On 9 November 1985, MRTA gunmen threw dynamite sticks at the U.S. Embassy and raked it with machine-gun fire. On 4 April 1986, MRTA made a similar attack on the Peruvian-U.S.

Cultural Institute, wounding a guard, as well as attacking two Citibank offices, an IBM warehouse, and a Sears office. On 9 June 1990, MRTA launched mortars at the U.S. Ambassador's residence and on 18 July 1990, bombed the U.S. Embassy, wounding three guards. MRTA also bombed the courtyard of the Interior Ministry on 25 July 1985 and attacked the Presidential Palace and the airplane carrying newly elected President Alberto Fujimori in November 1991.

The membership is estimated at 1,000 to 2,000. Whereas they were mainly active only in Lima in the 1980s, more recently they have carried out activities in Cuzco, Peru, and in areas bordering Bolivia. The appearance of MRTA in highly visible urban operations in 1984 may have moved Sendero Luminoso (q.v.) to open its campaign within the cities rather than relying solely on the rural guerrilla strategy of "encircling the cities" in order to prevent its new rival from taking center stage within Peru.

TUPAMAROS. The Uruguayan *Movimiento de Liberación Nacional* (MLN) was a leftist guerrilla group that sought to overthrow the Uruguayan state and to drive out foreign, particularly U.S. and Brazilian, interests. The group first surfaced on 31 July 1963 with an attack on a gun club and carried out robberies and precise bombings against U.S. and Brazilian diplomatic vehicles and against the homes of high-ranking civilian politicians and bureaucrats. Because the group was believed to have Cuban backing, Uruguay severed diplomatic ties with Cuba in September 1964.

In 1966 the MLN embarked on a campaign of urban terrorism and took the name "Tupamaro" from that of the Peruvian Inca pretender Tupac Amaru executed by the Spaniards in 1782. From January 1968 to July 1972, the Tupamaros engaged in the bombings of institutional targets and conducted nine major bank robberies. The Tupamaros also conducted a campaign of distributing money seized from their robberies to the urban poor and also of publishing financial records they had stolen supposedly documenting alleged corruption among the ruling circles of Uruguay.

Tupamaro terrorism became of international concern with the abduction on 31 July 1970 of a U.S. Agency for International Development employee, Daniel A. Mitrione, who was murdered on 9 August 1970. On 8 January 1971 British Ambassador Geoffrey Jackson was abducted and held eight months in a Tupamaro "people's prison." The Tupamaros had contacts with the Chilean Movement of the Revolutionary Left (MIR, q.v.) and the Argentinean People's Revolutionary Army (ERP, q.v.).

By 1972, Tupamaros began to target members of the Uruguayan military and security forces, a move that drew forth a declaration of internal war by the Uruguayan government, which unleashed the military on the Tupamaros. By May 1972, the military had penetrated the Tupamaro network, uncovering an impressive infrastructure of over 200 safe houses, including a clandestine hospital complete with operating theater and a covert arms factory. By November 1972, some 2,600 members and supporters were arrested and 42 killed. The leader, Raul Sendic Antonaccio, was captured and the movement collapsed. Ironically, the Tupamaros had succeeded in destroying Uruguayan democracy since the military seized power shortly after the crackdown on the Tupamaros; the military, however, then pursued its own ruthless suppression of leftists and subversives that precluded any mass-based leftist revolution. Following the restoration of civilian rule in 1984, a general amnesty was declared in 1985. Upon his release from prison, Sendic and other surviving Tupamaros reconstituted themselves as a legal political party.

TURBAS DIVINAS, LOS. The "divine mobs" were Nicaraguan state-sponsored groups used to intimidate and suppress domestic opponents of the Sandinista regime in Nicaragua. These mobs consisted of FSLN (Frente Sandinista de Liberación Nacional) activists and members of the Sandinista

Defense Committees, a network of block-watch organizations. The turbas divinas and Defense Committees were under the control of Department F-8 for "Mass Organizations" within the General Directorate of State Security (DGSE).

During the first year following the 17 July 1979 Sandinista victory, the FSLN appeared to share power with a number of non-Marxist democratic groups. As hard-line Marxist Tomás Borge Martínez consolidated FSLN control over the Interior Ministry, toleration of non-FSLN political groups ended. On 7 November 1980, organized mobs attacked an opposition rally at Nandaime led by Nicaraguan Democratic Movement leader Alfonso Robelo, and on 9 November, mobs attacked the Nicaraguan Democratic Movement's (NDM) offices, destroying files and equipment and torching an NDM vehicle. When the non-FSLN paper *La Prensa* sought to publish details of the attack it was put under censorship by the Interior Ministry. Sandinista National Directorate member Daniel Ortega is reputed to have dubbed these FSLN-organized mobs as the "turbas divinas" and after his election as president, publicly threatened to unleash the turbas upon Nicaraguan opposition groups.

The turbas divinas destroyed the home of NDM leader Alfonso Robelo, who later left Nicaragua and joined the contras (q.v.). In March 1981, the turbas began painting slogans and insults each night upon the walls of the home of Violeta Chamorro, widow of Pedro Joaquín Chamorro Cardenal, the *La Prensa* editor believed to have been murdered by right-wing Somoza supporters before the Sandinista revolution. Also in 1981, turbas stoned the jeep of Archbishop Miguel Obando y Bravo, a critic of the Sandinistas. On 20 July 1982, turbas beat up the auxiliary bishop of Managua, and in August 1982, stripped Rev. Bismarck Carballo, the Archbishop's spokesman, along with a female parishioner and paraded both of them naked in front of photographers, claiming they had been caught in adultery. In late 1982, the turbas attacked and vandalized a Mormon church in the San Judas neighborhood of Managua. In March 1983, during the visit of Pope John Paul II to Nicaragua, turbas mobbed the Pope and drowned out his public address in Managua with revolutionary and anticlerical slogans. In January 1985, turbas attacked the Conservative Party headquarters after the Conservatives accused the FSLN of rigging the national elections. In August 1987 the turbas attacked two human rights groups, the Permanent Commission on Human Rights and the January 22 Movement of Mothers of Political Prisoners.

The turbas generally attacked the homes and businesses of anyone suspected of being anti-Sandinista, often beating or maiming their victims as well. With the electoral defeat of the FSLN and the installation of Violeta Chamorro as Nicaragua's president on 25 February 1990, the turbas ceased to be a state-sponsored group and their activity largely ceased.

TURKISH PEOPLE'S LIBERATION ARMY. TPLA was a Soviet-sponsored Turkish leftist revolutionary group that specialized in abductions of U.S. servicemen stationed at NATO bases within Turkey, murders of right-wing Turks, as well as bank robberies and bombing right-wing and U.S. targets. The group was founded in 1968 or shortly thereafter by leftist students from the Middle East Technical University in Ankara who underwent guerrilla training in Al Fatah (q.v.) camps within Jordan and Lebanon and who also established contacts with leftist Army officers and cadets. Following the abduction of four U.S. servicemen on 4 March 1971, later released unharmed, about 18 members of the TPLA, including its leader, Deniz Gezmi, were arrested.

Gezmi was executed along with two comrades in 1972, but when the rest of his colleagues were released in 1974 under a general amnesty, they reactivated the organization. The TPLA members expanded their ranks by recruiting from leftist university students in Ankara and Istanbul who received training and arms from Soviet-bloc countries. By

1977, TPLA assassinations had claimed 260 lives. In 1979, around 2,000 people were killed due to death-squad activities of the TPLA and similar groups. The military crackdown in September 1980 led to the suppression of most activities of the TPLA, which then ceased to be active.

Disagreements within the TPLA led to the splitting off in 1975 of a faction, known as *Dev Yol*, or the Revolutionary Road, which did not engage in terrorism or violence. In 1978 a split emerged in Dev Yol leading to the creation of *Dev Sol* (q.v.), or the Revolutionary Left, which acted mainly as an antirightist death squad in the environs of Ankara and is one of the few leftist terrorist groups in Turkey that survived the crackdown of 1980 and has made a comeback in the late 1980s.

TURKISH PEOPLE'S LIBERATION FRONT. The TPLF was the armed wing of the Turkish People's Liberation Party. Like the Turkish People's Liberation Army (q.v.), with which it had no direct connection, the TPLF sought to overturn the constitutional democracy in Turkey in favor of a Marxist-Leninist state and its members also received training in Al Fatah (q.v.) camps as well as covert Soviet-bloc support. On 17 May 1971, the TPLF kidnapped Ephraim Elrom, the Israeli consul general in Istanbul, later murdered on 22 May.

The leader of the TPLF, Mahir Çayan, escaped after briefly being imprisoned and kidnapped three NATO radar technicians on 27 March 1972, who were later murdered by the terrorists, in order to force Turkish officials to release another comrade still in prison. Instead the Turkish police hunted down and killed Çayan and nine of his companions in their hideout near the Black Sea. The widow of Mahir Çayan later helped found the Marxist-Leninist Armed Propaganda Unit (q.v.).

TPLF members later hijacked two Turkish airliners, once in May 1972 and again in October 1972, demanding the release of imprisoned comrades in exchange for the hostages' lives. On each occasion the Turkish government refused their demands and the hijackers took their planes to Bulgaria where they sought political asylum. The TPLF continued to operate until September 1980 when it was suppressed in the overall crackdown of the Turkish military against leftist groups.

- U -

ULSTER DEFENSE ASSOCIATION. The UDA is a northern Irish Protestant militia founded in September 1971, committed to maintaining Protestant supremacy in the political and social life of northern Ireland, while its ostensible purpose is to protect Protestant neighborhoods from IRA (q.v.) attacks. Most of its numbers and resources, in fact, are devoted to defending Protestant neighborhoods, but it is widely believed to support death squad activities involving smaller, specialized units that often assume their own names and maintain their independence from the UDA; such is believed to be the case with the Ulster Freedom Fighters (q.v.). The UDA enjoys effective state support from the Ulster Defense Regiment, an official security organization dominated by sectarian Protestant militiamen. The relationship with the British Army is more problematic, since from September to October 1972 they had considered the British Army to be in league with their Catholic enemies. Since then, it has maintained a truce with British forces and acts, in effect, as an ally. This may explain why the UDA alone maintains its legal status of all Northern Irish paramilitary groups. Proscription available under the Special Powers Act of 1922 has not been sought because British security forces must rely on the UDA for auxiliary support. The membership of the UDA has been estimated in the range of 40,000 to 60,000.

The UDA leader, Andy Tyrie, explained the UDA mission as follows: "We're a counterterrorist organization. The only way we'll get peace here is to terrorize the terrorists." The

UDA finances itself partly through protection rackets, ironically the same way the Provisional IRA finances itself. The UDA is affiliated with the Ulster Loyalist Democratic Party and the New Ulster Political Research Group. The latter makes contingency plans for creating an independent Ulster state in the event Ulster Protestants decide to go it alone in the future. During the pro-unionist Ulster Workers' Council general strike in 1974, directed against a British-sponsored plan to share power in Ulster with Catholics, the UDA openly joined ranks with proscribed death squads such as the Ulster Volunteer Force (q.v.), Red Hand Commandos (q.v.), and other illegal militias, to form an Ulster Army Council to enforce the general strike.

Beginning in mid-1980 and lasting into 1981 an assassination campaign was waged against republicans and nationalists in the north. John Turnley, a nationalist member of the Westminster parliament who had unseated the ultra-unionist Ian Paisley in 1979, was shot dead in June 1980. On 16 January 1981, a republican, the former member of the Westminster parliament, Bernadette Devlin McAlisky, and her husband were wounded by gunmen in their home. Later UDA men were convicted of the Turnley murder and attempted murders of the McAliskys. Three other nationalists were also killed this way, suggesting that the UDA was behind the wave of killings. IRA supporters believed that the UDA had to have enjoyed the cover of British army patrols to have been able to penetrate the largely Catholic areas in which these murders took place.

ULSTER FREEDOM FIGHTERS. The UFF was a splinter group that emerged from the Ulster Defense Association (q.v.). Like its parent group, the UFF was an anti-Catholic militia formed of Ulster Protestants but was much more prone to violence and rowdyism. Although the UFF was banned by the British government in 1973, it continued to carry out numerous assassinations and bombings. Some observers believe that the UFF is actually nothing more than a death squad covertly operated by the Ulster Defense Association.

The UFF murdered not only IRA activists and sympathizers but also carried out random killings of Catholics not associated with anti-unionist groups in order to terrorize the Roman Catholic community. In 1976, it murdered a former Sinn Fein activist, Marie Drumm, in her bed at Belfast's Mater Hospital where she was being treated for cataracts. On 14 March 1984, it shot and wounded Sinn Fein President Gerry Adams as he was being driven through downtown Belfast. On 7 November 1986, two bombs planted by the UFF exploded in garbage cans on Dublin's main street causing no injuries. Two others were found and deactivated. These bombs had been planted to protest the recently concluded Anglo-Irish Agreement. On 12 February 1989, UFF members entered the home of a prominent Catholic lawyer, Pat Finucane, and killed him in the presence of his family at the dinner table. While they claimed that he had been an IRA member, this appeared to be another example of the UFF campaign of killing prominent Catholics of whatever political complexion.

ULSTER VOLUNTEER FORCE. The Ulster Volunteer Force (UVF) was a northern Irish Protestant death squad used to repress suspected IRA (q.v.) members; it had effective state support from the Ulster Defense Regiment, an official security organization dominated by sectarian Protestant militiamen. The original UVF was formed from the unification of all Ulster Protestant militias in 1913 in order to oppose the grant of an autonomous government to Ireland in which Protestants would have formed a minority. At that time many British officers gave the UVF covert support. Upon the partition of Ireland under the Irish Free State Act of 1922, the Royal Irish Constabulary was dissolved throughout Ireland while the Royal Ulster Constabulary (RUC) took its place in the north. Most UVF members entered the RUC at that time and continued to fight those IRA members who rejected partition. Although the UVF ceased to exist officially, the corps of its members remained within the RUC and also later entered the Ulster Special Constabulary.

A former British military policeman, Augustus Spence (b. 1933), declared the UVF revived in 1966 in a special newspaper advertisement on 21 May 1966. This ad declared the UVF "a military body dedicated to upholding the constitution of Ulster by force of arms if necessary" and declared war on all IRA members, threatening to kill them summarily. By the "constitution of Ulster" Spence meant Protestant supremacy in the political and social life of northern Ireland rather than any constitutional rule of law as such. The new UVF engaged in a campaign of fire-bombings of Catholic homes and businesses. The Special Powers Act (1922) banning the IRA was amended on 23 June 1966 to proscribe the UVF as well. On 26 May 1966, UVF shot one John Scullion, who died two weeks later, for singing republican songs in public. On 25 June 1966, Augustus Spence and other UVF members shot four Catholics leaving a pub in the Shankill area, killing one of them. The UVF then carried out a bombing campaign in 1969, which was blamed on the IRA, that forced the moderate prime minister of North Ireland, Terence O'Neill, to resign.

The UVF was legalized again in 1973. On 31 July 1975, UVF members murdered three members of the southern Irish Miami Showcase Band outside Newry. The UVF had tried to rig the band's van with a bomb, which detonated, killing two of their own numbers as well. One of the two UVF dead happened to be a sergeant in the Ulster Defense Regiment, the successor to the Ulster Special Constabulary. The overlapping membership of the UDR and UVF and the direct material support given by UDR members to the UVF made the latter, in effect, a state-sponsored group. The UVF also had relations with the Red Hand Commandos, who were suspected of bombing downtown Dublin and the southern Irish town of Monaghan on 17 May 1974, killing 30 and wounding 151.

The UVF had perhaps 500 members at its height. In 1976, the UVF pledged to refrain from violence; in the following three years, however, 43 members were tried and convicted on charges ranging from illegal possession of arms to murder.

UMKHONTO WE SIZWE. The *Spear of the Nation* (MK) is the military wing of the African National Congress (ANC) established by Nelson Mandela in 1961. With the legal recognition of the African National Congress by the South African government in 1990, the MK is technically dissolved, though in fact high levels of racial violence persist into South Africa's transitional period. Following the withdrawal of Portugal from Mozambique and Angola in 1975, the MK was afforded state support channeled to it through the ANC from the African national regimes established in those lands as well as Cuban military training and material support from the Soviet Union and eastern bloc. The object of MK was to destroy the South African apartheid regime through political agitation, sabotage, and terrorism.

From 1961 to 1977, the MK confined its attacks largely to sabotaging power pylons and commercial property and avoided targeting civilians. In 1977, in response to the South African Defense Forces killing hundreds of blacks in South African townships, MK started its ''second campaign'' in which it targeted police and military officials as well as property. In this phase, lasting until 1983, MK conducted over 200 terrorist attacks. In 1977, MK shot two whites in Johannesburg and embarked on more extensive bombing operations. On 1 June 1980 MK bombed the three South African Coal, Gas and Oil Conversion (SASOL) plants simultaneously at midnight, one in the Orange Free State and two in Transvaal, causing $7 million in damages and wounding one guard. On 13 August 1981, MK launched several rockets against the Voortrekkerhoogte military academy near Pretoria, causing damages but only two casualties. On 21 December 1982, MK exploded four bombs in the Koeburg nuclear plant near Capetown, which was fueled but not in operation at that time. On 20 May 1983, MK car bombed the South Africa air force headquarters outside Pretoria in which 17 persons were killed and around 200 wounded, although virtually no damage was inflicted on the military facility itself. Attacks were also made on civilian targets, such as the 24 June 1986 bombing of Wimpy Burgers in Johannesburg, wounding 17 customers and the bombing of the Holiday Inn-owned President Hotel the same day in which 2 were wounded.

Since 1983, the program of MK has been to terrorize white farmers, to sabotage the industrial base of South Africa, to terrorize black policemen and politicians as collaborators of the apartheid regime, and to conduct urban terrorism in the white-inhabited urban areas. As is often the case with mass-based movements, a number of terrorist incidents against whites and black collaborators have occurred for which no group has claimed credit. In the late 1980s, black "football clubs" appeared, which were, in fact, youth gangs that would terrorize or kill blacks who did not support the ANC. A particularly grisly form of murder called "neck-lacing" was perpetrated against blacks suspected of being police informants in which an automobile tire filled with gasoline-soaked rags would be placed around the victim's neck and set afire.

With the legalization of the African National Congress and release from imprisonment of Nelson Mandela, the activities of Umkhonto we Sizwe have been suspended. Yet, Mandela and other ANC leaders threatened in mid-1992 to resume guerrilla warfare and terrorism if what they claimed were South African police-inspired killings of black nationalists continued.

UNITED FREEDOM FRONT. The United Freedom Front (UFF) was a non-state U.S. leftist group that engaged in terrorism for the limited purpose of protesting U.S. policy in Central America and South Africa. Its main terrorist activity consisted of bombings against military and defense-related industrial targets in the New York metropolitan area.

On 12 May 1983 UFF bombed the U.S. Army Reserve facility in Uniondale, N.Y. The following night they bombed the Naval Reserve center in Queens. The UFF accomplished its tenth major bombing by 19 March 1984 when it bombed an IBM facility near Purchase, N.Y., its third such attack on IBM. On 27 September 1984, the UFF bombed a Union Carbide office to protest the company's investments in South Africa. UFF also had bombed facilities of Honeywell, the U.S. National Guard, and a Navy recruiting center.

Such left-wing groups as the United Freedom Front, Armed Resistance Unit, or New World Liberation Front tended to pick bombing targets for symbolic value and to target property rather than human life. These groups generally would use the terrorist event as "armed propaganda" for specific issues or causes rather than as direct military tactics to achieve revolution. Therefore, UFF used to deposit leaflets near targets and to call news agencies to give communiqués explaining their motives and cause. Instead of mobilizing widespread discussion of their specific issue of interest, however, the net result of the UFF bombing campaign was to motivate targeted firms and similar companies to adopt costly antiterrorist security measures, such as antibomb blast walls.

The United Freedom Front was effectively ended with the arrests of its seven members from November 1984 until April 1985, who were convicted on 13 March 1985 on charges arising from the bombings conducted by the group. The similarity of the tactics and language used by such groups as the United Freedom Front, the Sam Melville-Jonathan Jackson Unit (q.v.), and the Armed Resistance Unit (q.v.) have led many analysts to conclude that these were either one group or branches from a single original group.

URNG. See Guatemalan National Revolutionary Union

- W -

WEATHERMEN/WEATHER UNDERGROUND. The Weather Underground was an anarchistic, leftist terrorist group active from 7 October 1969 to about 1976 that was formed in the student radicalism of the late 1960s, much in the same way as the Baader-Meinhof Red Army Faction (RAF, q.v.), as well as several other terrorist groups drawn from middle-class university students. Such groups rationalized their terrorism in revolutionary leftist terms but in actuality appeared to pursue terrorist violence as an end in itself rather than as a strategy to achieve revolution. These groups can be considered ''leftist'' insofar as they despised capitalism, believed in the superiority of a socialist state, and often spoke in Marxist jargon. They were also anarchistic insofar as they limited their purposes to destroying the existing capitalist states rather than building the foundations of some successor socialist state.

The Weathermen emerged out of the Students for a Democratic Society (SDS), a student leftist antiwar group, in June 1969 during an SDS conference. Their name is taken from some Bob Dylan lyrics—''You don't need to be a weatherman to know which way the wind blows'' which were used as the title of the position paper of the SDS leadership cadre advocating armed revolutionary struggle. While the majority of SDS members rejected this proposal, the Weathermen core stuck to the proposal, imagining themselves as the vanguard that would kindle the revolution at large.

Their proposal involved acts of armed propaganda aimed at pitting antiwar youth against the police. To this end, they planned to incite a spontaneous riot in the so-called ''days of rage,'' that is, a premeditated re-enactment of the demonstrations and police riot that had occurred a year earlier at the 1968 Democratic Convention in Chicago. On 7 October 1969, they bombed the Chicago policeman's statue in Haymarket Square. During October 8–11, the 200 or so Weathermen assembled in Grant Park and were arrested for disorderly conduct. In December 1969, the Weathermen "war council" decided to go underground and accordingly failed to appear for their trials rising from the Grant Park demonstrations, so becoming fugitives. On 6 March 1970, the Weathermen's hideout in Greenwich Village, N.Y., was blown up, killing three leaders due to an error one of them made while trying to assemble a bomb. Despite this mishap, the group undertook its program of armed propaganda. On 1 August 1970 they blasted the exterior of the New York branch of the Bank of Brazil with a pipe bomb. On 13 September 1970, they arranged the jail escape of Timothy Leary. On 8 October 1970, they bombed the ROTC building on the University of Washington campus, the Santa Barbara National Guard Armory, and a courthouse in San Rafael, Calif.

Sometime in the period of 1970–1971, the group's name was changed to the Weather Underground, partly to emphasize their voluntary decision to go underground but also because of an increasing sensitivity within the group to feminist concerns about sexism. On 1 March 1971, they bombed the U.S. Senate wing of the Capitol building. Other targets included the Pentagon and the State Department on 29 January 1975, having conducted 17 bombings to date.

An internal purge destroyed the organization sometime in 1976–1977. Their decision to go underground in 1970 left them isolated from society at large. The aboveground support network, known as the Prairie Fire Organizing Committee, faulted the underground cadre for lagging behind in their commitment to combatting sexism and racism, which had filled the vacuum in the New Left's agenda once filled by the antiwar movement. The Weather Underground members then turned upon one another in internal ideological debates and purges of the insufficiently "committed." Those original Weatherman leaders who were banished eventually gave themselves up to law enforcement officials: Mark Rudd in 1977, and Bernadine Dohrn and William Ayers in 1981. The

ideological hard-liners went on to create the May 19th
Communist Coalition (q.v.), which created the Revolutionary Armed Task Force (q.v.) by merging the remnants of
the Weather Underground and the Black Liberation Army.
With the surrender of Jeffrey David Powell on 6 January
1994 the last of the six Weathermen wanted by the FBI had
surfaced.

WHITE HAND. "Mano Blanca" was a state-sponsored vigilante
group established in 1966 to suppress communist insurgents
in Guatemala. The organization was supposedly founded by
Colonel Enrique Trinadad Oliva and later led by the national
police chief. It eventually turned into a right-wing death
squad that targeted any prominent citizens suspected of
harboring leftist sympathies, including trade union officials
and Roman Catholic priests and prelates. The word "Mano"
in the group's name originally stood for *Movimiento de
Acción Nacionalista Organizada*.

On 17 March 1968, White Hand abducted the Archbishop
of Guatemala, Monsignor Mario Casariego Acevedo, whom
it held for a few days before releasing him. The organization
had hoped by this action to frame leftist groups in order to
create an antileftist backlash among church and army officials. In 1970, Colonel Carlos Arana Osorio, the counterinsurgency military commander who had destroyed two of the
largest leftist guerrilla groups in the countryside, was elected
president. During his presidency, White Hand, along with
other right-wing groups, was permitted to conduct a terror
campaign against suspected leftist elements in the cities.

WHITE PATRIOT ARMY. The WPA is a nonstate paramilitary
white supremacist organization that seeks to undertake a
revolutionary "war" against the "Zionist Occupation Government" of the United States. The main figure behind this
organization is Frazier Glenn Miller, a former Green Beret
Vietnam combat veteran, onetime member of the American
Nazi Party, and leader of the Carolina Knights of the Ku

Klux Klan, from which the WPA drew most of its members. Miller and other members, who later formed the WPA, were responsible for the 1979 massacre in Greensboro, N.C., in which they gunned down five anti-Klan demonstrators belonging to the Communist Workers Party.

In 1986, Miller and three other members of the WPA were arrested for conspiracy to steal military explosives in order to bomb the Southern Poverty Law Center of Montgomery, Ala., an anti-Klan group that had obtained a court order restraining Miller from his paramilitary activities in 1985. The bombing was also intended to murder Morris Dees, the director of the Center and personal nemesis of Miller. FBI investigations revealed that all WPA members were also affiliated with the Carolina Klan and that three of them also were members of the Order (q.v.) from which Miller had accepted $300,000 in stolen funds. Searches of Miller's property in Missouri also revealed stockpiles of contraband military arms and explosives. Miller was imprisoned for failing to obey the 1985 injunction.

While the membership of the WPA, and similar white supremacist organizations, is not known with precision due to these organizations' secretive nature, United Press International reported that several marches staged by the WPA in North Carolina during 1984 each involved over 300 participants.

WHITE WARRIORS' UNION. The UGB, *Unión de Guerreros Blancos*, "White Warriors' Union," or, *Unión Guerrera Blanca*, "White Fighting Union," was a nonstate group founded in 1976 by Roberto D'Aubuisson for the limited purpose of repressing leftist elements in Salvadoran society. Due to the involvement of the Society of Jesus and other Roman Catholic educators with liberation theology (q.v.) and espousal of leftist causes, this group was pronouncedly anti-Jesuit although it claimed itself to be loyal to the traditional values of Catholicism. In 1977, UGB claimed credit for killing two priests in San Salvador and also bombed the home of a trade union leader. In 1979, UGB killed several teachers.

Roberto D'Aubuisson was a protégé of General José Alberto Medrano, who had organized ORDEN (q.v.), the peasant militia that evolved into a death squad that was officially abolished but not fully suppressed in November 1979. From 1979 until 1982, UGB was only one of numerous right-wing death squads operating in El Salvador. During this period, killings by death squads sometimes exceeded 800 people each month and included among their victims Archbishop Oscar Romero y Galdamez killed on 24 March 1980. In 1982, D'Aubuisson founded and led the rightist Republican National Alliance Party (ARENA, q.v.), itself suspected of sponsoring death squad activities. ARENA won the largest share of seats in the new Constituent Assembly in 1982. With the ascendancy of ARENA, both the remnants of ORDEN and UGB were absorbed into D'Aubuisson's new political organization.

WORLD TRADE CENTER BOMBING. On 26 February 1993 at 12:18 P.M. a rented van packed with home-made explosives detonated in the parking lot under the north tower of the World Trade Center in downtown Manhattan. The blast killed six people and injured over 1,000 more and is perhaps the worst terrorist incident to have occurred within the United States. The blast crater extended through five stories of the underground parking lot. The bomb is estimated to have consisted of 1,000 pounds of explosives presumably manufactured from urea, sulfuric and nitric acid, materials later found in the possession of some of the suspects. The bomb is believed to have been rigged with hydrogen gas cylinders and nitroglycerin blasting caps to amplify the explosive effect of the resulting fireball.

Forensic analysis of the remaining fragments of the vehicle bomb revealed the vehicle identification number that allowed the FBI to identify Mohammed A. Salameh (b. 1971) as the person who rented the van and who was arrested within five days of the bombing. Salameh also had rented a storage locker in New Jersey where the bomb-making materials were stored. He shared an apartment with Nidal A. Ayyad, the chemical engineer who apparently had mixed the explosives. Salameh and Ayyad also shared a bank account which funded the purchase of the explosives and rental of the van. A New York taxi-driver, Mahmud Abouhalima (b. 1960), who had helped prepare the explosives and who had bought fuel for the van, was arrested in Egypt and extradited to the United States. Fingerprints on military bomb-making manuals found in Salameh's apartment and records of telephone calls with Salameh led police to another suspect, Ahmad M. Ajaj (b. 1966), who was imprisoned at the time of the bombing.

Two other key suspects named in federal indictments, Abdul Rahman Yasin and Razmi Ahmad Yousef, had already fled the country. It is now believed that Yousef, an Iraqi national who had entered the United States from Pakistan six months before the bombing, was the actual mastermind behind the bombing and that he entered the country with the specific intent of carrying out a terrorist attack on U.S. soil.

With the exception of Abouhalima, who was Egyptian, the arrested suspects were all Palestinian. Based on the evidence presented in their trial all four defendants were convicted on 4 March 1994 on charges of conspiracy, explosive destruction of property, interstate transportation of explosives, assault on a Federal officer, and using a destructive device in the course of a violent crime.

Among the unresolved questions of this case is the possible relationship of this crime to the world-wide resurgence of Islamic fundamentalism, and what national government, if any, had sponsored this action.

Shortly after the arrest of Salameh and Ayyad it was learned that both had regularly attended a New Jersey mosque, the *Masjid as Salaam*, where the resident prayer leader was none other than Sheikh Umar Abdul Rahman, the blind Egyptian preacher and leader of the *Jamaa Al Islami* group in Egypt who had issued the decree of *takfir* to members of the Munazzamat al Jihad (q.v.) that authorized the killing of Anwar Sadat. Although his name was included in an official list of suspected terrorists prohibited from entering the United States, he had managed nonetheless to obtain a visa from a U.S. consulate in the Sudan. Although Sheikh Abdul Rahman afterwards declared the bombing to have been contrary to Islam, such strong circumstantial evidence had linked him to the other suspects and to evidence regarding a broader conspiracy to bomb public places that he was arrested in June 1993 to await a separate trial.

Most Muslim religious scholars throughout the world and most ordinary Muslims living within the United States state that such bombings are abhorrent and contrary to Islamic law. Nonetheless the undoubted fundamentalist convictions of those convicted for the bombing and of their mentor, Sheikh Umar Abdul Rahman, and his own connection with fundamentalist violence in Egypt directed at Western tourists suggest strongly that this event may have stemmed from the Islamic resurgence at large even if the act itself was incompatible with Islamic norms.

Not altogether separate from the question of a fundamentalist inspiration behind the bombing is the question of possible state sponsorship. Sheikh Abdul Rahman, Salameh, and Ayyad all received funds from unknown sources abroad. Ahmad Ajaj and Razmi Ahmad Yousef both had guerrilla training with Afghan rebels and possessed several false passports. Yousef, an Iraqi citizen, moved about freely between Pakistan and the United States despite the travel and foreign exchange restrictions that Iraq imposes on ordinary citizens. These circumstances suggest, but by no means prove, possible state sponsorship.

On the basis of such circumstantial clues as well as content analysis of the speeches and declarations of Islamic fundamentalist leaders, Yossef Bodansky, a former director of the House Republican Task Force on Terrorism, has argued that the Islamic Republic of Iran was the main sponsor behind the bombing. His argument, however, rests on certain assumptions of strategic and tactical coordination between such unlikely allies as Saddam Hussein, Iran's fundamentalist leaders, Hafez al-Asad and the Muslim Brotherhood. Egyptian security officials claimed that Abouhalima had confessed under interrogation to having met two Iranian intelligence operatives. None of the defendants indicated outside state support, however, when questioned by U.S. interrogators.

The coincidence of the date of the bombing with the anniversary of Iraq's defeat in Operation Desert Storm suggests Iraq as a possible state sponsor. During the Persian Gulf war Sheikh Abdul Rahman also had given many vehement sermons denouncing the U.S.-led coalition and championing Saddam Hussein. However the available evidence based on open sources is insufficient to indict either Iran or Iraq for such sponsorship, in spite of whatever incidental benefits or satisfaction either state may have derived from the bombing.

The World Trade Center bombing does, however, raise important questions about U.S. preparedness and security measures. Even if no state sponsorship was involved, the demonstration effect of this event still might encourage possible state sponsors to pursue more active anti-U.S. terrorism on U.S. soil. The investigations into the linkages of certain defendants with the Jersey City mosque, with a Hamas support infrastructure in the United States, and with fundamentalist groups in Egypt and Afghanistan, as well as the ease with which they gained permanent U.S. resident status as alleged political refugees, also raise questions about the transnational impact of foreign terrorist groups and their support networks within our own borders.

- Z -

ZEALOTS. Also known as the *Sicarii* (dagger-wielders), the Zealots were first century A.D. Jewish religious nationalists in the Roman province of Judea who carried out terrorist attacks on Roman officials and Jews considered to be Roman collaborators as well as waging an open insurgency against Rome in the period from 66–70 A.D. The immediate goal of the Zealots was to purge Hellenistic cultural influences from Jewish life as well as to rid Judea of Roman domination. Their ultimate goal was actually to initiate the advent of the Messiah by forcing an apocalyptic confrontation between Rome and the Jewish nation. As Judea lacked sufficient human resources to withstand Rome's military power, the Zealots believed that by provoking such a crisis they could force God's direct intervention to save the people of Israel according to His Covenant.

The historian Josephus Flavius recorded most of the activity of the Zealots-Sicarii as having occurred in the twenty-five years preceding the destruction of Jerusalem by Roman forces in 70 A.D. The Gospel of Luke also mentioned one of the disciples of Jesus as being one ''Simon who was called the Zealot,'' (Luke 6:15) while later Roman historians recorded two subsequent revolts in Judea as late as the second century that recalled the tactics of the Zealots. At least two separate groups were known as the Sicarii while another group was known as the Zealots but their common tactics and goals suggest that these various groups were either independent manifestations of a continuing resurgence movement in Judea or cellular groups emanating from the same organized conspiracy.

The tactics of the Zealots included assassination in broad daylight of Roman officials and members of the Temple priesthood, usually by stabbing with a dagger (*sica*) in the midst of milling crowds into which the assassin then escaped. They also took hostages for ransom and extorted protection payments from Jewish landowners. Finally they also engaged both in guerrilla warfare and in open engagements with Roman troops. The Zealots also resorted to the first recorded instances of using the tactic of massive passive resistance by staging sit-in demonstrations involving unarmed men, women, and children in the streets of Jerusalem to protest instances of Roman disregard for Jewish religious sensitivities. The Zealots timed both their assassinations and these protests to coincide with certain holy days during which Jerusalem would be packed with throngs of Jewish pilgrims. Roman officials were faced with the dilemma of backing away from confrontation, in which case more resistance to Roman authority would be encouraged, or else employing force against civilians, so providing the Zealots with more instances of Roman sacrileges with which to fuel their cause. These efforts prefigured later efforts by modern urban guerrilla groups to instigate mass uprisings by provoking authorities into indiscriminate repression in reprisal for terrorist attacks.

In spite of the success of the Zealots in provoking the mass revolt against Roman rule in Judea, ultimately Roman forces besieged and destroyed Jerusalem, including the Second Temple, and killed or enslaved the surviving Jewish population in the countryside which was sent into exile. Josephus recorded that the surviving Zealots were besieged in the fortress of Masada near the southern end of the Dead Sea. When capture of the fortress by Roman forces following a year-long siege seemed imminent the Zealots reportedly committed mass suicide rather than allowing themselves to be enslaved by the Romans.

THE BIBLIOGRAPHY:

TABLE OF CONTENTS

INTRODUCTION

The literature on terrorism has burgeoned so much within the last two decades that a few key bibliographies and general references are necessary starting points for any systematic research of the existing literature on terrorism. The *International Terrorism: An Annotated Bibliography and Research Guide* by Augustus R. Norton and Martin H. Greenberg covers most of the literature until 1980 fairly comprehensively with summary descriptions of key works. Amos Lakos's *Terrorism, 1980–1990: A Bibliography* is comprehensive but the volume of the literature on terrorism grew so much in that decade that few bibliographies could succeed in being annotated and comprehensive. Edward F. Mickolus's *The Literature of Terrorism: A Selectively Annotated Bibliography* treats the more seminal books and articles and can be used in conjunction with Lakos's work.

The key work for the theory and concepts of terrorism is Alex P. Schmid and Albert J. Jongman's *Political Terrorism: A New Guide to Actors, Authors, Concepts, Databases and Literature* in its revised edition of 1988. A more abbreviated yet thorough conceptual treatment of the key concepts and categories is also to be found in John R. Thackrah's *Encyclopedia of Terrorism and Political Violence.*

Fortunately a number of comprehensive data bases and chronologies have been produced within the last 10 years that simplify greatly the task of researchers and students. Yonah Alexander helped to compile and organize a microforms data base compiling the leading articles on terrorism arranged by geographic areas and also by subject matter, namely, *Terrorism: An International Resource File,* available through University Microforms Incorporated, Ann Arbor, Mich. Complete chronologies are also indispensable, and Edward F. Mickolus's three major chronologies spanning the periods 1968–1979, 1980–1983, and 1984–1987 reproduce much of the material Mickolus included in his ITERATE (International Terrorism: Attributes of Terrorist Events) data base. Because of their emphasis on international terrorism, however, these chronologies do not deal much with purely domestic U.S. terrorism or with terrorist insurgencies that neither cross borders nor victimize foreign nationals. The Rand Corporation has also produced a series of annual terrorist chronologies that, like the ITERATE data base, seek to categorize incidents geographically and by terrorist tactics.

A number of handbooks or general reference books have been produced also in the last 10 years that can be of help as starting points for research. One general caveat pertains to all attempts to produce single-volume encyclopedias or dictionaries of terrorism, however. Due to the sheer multiplicity of terrorist groups, events, and personalities to the extent that any general reference seeks to be complete and comprehensive, it will also tend to be summary in its treatment of any given entry. Likewise to the extent that such a work tries to deal with its entries in greater depth it will have to limit itself to covering a sample of the universe of possible entries. For a detailed treatment of leading terrorist groups and organizations, Peter Janke's *Guerrilla and Terrorist Organisations: A World Directory and Bibliography* is both comprehensive and scholarly. A handbook that is much more ambitious in its scope is the *Almanac of Modern Terrorism* (1990) by Jay Shafritz and his colleagues, which tries to deal with leading groups, ideas, personalities, events, and technical details of weapons and tactics. Most entries in this almanac have references to more detailed sources, allowing the user to gain a basic knowledge from each entry but also enabling the researcher to pursue more detailed sources if desired. Other handbooks in the public domain include the U.S. Department of Defense's *Profiles of Terrorist Groups* and the U.S. Department of State's annual report *Patterns of Global Terrorism,* which includes a basic chronology, descriptive guide to leading active terrorist groups, and analysis of terrorism by geographic region and by state sponsors. The latter report also often includes special appendices dealing in more depth with major events or controversies as well as statistical summaries using graphs and maps. George Rosie's *Directory of International Terrorism* deals with a select sampling of groups, events, and personalities in great detail.

Political science literature contains a few journals devoted exclusively to political violence, insurgency, and terrorism. The Crane Russak publishers produced the journals *Conflict* and *Terrorism*, which were combined in 1992 as a new publication, *Studies in Conflict and Terrorism*, whose first volume (Volume 15, 1992) continues to follow the numbering of issues used in its predecessor *Terrorism*. The Frank Cass publishers produce the journal *Terrorism and Political Violence* while another specialty journal is *Conflict Quarterly* published by the Centre for Conflict Studies of the University of New Brunswick, Fredericton. The *TVI Report: Comprehensively Reporting Terrorism, Violence, and Insurgency Worldwide* covers matters of interest to law enforcement agencies and multinational firms as well as to academic users and is published by TVI, Inc., (P.O. Box 1055, Beverly Hills, CA, 90213–9940). Occasional papers on various terrorist topics can be found in various issues of the *Adelphi Papers* of the International Institute for Strategic Studies, the *Washington Papers* of the Center for Strategic and International Studies, as well as *Conflict Studies*. Certain standard periodical indexes, such as the *Public Affairs Information Service* and the *ABC POLI SCI: Bibliography of Contents, Political Science and Government* will generally list most titles of occasional articles dealing with terrorism in leading political science and administrative journals.

The following bibliography draws on all of these sources to include as many of the seminal articles germane to terrorism and current controversies in this field as possible. It is a starting point from which, the authors hope, the diligent researcher will be able to generate further references from those provided in the articles cited here, which could not themselves also have been contained within the space allotted here.

I. GENERAL REFERENCE WORKS

1. Bibliographies and Dictionaries

Atkins, Stephen F. *Terrorism: A Reference Handbook.* Santa Monica, Calif.: ABC-CLIO, 1992. 199 p.

Lakos, Amos. *Terrorism, 1980–1990: A Bibliography.* Boulder, Colorado: Westview Press, 1991. 443 p.

Lentz, Harris M., III. *Assassinations and Executions: An Encyclopedia of Political Violence, 1865–1986.* Jefferson, North Carolina: McFarland & Company, Inc., Publishers, 1988.

Mickolus, Edward F. *The Literature of Terrorism: A Selectively Annotated Bibliography.* Westport, Connecticut, Greenwood Press, 1980.

Mickolus, Edward F. and Peter A. Flemming. *Terrorism, 1980–1987: A Selectively Annotated Bibliography.* Westport, Connecticut, Greenwood Press, 1988.

Newton, Michael and Judy Ann Newton. *Terrorism in the United States and Europe, 1800–1959: An Annotated Bibliography,* New York: Garland Publishing, Inc., 1988. 508 p.

Norton, Augustus R. and Martin H. Greenberg. *International Terrorism: An Annotated Bibliography and Research Guide.* Boulder, Colorado: Westview Press, 1980. 218 p.

Ontiveros, Suzanne Robitaille (ed.) *Global Terrorism: A Historical Bibliography.* Santa Barbara, California: ABC-CLIO, 1986. 168 p.

Picard, Robert G. and Rhonda S. Sheets. ''Terrorism and the News Media: A Research Bibliography, Part III,'' *Political Communication and Persuasion,* 4, 3 (1987): 217 et seq.

Picard, Robert G. and Rhonda S. Sheets. "Terrorism and the News Media: A Research Bibliography, Part IV," *Political Communication and Persuasion,* 4, 4 (1987): 325 et seq.

Schmid, Alex P. *Political Terrorism: A Research Guide to Concepts, Theories, Databases and Literature.* Amsterdam: North-Holland, 1983. 585 p.

Schmid, Alex P., and Albert J. Jongman. *Political Terrorism: A New Guide to Actors, Authors, Concepts, Databases and Literature.* (Revised edition) New Brunswick, New Jersey: Transaction Books, 1988. 700 p.

Sifakis, Carl. *Encyclopedia of Assassinations.* New York: Facts on File, 1991. 228 p.

Smith, Myron J. *The Secret Wars: A Guide to Sources in English.* Santa Barbara, California: ABC-CLIO, 1980–1981. (3 volumes).

Thackrah, John Richard. *Encyclopedia of Terrorism and Political Violence.* New York: Routledge & Kegan Paul, 1987. 308 p.

Wilson, Colin and Donald Seaman. *The Encyclopedia of Modern Murder, 1962–1982.* New York: G. P. Putnam's Sons, 1983.

2. Directories and Yearbooks

Alexander, Yonah and A. H. Foxman, eds. *The 1988–89 Annual on Terrorism.* Dordrecht: Martinus Nijhoff, 1990.

Janke, Peter. *Guerrilla and Terrorist Organisations: A World Directory and Bibliography.* (New York: Macmillan, 1983). 401 p.

Rosie, George. *The Directory of International Terrorism.* Edinburgh: Mainstream Publishing, 1986. 310 p.

Schechterman, Bernard and Martin Slann, eds., *Violence and Terrorism 91/92.* Sluice Dock, Guilford, Connecticut: Dushkin Publishing Group, Inc. 243 p.

Shafritz, Jay M., E. F. Gibbons, Jr., and Gregory E. J. Scott. *Almanac of Modern Terrorism.* New York: Facts On File, 1991. 290 p.

U.S. Department of Defense. *Terrorist Group Profiles.* Washington, D.C. [Dept. of Defense]; for sale by the Superintendent of Documents, U.S. Government Printing Office, 1988. 131 p.

U.S. Department of State. *Patterns of Global Terrorism: 1987,* (U.S. Government Printing Office, August 1988): pp. 12, 36.

3. Chronologies and Data Bases

Alexander, Yonah ed., *Terrorism: An International Resource File, 1986,* Ann Arbor, Michigan: University Microforms Incorporated, 1987. 332 p.

Alexander, Yonah ed., *Terrorism: An International Resource File, 1987,* Ann Arbor, Michigan: University Microforms Incorporated, 1988. 177 p.

Alexander, Yonah ed., *Terrorism: An International Resource File, 1988,* Ann Arbor, Michigan: University Microforms Incorporated, 1989. 316 p.

Gardela, Karen and Bruce Hoffman. RAND/R-3890-RC, *The RAND Chronology of International Terrorism for 1986.* Santa Monica, California: Rand Corporation, 1990. 105 p.

Gardela, Karen and Bruce Hoffman. RAND/R-4006-RC, *The RAND Chronology of International Terrorism for 1987.* Santa Monica, California: Rand Corporation, 1991. 107 p.

Lentz, Harris M., III. *Assassinations and Executions: An Encyclopedia of Political Violence, 1865–1986.* Jefferson, North Carolina: McFarland & Co., 1988. 275 p.

Mickolus, Edward F. "Chronology of Transnational Terrorist Attacks Upon American Business People, 1968–1976." *Terrorism,* 1 (1978): 217–235.

Mickolus, Edward F. *Transnational Terrorism: A Chronology of Events, 1968–1979.* Westport, Connecticut: Greenwood Press, 1980. 967 p.

Mickolus, Edward F., Todd Sandler, and Jean M. Murdock. *International Terrorism In the 1980s: A Chronology of Events, Volume I, 1980–1983.* Ames, Iowa: Iowa State University Press, 1989. 539 p.

Mickolus, Edward F., Todd Sandler, and Jean M. Murdock. *International Terrorism In the 1980s: A Chronology of Events, Volume II, 1984–1987.* Ames, Iowa: Iowa State University Press, 1989. 776 p.

Mickolus, Edward F. *Codebook: ITERATE (International Terrorist: Attributes of Terrorist Events).* Inter-University Consortium for Political and Social Research, University of Michigan, 1976.

II. GENERAL DESCRIPTIVE AND THEORETICAL WORKS

Adams, James. *The Financing of Terror.* London: New English Library, 1986. p. 294.

Alexander, Yonah, ed. *International Terrorism: National, Regional and Global Perspectives.* New York: Praeger Publishers, 1976.

Alexander, Yonah, and Seymour M. Finger, eds. *Terrorism: Interdisciplinary Perspectives.* New York: The John Jay Press, 1977. 393 p.

Alexander, Yonah, and Robert A. Kilmarx, eds. *Political Terrorism and Business: The Threat and Response.* New York: Praeger Publishers, 1979.

Amos, John W., II. and Russel H. S. Stolfi. "Controlling International Terrorism: Alternatives Palatable and Unpalatable," *Annals of the American Academy of Political and Social Science,* 463 (September 1982): 69–83.

Ansari, Masud. *International Terrorism: Its Causes and How to Control It.* Washington, D.C.: Mas-Press, 1988. 272 p.

Bell, J. Bowyer. "Transnational Terror and World Order," *South Atlantic Quarterly,* 74, 4 (1975): 404–417.

Beres, Louis Rene. "Guerrillas, Terrorists, and Polarity: New Structural Models of World Politics," *Western Political Quarterly,* 27, 4 (1974): 624–636.

Blair, Robert A. "Fighting Terrorism: A Dissenting View," *World Affairs,* 146, 1 (Summer 1983): 114–116.

Blaufarb, Douglas S. "Terrorist Trends and Ties," *Problems of Communism,* 31, 3 (1982): 73–77.

Book Review. "Terrorist Facts and Fancies," *World Today,* 44, 2 (1988): 35 et seq.

Brainerd, Gideon H., Jr. "Terrorism: The Theory of Differential Effects," *Conflict,* 5, 3 (1984): 233–244.

Burton, Anthony M. *Urban Terrorism: Theory, Practice and Response.* New York: The Free Press, 1975. 259 p.

Cetron, Marvin J. "The Growing Threat of Terrorism," *The Futurist* (July-August 1989) in Schechterman, Bernard and Slann, Martin, eds., *Violence and Terrorism 91/92*. Sluice Dock, Guilford, Connecticut: Dushkin Publishing Group, Inc. pp. 222–225.

Chapman, Robert D. "State Terrorism," *Conflict: An International Journal for Conflict and Policy Studies,* 3, 4 (1982): 283–298.

Chomsky, Noam. *The Culture of Terrorism.* Boston: South End Press, 1988. 269 p.

Clawson, Patrick. "Terrorism in Decline?," *Orbis,* 33, 3 (1989): 263–276.

Cline, Ray, and Yonah Alexander. *Terrorism as State-Sponsored Covert Warfare.* Fairfax, Virginia: Herobook, 1986. 128 p.

Clutterbuck, Richard. *Guerrillas and Terrorists.* London: Faber and Faber Limited, 1977.

Clutterbuck, Richard. *Kidnap and Ransom: The Response.* London: Faber and Faber Limited, 1978.

Crenshaw, Martha. "The Causes of Terrorism," *Comparative Politics,* 13, 4 (1981): 379–400.

Crenshaw, Martha. "An Organizational Approach to the Analysis of Political Terrorism," *Orbis,* 29, 3 (1985): 465–489.

Crenshaw, Martha. "Current Research on Terrorism: The Academic Perspective," *Studies in Conflict and Terrorism,* 15, 1 (1992): 1–12.

Derriennie, Jean Pierre. "The Nature of Terrorism and the Effective Response," *International Perspective* (Canada), 3 (1975): 7–10.

Devine, Philip E. and Robert J. Rafalko. "On Terror," *Annals of the American Academy of Political and Social Science,* 463 (September 1982): 39–53.

Dobson, Christopher, and Ronald Payne. *The Carlos Complex: A Study in Terror.* New York: G. P. Putnam's Sons, 1977.

Dobson, Christopher, and Ronald Payne. *Terror! The West Fights Back.* London: Macmillan, 1982.

Dobson, Christopher, and Ronald Payne. *The Terrorists, Their Weapons, Leaders and Tactics.* New York: Facts on File, 1982. 279 p.

Dobson, Christopher. *War Without End: The Terrorists, An Intelligence Dossier.* London: Harrap, 1986. 269 p.

Dugard, John. "International Terrorism: Problems of Definition," *International Affairs* (United Kingdom), 50, 1 (1974): 67–81.

Duvall, Raymond and Michael Stohl. *The Politics of Terrorism,* third edition. New York: Marcel Dekker, 1988. 622 p.

Emerson, Steven. *Secret Warriors.* New York: G. P. Putnam's Sons, 1993.

Enders, Walter and Todd Sandler. "Causality Between Transnational Terrorism and Tourism: The Case of Spain," *Terrorism,* 14, 1 (1991): 49–58.

Falk, Richard. *Revolutionaries and Functionaries: The Dual Face of Terrorism.* New York: E. P. Dutton, 1988. 222 p.

Finger, Seymour Maxwell. "The United Nations and International Terrorism," *Jerusalem Journal of International Relations,* 10, 1 (1988): 12–43.

Ford, Franklin L. *Political Murder: From Tyrannicide to Terrorism.* Cambridge, Massachusetts: Harvard University Press, 1985. 440 p.

Freedman, Lawrence Zelic, and Yonah Alexander, eds. *Perspectives on Terrorism.* Wilmington, Delaware: Scholarly Resources Inc., 1983. 254 p.

Freedman, Lawrence Zelic, et al. *Terrorism and International Order.* London: Routledge and Kegan Paul, 1987. 107 p.

Frey, R. G. and Christopher W. Morris, eds. *Violence, Terrorism, and Justice.* Cambridge: Cambridge University Press, 1991.

Friedlander, Robert A. *Terrorism: Documents of International and Local Control,* 5 volumes. Dobbs Ferry, New York: Oceana Publications, 1979. Volume 1, 572 p.; volume 2, 753 p.; volume 3, 614 p.; volume 4, 595 p.; volume 5, 425 p.; and Appendix, 100 p.

George, Alexander, ed. *Western State Terrorism.* New York: Routledge, Chapman and Hall, Inc., 1991. 264 p.

Grosscup, Beau. *The Explosion of Terrorism.* Far Hills, New Jersey: New Horizon Press, 1987. 320 p.

Guillen, Abraham. *Philosophy of the Urban Guerrilla.* Donald C. Hodges, ed. New York: William Morrow, 1973. 305 p.

Gutteridge, William ed. *Contemporary Terrorism.* New York: Facts on File, 1986. 225 p.

Hanle, Donald J. *Terrorism: The Newest Face of Warfare.* Pergamon-Brassey Terrorism Library, Vol. 1, Washington, D.C.: Pergamon Press, 1989. 272 p.

Hocking, Jenny. "Orthodox Theories of 'Terrorism': The Power of Politicized Terminology," *Politics,* 19, 2 (1984): 103–111.

Hof, Frederic C. "The Beirut Bombing of October 1983: An Act of Terrorism?," *Parameters: Journal of the US Army War College,* 15, 2 (1985): 69–74.

Hoffman, Bruce. "Current Research on Terrorism and Low-Intensity Conflict," *Studies in Conflict and Terrorism,* 15, 1 (1992): 25–38.

Hoffman, Bruce. "The Contrasting Ethical Foundations of Terrorism in the 1980s," *Terrorism and Political Violence,* (July 1989) in Schechterman, Bernard and Slann, Martin, eds., *Violence and Terrorism 91/92.* Sluice Dock, Guilford, Connecticut: Dushkin Publishing Group, Inc. pp. 226–231.

Hunter, Shireen. "Terrorism: A Balance Sheet," *Washington Quarterly,* 12, 3 (1989): 17–32.

Jenkins, Brian M. "The Future Course of International Terrorism," in Paul Wilkinson, ed. *Contemporary Research on Terrorism.* (Aberdeen: Aberdeen University Press, 1987). pp. 581–85.

Jenkins, Brian M. "Defense against Terrorism," *Political Science Quarterly,* 101, 5 (1986): 773–786.

Jenkins, Brian M. "Will Terrorists Go Nuclear?," *Orbis,* 29, 3 (1985): 507–516.

Jenkins, Brian Michael. "New Modes of Conflict," *Orbis,* 28, 1 (Spring 1984): 5–16.

Jenkins, Brian M. "Statements about Terrorism," *Annals of the American Academy of Political and Social Science,* 463 (September 1982): 11–23.

Jenkins, Brian M. "Statements about Terrorism," *Annals of the American Academy of Political and Social Science,* 463 (September 1982): 11–23.

Jenkins, Brian M. "International Terrorism: Trends and Potentialities," *Journal of International Affairs,* (Spring/Summer 1978), 115–123.

Jenkins, Philip. "Whose Terrorists? Libya and State Criminality," *Contemporary Crises,* 12, 1 (1987): 5–24.

Kidder, Rushworth. "State-Sponsored Terrorism," *The Christian Science Monitor,* (May 14, 1986): 11–24.

Kirk, Richard M. "Political Terrorism and the Size of Government: A Positive Institutional Analysis of Violent Political Activity," *Public Choice,* 40, 1 (1983): 41–52.

Kupperman, Robert H. "Terror, the Strategic Tool: Response and Control," *Annals of the American Academy of Political and Social Science,* 463 (September 1982): 24–38.

Kurz, Anat, ed., *Contemporary Trends in World Terrorism.* New York: Praeger, 1987. 170 p.

Laqueur, Walter, and Yonah Alexander, eds. *The Terrorism Reader: A Historical Anthology.* New York: New American Library, 1987. 405 p.

Laqueur, Walter. *The Age of Terrorism.* Boston: Little, Brown and Company, 1987. 385 p.

Laqueur, Walter. "Reflections on Terrorism," *Foreign Affairs,* 65 (Fall 1986): 86–100.

Laqueur, Walter. *Terrorism.* Boston: Little, Brown and Company, 1977. 277 p.

Laqueur, Walter. "The Origins of Guerrilla Doctrine," *Journal of Contemporary History,* 10 (July 1975).

Ledeen, Michael. "Syllogisms and Stereotypes," *Society,* 19, 4 (1982): 77–79.

Ledeen, Michael. "Syllogisms and Stereotypes," *Society,* 4, 3 (March-April 1982): 77–79.

Leeman, Richard W. "Terrorism as Rhetoric: An Argument of Values," *Journal of Political Science,* 14, 1–2 (1986): 33–42.

Levitt, Geoffrey M. *Democracies Against Terror.* New York: Praeger Press, 1988. 142 p.

Livingston, Marius H., ed.; with Kress, Lee B., and Wanek, Marie G. *International Terrorism in the Contemporary World: Proceedings of the 1976 Glassboro State College International Symposium.* Contributions in Political Science, No. 3. Westport, Connecticut: Greenwood Press, 1978. 522 p.

Livingston, Neil C. *The War against Terrorism.* Lexington, Massachusetts: Lexington Books, 1982. 291 p.

Livingston, Neil C. "States in Opposition: The War Against Terrorism," *Conflict: An International Journal for Conflict and Policy Studies,* 3, 2–3 (1981): 83–142.

Livingston, Neil C. "The Wolves among Us: Reflections on the Past Eighteen Months and Thoughts on the Future," *World Affairs,* 146, 1 (Summer 1983): 7–22.

Livingston, Susan Morrisey. "Terrorism: 'The Original Cheap Shot': An Interview with Ambassador Diego Asencio," *World Affairs,* 146, 1 (Summer 1983): 42–53.

Livingston, Susan Morrisey. "Terrorist Wrongs versus Human Rights: An Interview with Assistant Secretary of State Elliott Abrams," *World Affairs,* 146, 1 (Summer 1983): 69–78.

Long, David E. *The Anatomy of Terrorism.* New York: The Free Press, 1990. 244 p.

Long, Kenneth J. "Understanding and Teaching the Semantics of Terrorism: An Alternative Perspective," *Perspectives on Political Science,* 19, 4 (1990): 203–208.

Maranto, Robert. "The Rational Terrorist: Toward a New Theory of Terrorism," *Journal of Political Science,* 14, 1–2 (1986): 16–24.

McForan, Desmond. *The World Held Hostage: The War Waged by International Terrorism.* London: Oak-Tree Books, 1986. 262 p.

Merari, Ariel. "Classification of Terrorist Groups," *Terrorism,* 1 (1978): 331–346.

Merkl, Peter H. ed. *Political Violence and Terror: Motifs and Motivations.* Berkeley: University of California Press, 1986. 380 p.

Mickolus, Edward F. "Statistical Approaches to the Study of Terrorism," in Alexander, Yonah, and Finger, Seymour M., eds. *Terrorism: Interdisciplinary Perspectives.* New York: The John Jay Press, 1977. pp. 209–269.

Mickolus, Edward F. "Comment-Terrorists, Governments, and Numbers: Counting Things Versus Things That Count," *Journal of Conflict Resolution,* 31, 1 (1987): 54–62.

Mickolus, Edward F. "What Constitutes State Support to Terrorists?," *Terrorism and Political Violence,* (July 1989), in

Schechterman, Bernard and Slann, Martin, eds., *Violence and Terrorism 91/92*. Sluice Dock, Guilford, Connecticut: Dushkin Publishing Group, Inc. pp. 38–40.

Miller, Abraham. "The Evolution of Terrorism," *Conflict Quarterly,* 5, 4 (Fall 1985): 5–16.

Miller, David. "The Use and Abuse of Political Violence," *Political Studies,* 32, 3 (1984): 401–419.

Miller, Reuben. "Acts of International Terrorism: Governments' Responses and Policies," *Comparative Political Studies,* 19, 3 (1986): 385–414.

Mozaffari, Mehdi. "The New Era of Terrorism: Approaches and Typologies," *Cooperation and Conflict,* 23, 4 (1988): 179–196.

Newman, Graeme R. and Michael J. Lynch. "From Feuding to Terrorism: The Ideology of Vengeance," *Contemporary Crises,* 11, 3 (1987): 223–242.

Norton, Augustus R., and Martin H. Greenberg, eds. *Studies in Nuclear Terrorism.* Boston: G. K. Hall and Company, 1979. 465 p.

Norton, Graham. "Tourism and International Terrorism," *World Today,* 43, 2 (1987): 30–32.

Oakley, Robert. "International Terrorism," *Foreign Affairs,* 65, 3 (1987): 611–629.

Ochberg, Frank M. and David A. Soskis, *Victims of Terrorism.* Boulder, Colorado: Westview Press, 1982. 200 p.

O'Neill, Bard E. *Insurgency and Terrorism: Inside Modern Revolutionary Warfare.* New York: Pergamon Press, 1990. 171 p.

O'Neill, Bard E., Donald J. Alberts and William R. Henton. *Insurgency in the Modern World.* Boulder, Colorado: Westview Press, 1980. 291 p.

O'Sullivan, Noel, ed. *Terrorism, Ideology and Revolution.* Brighton, U.K.: Wheatsheaf Books Ltd., 1986. 232 p.

Pierre, Andrew J. "The Politics of International Terrorism." *Orbis,* 19, 4 (1976): 1251–1269.

Pluchinsky, Dennis. "Terrorist Documentation," *Terrorism,* 14, 4 (1991): 241–252.

Pluchinsky, Dennis A. "Academic Research on European Terrorist Developments: Pleas from a Government Terrorism Analyst," *Studies in Conflict and Terrorism,* 15, 1 (1992): 13–24.

Poland, James M. *Understanding Terrorism: Groups, Strategies, and Responses.* Englewood Cliffs, New Jersey: Prentice Hall, 1988. 265 p.

Price, H. Edward Jr. "The Strategy and Tactics of Revolutionary Terrorism." *Comparative Studies in Society and History,* 19 (January 1977): 52–66.

Rapoport, David C., ed. *Inside Terrorist Organizations.* New York: Columbia University Press, 1988. 259 p.

Rapoport, David C. and Yonah Alexander, eds. *The Morality of Terrorism: Religious and Secular Justifications.* New York: Pergamon Press, 1982. 375 p.

Reich, Walter, ed. *Origins of Terrorism: Psychologies, Ideologies, Theologies, States of Mind.* Cambridge: Cambridge University Press, 1990. 289 p.

Rubenstein, Richard. *Alchemists of Revolution: Terrorism in the Modern World.* New York: Basic Books, 1987. 266 p.

Sandler, Todd, John T. Tschirhart, and Jon Cauley. "A Theoretical Analysis of Transnational Terrorism," *American Political Science Review,* 77, 1 (1983): 36–54.

Schaerf, Carlo, and David Carlton, eds. *Contemporary Terror: Studies in Substate Violence.* New York: St. Martin's Press, 1978. 231 p.

Schlagheck, Donna. *International Terrorism: An Introduction to the Concepts and Actors.* Lexington, Massachusetts: Lexington Books, 1988. 163 p.

Sederberg, Peter C. "Defining Terrorism," *Terrorism: Contending Trends in Contemporary Research,* in Schechterman, Bernard and Slann, Martin, eds., *Violence and Terrorism 91/92.* Sluice Dock, Guilford, Connecticut: Dushkin Publishing Group, Inc. pp. 6–8.

Segaller, Stephan. *Invisible Armies: Terrorism into the 1990s.* London: Sphere, 1987. 323 p.

Shafer, D. Michael. *Deadly Paradigms: The Failure of U.S. Counterinsurgency Policy.* Princeton: Princeton University Press, 1988. 331 p.

Shain, Yossi. "The War of Governments against Their Opposition in Exile," *Government and Opposition,* 24, 3 (1989): 341–356.

Sick, Gary. "Terrorism: Its Political Uses and Abuses," *SAIS Review,* 7, 1 (1987): 11–26.

Slann, Martin and Bernard Schechtermann, eds. *Multidimensional Terrorism.* Boulder, Colorado: Lynne Rienner, 1987. 138 p.

Sobel, Lester A., ed. *Political Terrorism, 1975–1978.* 2 volumes. New York: Facts on File, 1978. Volume 1, 328 p., volume 2, 292 p.

Sproat, Peter Alan. "Can the State Be Terrorist?," *Terrorism,* 14, 1 (1991): 19–30.

Sterling, Claire. *The Terror Network: The Secret War of International Terrorism.* New York: Holt, Rinehart, and Winston, 1981. 357 p.

Stohl, Michael. "National Interests and State Terrorism in International Affairs," *Political Science,* 36, 1 (1984): 37–52.

Stohl, Michael. *Terrible Beyond Endurance? The Foreign Policy of State Terrorism.* New York: Greenwood, 1988. 360 p.

Tugwell, Maurice A., "Guilt Transfer," in Rapoport, David C. and Yonah Alexander, eds. *The Morality of Terrorism: Religious and Secular Justifications.* New York: Pergamon Press, 1982. pp. 275–289.

Wallack, Michael. "Terrorism and 'Compellence'," *International Perspectives,* (November-December 1987): 13–16.

Weinberg, Leonard and Paul Davis. *Introduction to Political Terrorism.* New York: McGraw-Hill, 1989.

Wilkinson, Paul. "The Future of Terrorism," *Futures,* 20, 5 (1988): 493–505.

Wilkinson, Paul and Alasdair M. Stewart, eds. *Contemporary Research on Terrorism.* (Aberdeen: Aberdeen University Press, 1987). 634 p.

Wilkinson, Paul, ed. *British Perspectives on Terrorism.* London: George Allen & Unwin, 1991.

Wilkinson, Paul. *Terrorism and the Liberal State.* New York: John Wiley and Sons, 1978. 257 p.

Wilkinson, Paul. *Political Terrorism.* New York: John Wiley and Sons, 1974. 159 p.

Windsor, Philip. "Terrorism and International Order," *Atlantic Community Quarterly,* 25, 2 (1987): 201–209.

III. OPERATIONAL ASPECTS OF TERRORISM

Badolato, Edward V. "Environmental Terrorism: A Case Study," *Terrorism,* 14, 4 (1991): 237–240.

Diehl, Paul F. "Avoiding Another Beirut Disaster for the Employment of U.S. Troops in Peacekeeping Roles," *Conflict,* 8, 4 (1988): 261–270.

Dobson, Christopher, and Ronald Payne. *The Terrorists, Their Weapons, Leaders and Tactics.* New York: Facts on File, 1982.

Holden, Robert T. "The Contagiousness of Aircraft Hijacking," *American Journal of Sociology,* 91, 4 (1986): 874–904.

Jenkins, Brian M. "Defense against Terrorism," *Political Science Quarterly,* 101, 5 (1986): 773–786.

Livingston, Neil C. "Death Squads," *World Affairs* 146 (Winter 1984): 42–53.

Livingston, Neil C. "Fighting Terrorism: The Private Sector," *Conflict: An International Journal for Conflict and Policy Studies,* 3, 2–3 (1982): 177–222.

McGeorge, Harvey J., II. "Kinetics of Terrorism," *World Affairs,* 146, 1 (1983): 23–41.

Sandler, Todd, and John L. Scott. "Terrorist Success in Hostage-Taking Incidents: An Empirical Study," *Journal of Conflict Resolution,* 31, 1 (1987): 35–53.

Sloan, Stephen. "International Terrorism: Academic Quest, Operational Art and Policy Implications," *Journal of International Affairs,* 32 (Spring/Summer 1978): 1–5.

Sloan, Stephen. *Simulating Terrorism.* Norman, Oklahoma: University of Oklahoma Press, 1981. 158 p.

Snitch, Thomas H. "Terrorism and International Assassinations: A Transnational Assessment, 1968–1980," *Annals of the American Academy of Political and Social Science,* 463 (September 1982): 54–68.

Wolf, John B. "Organization and Management Practices of Urban Terrorist Groups." *Terrorism,* 1, 2 (1978): 169–186.

Wolf, John B. "Urban Terrorist Operations." *Police Journal* (England), 49 (October-December 1976): 277–284.

Zawodny, J. K. "In Organizational Problems and the Sources of Tensions of Terrorist Movements as Catalysts of Violence," *Terrorism: An International Journal,* 1, 3 & 4 (1978): 277–285.

Zawodny, J. K. "Infrastructures of Terrorist Organizations," in Freedman, Lawrence Zelic and Yonah Alexander, eds. *Perspectives on Terrorism.* Wilmington, Delaware: Scholarly Resources Inc., 1983. 254 p.

IV. INTERNATIONAL AND DOMESTIC LEGAL ISSUES

Abramovsky, Abraham. "Multilateral Conventions for the Suppression of Unlawful Seizure and Interference with Aircraft,'' *Columbia Journal of Transnational Law,* 14, 1–3 (1975): (1) 381–405, (2) 268–300, and (3) 451–484.

Achille Lauro Affair (Legal Documents). ''United State Legislation; Act for the Prevention and Punishment of the Crime of Hostage-Taking and Aircraft Sabotage; Arrest Warrant and Criminal Complaint for Individuals in *Achille Lauro* Incident Based on the Act; International Security and Development Cooperation Act of 1985, Title V on International Terrorism and Foreign Airport Security; House and Concurrent Resolution 228 on International Cooperation in Combatting Terrorism,'' *International Legal Materials,* 24, 6 (1985): 1551–1564.

Achille Lauro Affair (Legal Documents). ''United Nations Statement by the President of the Security Council Condemning Terrorism,'' *International Legal Materials,* 24, 6 (1985): 1565–1566.

Almond, Harry H. Jr. ''The Legal Regulation of International Terrorism,'' *Conflict: An International Journal for Conflict and Policy Studies,* 3, 2–3 (1982): 143–166.

Bassiouni, M. Cherif, ed. *International Terrorism and Political Crimes: Proceedings of the Third Conference on Terrorism and Political Crimes, Syracuse, Italy.* Springfield, Illinois: Charles C. Thomas, 1974. 594 p.

Berman, Jerry J. and Morton H. Halperin. ''Protecting Our Freedoms,'' *Society,* 4, 3 (March-April 1982): 71–74.

Borkowski, George M. ''Use of Force: Interception of Aircraft,'' *Harvard International Law Review,* 27, 2 (1986): 761 et seq.

Braungart, Richard G. and Margaret M. Braungart. ''International Terrorism: Background and Response,'' *Journal of Political and Military Sociology,* 9, 2 (1981): 263–288.

Caras, James. ''Economic Sanctions: United States Sanctions Against Libya,'' *Harvard International Law Review,* 27, 2 (1986): 672–678.

Cassese, Antonio. *Terrorism, Politics, and Law: The Achille Lauro Affair.* London: Basil Blackwell, 1989. 162 p.

Chamberlain, Kevin. ''Collective Suspension of Air Services with States Which Harbour Hijackers,'' *International and Comparative Law Quarterly,* 32, 3 (1983): 616–632.

Chinkin, Christine. ''The Foreign Affairs Powers of the U.S. President and the Iranian Hostages Agreement: Dames and Moore v. Regan,'' *International and Comparative Law Quarterly,* 32, 3 (July 1983): 600–615.

Dean, Benjamin P. ''Self-Determination and U.S. Support of Insurgents: A Policy-Analysis Model,'' *Military Law Review,* 122, (Fall): 149–220.

Donelan, Michael. ''Terrorism: Who Is a Legitimate Target?,'' *Review of International Studies,* 13, 3 (1987): 229–234.

Dowling, Kathryn. ''Civil Rights, Human Rights, and Terrorism in Northern Ireland,'' *Journal of Intergroup Relations,* 7, 4 (1979–80): 3–23.

Feith, Douglas J. ''The Law of War: The Terrorists Are Rolled Back,'' *Atlantic Community Quarterly,* 25, 2 (1987): 210–212.

Frey, Bruno S. ''Fighting Political Terrorism by Refusing Recognition,'' *Journal of Public Policy,* 7, 2 (1987): 179–188.

Gilbert, Geoffrey S. ''Terrorism and the Political Offense Exemption Reappraised,'' *International and Comparative Law Quarterly,* 34, 4 (1985): 695–723.

Halberstam, Malvina. "Terrorism on the High Seas: The *Achille Lauro,* Piracy, and IMO Convention on Maritime Safety," *American Journal of International Law,* 82, 2 (1988): 269–310.

International Civil Aviation Organization. "Excerpts from Report of ICAO Fact-Finding Investigation pursuant to Decision of ICAO Council of July 14, 1988," *American Journal of International Law,* 83, 2 (1989): 332–347.

Kuber, Douglas. "A Sewing Lesson in Political Offense Determinations: Stitching-Up the International Terrorist's Loophole," *Hastings International and Comparative Law Review,* 10, 2 (1987): 499–524.

Murphy, John F. *State Support of International Terrorism: Legal, Political, and Economic Dimensions.* Boulder, Colorado: Westview Press, 1989. 128 p.

Murphy, John F. "The Need for International Cooperation in Combatting Terrorism," *Terrorism,* 13, 6 (1990): 381–396.

Paasche, Franz W. "The Use of Force in Combatting Terrorism," *Columbia Journal of Transnational Law,* 25, 2 (1987): 377–402.

Paust, Jordan J. "The Link Between Human Rights and Terrorism and Its Implications for the Law of State Responsibility," *Hastings International and Comparative Law Review,* 11, 1 (1987): 41–54.

Paust, Jordan J. "Terrorism and 'Terrorism-Specific' Statutes," *Terrorism,* 7, 2 (1984): 233–239.

Porter, Jack Nusan, ed. *Genocide and Human Rights.* Washington, D.C.: University Press of America, 1982. 353 p.

Quigley, John. "Government Vigilantes at Large: The Danger to Human Rights from Kidnapping of Suspected Terrorists," *Human Rights Quarterly,* 10, 2 (1988): 193–213.

Rajput, R. S. "International Conventions on Aerial Hijacking: An Approach to Combat Terrorism," *Indian Journal of Political Science,* 51, 1 (1990): 98–125.

Rubin, Alfred P. "Current Legal Approaches to International Terrorism," *Terrorism,* 13, 4–5 (1990): 277–298.

Rubner, Michael. "Antiterrorism and the Withering Away of the 1973 War Powers Resolution," *Political Science Quarterly,* 102, 2 (1987): 193–216.

Schachter, Oscar. "Self-Help in International Law: U.S. Action in the Iranian Hostage Crisis," *Journal of International Studies,* 37, 2 (1984): 231–246.

Schlaefer, Cindy Verne. "American Courts and Modern Terrorism: The Politics of Extradition," *New York University Journal of International Law and Politics,* 13, 3 (1981): 617–643.

Schuetz, G. Gregory. "Apprehending Terrorists Overseas under United States and International Law: A Case Study of the Fawaz Younis Arrest," *Harvard International Law Journal,* 29, 2 (1988): 499–532.

Smith, Brent L. "Antiterrorism Legislation in the United States: Problems and Implications," *Terrorism,* 7, 2 (1984): 213–31.

Sofaer, Abraham D. "Terrorism and the Law," *Foreign Affairs,* 64, 5 (1986): 901–923.

Stein, Ted L. "Contempt, Crisis, and the Court: The World Court and the Hostage Rescue Attempt," *American Journal of International Law,* 76, 3 (1982): 499–531.

Temple, Caleb L. "Terrorism and International Law: Two Barriers to Consensus," *Conflict,* 10, 3 (1990): 215–226.

Tharp, Paul A., Jr. "The Laws of War as a Potential Legal Regime for the Control of Terrorist Activities," *Journal of International Affairs,* 32 (Spring/Summer 1978): 81–100.

Warbrick, Colin. "The Prevention of Terrorism (Temporary Provisions) Act 1976 and the European Convention on Human Rights: The McVeigh Case," *International and Comparative Law Quarterly,* 32, 3 (July 1983): 757 et seq.

V. POLICE AND LAW-ENFORCEMENT ISSUES

Aggarwala, Narinder. "Political Aspects of Hijacking," *International Conciliation,* 585 (1971): 7–27.

Blair, Bruce G. and Garry D. Brewer. "The Terrorist Threat to World Nuclear Programs," *Journal of Conflict Resolution,* 21, 3 (1977): 379–403.

Bolz, Frank, Jr., Kenneth J. Dudonis, and David P. Schulz. *The Counter-Terrorism Handbook: Tactics, Procedures, and Techniques.* Elsevier Series in Practical Aspects of Criminal and Forensic Investigations, No. 16. New York: Elsevier Science Publishing Co., 1990. 233 p.

Boyce, Daniel. "Narco-Terrorism," *FBI Law Enforcement Bulletin,* 56, 11 (October 1987): 24–27.

Brock, David. "The World of Narcoterrorism," *American Spectator,* 22 (June 1989): 24–28.

Clutterbuck, Richard. "Air Piracy: A Gleam of Hope for the World," *Army Quarterly and Defence Journal,* 104, 4 (1974): 402–408.

Courter, Jim. "Protecting Our Citizens," *Policy Review,* 36 (Spring 1986): 10–17.

Crenshaw, William A. "Civil Aviation: Target for Terrorism," *Annals of the American Academy of Political and Social Science,* 498 (July 1988): 60–69.

Fenello, Michael. "Technical Prevention of Air Piracy," *International Conciliation,* 585 (1971): 28–41.

Gregory, F.E.C. "The British Police and Terrorism," *Terrorism,* 5, 1–2 (1981): 107–123.

Gregory, F.E.C. "Police Cooperation and Integration in the European Community: Proposals, Problems and Prospects," *Terrorism,* 14, 3 (1991): 145–156.

Harris, John W., Jr.. "Domestic Terrorism in the 1980's," *FBI Law Enforcement Bulletin,* 56, 11 (October 1987): 5–13.

Horchem, Hans J. "Terrorism and Government Response: The German Response," *Jerusalem Journal of International Relations,* 4, 3 (1980): 43–55.

Hughes, Martin. "Terror and Negotiation," *Terrorism and Political Violence,* 2, 1 (Spring 1990) in Schechterman, Bernard and Slann, Martin, eds., *Violence and Terrorism 91/92.* Sluice Dock, Guilford, Connecticut: Dushkin Publishing Group, Inc. pp. 202–205.

Jenkins, Brian Michael. "Terrorist Threat to Commercial Aviation," *IDF Journal,* (Fall 1989) in Schechterman, Bernard and Slann, Martin, eds., *Violence and Terrorism 91/92.* Sluice Dock, Guilford, Connecticut: Dushkin Publishing Group, Inc. pp. 218–221.

Landes, William M. "An Economic Study of U.S. Aircraft Hijacking, 1961–1976," *Journal of Law and Economics*, 21, 1 (1978): 1–31.

Martell, D. F. "FBI's Expanding Role in International Terrorism Investigations," *FBI Law Enforcement Bulletin*, 56, 11 (October 1987): 28–32.

Pizer, Harry and Stephen Sloan. *Corporate Aviation Security: The Next Frontier in Aerospace Operations*. Norman, Oklahoma: University of Oklahoma Press, 1992. 161 p.

Pockrass, Robert M. "The Police Response to Terrorism," *Conflict*, 6, 4 (1986): 287–306.

Pockrass, Robert M. "Building a Civil Police Counter-Terrorist Team," *Conflict*, 8, 4 (1988): 327–332.

Pomerantz, Steve L. "The FBI and Terrorism," *FBI Law Enforcement Bulletin*, 56, 11 (October 1987): 14–17.

Revell, Oliver B. "Terrorism Today," *FBI Law Enforcement Bulletin*, 56, 11 (October 1987): 1–4.

Sessions, William S. "The FBI's Mission in Countering Terrorism," *Terrorism*, 13, 1 (1990): 1–6.

St. John, Peter. *Air Piracy, Airport Security, and International Terrorism: Winning the War Against Hijackers*. New York: Quorum Books, 1991. 280 p.

Stone, J.L., Jr. "Irish Terrorism Investigations," *FBI Law Enforcement Bulletin*, 56, 11 (October 1987): 18–23.

U.S. Department of Justice, Law Assistance Administration. *Disorders and Terrorism: Report of the Task Force on*

Disorders and Terrorism. Washington, D.C.: Government Printing Office, 1976.

U.S. Department of State. "Patterns of Global Terrorism," *Terrorism,* 14, 4 (1991): 253 et seq.

Vincent, Billie H. "Aviation Security and Terrorism," *Terrorism,* 13, 6 (1990): 397–440.

Wolf, John B. "Analytical Framework for the Study and Control of Agitational Terrorism." *Police Journal* (England), 49 (July-September 1976): 165–171.

VI. NATIONAL SECURITY POLICY AND COUNTERTERRORISM

Alexander, Yonah. "Special Report: Technology Against Terrorism, The Federal Effort," *Terrorism,* 14, 2 (1991): 111 et seq.

Alexander, Yonah. "Will Terrorists Use Chemical Weapons?," *JINSA Security Affairs,* (June-July 1990) in Schechterman, Bernard and Slann, Martin, eds., *Violence and Terrorism 91/92.* Sluice Dock, Guilford, Connecticut: Dushkin Publishing Group, Inc. pp. 157.

Alexander, Yonah. "Fighting International Terrorism: What Does and What Does Not Work," *The World & I,* (March 1989) in Schechterman, Bernard and Slann, Martin, eds., *Violence and Terrorism 91/92.* Sluice Dock, Guilford, Connecticut: Dushkin Publishing Group, Inc. pp. 194–197.

Amit, Meir. "Diminishing the Threat Against Terrorism: Intelligence and the War Against Terrorism," *IDF Journal,* (Fall 1989) in Schechterman, Bernard and Slann, Martin, eds., *Violence and Terrorism 91/92.* Sluice Dock, Guilford, Connecticut: Dushkin Publishing Group, Inc. pp. 200–201.

Behm, Allan J., and Michael J. Palmer. "Coordinating Counterterrorism: A Strategic Approach to a Changing Threat,"
Terrorism, 14, 3 (1991): 171–194.

Berman, Jerry J. and Morton H. Halperin. "Protecting Our
Freedoms," *Society,* 4, 3 (March-April 1982): 71–74.

Bernstein, Alvin H. "Iran's Low-Intensity War against the United
States," *Orbis,* 30, 1 (1986): 149–167.

Bishop, Joseph W., Jr. "Can Democracy Defend Itself Against
Terrorism?," *Commentary,* 65, 5 (1978): 55–62.

Bodansky, Yossef. *Target America: Terrorism in the U.S. Today.*
New York, N.Y.: Shapolsky Publishers, Inc., 1993. 461 p.

Borchgrave, Arnaud de. "Disseminating Disinformation," *Society,* 4, 3 (March-April 1982): 79–81.

Bremer, L. Paul, III. "Continuing the Fight against Terrorism,"
Terrorism, 12, 2 (1989): 81–88.

Bremer, L. Paul, III. "Terrorism: Myth and Reality," U.S.
Department of State, *Current Policy No. 1047* (February 4,
1988), in Schechterman, Bernard and Slann, Martin, eds.,
Violence and Terrorism 91/92. Sluice Dock, Guilford, Connecticut: Dushkin Publishing Group, Inc. pp. 13–14.

Brenchley, Frank. "Living With Terrorism: The Problem of Air
Piracy," *Conflict Studies,* 184 (1986).

Brenchley, Frank. "Diplomatic Immunities and State-Sponsored
Terrorism," *Conflict Studies,* 164 (1984).

Burgess, William H., III. "Iranian Special Operations in the Iran-
Iraq War: Implications for the United States," *Conflict,* 8, 1
(1988): 22–40.

Bush, George. "Prelude to Retaliation: Building a Governmental Consensus on Terrorism," *SAIS Review*, 7, 1 (1987): 1–10.

Celmer, Marc A. *Terrorism, U.S. Strategy, and Reagan Policies.* Westport, Connecticut: Greenwood Press, 1987. 132 p.

Clutterback, Richard. *Terrorism and Guerrilla Warfare: Forecasts and Remedies.* London: Routledge, Chapman and Hall, Inc., 1990. 235 p.

Clutterback, Richard. *Kidnap, Hijack and Extortion: The Response.* London: Macmillan Press, Ltd., 1987.

Corr, Edwin G., and Stephen Sloan, eds., *Low Intensity Conflict: Old Threats in a New World.* Boulder, Colorado: Westview, 1992. 317 p.

Crabtree, Richard D. "U.S. Policy for Countering Terrorism: The Intelligence Dimension," *Conflict Quarterly*, 6, 1 (Winter 1986).

Crenshaw, William A. "Civil Aviation: Target for Terrorism," *Annals of the American Academy of Political and Social Science*, 498 (July 1988): 60–69.

DiLaura, Arnold E. "Preventing Terrorism: An Analysis of National Strategy," *SAIS Review*, 7, 1 (1987): 27–38.

Donelan, Michael. "Terrorism: Who Is a Legitimate Target?," *Review of International Studies*, 13, 3 (1987): 229–234.

Earl, Robert L. "A Matter of Principle," *U.S. Naval Institute Proceedings*, 109, 2 (1983): 29–36.

Frey, Bruno S. "Fighting Political Terrorism by Refusing Recognition," *Journal of Public Policy*, 7, 2 (1987): 179–188.

Gal-Or, Noemi, ed. *Tolerating Terrorism in the West: An International Survey.* London: Routledge, Chapman and Hall, 1991. 172 p.

Goldman, John Richard. "Terrorism and the Role of Security Strategies," *Journal of Political Science,* 14, 1–2 (1986): 1–9.

Green, L. C. "Terrorism and Its Response," *Terrorism,* 8 (1985): 33–77.

Hastedt, Glenn. "Intelligence Failure and Terrorism: The Attack on the Marines in Beirut," *Conflict Quarterly,* 8, 2 (Spring 1988): 7–22.

Hudson, Rex A. "Dealing with International Hostage-Taking: Alternatives to Reactive Counterterrorist Assaults," *Terrorism,* 12, 3 (1989): 321 et seq.

Jenkins, Brian M. RAND/R-3302-AF, *International Terrorism: The Other World War.* Santa Monica, California: Rand Corporation, 1985. 29 p.

Jenkins, Brian M. "A U.S. Strategy for Combatting Terrorism," *Conflict: An International Journal for Conflict and Policy Studies,* 3, 2–3 (1981): 167–176.

Johns, Milton C. "The Reagan Administration's Response to State-Sponsored Terrorism," *Conflict,* 8, 4 (1988): 241–260.

Jones, William F. W. "Terrorism and Electrical Energy Interrruption: The Role of The Federal Emergency Management Agency," *Terrorism,* 13, 6 (1990): 441–446.

Kerr, Donald M. "Coping With Terrorism," *Terrorism,* 8 (1985): 113–126.

Klare, Michael T. and Peter Kornblush, eds. *Low Intensity Warfare: Counterinsurgency, Proinsurgency, and Antiterrorism in the Eighties.* New York: Pantheon, 1988. 250 p.

Kumamoto, Robert. "Diplomacy from Below: International Terrorism and American Foreign Relations, 1945–1962," *Terrorism,* 14, 1 (1991): 31–48.

Larsen, David L. "The American Response to the Iranian Hostage Crisis: 444 Days of Decision," *International Social Science Review,* 57, 3–4 (1982): 195–209.

Lee, Dwight R. and Todd Sandler. "On The Optimal Retaliation against Terrorists: The Paid-Rider Option," *Public Choice,* 6, 2 (1989): 141–152.

Leventhal, Paul L., and Milton M. Hoenig. "The Hidden Danger: Risks of Nuclear Terrorism," *Terrorism,* 10, 1 (1987): 1–22.

Livingston, Neil C. "Fighting Terrorism: The Private Sector," *Conflict: An International Journal for Conflict and Policy Studies,* 3, 2–3 (1982): 177–222.

MacWilson, Alastair C. *Hostage-Taking Terrorism: Incident-Response Strategy.* New York: St. Martin's Press, 1992. 263 p.

Martin, David and John Walcott. *Best Laid Plans: The Inside Story of America's War Against Terrorism.* New York: Harper & Row, 1988. 392 p.

Maury, John M. "Intelligence Secrets?," *Society,* 4, 3 (March-April 1982): 76–77.

McGeorge, Harvey J., II. "Plan Carefully, Rehearse Thoroughly, Execute Violently: The Tactical Response to Hostage Situations," *World Affairs,* 146, 1 (1983): 59–68.

McGeorge, Harvey J., II. "Kinetics of Terrorism," *World Affairs,* 146, 1 (Summer 1983): 23–41.

Mullins, Wayman C. "Stopping Terrorism . . . The Problems Posed by the Organizational Infrastructure of Terrorist Organizations," *Journal of Contemporary Criminal Justice,* (December 1988) in Schechterman, Bernard and Slann, Martin, eds., *Violence and Terrorism 91/92.* Sluice Dock, Guilford, Connecticut: Dushkin Publishing Group, Inc. pp. 92–96.

Netanyahu, Benjamin, ed. *Terrorism: How the West Can Win.* New York: Farrar, Straus, Giroux, 1986. 254 p.

Ofri, Arie. "Intelligence and Counterterrorism," *Orbis,* 28, 1 (1984): 41–52.

O'Neill, Bard E. *Insurgency and Terrorism: Inside Modern Revolutionary Warfare.* New York: Pergamon Press, 1990. 171 p.

O'Neill, Bard E., William R. Henton, and Donald J. Alberts. *Insurgency in the Modern World.* Boulder, Colorado: Westview Press, 1980. 291 p.

Oots, Kent L. "Bargaining with Terrorists: Organizational Considerations," *Terrorism,* 13, 2 (1990): 145–158.

Post, Jerrold M. "Prospects for Nuclear Terrorism: Psychological Motivations and Constraints," *Conflict Quarterly,* 7, 3 (Summer 1987): 47–58.

Prince, James. "Is There a Role for Intelligence in Combatting Terrorism?," *Conflict,* 9, 3 (1989): 301–318.

Probst, Peter. "Future Trends: Some Observations," *Terrorism,* 14, 4 (1991): 233–236.

Raufer, Xavier, "Gray Areas: A New Security Threat," *Political Warfare: Intelligence, Activities, Measures and Intelligence Report*, 20 (Spring 1992): 1.

Revell, Oliver B. "Structure of Counterterrorism Planning and Operations in the United States," *Terrorism*, 14, 3 (1991): 135–144.

Rubin, Barry, ed. *Terrorism and Politics*. New York: St. Martin's Press, 1991. 174 p.

Rubin, Barry, ed. *The Politics of Counterterrorism: The Ordeal of Democratic States*. Washington, D.C.: Johns Hopkins Foreign Policy Institute, 1990. 222 p.

Schultz, Richard H., and Stephen Sloan, eds. *Responding to the Terrorist Threat: Security and Crisis Management*. New York: Pergamon Press, 1980. 261 p.

Schultz, Richard H., and Stephen Sloan. "International Terrorism: The Nature of the Threat," in R. H. Schultz, and S. Sloan, eds., *Responding to the Terrorist Threat: Security and Crisis Management*. New York: Pergamon Press, 1980. pp. 1–7.

Schultz, Richard H., and Stephen Sloan. "Terrorism: An Objective Act, A Subjective Reality," in R. H. Schultz, and S. Sloan, eds., *Responding to the Terrorist Threat: Security and Crisis Management*. New York: Pergamon Press, 1980. pp. 245–254.

Shafer, D. Michael. "The Unlearned Lessons of Counterinsurgency," *Political Science Quarterly*, 103, 1 (1988): 57–80.

Simon, Jeffrey D. RAND/R-3840-C3I, *U.S. Countermeasures Against International Terrorism*. Santa Monica, California: Rand Corporation, 1990. 44 p.

Simon, Jeffrey D. RAND/R-3423-RC, *Misperceiving the Terrorist Threat.* Santa Monica, California: Rand Corporation, 1987. 17 p.

Sloan, Stephen. "In Search of a Counterterrorism Doctrine," *Military Review,* 66, 1 (June 1986): 44–48.

Sloan, Stephen. *Beating International Terrorism: An Action Strategy for Preemption and Punishment.* Maxwell Air Force Base, Alabama: Air University Press, 1986. 63 p.

Sloan, Stephen. "U.S. Anti-Terrorism Policies: Lessons to be Learned to Meet an Enduring and Changing Threat," *Terrorism and Political Violence,* 5, 1 (Spring 1993): 106–131.

Sloan, Stephen, and Richard Kearney. "Non-Territorial Terrorism: An Empirical Approach to Policy Formation," *Conflict: An International Journal for Conflict and Policy,* 1 (1978): 131–144.

Smith, G. Davidson. *Combatting Terrorism.* London: Routledge, Chapman and Hall, Inc., 1990. 307 p.

Soule, John W. "Problems in Applying Counterterrorism to Prevent Terrorism: Two Decades of Violence in Northern Ireland Reconsidered," *Terrorism,* 12, 1 (1989): 31–46.

Sterling, Claire. "Theft from Left and Right," *Society,* 4, 3 (March-April 1982): 82–83.

St. John, Peter. "Analysis and Response of a Decade of Terrorism," *International Perspectives,* (September-October, 1981): 2–5.

Stohl, Michael. "National Interests and State Terrorism in International Affairs," *Political Science,* 36, 1 (1984): 37–52.

Thompson, Leroy. *The Rescuers: The World's Top Anti-Terrorist Units.* Trowbridge, Wiltshire, U.K.: David and Charles Publishers, 1986. 255 p.

U.S. Congress. "Act for the Prevention and Punishment of the Crime of Hostage Taking and Aircraft Sabotage," *International Legal Materials,* 24, 6 (1985): 1551–1552.

Vice President's Task Force on Combatting Terrorism. Public Report of the Vice President's Task Force on Combatting Terrorism. Washington, D.C.: U.S. Government Printing Office, 1986.

Wagner-Pacifici, Robin. "Negotiation in the Aldo Moro Affair: The Suppressed Alternative in a Case of Symbolic Politics," *Politics and Society,* 12, 4 (1983): 487–517.

Waugh, William L., Jr. *Terrorism and Emergency Management: Policy and Administration.* New York: Marcel Dekker, Inc., 1990. 215 p.

Williard, Richard K. "Maintaining Security," *Society,* 4, 3 (March- April 1982): 75–76.

Wolf, John B. "Terrorist Manipulation of the Democratic Process," *Police Journal* (England), 48 (April-June 1975): 102–112.

Wright, Jeffrey W. "Terrorism: A Mode of Warfare," *Military Review,* 64, 10 (1984): 35–45.

Zamir, Meir. "Iran: Consequences of the Abortive Attempt to Rescue the American Hostages," *Conflict,* 3, 1 (198): 55–77.

VII. TERRORISM AND THE MASS MEDIA

Alexander, Yonah. "Terrorism, the Media and the Police," *Journal of International Affairs,* 32, 1 (1978): 101–113.

Bassiouni, M. Cherif. "Media Coverage of Terrorism: The Law and the Public," *Journal of Communication,* 32, 2 (1982): 128–143.

Bremer, L. Paul, III. "Terrorism, the Media, and the Government," *Parameters: U.S. Army War College Quarterly,* 18, 1 (1988): 52–59.

Bremer, L. Paul, III. "Terrorism and the Media," U.S. Department of State, *Current Policy No. 986* (June 25, 1987) in Schechterman, Bernard and Slann, Martin, eds., *Violence and Terrorism 91/92.* Sluice Dock, Guilford, Connecticut: Dushkin Publishing Group, Inc. pp. 114–116.

Clutterback, Richard. *The Media and Political Violence.* London: Macmillan Press, Ltd., 1987.

Crelinsten, Ronald D. "Images of Terrorism in the Media," *Terrorism,* 12, (1989): 167–198.

Dowling, Ralph E. "Terrorist Motivation: Media Coverage or Human Social Action?," *Conflict Quarterly,* 9, 3 (Summer 1989): 41–53.

Farnen, Russell F. "Terrorism and the Mass Media: A Systemic Analysis of a Symbiotic Process," *Terrorism,* 13, 2 (1990): 99–144.

Lumley, Bob and Philip Schlesinger. "The Press, the State and Its Enemies: The Italian Case," *Sociological Review* (United Kingdom), 30, 4 (1982): 603–626.

Miller, Abraham H. "Terrorism and the Media: Lessons from the British Experience," *The Heritage Foundation Lectures* (1990) in Schechterman, Bernard and Slann, Martin, eds., *Violence and Terrorism 91/92.* Sluice Dock, Guilford, Connecticut: Dushkin Publishing Group, Inc. pp. 129–133.

Nacos, Brigitte, David P. Fan, and John T. Young. "Terrorism and the Print Media: The 1985 TWA Hostage Crisis," *Terrorism,* 12, 2 (1989): 107–116.

Picard, Robert G., and Rhonda S. Sheets. "Terrorism and the News Media: A Research Bibliography, Part III," *Political Communication and Persuasion,* 4, 3 (1987): 217 et seq.

Picard, Robert G., and Rhonda S. Sheets. "Terrorism and the News Media: A Research Bibliography, Part IV," *Political Communication and Persuasion,* 4, 4 (1987): 325 et seq.

Schlesinger, Philip. " 'Terrorism,' the Media, and the Liberal-Democratic State: A Critique of the Orthodoxy," *Social Research,* 48, 1 (1981): 74–99.

Tugwell, Maurice A. "Terrorism and Propaganda: Problem and Response," *Conflict Quarterly,* 6, 2 (1986): 5–15.

Weimann, Gabriel. "Conceptualizing the Effects of Mass-Mediated Terrorism," *Political Communication and Persuasion,* 4, 3 (1987): 213–216.

World Press Review. "Colombian Journalists Vs. Drug Terrorists," *World Press Review,* (January 1990), pp. 38–41, in Schechterman, Bernard and Slann, Martin, eds., *Violence and Terrorism 91/92.* Sluice Dock, Guilford, Connecticut: Dushkin Publishing Group, Inc. pp. 154–156.

VIII. SOCIOLOGICAL STUDIES

Beeman, William O. "Terrorism: Community Based or State Supported," *American-Arab Affairs,* 16 (Spring 1986): 1–8.

Crenshaw, Martha. "The Logic of Terrorism: Terrorist Behavior as a Product of Strategic Choice," in Walter Reich, ed. *Origins of Terrorism: Psychologies, Ideologies, Theologies,*

States of Mind. Cambridge: Cambridge University Press, 1990. pp. 7–24.

Elliott, Deni. "Family Ties: A Case Study of Coverage of Families and Friends during the Hijacking of TWA 847," *Political Communication and Persuasion*, 5, 1 (1988): 67–76.

Ferracuti, Franco. "A Sociopsychiatric Interpretation of Terrorism," *Annals of the American Academy of Political and Social Science*, 463 (September 1982): 129–140.

Georges-Abeyie, Daniel E. "Political Criminogenesis of Democracy in the Criminal Settler-State: Terror, Terrorism, and Guerrilla Warfare," *Terrorism*, 14, 1 (1991): 145–156.

Hewitt, Christopher. "Terrorism and Public Opinion: A Five Country Comparison," *Terrorism and Political Violence*, (Summer 1990) in Schechterman, Bernard and Slann, Martin, eds., *Violence and Terrorism 91/92*. Sluice Dock, Guilford, Connecticut: Dushkin Publishing Group, Inc. pp. 158–165.

Holden, Robert T. "The Contagiousness of Aircraft Hijacking," *American Journal of Sociology*, 91, 4 (1986): 874–904.

Mason, T. David. "Nonelite Response to State-Sanctioned Terror," *Western Political Quarterly*, 42, 4 (1989): 467–492.

Oots, Kent Layne. "Organizational Perspectives on the Formation and Disintegration of Terrorist Groups," *Terrorism*, 12, 3 (1989): 99–144, 149–152.

Rapoport, David C. "Fear and Trembling in Three Religious Traditions," *American Political Science Review*, 78, 3 (1984): 658–678.

Rapoport, David C. *Assassination and Terrorism.* Toronto: Canadian Broadcasting Company, 1971.

Rapoport, David C. "Why Does Religious Messianism Produce Terror?," in Paul Wilkinson, ed. *Contemporary Research on Terrorism.* (Aberdeen: Aberdeen University Press, 1987). pp. 72–88.

Rapoport, David C. "Messianic Sanctions for Terror," *Comparative Politics,* 20, 2 (1988): 195–214.

Rapoport, David C. "Sacred Terror: A Contemporary Example From Islam," in Walter Reich, ed. *Origins of Terrorism: Psychologies, Ideologies, Theologies, States of Mind.* (Cambridge: Cambridge University Press, 1990). pp. 103–130.

Tugwell, Maurice A. "Terrorism and Propaganda: Problem and Response," *Conflict Quarterly,* 6, 2 (Spring 1986): 5–15.

Turk, Austin T. "Social Dynamics of Terrorism," *Annals of the American Academy of Political and Social Science,* 463 (September 1982): 119–128.

Wasmund, Klaus. "The Political Socialization of Terrorist Groups in West Germany," *Journal of Political and Military Sociology,* 11, 2 (1983): 223–239.

IX. TERRORISM BY REGION

1. North America (Canada and the United States)

Aho, James A. *The Politics of Righteousness: Idaho Christian Patriotism.* Seattle: University of Washington Press, 1990. 323 p.

Anti-Defamation League of B'nai B'rith: Civil Rights Division. "Neo-Nazi Skinheads: A 1990 Status Report." *Terrorism,* 13, 3 (1990): 243–275.

Anti-Defamation League of B'nai B'rith. *Extremism on the Right.* New York: Anti-Defamation League of B'nai B'rith, 1983.

Arostegui, Martin C. "Terrorism in the United States," *Clandestine Tactics and Technology: Group and Area Studies,* 9, 2 (n.d.): 4.

Audsley, David. "Posse Comitatus: An Extremist Tax Protest Group," *TVI Journal,* 6, 1 (Summer 1985): 13–16.

Bell, Robert G. "The U.S. Response to Terrorism Against Civil Aviation," *Orbis,* 19, 4 (1976): 1326–1343.

Center for Democratic Renewal. *Aryan Nations Far Right Underground Movement.* Atlanta, Georgia: Center for Democratic Renewal, 1986. 64 p.

Chapman, Robert D. "State Terrorism," *Conflict,* 3, 4 (1982): 283–298

Clark, Lorne S. "Canada's Initiatives to Combat the Latest Scourge of the Skies," *International Perspectives* (Canada), 1 (1973): 47–51.

Clawson, Patrick. "Coping with Terrorism in the United States," *Orbis,* 33, 3 (1989): 341–357.

Coates, James. *Armed and Dangerous: The Rise of the Survivalist Right.* New York: Hill and Wang, 1987. 294 p.

Collins, J. G. "Terrorism and Animal Rights," *Science* 6 (1990): 4–5.

Coplon, Jeff. "Skinhead Nation," *Rolling Stone,* December 1, 1988, pp. 57–58.

Daley, R. *Target Blue.* New York: Delacorte Press, 1973.

Dennis, Stuart. "The Weathermen," *Government and Opposition* (United Kingdom), 9, 4 (1974): 430–459.

Dolgin, Janet L. *Jewish Identity and the JDL.* Princeton, New Jersey: Princeton University Press, 1977. 189 p.

Edgar, David. "A Crime to Disagree," *New Statesman,* 104 (July 23, 1982).

Flynn, Kevin, and Gary Gerhardt. *The Silent Brotherhood: Inside America's Racist Underground.* New York: The Free Press, 1989. 419 p.

George, John and Laird Wilcox. *Nazis, Communists, Klansmen, and Others on the Fringe: Political Extremism in America.* Buffalo, N.Y.: Prometheus Books, 1992. 523 p.

Gleason, John M. "A Poisson Model of Incidents of International Terrorism in the United States," *Terrorism,* 4, 1–4 (1980): 259–265.

Harris, J. W., Jr. "Domestic Terrorism in the 1980s," *FBI Law Enforcement Bulletin,* 56 (1987): 5–13.

Hoffman, Bruce. "The Cuban Anti-Castro Terrorist Movement," *TVI Journal,* Spring 1984: 15–21.

Hoffman, Bruce. RAND/R-3351, *Terrorism in the United States and the Potential Threat to Nuclear Facilities.* Santa Monica: Rand Corporation, 1986. 56 p.

Hoffman, Bruce. RAND/R-3618, *Recent Trends and Future Prospects of Terrorism in the United States.* Santa Monica: Rand Corporation, May 1988. 71 p.

Holt, Simma. *Terrorism in the Name of God.* Toronto: McClelland and Stewart, 1964.

LaPierre, Laurier. "Quebec: October, 1970," in "The Quebec Question: Two Views," *North American Review,* 256, 3 (1971): 23–33.

Lewis, Gregory L. "The Hood, the Swastika and the Cross: Hate Terrorism in the United States," *Clandestine Tactics and Technology: Technical Notes.* Arlington, Virginia: International Association of Chiefs of Police, 1989.

Marshall, Peter. "Quebec: After the English Conquest," in "The Quebec Question: Two Views," *North American Review,* 256, 3 (1971): 9–23.

Monroe, Charles P. "Addressing Terrorism in the United States," *Annals of the American Academy of Political and Social Science,* 463 (September 1982): 141–148.

Monti, Daniel J. "The Relation Between Terrorism and Domestic Civil Disorders," *Terrorism,* 4, 1–4 (1980): 123–141.

Mulgannon, Terry. "The Animal Liberation Front," *TVI Journal* 5 (Spring 1985).

Mullins, Wayman C. *Terrorist Organizations in the United States.* Springfield, Illinois: Charles C. Thomas Books, 1988. 228 p.

New York State Policy Group on Terrorism, Report on the Brinks Incident. *Terrorism,* 9 (1987): 169–206.

Nice, David C. "Abortion Clinic Bombings as Political Violence," *American Journal of Political Science,* 32 (February 1988): 178–195.

Ross, Jeffrey Ian, and Ted Robert Gurr. "Why Terrorism Subsides: A Comparative Study of Canada and the United States," *Comparative Politics,* 21, 4 (1989): 405–426.

Ross, Jeffrey Ian. "Attributes of Domestic Political Terrorism in Canada," *Terrorism,* 11 (1988): 213–233.

Seymore, Sheri. *Committee of the States.* Mariposa, Calif.: Camden Place Communications Inc., 1991. 406 p.

Stanton, Bill. *Klanwatch: Bringing the Ku Klux Klan to Justice.* New York: Grove Weidenfeld, 1991. 277 p.

Suall, Irwin, and David Lowe. "The Hate Movement Today: A Chronicle of Violence and Disarray," *Terrorism,* 10, 4 (1987): 345–364.

U.S. Senate (1975). United States Senate Committee on the Judiciary: The Weather Underground, Report of the Sub-committee to Investigate the Administration of the Internal Security Act and other Internal Security Laws: Ninety-fourth Congress, First Session; SD catalogue no. Y 4.J 89/2:S.W37.

Wilcox, Michele, and John Lynxwiler. "Abortion Clinic Violence as Terrorism," *Conflict,* 8 (Summer 1988): 5–26.

Woodcock, George, and Ivan Avakumovic. *The Doukhobors.* Toronto: McClelland and Stewart, 1977.

Yerbury, J. C. "The 'Sons of Freedom' Doukhobors and the Canadian State," *Canadian Ethnic Studies,* 16, 2 (1984): 47–70.

2. Central and South America

Adams, James. "The Narc-Farc Connection," in *The Financing of Terror.* London: New English Library, 1986. 293 p.

Anderson, Thomas P. "The Ambiguities of Political Terrorism in Central America," *Terrorism,* 4 , 1–4 (1980): 267–276.

Andreas, Peter and Coletta Youngers. " 'Busting' The Andean Cocaine Industry: America's Counterproductive War on Drugs,'' *World Policy Journal,* 6, 3 (1989): 529–562.

Angell, Alan. "The Chilean Road to Militarism," *International Journal* [Canada], 29, 3 (1974): 393–411.

Asencio, Diego, Nancy Asencio, and Ron Tobias. *Our Man Is Inside.* Boston: Little, Brown, 1983. 244 p.

Bagley, Bruce Michael. "Colombia: The Wrong Strategy," *Foreign Policy,* 77 (Winter 1989–90): 154–171.

Bagley, Bruce Michael. "Colombia and the War on Drugs," *Foreign Affairs,* 67, 1 (1988): 70–92.

Bagley, Bruce Michael. "Colombian Politics: Crisis or Continuity?" *Current History,* 86, 516, (January 1987): 21–24, 40–41.

Baratta, Robert Thomas. "Political Violence in Ecuador and the AVC," *Terrorism,* 10, 3 (1987): 165–174.

Belli, Humberto. *Breaking Faith: The Sandinista Revolution and its Impact on Freedom and Christian Faith in Nicaragua.* Winchester, Illinois: Crossway Books, 1983. 271 p.

Black, George. *Garrison Guatemala.* New York: Monthly Review Press, 1984. 208 p.

Blake, Samuel W. "Totalitarianism in Sandinista Nicaragua," *Studies in Conflict and Terrorism,* 15, 3 (1992): 201–224.

Bonner, Raymond. *Weakness and Deceit: U.S. Policy and El Salvador.* New York: Times Books, 1984. 408 p.

Booth, John A. "Guatemalan Nightmare: Levels of Political Violence," *Journal of Interamerican Studies and World Affairs,* 22, 2 (1980): 195–225.

Browning, David. "Conflicts in El Salvador," *Conflict Studies,* 168 (1984).

Chapman, Robert D. "State Terrorism," *Conflict,* 3, 4 (1982): 283–298

Christian, Shirley. *Nicaragua: Revolution in the Family.* New York: Vintage, 1986. 415 p.

Collett, Merrill. "The Myth of the 'Narco-Guerrillas'," *Nation,* 247, 4 (August 13–20, 1988): 1, 130–34.

Corr, Edwin G., and Courtney E. Prisk. "El Salvador: The FMLN Insurgency and the Prospects for Democracy and Peace," in Edwin G. Corr and Stephen Sloan eds., *Low Intensity Conflict: Old Threats in a New World.* Boulder, Colorado: Westview, 1992. pp. 223–253.

Cross, Benedict (pseud.). "Marxism in Venezuela," *Problems of Communism,* 22 (November-December 1973): 51–70.

Dickey, Christopher. "Behind the Death Squads: Who They Are, How They Work, and Why No One Can Stop Them," *The New Republic,* 189, (December 26, 1983): 16–21.

Falcoff, Mark. *Modern Chile: 1970–1989: A Critical History.* New Brunswick (U.S.A.): Transaction Publishers, 1989.

Fontaine, Roger W. *Terrorism: The Cuban Connections.* New York: Crane Russak, 1988. 199 p.

Gillespie, Richard. *Soldiers of Peron: Argentina's Monteneros.* Oxford: Oxford University Press, 1982. 310 p.

Gott, Richard. *Guerrilla Movements in Latin America.* Garden City: Doubleday, 1972. 626 p.

Halperin, Ernst. *Terrorism in Latin America.* The Washington Papers, No. 33. Beverly Hills: Sage Publications, 1976. 89 p.

Hoffman, Bruce. "The Cuban Anti-Castro Terrorist Movement," *TVI Journal,* Spring 1984: 15–22.

Hoskin, Gary, "Columbia's Political Crisis," *Current History,* 87, 528 (January 1988): 9–12, 38–39.

International Court of Justice. *Military and Paramilitary Activities in and against Nicaragua* (Nicaragua v. United States of America), Merits, 1986.

International Court of Justice. *Nicaragua v. United States of America,* Uncorrected Verbatim Record. September 12, 1985, CR 85/19-September 20, 1985, CR 85/27.

Janke, Peter. "Terrorism in Argentina," *Journal of the Royal United Services Institute for Defense Studies* (United Kingdom), 119, 3 (1974): 43–48.

Johnson, Kenneth F. "On the Guatemalan Political Violence," *Politics and Society,* 4, 1 (1973): 55–82.

Klette, Immanuel J. "U.S. Assistance to Venezuela and Chile in Combatting Insurgency, 1963–1964: Two Cases," *Conflict,* 3, 4 (1982): 227–244.

Lefever, Ernest W. "Murder in Montevideo: The AID/Mitrione Story," *Freedom At Issue,* 21 (1973): 14–16.

LeMoyne, James. "El Salvador's Forgotten War," *Foreign Affairs,* 68 (Summer 1989): 105–125.

Livingston, Neil C. "Death Squads," *World Affairs* 146, 3 (1983–1984): 239–248.

Livingston, Susan Morrisey. "Terrorism: 'The Original Cheap Shot': An Interview with Ambassador Diego Asencio," *World Affairs,* 146, 1 (1983): 42–53.

Mason, T. David, and Dale A. Krane. "The Political Economy of Death Squads: Toward a Theory of the Impact of State-Sanctioned Terror," *International Studies Quarterly,* 33, 2 (1989): 175–198.

Maullin, Richard L. *Soldiers, Guerrillas, and Politics in Colombia.* Lexington, Massachusetts: Lexington Books, 1973. 168 p.

McCormick, Gordon H. *The Shining Path and the Future of Peru,* RAND/ R-3781-DOS/OSD. Santa Monica, California: Rand Corporation, 1990. 58 p.

Nolan, David. *The Ideology of the Sandinista and the Nicaraguan Revolution.* Coral Gables, Florida: Institute of Interamerican Studies, University of Florida, 1984. 203 p.

d'Oliveira, Sergio L. "Uruguay and the Tupamaro Myth," *Military Review,* 53, 4 (1973): 25–36.

Palmer, David Scott. "Rebellion in Rural Peru: The Origins and Evolution of Sendero Luminoso," *Comparative Politics,* 18, 2 (January 1986): 127–146.

Pardo-Maurer, Rogelio. *The Contras, 1980–1989: A Special Kind of Politics.* The Washington Papers, No. 147. New York: Praeger Press, 1990. 151 p.

Petras, James. "The Anatomy of State Terror: Chile, El Salvador, and Brazil," *Science and Society,* 51, 3 (1987): 314–338.

Phillips, Dion E. ''Terrorism and Security in the Caribbean: The 1976 Cubana Disaster Off Barbados,'' *Terrorism,* 14, 4 (1991): 209–220.

Porzecanski, Arturo L. *Uruguay's Tupamaros: The Urban Guerrilla.* New York: Praeger Press, 1973. 80 p.

Radu, Michael S. ''Terror, Terrorism, and Insurgency in Latin America,'' *Orbis,* 28, 1 (Spring 1984): 27–40.

Ramsey, Russell W. ''The Urban Guerrilla in Latin America: A Select Bibliography,'' *Latin American Research Review,* 8, 1, (1973): 3–44.

Rensselaer, Lee, III. ''Dimensions of the South American Cocaine Industry,'' *Journal of InterAmerican Studies and World Affairs,* 30 (Summer/Fall 1988): 87–104.

Rosenberg, Tina. *Children of Cain: Violence and the Violent in Latin America.* New York: William Morrow and Co., 1991. 394 p.

Russell, Charles A., James A. Miller, and Robert E. Hildner. ''The Urban Guerrilla in Latin America: A Select Bibliography,'' *Latin American Research Review,* 9, 1, (1974): 37–80.

Russell, Charles A. ''Latin America: Regional Review,'' *Terrorism,* 4, 1–4 (1980): 277–292.

Sater, William. *The Revolutionary Left and Terrorist Violence in Chile,* RAND/ N-2490-AF. Santa Monica, California: Rand Corporation, 1986. 19 p.

Sereseres, Caesar. ''Guatemala: A Country Response Without Outside Help,'' in Edwin G. Corr and Stephen Sloan, eds. *Low Intensity Conflict: Old Threats in a New World.* Boulder, Colorado: Westview, 1992. pp. 101–123.

Simpson, John, and Jana Bennett. *The Disappeared and the Mothers of the Plaza: The Story of the 11,000 Argentinians Who Vanished.* New York: St. Martin's Press, 1985. 416 p.

Steinitz, Mark S. "Insurgents, Terrorists, and the Drug Trade," *Washington Quarterly,* 8, 4 (1985): 141–153.

Strong, Simon. "Where the Shining Path Leads," *The New York Times Magazine,* 24 May 1992, pp. 12–17, 35.

Tarazona-Sevillano, Gabriela, with John B. Reuter. *Sendero Luminoso and the Threat of Narcoterrorism.* The Washington Papers, No. 144. New York: Praeger Press, 1990. 168 p.

Taylor, Robert W., and Harry E. Vanden. "Defining Terrorism in El Salvador: 'La Matanza'," *Annals of the American Academy of Political and Social Science,* 463 (September 1982): 106–118.

Turner, Robert F. *Nicaragua v. United States: A Look at the Facts.* Washington, D.C.: Pergamon-Brassey's, 1987. 165 p.

U.S. Department of State, Coordinator of Public Diplomacy for Latin America and the Caribbean. *"The 72-Hour Document": The Sandinista Blueprint For Constructing Communism in Nicaragua.* Washington, D.C.: Government Printing Office, 1986.

U.S. Department of State, Coordinator of Public Diplomacy for Latin America and the Caribbean. *Inside the Sandinista Regime: A Special Investigator's Perspective.* Washington, D.C.: Government Printing Office, 1986.

Villalobos, Joaquin. "A Democratic Revolution for El Salvador," *Foreign Policy,* 74 (Spring 1989): 103–122.

Wardlaw, Grant. "Linkages Between the Illegal Drugs Traffic and Terrorism," *Conflict Quarterly,* 8, 3 (Summer 1988).

Werlich, David P. "Peru: The Shadow of the Shining Path," *Current History,* 83, 481, (February 1984): 78–82, 90.

Werlich, David P. "Debt, Democracy, and Terrorism in Peru," *Current History,* 86, 516, (January 1987): 29.

World Press Review, "Colombian Journalists Vs. Drug Terrorists," *World Press Review,* (January 1990), pp. 38–41, in Schechterman, Bernard and Slann, Martin, eds., *Violence and Terrorism 91/92.* Sluice Dock, Guilford, Connecticut: Dushkin Publishing Group, Inc. pp. 154–156.

3. British Isles and Europe

Alexander, Yonah, and Dennis A. Pluchinsky, eds. *European Terrorism: Today and Tomorrow.* Brassey's Terrorism Library. Washington, D.C.: Brassey's (US), Inc., 1992. 208 p.

Alexander, Yonah and Alan O'Day, eds. *Terrorism in Ireland.* New York: St. Martin's Press, 1984. 277 p.

Alexiev, Alex. "The Kremlin and the Pope," *Ukrainian Quarterly,* 39, 4 (1983): 378–388.

Aston, Clive C. "Political Hostage Taking in Western Europe," *Conflict Studies,* 157 (1984).

Bahry, Donna, and Brian D. Silver. "Intimidation and the Symbolic Uses of Terror in the USSR," *American Political Science Review,* 81, 4 (1987): 1065–1098.

Baldy, Tom F. *Battle for Ulster.* Washington, D.C.: National Defense University Press, 1987. 136 p.

Bell, J. Bowyer. "The Escalation of Insurgency: The Provisional Irish Republican Army's Experience, 1969–71," *Review of Politics,* 35, 3 (1973): 398–411.

Billig, Michael, and Raymond Cochrane. "The National Front and Youth," *Patterns of Prejudice,* 15, 4 (1981): 3–15.

Boyce, D. George. "Normal Policing: Public Order in Northern Ireland since Partition," *Eire-Ireland,* 14, 4 (1979): 35–52.

Carr, Gordon. *The Angry Brigade: The Cause and the Case.* London: Gollancz, 1975.

Catanzaro, Raimondo. *The Red Brigades and Left-Wing Terrorism in Italy.* New York: St. Martin's Press, 1991. 216 p.

Clissold, Stephen. "Croat Separatism: Nationalism, Dissidence, and Terrorism," *Conflict Studies,* 103 (1979).

Clutterback, Richard. "Terrorism and the Security Forces in Europe," *Army Quarterly and Defence Journal,* 111, 1 (1981): 12–29.

Clutterback, Richard. "Intimidation of Witnesses and Juries," *Army Quarterly and Defence Journal,* 104, 3 (1974): 285–289.

Clutterback, Richard. "Terrorist International," *Army Quarterly and Defence Journal,* 104, 2 (1974): 154–159.

Collin, Richard Oliver. "When Reality Became Unglued: Antonio Savasta and the Italian Red Brigades," *Violence, Aggression and Terrorism,* 3, 4 (1989) in Schechterman, Bernard and Slann, Martin, eds., *Violence and Terrorism 91/92.* Sluice Dock, Guilford, Connecticut: Dushkin Publishing Group, Inc. pp. 176–189.

Collins, J. G. "Terrorism and Animal Rights," *Science,* 249, 4967 (1990): 345.

Corsun, Andrew. "Group Profile: The Revolutionary Organization 17 November in Greece," *Terrorism,* 14, 2 (1991): 77–104.

Drake, Richard. *The Revolutionary Mystique and Terrorism in Contemporary Italy.* Bloomington: Indiana University Press, 1989. 218 p.

Enders, Walter, and Todd Sandler. "Causality Between Transnational Terrorism and Tourism: The Case of Spain," *Terrorism,* 14, 1 (1991): 49–58.

Francis, Samuel T. "Terrorist Renaissance: France, 1980–1983," *World Affairs,* 146, 1 (Summer 1983): 54–58.

Frankland, Erich. "The Basque Nationalist Insurgency and Spanish Democracy." In Yonah Alexander, ed. *Annual on Terrorism: 1990–92,* Dordrecht, The Netherlands: Martinus Nijhoff, 1992.

Golan, Galia. *Gorbachev's "New Thinking" on Terrorism.* The Washington Papers, No. 141. New York: Praeger Press, 1990. 117 p.

Gregory, F.E.C. "Police Cooperation and Integration in the European Community: Proposals, Problems and Prospects," *Terrorism,* 14, 3 (1991): 145–156.

Henze, Paul. *The Plot to Kill the Pope.* New York: Charles Scribner's Sons, 1985. 216 p.

Herman, Valentine, and Rob van der Laan Bouma. "Nationalists Without a Nation: South Moluccan Terrorism in the Netherlands," *Terrorism,* 4, 1–4 (1980): 223–257.

Hoffman, Bruce. "Right-Wing Terrorism in Europe," *Orbis,* 28, 1 (Spring 1984): 16–26.

Horchem, Hans J. "Terrorism in West Germany," *Conflict Studies,* 186 (April 1986): 1–20.

Horchem, Hans J. "Terrorism in Germany: 1985," in Paul Wilkinson and Alasdair M. Stewart, eds. *Contemporary Research on Terrorism.* (Aberdeen: Aberdeen University Press, 1987). 141–163.

Horchem, Hans J. "European Terrorism: A German Perspective," *Terrorism,* 6, 1 (1982): 27–51.

Institute for the Study of Conflict. "Northern Ireland: An Anglo-Irish Dilemma?," *Conflict Studies,* 185 (1986).

Ivansky, Zeev. "Provocation at the Center: A Study in the History of Counter-Terror," *Terrorism,* 4, 1–4 (1980): 53–88.

Jamieson, Alison. *The Heart Attacked: Terrorism and Conflict in the Italian State.* London: Marion Boyars, 1989. 306 p.

Jamieson, Alison. "Political Kidnapping in Italy," *Conflict,* 8, 1 (1988): 41–48.

Jenkins, Philip. "The Assassination of Olof Palme: Evidence and Ideology," *Contemporary Crises,* 13, 1 (1989): 15–33.

Kelley, Kevin J. *The Longest War: Northern Ireland and the IRA.* Westport, Connecticut: Lawrence Hill & Co. Inc., 1988. 395 p.

Lee, Alfred McClung. *Terrorism in Northern Ireland.* Bayside, New York: General Hall Inc., 1988. 257 p.

Lee, Alfred McClung. "The Dynamics of Terrorism in Northern Ireland," *Social Research,* 48, 1 (1981): 100–134.

Lee, Martin A. "Hitler's Offspring," *The Progressive,* March 1993: 28–31.

Meade, Robert C., Jr. *Red Brigades: the Story of Italian Terrorism.* New York: St. Martin's Press, 1990. 301 p.

Merkl, Peter H. "Rollerball or Neo-Nazi Violence," in Peter H. Merkl ed. *Political Violence and Terror: Motifs and Motivations,* (Berkeley: University of California Press, 1986.) pp. 229–255.

Moss, David. "The Kidnapping and Murder of Aldo Moro," *European Journal of Sociology* (United Kingdom), 22, 2 (1981): 265–295.

Moxon-Brown, Edward P. "Spain and the ETA: The Bid for Basque Autonomy," *Conflict Studies,* 201 (1987).

Moxon-Brown, Edward P. "Alienation: The Case of the Catholics in Northern Ireland," *Journal of Political Science,* 14, 1–2 (1986): 74 et seq.

Moxon-Brown, Edward P. "The Water and the Fish: Public Opinion and the Provisional IRA in Northern Ireland," *Terrorism,* 5, 1–2 (1981): 41–72.

Mulgannon, Terry. "The Animal Liberation Front," *TVI Journal* 5 (Spring 1985).

O'Ballance, Edgar. "IRA Leadership Problems," *Terrorism,* 5, 1–2 (1981): 73–82.

Payne, Stanley G. "Terrorism and Democratic Stability in Spain," *Current History,* 77, 451 (1979): 167–171, 182–183.

Pisano, Vittorfranco S. "Genesis, Rise, and Decline of Italian Terrorism," *Conflict,* 10, 3 (1990): 227–238.

Pluchinsky, Dennis. "Middle Eastern Terrorist Activity in Western Europe: A Diagnosis and Prognosis," *Conflict Quarterly,* 6, 3 (Summer 1986): 40–52.

Preston, Paul. "Walking the Terrorist Tightrope," *Contemporary Review* (United Kingdom), 234, 1358 (1979): 119–123.

Ramet, Pedro. "Yugoslavia and the Threat of Internal and External Discontents," *Orbis,* 28, 1 (Spring 1984): 103–122.

Reinares, Fernando. "Nationalism and Violence in Basque Politics," *Conflict,* 8, 2–3 (1988): 141–155.

Robertson, Ken. "Terrorism: Europe Without Borders," *Terrorism,* 14, 2 (1991): 105–110.

Ronchey, Alberto. "Guns and Gray Matter: Terrorism in Italy," *Foreign Affairs,* 57, 4 (1979): 921–940.

Russell, Charles A. "Europe: A Regional View, 1970–78," *Terrorism,* 3, 1–2 (1979): 157–171.

Salvioni, Daniela, and Anders Stephanson. "Reflections on the Red Brigades," *Orbis,* 29, 3 (1985): 489–506.

Scherer, John L. "The Plot to Kill the Pope," *Terrorism,* 7 (1985): 351–366.

Schiller, David T. "Germany's Other Terrorists," *Terrorism,* 9 (1987): 87–99.

Smith, G. Davidson. "Political Violence in Animal Liberation," *Contemporary Review* 247, 1434 (1985): 26–31.

Smith, G. Davidson. "Issue Group Terrorism: Animal Rights Militancy in Britain," *TVI Journal* 5:4 (1984): 44–47.

Solomon, Gerald B. H., and Robert M. Jenkins. "The Impact of EC 1992 on Terrorism and Drug Trafficking in Europe: U.S. Concerns," *Terrorism,* 13, 1 (1990): 15–22.

Sterling, Claire. "Italian Terrorists: Life and Death in a Violent Generation," *Encounter* (United Kingdom), 57, 1 (1981): 18–31.

Terchek, Ronald J. "Conflict and Cleavage in Northern Ireland," *Annals of the American Academy of Political and Social Science,* 422 (1977): 47–59.

Tugwell, Maurice A. "Politics and Propaganda of the Provisional IRA," *Terrorism,* 5, 1–2 (1981): 13–40.

Weinberg, Leonard, and William Eubank. *The Rise and Fall of Italian Fascism.* Boulder, Colorado: Westview Press, 1987. 155 p.

Weinberg, Leonard, and William Lee Eubank. "Change and Continuity in the Recruitment of Italian Political Terrorists," *Journal of Political Science,* 14, 1–2 (1986): 43–57.

Wieviorka, Michel. "France Faced with Terrorism," *Terrorism,* 14, 3 (1991): 157–170.

Wright, Joanne. *Terrorist Propaganda: The Red Army Faction and the Provisional IRA, 1968–86.* New York: St. Martin's Press, 1990. 281 p.

Zasloff, Joseph J. "The KGB Abroad: 'Wet Affairs': Soviet Use of Assassination and Kidnapping," *Survey* (United Kingdom), 27 (1983): 68–79.

4. Middle East (North Africa and Southwest Asia)

Abrahamian, Ervand. *The Iranian Mojahedin.* New Haven: Yale University Press, 1989. 307 p.

Ahrari, Mohammed E. "Theological Insurgency: Iran in the Region," *Washington Quarterly,* 8, 2 (1985): 47–60.

Ajami, Fouad. *The Vanished Imam: Musa al Sadr and the Shia of Lebanon.* Ithaca, New York: Cornell University Press, 1986. 228 p.

Akhavi, Shahrough. "Post-Khomeini Iran: Global and Regional Implications," *SAIS Review,* 10, 1 (1990): 149–162.

Akhtar, Shameen. "PLO In-Fighting," *Pakistan Horizon,* 36, 3 (1983): 100–120.

Alexander, Yonah. "The Legacy of Palestinian Terrorism," *International Problems* (Israel), 15, 3–4 (1976): 57–64.

Alexander, Yonah. "Middle Eastern Fundamentalism and Terrorism: Interdisciplinary Perspectives," *Terrorism,* 11, 5 (1988): 345.

Ali, Yasser Hammad al-Hassan. "Killing Collaborators: A Hamas How-To," [Videotape Transcript], *Harper's Magazine,* May 1993: 10–13.

Alpher, Joseph. "The Khomeini International," *Washington Quarterly,* 3, 4 (1980): 55–57.

Anderson, Sean K. "Iranian State-Sponsored Terrorism," *Conflict Quarterly,* 11, 4 (1991): 19–34.

Anderson, Sean K. *The Impact of Islamic Fundamentalist Politics Within the Islamic Republic of Iran on Iranian State Spon-*

sorship of Transnational Terrorism, (unpublished dissertation). Norman, University of Oklahoma, 1993. 460 p.

Asaf, Hussain. *Islamic Iran: Revolution and Counterrevolution.* New York: St. Martin's Press, 1985. 225 p.

Asaf, Hussain. *Political Terrorism and the State in the Middle East.* London: Mansell Publishing Ltd., 1985. 225 p.

Ashrawi, Hanan. "Impact on the Palestinians," *American-Arab Affairs,* 31 (Winter 1989–90): 33–37.

Beres, Louis Rene. "Terrorism and the Nuclear Threat in the Middle East," *Current History,* 70, 412 (1976): 27–29.

Bernstein, Alvin H. "Iran's Low-Intensity War against the United States," *Orbis,* 30, 1 (1986): 149–167.

Bill, James A. "Power and Religion in Revolutionary Iran," *Middle East Journal,* 36, 1 (1982): 22–47.

Brand, Laurie. "Palestinians in Syria: The Politics of Integration," *Middle East Journal,* 42, 4 (August 1988): 621–638.

Brynen, Rex. *Sanctuary and Survival: The PLO Lesson in Lebanon.* Boulder, Colorado: Westview Press, 1990. 255 p.

Burgess, William H., III. "Iranian Special Operations in the Iran-Iraq War: Implications for the United States," *Conflict,* 8, 1 (1988): 22–40.

Chapman, Robert D. "State Terrorism," *Conflict,* 3, 4 (1982): 283–298.

Cobban, Helena. *The Palestine Liberation Organization: People, Power, and Politics.* New York: Cambridge University Press, 1983. 305 p.

Cobban, Helena. "Relationships Between Palestinians Inside and Outside," *American-Arab Affairs,* 31 (Winter 1989–90): 38–41.

CSIS Intifada Conference. CSIS Conference Excerpts "Two Years of Intifada: Its Impact on the American, Israeli, and Palestinian Political Climates," *American-Arab Affairs,* 31 (Winter 1989–1990): 29.

Deeb, Marius. *Militant Islamic Movements in Lebanon: Origins, Social Basis, and Ideology.* Washington, D.C.: Center for Contemporary Arab Studies, Georgetown University, 1986. (Occasional Papers Series). p. 27.

Diskin, Abraham. "Trends in Intensity [and] Variation of Palestinian Military Activity: 1967–1978," *Canadian Journal of Political Science,* 16, 2 (1983): 335–348.

Don-Yehiya, Eliezer. "Jewish Messianism, Religious Zionism, and Israeli Politics: The Impact and Origins of Gush Emunim," *Middle Eastern Studies,* 23, 2 (1987): 215–234.

Duran, Khaled. "The Second Battle of Algiers," *Orbis,* 33, 3 (1989): 403–422.

Elliott, Deni. "Family Ties: A Case Study of Coverage of Families and Friends during the Hijacking of TWA 847," *Political Communication and Persuasion,* 5, 1 (1988): 67–76.

Emerson, Steven and Brian Duffy. *The Fall of Pan Am 103: Inside the Lockerbie Investigation.* New York: G.P. Putnam's Sons, 1990. pp. 56–65, 199–205.

Fay, James R. "Terrorism in Turkey: Threat to NATO's Troubled Ally," *Military Review,* 61, 4 (1981): 16–26.

Ferdows, Amir H. ''Khomaini and Fadayan's Society and Politics,'' *International Journal of Middle East Studies,* 15, 2 (May 1983): 241–258.

Fisk, Robert. *Pity the Nation:: The Abduction of Lebanon.* New York: Simon and Schuster, 1990. 678 p.

Friedman, Thomas L. *From Beirut to Jerusalem.* New York: Doubleday, 1989. 541 p.

Garfincle, Adam M. ''Sources of the Al-Fatah Mutiny,'' *Orbis,* 27, 3 (1983): 603–640.

Gilmour, Ian, and Andrew Gilmour. (Book Review), ''Terrorism,'' *Journal of Palestine Studies,* 17, 2 (1988): 129–142.

Goldberg, Giora. ''Haganah, Irgun and 'Stern': Who Did What?,'' *Jerusalem Quarterly,* 25 (1982): 116–120.

Gordon, David C. *The Republic of Lebanon: Nation in Jeopardy.* Boulder, Colorado: Westview Press, 1983. 171 p.

Gowers, Andrew, and Tony Walker. *Behind the Myth: Yasser Arafat and the Palestinian Revolution.* New York: Olive Branch Press, 1992. 407 p.

Green, Jerrold D. ''Countermobilization as a Revolutionary Form,'' *Comparative Politics,* 16, 2 (1984): 153–170.

Gresh, Alain. *The PLO: The Struggle Within* (revised and updated edition). London: Zed Books Ltd., 1988. 270 p.

Gunter, Michael. *The Kurds in Turkey: A Political Dilemma,* Boulder, Colorado: Westview Press, 1990. 151 p.

Gunter, Michael. ''Cycles of Terrorism: The Question of Contemporary Turkish Counterterror and Harassment against the

Armenians," *Journal of Political Science,* 14, 1–2 (1986): 58–73.

Gunter, Michael. "Contemporary Armenian Terrorism," *Terrorism,* 8 (1986): 213–253.

Gunter, Michael M. "The Armenian Terrorist Campaign Against Turkey," *Orbis,* 27, 2 (1983): 447–477.

Gutteridge, William ed. "Libya: Still A Threat To Western Interests?," *Conflict Studies,* 160 (1984).

Hamden, Raymond H. *The Psychological Aspects of IsTishShad: Suicide or Sacrifice?,* Paper presented before the U.S. Senate Anti-Terrorism Caucus on 26 March 1986, from Yonah Alexander, ed., *Terrorism: An International Resource File, 1986,* Microfiche Collection No. T-354.

al Hassan, Khaled. "The PLO and the Intifada," *American-Arab Affairs,* 31 (Winter 1989–1990): 42–48.

Hof, Frederic C. "The Beirut Bombing of October 1983: An Act of Terrorism?," *Parameters: Journal of the US Army War College,* 15, 2 (1985): 69–74.

Hoffman, Bruce. Rand/P-7116 *Shia Terrorism: The Conflict in Lebanon and the Hijacking of TWA Flight 847.* Santa Monica: Rand Corporation, 1985. 3 p.

Hoffman, Bruce. RAND/R-3783-USDP, *Recent Trends and Future Prospects of Iranian Sponsored International Terrorism.* Santa Monica: Rand Corporation, 1990. 43 p.

Hudson, Michael C. "The Palestinians: Retrospect and Prospects," *Current History,* 78, 453 (1980): 22–25, 31, 39–41, 48.

Hudson, Michael C. "The Palestinian Factor in the Lebanese Civil War," *Middle East Journal* 32, 3 (1978): 261–278.

Hunter, F. Robert. *The Palestinian Intifada: A War by Other Means.* Berkeley: University of California Press, 1991. 292 p.

Hunter, Shireen. "Islamic Fundamentalism: What It Really Is and Why It Frightens the West," *SAIS Review,* 6, 1 (1986): 189–200.

Hyland, Francis P. *Armenian Terrorism: The Past, the Present, the Prospects.* Boulder, Colorado: Westview Press, 1991. 248 p.

(Iran Air 655 Disaster Legal Documents). "International Court of Justice: Application Instituting Proceedings in Case concerning Aerial Incident of 3 July 1988 (Iran v. United States)," *International Legal Materials,* 28, 4 (1989): 842–846.

(Iran Air 655 Disaster Legal Documents). "International Civil Aviation Organization: Resolution and Report concerning the Destruction of Iran Air Airbus on July 3, 1989," *International Legal Materials,* 28, 4 (1989): 896–943.

Isby, David. "Afghanistan: Low Intensity Conflict with Major Power Intervention," in Edwin G. Corr and Stephen Sloan eds. *Low Intensity Conflict: Old Threats in a New World.* Boulder, Colorado: Westview, 1992. pp. 197–220.

Israeli, Raphael. "The Charter of Allah: The Platform of the Islamic Resistance Movement," in Yonah Alexander and A. H. Foxman, eds. *The 1988–89 Annual on Terrorism.* Dordrecht: Martinus Nijhoff, 1990. pp. 99–134.

Jansen, Johannes J. G. *The Neglected Duty: The Creed of Sadat's Assassins and Islamic Resurgence in the Middle East.* New York: Macmillan Publishing Company, 1986. 245 p.

Jenkins, Philip. "Whose Terrorists? Libya and State Criminality," *Contemporary Crises,* 12, 1 (1987): 5–24.

Katzman, Kenneth. *The Warriors of Islam: Iran's Revolutionary Guard.* Boulder, Colorado: Westview Press, 1993. 192 p.

Khalidi, Rashid. *Under Siege: PLO Decision-Making During the 1982 War.* New York: Columbia University Press, 1986. 241 p.

Kostiner, Joseph. "The Rise and Fall of Militant Opposition Movements in the Arabian Peninsula," in Anat Kurz, ed., *Contemporary Trends in World Terrorism.* (New York: Praeger, 1987). pp. 43–52.

Kostiner, Joseph. "War, Terror, Revolution: The Iran-Iraq Conflict," in Barry Rubin ed. *The Politics of Terrorism: Terror as a State and Revolutionary Strategy.* Lanham, Maryland: University Press of America, 1989. pp. 27–66.

Kramer, Martin. "Shiite Terrorism," in Martin Kramer, ed., *Anti-Terrorism—IDENTA—85.* (Boulder, Colorado: Westview, 1985). pp. 417–24.

Kramer, Martin. "The Structure of Shiite Terrorism," in Anat Kurz, ed., *Contemporary Trends in World Terrorism* (New York: Praeger, 1987). pp. 43–52.

Kramer, Martin. "The Moral Logic of Hizballah," in Walter Reich, ed. *Origins of Terrorism: Psychologies, Ideologies, Theologies, States of Mind.* (Cambridge: Cambridge University Press, 1990). pp. 131–157.

Kramer, Martin. "Tragedy in Mecca," *Orbis,* 32, 2 (1988): 231–248.

Kuriyama, Yoshihiro. "Terrorism at Tel Aviv Airport and A 'New Left' Group in Japan," *Asian Survey,* 13, 3 (1973): 336–346.

Kurz, Anat, and Ariel Merari. *ASALA: Irrational Terror or Political Tool?* Boulder, Colorado: Westview, 1985. 118 p.

Livingston, Neil C. and David Halevy. *Inside the PLO: Covert Units, Secret Funds, and the War Against Israel and the United States.* 336 p.

Lustick, Ian S. "Israel's Dangerous Fundamentalists," *Foreign Policy,* 68 (Fall 1987): 118–139.

Mead, James M. "Lebanon Revisited," *Marine Corps Gazette,* 67, 9 (1983): 64–73.

Media Analysis Center. "The Covenant of the Islamic Resistance Movement (Hamas)." Jerusalem: Media Analysis Center, 1988. 12 p. (Mideast Backgrounds, 251.) Also in Yonah Alexander ed., *Terrorism: An International Resource File, 1988,* microfiche T-831.

Merari, Ariel, et al. "Shiite Terrorism in 1985," in *Inter 85: A Review of International Terrorism in 1985.* (Boulder, Colorado: Westview, 1985). pp. 55–70.

Merari, Ariel. "The Readiness to Kill and Die: Suicidal Terrorism in the Middle East," in W. Reich, ed. *Origins of Terrorism.* Cambridge: Cambridge University Press, 1990. pp. 192–210.

Metz, Steven. "The Ideology of Terrorist Foreign Policies in Libya and South Africa," *Conflict,* 7, 4 (1987): 379–402.

Miller, Aaron David. "U.S. Policy [Regarding the Intifada]," *American-Arab Affairs,* 31 (Winter 1989–1990): 29–32.

Mohaddessin, Mohammad. *Islamic Fundamentalism: The New Global Threat.* Washington, D.C.: Seven Locks Press, 1993. 224 p.

Momayezi, Nasser. "Economic Correlates of Political Violence: The Case of Iran," *Middle East Journal,* 40, 1 (1986): 68–81.

Muslih, Muhammad Y. "Moderates and Rejectionists Within the Palestine Liberation Organization," *Middle East Journal,* 2 (1976): 127–140.

Norton, Augustus R. *Amal and the Shia: Struggle for the Soul of Lebanon.* Austin: University of Texas Press, 1987. p. 238.

Norton, Graham. "The Terrorist and the Traveller: A Gulf Aftermath Assessment," *World Today,* 47, 5 (1991): 80–82.

Note on Libyan Raid of 1986. "The Libya Raid: A Provisional Balance-Sheet," *World Today,* 42, 6 (June 1984): 95–96.

O'Neill, Bard E. "Towards A Typology of Political Terrorism: The Palestinian Resistance Movement," *Journal of International Affairs,* 32, 1 (1978): 17–42.

Orlow, Dietrich. "Political Violence in Pre-Coup Turkey," *Terrorism,* 6, 1 (1982): 53–71.

Peretz, Don. "Intifadeh: the Palestinian Uprising," *Foreign Affairs,* 66 (Summer 1988): 964–980.

Perry, Victor. "Terrorism Incorporated," *Midstream,* 28, 2 (1982): 7–10.

Pipes, Daniel. "The Scourge of Suicide Terrorism." *The National Interest.* 4 (Summer 1986): 95–99.

Pipes, Daniel. "Fundamentalist Muslims between America and Russia." *Foreign Affairs,* 64, 5 (Summer 1986): 939–959.

Pipes, Daniel. "Why Asad's Terror Works and Qadhdhafi's Does Not," *Orbis,* 33, 4 (1989): 501–508.

Pluchinsky, Dennis. "Middle Eastern Terrorist Activity in Western Europe: A Diagnosis and Prognosis," *Conflict Quarterly,* 6, 3 (Summer 1986): 40–52.

Quester, George. "Some Explanations for State-Supported Terrorism in the Middle East," in Michael Stohl and George A. Lopez ed. *Terrible Beyond Endurance?: The Foreign Policy of State Terrorism.* New York: Greenwood Press, 1988. pp. 223–46.

Rapoport, David C. "Why Does Religious Messianism Produce Terror?," in Paul Wilkinson, ed. *Contemporary Research on Terrorism.* Aberdeen: Aberdeen University Press, 1987. pp. 72–88.

Rapoport, David C. "Messianic Sanctions for Terror," *Comparative Politics,* 20, 2 (1988): 195–214.

Rapoport, David C. "Fear and Trembling in Three Religious Traditions," *American Political Science Review,* 78, 3 (1984): 658–678.

Rapoport, David C. "Sacred Terror: A Contemporary Example From Islam," in Walter Reich, ed. *Origins of Terrorism: Psychologies, Ideologies, Theologies, States of Mind.* Cambridge: Cambridge University Press, 1990. pp. 103–130.

Rose, Gregory. "Revolution, Culture, and Collective Action," *Journal of Political Science,* 14, 1–2 (1986): 25–32.

Rubin, Barry. "The Political Uses of Terrorism in the Middle East," in Barry Rubin ed. *The Politics of Terrorism: Terror as a State and Revolutionary Strategy*. Lanham, Maryland: University Press of America, 1989. pp. 27–66.

Satloff, Robert. "Islam in the Palestinian Uprising," *Orbis,* 33, 3 (1989): 389–402.

Schahgaldian, Nikola. RAND/R-3473, *The Iranian Military Under The Islamic Republic*. Santa Monica: Rand Corporation, March 1987. 165 p.

Schahgaldian, Nikola B. RAND/R-3788-USDP, *The Clerical Establishment in Iran*. Santa Monica: Rand Corporation, 1989. 140 p.

Schbley, Ayla H. "Religious Terrorists: What They Aren't Going to Tell Us," *Terrorism,* 13, 3 (1990): 237–242.

Schbley, Ayla H. "Resurgent Religious Terrorism: A Study of Some of the Lebanese Shia Contemporary Terrorism, *Terrorism,* 12, 4 (1989): 213–248.

Schechterman, Bernard and Bradford R. McGuinn. "Linkages between Sunni and Shii Radical Fundamentalist Organizations: A New Variable in Recent Middle Eastern Politics?," *The Political Chronicle,* 1, 1 (1989) in Schechterman, Bernard and Slann, Martin, eds., *Violence and Terrorism 91/92*. Sluice Dock, Guilford, Connecticut: Dushkin Publishing Group, Inc. pp. 136–144.

Schweitzer, Yoram. "Terrorism: A Weapon in the Shiite Arsenal," in Anat Kurz, ed., *Contemporary Trends in World Terrorism*. New York: Praeger, 1987. pp. 43–52.

Seale, Patrick. *Abu Nidal: A Gun for Hire*. New York: Random House, 1992. 339 p.

Seale, Patrick, and Maureen McConville. *Asad of Syria: The Struggle for the Middle East.* Berkeley: University of California Press, 1989. 552 p.

Shadid, Mohammad K. "The Muslim Brotherhood Movement in the West Bank and Gaza," *Third World Quarterly,* April 1988.

Shapira, Shimon. "The Origins of Hizballah," *The Jerusalem Quarterly,* 46 (Spring 1988): 115–130.

Sick, Gary. *October Surprise: America's Hostages in Iran and the Election of Ronald Reagan.* New York: Times Books, 1991. 277 p.

Sick, Gary. *All Fall Down: America's Tragic Encounter With Iran.* New York: Random House, 1985. 366 p.

Sick, Gary. "Iran's Quest for Superpower Status," *Foreign Affairs,* 65, 4 (1987): 697–715.

Sivan, Emmanuel. "Sunni Radicalism in the Middle East," *International Journal of Middle East Studies,* 21, 1 (1989): 1–30.

St. John, Ronald Bruce. "Terrorism and Libyan Foreign Policy, 1981–1986," *World Today,* 42, 7 (July 1984): 111–114.

Stoakes, Frank. "The Supervigilantes: The Lebanese Kataeb Party as Builder, Surrogate and Defender of the State," *Middle Eastern Studies* (United Kingdom), 11, 3 (1975): 215–236.

Taheri, Amir. *Nest of Spies: America's Journey to Disaster in Iran.* New York: Pantheon Books, 1988. 314 p.

Taheri, Amir. *Holy Terror: Inside the World of Islamic Terrorism,* (Bethesda, Maryland: Adler and Adler, 1987): 136–137.

Taheri, Amir. *The Spirit of Allah: Khomeini and the Islamic Revolution.* Bethesda, Maryland: Adler and Adler, 1986. 349 p.

U.S. Department of State. *The Hawari Group* (Washington, D.C.: U.S. Department of State, Office of the Ambassador-at-Large for Counter-Terrorism, October 31, 1988), 3 p. Also in Yonah Alexander ed., *Terrorism: An International Resource File,* microfiche T-786.

Wallach, Janet, and John Wallach. *Arafat: In the Eyes of the Beholder.* New York: Lyle Stuart Book/Carol Publishing Group, 1990. 465 p.

Wege, Carl Anthony. "The Abu Nidal Organization," *Terrorism,* 14, 1 (1991): 59 et seq.

Weiss, Ellen. "Islamic Terrorist Threat in U.S.," *TVI Journal,* 5, 1 (Summer 1984): 28–29.

Wilkinson, Paul. "After Tehran," *Contemporary Review* (United Kingdom), 238, 1385 (1981): 281–290.

Wright, Robin, *Sacred Rage: The Wrath of Militant Islam.* Simon & Schuster: New York, 1986. 315 p.

Wright, Robin. "The Islamic Resurgence: A New Phase?," *Current History,* 87, 526 (1988): 53–56, 85–86.

Wright, Robin. "Islam's New Political Face," *Current History,* 90, 552 (1991): 25–28.

Wright, Robin. *In the Name of God: The Khomeini Decade.* New York: Simon & Schuster, 1989. 284 p.

Yishai, Yael. "The Jewish Terror Organization: Past or Future Danger?," *Conflict,* 6, 4 (1986): 306–332.

Zabih, Sepehr. "Aspects of Terrorism in Iran," *Annals of the American Academy of Political and Social Science,* 463 (September 1982): 84–94.

Zamir, Meir. "Iran: Consequences of the Abortive Attempt to Rescue the American Hostages," *Conflict,* 3, 1 (198): 55–77.

5. Southern and Eastern Asia and Pacific

Akbar, M. J. *India: The Siege Within: Challenges to a Nation's Unity.* Bungay, Suffolk: Penguin Books, 1985. 325 p.

Austen, Dennis, and Anirudha Gupta. "Lions and Tigers: The Crisis in Sri Lanka," *Conflict Studies,* 211 (1988): 1–19.

Bermudez, Joseph S., Jr. *Terrorism: The North Korean Connection.* New York: Crane Russak, 1990. 220 p.

Dale, Stephen Frederic. "Religious Suicide in Islamic Asia: Anticolonial Terrorism in India, Indonesia, and the Philippines," *Journal of Conflict Resolution,* 32, 1 (1988): 37–60.

Farrell, William R. *Blood and Rage: The Story of the Japanese Red Army.* Lexington, Massachusetts: Lexington Books, 1990. 265 p.

George, T.J.S. *Revolt in Mindanao: The Rise of Islam in Philippine Politics.* Oxford: Oxford University Press, 1980.

Grewal, J. S. *The New Cambridge History of India (II.3) The Sikhs of the Punjab.* Cambridge: Cambridge University Press, 1990. 264 p.

Holtzappel, Coen. "The 30 September Movement: A Political Movement of the Armed Forces or an Intelligence Operation?," *Journal of Contemporary Asia* (Sweden), 9, 2 (1979): 216–240.

Jeffrey, Robin. *What's Happening to India? Punjab, Ethnic Conflict, Mrs. Gandhi's Death and the Test for Federalism.* New York: Holmes and Meier, 1986. 249 p.

Kim, Jae Taik. "North Korean Terrorism: Trends, Characteristics and Deterrence," *Terrorism,* 11 (1988): 309–322.

Kodikara, S. V. "The Separatist Eelam Movement in Sri Lanka: An Overview," *India Quarterly,* 37, 2 (1981): 194–212.

Kuriyama, Yoshihiro. "Terrorism at Tel Aviv Airport and A 'New Left' Group in Japan," *Asian Survey,* 13, 3 (1973): 336–346.

Nagarajan, K. V. "Troubled Paradise: Ethnic Conflict in Sri Lanka," *Conflict,* 6, 4 (1986): 333–354.

Noble, Pela Garner. "The Philippines: Autonomy for the Muslims," in John L. Esposito ed., *Islam in Asia: Religion, Politics and Society,* New York: Oxford University Press, 1987. 270 p.

Oberst, Robert C. "Sri Lanka's Tamil Tigers," *Conflict,* 8, 2–3 (1988): 185–202.

Reddy, N. Subba. "Crisis of Confidence among the Tribal People and the Naxalite Movement in Srikakulam District," *Human Organization,* 36, 2 (1977): 142–149.

Schultz, Richard. "The Limits of Terrorism in Insurgency Warfare: The Case of the Viet Cong," *Polity,* 11, 1 (1978): 67–91.

Steinhoff, Patricia G. "Portrait of a Terrorist: An Interview with Kozo Okamoto," *Asian Survey,* 16, 9 (1976): 830–845.

Takagi, Masayuki. "Right Wing Draws Public Attention," *Japan Quarterly,* 27, 4 (1980): 479–486.

Tanham, George K. RAND/N-3040-USDP, *New Caledonia: The Fragile Peace.* Santa Monica, California: Rand Corporation, June 1990. 32 p.

Weatherbee, Donald E. "Communist Revolutionary Violence in the ASEAN States," *Asian Affairs: An American Review,* 10, 3 (1983): 1–17.

Wickramanayake, D. "Harijan Terror in India," *Plural Societies* (Netherlands), 6, 3 (1975): 17–20.

Yaeger, Carl H. "Sikh Terrorism in the Struggle for Khalistan," *Terrorism,* 14, 4 (1991): 221–232.

Zasloff, Joseph J. "Materials on Massacre of Korean Officials in Rangoon," *Korea and World Affairs* (South Korea), 7, 4 (1983): 735–764.

6. Sub-Saharan Africa

Chapman, Robert D. "State Terrorism," *Conflict,* 3, 4 (1982): 283–298.

Clifford-Vaughan, F. M. "Terrorism and Insurgency in South Africa," *Journal of Social, Political and Economic Studies,* 12, 2 (1987): 259–276.

Friedland, Elaine A. "South Africa and Instability in Southern Africa," *Annals of the American Academy of Political and Social Science,* 463 (September 1982): 95–105.

Metz, Steven. "The Ideology of Terrorist Foreign Policies in Libya and South Africa." *Conflict,* 7, 4 (1987): 379–402.

Nimer, Benjamin. "Terrorism and Southern Africa," *Terrorism,* 13, 6 (1990): 447–454.

Rich, Raul. "Insurgency, Terrorism and the Apartheid System in South Africa," *Political Studies* (United Kingdom), 32, 1 (1984): 68–85.

ABOUT THE AUTHORS

STEPHEN SLOAN (B.A., M.A., and Ph.D., New York University) is Professor of Political Science at the University of Oklahoma. Dr. Sloan's interest in the study of terrorism is part of his long-term commitment to the study of political violence. His fieldwork in the Republic of Indonesia, coinciding with the abortive coup d'état of 1965 in which over 100,000 people were killed, led to the publication of his first book, *A Study in Political Violence: The Indonesian Experience* (Rand McNally, 1971). Since 1966 Dr. Sloan pioneered the development of simulations of terrorist incidents to assist domestic and foreign law-enforcement departments, as well as the U.S. Army and U.S. Air Force in developing counterterrorist operational skills. His policy and field training led to publication of a second book, *Simulating Terrorism* (University of Oklahoma Press, 1980). Dr. Sloan also has been deeply involved in formulating counterterrorism doctrine for the military, as well as contributing to an evaluation of U.S. policies toward terrorism. In 1986 he served as an expert contributor to the Vice President's Task Force on Combating Terrorism. Dr. Sloan's latest books include: *Low-Intensity Conflict: Old Threats in a New World,* coedited with Edwin G. Corr (Westview, 1992), and *Corporate Aviation Security: The Next Frontier in Aerospace Operations,* coauthored with Harry Pizer (University of Oklahoma Press, 1992).

SEAN K. ANDERSON (B.A., Western Washington University; M.A. and Ph.D., University of Oklahoma) is Assistant Professor of Political Science at Idaho State University. From 1980 to 1982, Dr. Anderson worked as chief editor in the International Department of the Pars News Agency (now the Islamic Republic News

Agency) in Tehran, Iran. In April 1980, he presented a paper, "Iranian State Sponsorship of Terrorism," at the third annual Counter-Terror Study Center conference held at Winnipeg, Manitoba, which was later revised and published in *Conflict Quarterly,* Volume 11, Number 4 (Fall 1991). He also contributed a chapter entitled, "Iran: Terrorism and Islamic Fundamentalism," to the book *Low-Intensity Conflict: Old Threats in a New World,* coedited by Stephen Sloan and Edwin G. Corr (Westview, 1992).